# The Contessa

# The Contessa

BENEDETTA CRAVERI

Translated from the Italian by Alex Andriesse

nyrb New York Review Books New York

**This is a New York Review Book**

*published by The New York Review of Books*

207 East 32nd Street, New York, NY 10016

www.nyrb.com



This book was translated, in part, thanks to a grant awarded by the Italian Ministry of Foreign Affairs and International Cooperation.

Library of Congress Cataloging-in-Publication Data
Names: Craveri, Benedetta, 1942– author | Andriesse, Alex translator
Title: The Contessa / by Benedetta Craveri; translated from the Italian by Alex Andriesse.
Other titles: Contessa. English
Description: New York: New York Review Books, [2026]
Identifiers: LCCN 2026006729 (print) | LCCN 2026006730 (ebook) | ISBN 9798896230465 paperback | ISBN 9798896230472 ebook
Subjects: LCSH: Castiglione, Virginia Oldoini, contessa di, 1835–1899 | Nobility—Italy | France—Court and courtiers | Favorites, Royal—France | Favorites, Royal—Italy | LCGFT: Biographies
Classification: LCC DC280.5.C3 C7313 2026 (print) | LCC DC280.5.C3 (ebook)
LC record available at https://lccn.loc.gov/2026006729
LC ebook record available at https://lccn.loc.gov/20260

ISBN 979-8-89623-046-5
Available as an electronic book; ISBN 979-8-89623-047-2

The authorized representative in the EU for product safety and compliance is eucomply OÜ, Pärnu mnt 139b-14, 11317 Tallinn, Estonia, hello@eucompliancepartner.com, +33 757690241.

Printed in the United States of America on acid-free paper.
10 9 8 7 6 5 4 3 2 1

# Contents

# Preface

"*Io* SON IO!" "*Moi c'est moi!*" At twenty as at forty, Virginia Verasis di Castiglione demanded, in both her languages of choice, the right to be herself—the right to live a life compatible with her social position, her needs, and her intellectual gifts. But these demands were ahead of their time.

As a teenager she was blessed with a beauty that her parents considered a "serious business," and she'd barely come of age when she became one of the glories of the past. A former queen of Parisian society pages and Napoleon III's ex-lover, she wasn't even permitted to choose the role of seductress for herself; she played it on behalf of third parties, in the interests of Italian independence. Used as political bait by Cavour and Victor Emmanuel II (both of whom, once the French–Savoyard alliance was signed, left her to her fate); separated from a husband she'd humiliated and driven to ruin; and beleaguered by hosts of lovers, Virginia swore a solemn oath never to have a master again. She wanted to be free because freedom was for her, as it is for cats, an irrepressible instinct. And she would adhere to this freedom unswervingly, staying loyal solely to the volatile standard of her ego, under a banner stitched with the motto I THINK FOR MYSELF.

She was a forerunner of the tabloid celebrity. In Paris, in London, in Baden-Baden, she played every role in the repertoire to perfection, from tease to woman of mystery, from femme fatale to eminence grise. She alternated between comedy and melodrama, adventure tale and romantic tragedy, wisely leaving gaps between her performances, which she punctuated with no less sensational withdrawals from the public eye, rather like today's movie stars. She found photography the most congenial means of expressing her whimsical creativity and immortalized her own beauty in a series of masterpieces that to us anticipate the art of a later day. But her real talent, her greatest invention, was to make a cult of her personality. She had a distinctive flair for being famous for being famous.

Long after she first mesmerized her contemporaries and launched her own legend—a legend Robert de Montesquiou enshrined in *La divine comtesse*—Virginia has continued to fascinate historians, essayists, and biographers, eliciting the posthumous admiration of legions of fans. Beginning with Alain Decaux—whose biography unearthed documents and letters jealously guarded by the countess—the countess's devotees have made up for a lack of primary sources by resorting to the many testimonials of the memoirists and journalists of her day, as well as to the excerpts from her correspondence printed in the catalog of the historic Drouot auction of 1953. Meanwhile, major exhibitions of her photographs at the Metropolitan Museum of Art in 1999 and at the Musée d'Orsay in 2000 have brought to light an extraordinary autobiography in images, suggesting new ways of understanding the countess's life.

This book takes a somewhat different approach, yielding the floor whenever possible to Virginia, and pairing her voice with the voices of people who knew her well: her mother, her father, her husband, her son, and the men who loved her most. A huge number of unpublished documents housed in Italian and French archives provide us with fresh data, allowing us to reconstruct Virginia's personality and life and, above all, her always problematic relationships with her family. Virginia's long entanglement with Victor Emmanuel II leaves us in no doubt that although Paris was her second homeland, Italy always remained the first. Not that the countess was ever shy about laying claim to her incontrovertible contribution to Italian unification.

As an adolescent, Virginia formed a party of herself alone and kept her real feelings hidden; she was haughty and shrouded in mystery, holding dozens of lovers in check without ever letting them have the slightest hold on her. Even today, Virginia might still represent an unalloyed enigma were it not for the letters she wrote, during a crucial period in her life, to the only man to whom she would ever say such things as "There is no love like ours." This man was Prince Giuseppe Poniatowski, an old family friend who became a senator of the empire and with whom, during her triumphant mission in Paris, Virginia came to trust implicitly. For years and years, he was the only person in the world with whom she indulged in the luxury of being herself. In the two thousand pages of this extraordinary epistolary monologue, we hear, as clear as a bell, Virginia's voice, speaking in an unstudied Italian taken straight from her childhood. In letter after letter, the young lady wonders how to regain control of her life, sternly surveying every means available to her. Her ferocious individualism, her trust in the irresistible power of her charm, and her will to avenge herself are at loggerheads with her loneliness, her anxiety, her fear, and her anger, which get the better of her, time after time. She desired freedom, and this desire culminated in an all-out rebellion against the rules of family-minded self-denial, modesty, submission, and respectability imposed on women by the ethos of the bourgeois century. That rebellion retains its incendiary force. To this day, the contessa continues to disturb, disconcert, and scandalize.

# Florence
## 1837–1858

FLORENCE—after the Napoleonic intermission and the return of the Lorraines—enjoyed a long stretch of stability and peace. "From 1814 to 1848," one leading figure in the cultural and political life of the era was later to recall,

> Tuscany was in a period of rest and ease. These were years when whoever was in office might well have said that everything was running smoothly, for it appeared to be running just as those in positions of power wished it to run . . . As far as Florence was concerned, these were three very good decades. The tolerant government, the lazy aristocracy, the well-fed populace, the citizenry happily observing and taking part in the universal jubilation, the devil-may-care foreigners confidently venturing all they had and greedily buying all they didn't, the politesse and complaisant conventions, and an easygoing attitude toward religion . . . all of this made Florence the most cheerful city in Italy.[1]

The capital had been accumulating a crowd of émigrés and counterrevolutionaries since the French Revolution. The most famous of them, perhaps, were Vittorio Alfieri and the Countess of Albany, whose salon on the Arno had become a cultural touchstone. Napoleon's fall produced a new wave of arrivals. Among the most prominent foreigners were various members of the Bonaparte family, including two of Napoleon's brothers, Louis and Jérôme, who—unseated from the thrones of Holland and Westphalia respectively—both took up residence in the Tuscan capital.[2] In her memoirs, Jérôme's daughter, Princess Mathilde (who in 1840 married the rich patron and Russian count Anatoly Demidov and was the reigning queen of Florentine society for twenty years) would celebrate, with full knowledge of the facts, the sweetness of life in those days:

> Tuscany was a fortunate nation, governed by the Grand Duke with wisdom and a light hand. It was a corner of the world where everyone, safe from worry, enjoyed his life, and where the ill-fated found safe haven. This brio, good cheer, and good humor gave the city its unparalleled physiognomy. The inhabitants looked happy and may well have been so.[3]

But it is Massimo d'Azeglio, who spent a happy childhood[4] in Florence and considered it "more [his] native city than Turin,"[5] who best explains the reasons for this climate of tolerance, which was quite exceptional in the Europe that came out of the Congress of Vienna. "Tuscany," he writes in his memoirs,

> lived under a law not written in any statute book—a law devoid of any apparent function, yet no less respected and obeyed than the English constitution, so that it might rightly be called the Magna

> Carta of Tuscany. Whether he liked it or not, the Grand Duke himself was subject to it, and if he had wanted to disobey it, he would have been left high and dry. No official formulation of this law exists. It is felt and followed but never given verbal form. If I had to put it in language, I would use three simple words: *Let it go.*
>
> The applications in public and private and government matters were constant and countless. If a young man was a scatterbrain, or a girl was making love, or a woman was flirting, after a bit of brouhaha . . . *Let it go.* If a family went to rack and ruin, if the peasants or the farmers stole, everybody shouted for a moment . . . then: *Let it go.* If the police declared a law and nobody obeyed it, the hammer came down for twenty-four hours, and then . . . *Let it go.*[6]

In this oasis of liberty and merry hedonism scarcely touched by the winds of the Restoration, the future Countess of Castiglione was born on March 22, 1837, and spent the first sixteen years of her life.

Her parents (first cousins[7]), Marquis Filippo Oldoini and Isabella Lamporecchi, were married in Florence in 1836, when they were still in their teens.[8] At her birth they gave her the names Virginia, Elisabetta, Luisa, Carlotta, and Antonietta. Close relations were soon calling the girl Ninny, Niny, Nini, Ninì, Nicchia, and Bisisi.[9] She was to be the couple's only child.

Born in La Spezia on February 15, 1817, her father was descended from an old Cremona family who had moved to Genoa in 1424 before moving on to La Spezia, where at some point in the eighteenth century they took the surname Rapallini.[10] Filippo—a subject of the Savoy kingdom—was a handsome, elegant, rather decorous man, proud of his properties in La Spezia and his social prestige. After two terms as Ligurian deputy in the Parlamento Subalpino,[11] in 1848 he opted for a career in diplomacy, which was an occupation better befitting a gentleman. Thanks to his friend Massimo d'Azeglio,[12] who'd just been appointed president of the Council of Ministers of the Sardinian government, Filippo, after a brief apprenticeship at the ministry, was made a secretary of legation and sent first to Dresden and then, in 1852, to London. But this second and more important assignment—which had benefited from the obliging endorsement of Massimo's nephew Emanuele d'Azeglio, who was in charge of the Savoy legation to Her Britannic Majesty—was the subject of more than one malicious comment. No one in diplomatic circles had a high opinion of Oldoini.[13] And Cavour expressed frank misgivings about d'Azeglio, whom he was planning to supersede as president of the council. "When it comes to doing favors for those near and dear to him," he writes to General La Marmora, "Azeglio gives no consideration either to diplomatic interests or to public opinion." Cavour then goes on to compose a portrait of the minister's protégé worthy of a moralist of the Grand Siècle:

> Oldoini has all the defects of [Emanuele] d'Azeglio and no advantages at all. Both of them are supercilious and frivolous. But Azeglio is supercilious wittily, whereas Oldoini is supercilious stupidly! Azeglio dresses bizarrely, but women like it. And by appealing to the women he sometimes manages to get what he needs from their husbands. But no one likes Oldoini, not even his own wife. Finally, Azeglio, being Massimo's nephew, is well positioned in London society, where men and family are taken very seriously, while Oldoini, being married to a *femme galante*, is held in low esteem in London drawing-rooms.[14]

Though far from chivalrous, considering the woman he stigmatized as a *femme galante* was a sincere friend whom he himself had wooed,[15] Cavour's judgment was a verdict without appeal. He soon succeeded Azeglio as president of the council[16] and made no secret of his contempt for the marquis, calling him a "*ciola*" (fool)[17] and turning a deaf ear when he asked for promotions. Oldoini, meanwhile, was quite confident in his professional abilities and general savoir faire. He was psychologically unstable, a hypochondriac, splenetic, and perennially unsatisfied, always on the lookout for new destinations. His chief advocate was his wife, who good-naturedly mitigated criticisms ("He may not be Metternich but he does his job well") and never tired of recommending him to friends and acquaintances.[18]

Born in Florence a year before her husband[19]—and a force of nature from the first—Isabella was the daughter of Cavaliere Ranieri Lamporecchi,[20] a well-known jurist and lawyer at the Florentine court, reputed for his moral integrity and erudition. Despite his republican ideas and enthusiastic support of Napoleon's political reforms, and despite the fact that he didn't hide his high opinion of the emperor, to whom he dedicated a long poem,[21] Lamporecchi retained his credibility even after the Lorraines regained power. Furthermore, thanks to his talent as a lawyer and mediator, he was able to amass a fortune large enough to allow him, in 1846, to buy the prestigious Palazzo Gianfigliazzi on the Lungarno Corsini, once owned by the Countess of Albany and home to Louis Bonaparte, the father of the future Napoleon III.

Lamporecchi was a gruff but affectionate patriarch. But his sons were unscrupulous[22] and went through money like water. After he was widowed in 1852, he relied on Isabella to keep the family together.

The young Marquise Oldoini was a doting daughter, intelligent and generous, though not exactly a model of thrift or virtue. She was always ready to do all she could for her family, but she was also determined to make up for the romantic shortcomings of an arranged marriage by leading the pleasantest life possible. "Your whims and vices have already led you to squander a good part of your quite substantial patrimony,"[23] her affronted lawyer wrote in 1852. Eventually—though it was too little too late—she would try to make amends and save what could be saved. In fact, Isabella was the one who administered the properties of La Spezia and held the purse strings on behalf of her husband,[24] whose chief preoccupation was making a good impression as a diplomat.

Although they were always affectionate and supportive of one another, Virginia's parents gladly led separate lives,[25] and the marquise, whose husband was on diplomatic missions abroad more often than not, did nothing to discourage her admirers. But if Cavour's letter to La Marmora leaves us in no doubt about her reputation for *galanterie* and lets us see how, in the cloistered world of the Turinese nobility, such a reputation weighed like a boulder, in Florentine society—a cosmopolitan, hedonistic society inclined, as d'Azeglio says, to let things go—Isabella's straightforward nonchalance was completely unscandalous. Among the lovers attributed to her, two would figure in her daughter's life as well. The first was none other than Massimo d'Azeglio,[26] who, in addition to advancing Oldoini's career, developed a particular affection for little Virginia and warmly supported her marriage to Castiglione. The second was Prince Giuseppe Poniatowski.

Such was the Florence where Virginia spent a childhood that at first glance seems serene, with an unconventional but cohesive family in which everyone bent over backward to please her. And La Spezia—the family holdings, where each summer the marquise brought her daughter on holiday—soon became the mythic locale to which the girl alone held the keys. Even as a very young child, Virginia had been accustomed to imposing her own desires on the world around her, but as she approached adolescence she learned to mask these desires. "The Oldoini girl," Massimo d'Azeglio observed in the first days of spring 1849, "has changed with age. She too is throwing in with progress and has abdicated despotic power. She is now a pretty and respectable girl of twelve, and so has won me over completely."[27] This new, reserved, silence-keeping Virginia seldom risked opening her mouth, but she listened closely, observing the kaleidoscopic society around her.

This was the harsh, patriarchal society of Palazzo Lamporecchi, where magistrates, lawyers, professors, scholars, and important clients went to pay homage to her illustrious grandfather—a fact that filled her with pride. This was the elegant Florentine society of theaters, concerts, and parties, where her mother and uncle Alessandro, who were thick as thieves, reigned triumphant. Sandro—the youngest of her mother's brothers—was much admired for his elegance, wit, and imperturbable good humor.[28]

There were also the sumptuous and popular musical gatherings at the Palazzo Capponi, organized by Prince Stanisław Poniatowski, son of the brother of the last king of Poland, who had moved to Florence with his family at the invitation of the Grand Duke. And it was there, in Florence, at the Teatro Standish in 1838, that Stanisław's son Giuseppe[29] staged his first opera, *Giovanni da Procida*, and was appointed director of the philharmonic two years later.

But the most coveted invitations in good Florentine society were those of Henry Edward Fox, 4th Baron Holland, who from 1839 until 1846 was Britain's minister to the Grand Duchy of Tuscany.[30] Lord Holland had spent his childhood living all over the European continent, was a proponent of liberal ideals, and formed the central node in a network of contacts that ranged from Metternich to far-flung Bonapartes. In a word, he was a perfect gentleman, combining considerable cultivation with exquisite courtesy. His wife, Lady Mary Augusta—a woman tiny as a doll and blessed with an enchanting face, passionate about art and languages—helped make the Palazzo Amerighi and the Medician villa of Careggi favorite meeting places for Florence's cosmopolitan elite. Lady Holland had been deprived of the joy of motherhood and was extremely susceptible to beauty. Not surprisingly, she reserved a special welcome for the girl whom the Marquise Oldoini brought to visit her. The English grande dame—who rechristened her "Darling Beauty"[31]—became Virginia's first important conquest.

Isabella was not alone in her affection for the girl. Filippo, whose wife kept him informed of everything, likewise followed her progress. And Virginia herself wrote regularly to her father, bemoaning the distance between them. The young lady was quick-witted and intelligent and soon revealed herself to be an excellent student with a knack for languages. In addition to mastering French—the language of the Italian elite, which she used almost exclusively in her correspondence—she learned to speak English without an accent in a matter of months, under the guidance of Lady Holland. By the time she was twelve, she could write to her father in both English and German. In 1849, when Marquis Oldoini began his diplomatic career as a secretary of legation in Dresden, and again from 1851 to

1852, during his time in London, the many letters Virginia wrote to her "cher papa"—in a handwriting that transforms from childish scrawl into decisive, elegant script—are tender and affectionate.[32] In November 1852, the fifteen-year-old Virginia doesn't hide her sadness at the prospect of her father's absence from the family's Christmas dinner. And in another letter from the same period, she comforts the marquis, who is suffering from "spleen," leaving no doubt that she is perfectly familiar with the meaning of the word.

Catered to by everyone around her, Virginia, who by now occasionally accompanied her mother to the theater and society gatherings, was becoming more and more aware of her beauty and what it brought. When she was still just a child, her peers called her "the living Madonna,"[33] and when she was fifteen the biweekly Florentine newspaper *L'Arte*'s society page described her as "one of the most phenomenal Florentine beauties of the day... endowed with a grace that hardly seems of this world," whose appearance at the theater attracted the opera glasses "of the most fashionable spectators."[34]

"Her reputation is a serious business, and let me assure you, it's a serious business taking her around, looking more and more beautiful, wherever I go," Isabella wrote to her husband, enclosing a clipping from *L'Arte*.

> I've taken her to Cavalli's just twice, and see what they're saying about her on the page enclosed. She also has a reputation for having no feeling for anyone, about which I'm very pleased... Her rather resentful, peevish disposition is doubtless responsible for this stigma, but it goes to show that she is no coquette, as it is the law for girls to be these days.[35]

Yet Virginia wasn't shy about expressing her visceral attachment to whatever, in her conception, belonged to her. As Isabella reported to her husband, when Virginia learned that her parents intended to put one of the properties in La Spezia up for sale, she burst into tears.[36] And Virginia herself recorded in her diary that as a little girl, "by crying and laughing and sulking,"[37] she'd managed to acquire (complete with notarized deed) a seaside mill she'd considered part and parcel of her kingdom since infancy. Her mother was inclined, at the time, to attribute this proprietorial attitude to the child's uncommon sensitivity, which merely went to show that she "needed a husband who was kindness incarnate."[38]

The search for a suitable match for their prodigy was in fact a problem the Oldoinis were forced to face in the early 1850s, in large part for lack of money. The young woman in question did not, however, appear to share her parents' sense of haste. "Ninì doesn't want to see any suitors," Isabella reported to her husband, "because she says she doesn't want to get married or make commitments—that when winter is over she wants to go to Paris, see everything and everyone, and then make her choice..."[39] Many years later, the elderly Virginia would write: "If my mother hadn't been a fool, she would have taken me to Paris and the emperor would have married me and not Eugénie."

But the Oldoini family was neither prestigious nor rich enough to be able to marry their daughter into a great Florentine family—good matches were in short supply, Isabella confided to Filippo[40]—and so, when a suitor from Piedmont showed up with all his papers in order, Virginia's mother made no effort to hide her relief.[41]

Born in Turin on April 9, 1826, Francesco Verasis Asinari, 9th Count of Costigliole d'Asti and 6th Count of Castiglione Tinella, had arrived in La Spezia in July 1853 as the squire of Queen Maria Adelaide of Savoy. (Exhausted by eight successive pregnancies, Victor Emmanuel II's thirty-one-year-old wife had come to recuperate on the Ligurian coast.[42]) Castiglione was a dashing nobleman with impeccable manners who could boast of an impressive family tree and a significant inheritance, but life had already put him to the test: the count had been orphaned at a very early age and seen his young wife die in childbirth,[43] followed shortly afterward by the child.

Verasis was dazzled by Virginia's beauty and fell madly in love with her. The long letters he sent to her during the summer of 1853 are ample proof. We do not have Virginia's replies, but the count's anxiously proliferating declarations of love suggest the "peevish" sixteen-year-old's surprising skill in encouraging her suitor, then stringing him along. From his very first letter, Francesco gives himself over completely—"my fate is in your hands"—to his beloved. And when she agrees to send him a lock of her hair, he blesses her "a thousand times over for the treasure," confiding to her that when he held it in his hand his heart beat so hard that, for a moment, he thought it was going to burst. Eager to see Virginia's gesture not as an obvious move in keeping with romantic procedure but as the promise of a new life, Francesco did not hesitate to perform a sacrilegious symbolic act:

> I have a medallion in which I kept a lock trimmed from the head of my son, whose eyes were closed by eternal slumber. I have now replaced it with yours. Until now the memory of my lost little angel was the most precious thing I possessed; tell me, signorina, do you now believe me that my love is boundless? Could I offer you any more eloquent proof?[44]

The memory of his dead wife, too, was wiped out with a wave of the hand: "You are my first love that will last forever, I shall live only to make you happy."[45] But apparently this was not enough to convince Virginia—who showed herself jealous even of a rather improbable rival—of Francesco's unconditional surrender. "But what must I do to convince you of the immensity of my love?"[46] the poor man despaired, even as he went on seeking new metaphors to reiterate his amorous subjection: "For me, you are the deep mystery of the philosopher's stone, everything you touch turns to gold in my eyes, and I wouldn't trade this gold for all the riches in the world."[47] Finally Virginia yielded to his pleas. For the first time, she observed the magnetic power she was capable of exerting over men, and became enamored with unconditional love, of which the Count of Castiglione offered her the earliest example. Before July was out, an emotional Francesco recalled how, "with no witnesses but God," she had said yes in front of the Capuchin church, and how he'd promptly told Virginia's parents of his intentions. Marquis Oldoini—away in La Spezia—had by then had many opportunities to meet the count, get to know him, and entertain his appeals. Abiding by custom, Francesco had his younger brother Clemente take the initiative—a duty that would have fallen to their father, had he still been among the living—and officially ask the marquis for his daughter's hand on Francesco's behalf. In early September, just as the queen and her retinue were getting ready to go back to the Piedmontese capital, Oldoini thus received a letter from Clemente di Castiglione dated August 31. Getting straight to the point, Clemente took it for granted that Filippo by now knew his brother well enough to know that he was a "man of honor," that he had "the inclination" to marry Virginia, and that he would do anything in his power to make her happy.[48] No less formally, the marquis replied to him on September 3: "I was very glad to receive the request, and having just returned from Francesco's, I hasten to inform you that I have just given my daughter's hand to my future son-in-law with the certainty that I have ensured her happiness."[49] And so he indulged "the inclination."[50]

In fact, at first—unlike his wife, who'd immediately come out in favor of the Piedmontese suitor—the marquis did not hide his perplexity at the match.[51] The count had a reliable inheritance, yes, but he was a poor administrator, and by modernizing both the Castello di Costigliole and his residence in Turin so splendidly, he had gone deeply into debt. Yet with the help of his Castiglione ancestors, his prestigious position in the court of Savoy,[52] the favor of both the king and queen, not to mention the prospect of support in the diplomatic sphere, the influential patronage of Massimo d'Azeglio, and, last but not least, his daughter's own wishes, Oldoini was finally persuaded to give the count his consent. On January 9, 1854—once the laborious negotiations regarding the dowry and the protection of the patrimonial interests of both spouses were concluded (and not before the count completed one last assignment: a long summary of the history of Tuscany)—Virginia, looking splendid in her white *point de Venise* dress, married Count Francesco Verasis di Castiglione in the Church of the Most Holy Annunciation in Florence.[53] After a brief stop at La Spezia, on January 11 the couple set out for Turin, with a torrent of instructions from Marquise Oldoini—tireless when it came to telling her son-in-law to take the utmost care of her daughter, who was going to be away from her family for the first time in her life. Above all she urged him to keep an eye on her fragile health. And so it was that Virginia, who wasn't quite seventeen, started a new life with a husband who, as far as she was concerned, was a wild card, in a city whose customs and habits she knew only secondhand. The diary in which she almost daily recorded her doings, the correspondence between her and her parents, as well as the letters Castiglione sent to his in-laws, allow us to follow her closely in the two years after her marriage.

The palace—lavishly refurbished by her husband—where the couple took up residence was on via Lagrange,[54] in the heart of the eighteenth-century city, just ten minutes from the royal palace. One could come and go through the main entrance, which opened into a grand courtyard, or through a wrought-iron gate at the far end of the vast garden.

In a letter dated March 20, Francesco wrote to his father-in-law—with whom he'd established warm relations rooted in their "reciprocal bond of intimacy" and "affinity of thought"—regarding his wife's health. "Niny is blooming," he said. Yet neither of the two men seemed to think Virginia was mature enough to bear the burdens of her new marital duties, and both believed she needed to be discreetly steered along. Francesco kept his father-in-law scrupulously informed of his daughter's progress.

And so we witness Virginia going out of her way to be kind to the various members of the Castiglione family, "who are doing everything possible to win her affection";[55] admiring the decor in her new room (above all the big canopied bed with its gilded columns, which she will bring with her everywhere, through all her many moves); putting her personal touch on the arrangement of the furniture in her new home; and taking an interest in the garden.[56] But the couple's arrival at the ancestral Castello di Costigliole—a ritual that Francesco had gone to great lengths to organize—was, as he himself would later confide to Oldoini, a disappointment on all fronts:

"Rarely, I think, has a chatelaine been greeted like Niny: Triumphal Arches, Music, Poetry, Officials in Full Dress, Bells, Artillery Fire—but unfortunately, as you know, her character eschews such effusions, and she took them like medicine."[57] And four months later, in another letter addressed to his father-in-law from Costigliole, the count was forced to admit that his wife was ungovernable, that he simply had to accept her mood swings. "She is in very good spirits and if she continues," he wrote in English, before switching back to Italian, "we might make an offering to the Virgin Mary."[58]

Virginia's volatility might have come as a surprise to Francesco and, to a certain degree, to her father (who hadn't had much opportunity to see her in action during her adolescence), but it was certainly not news to her mother. The letters that the latter wrote to her husband, in which she told him what she heard from Turin, make this abundantly clear. However reassuring the initial news may have been, it wasn't enough to set her mind at ease. The marquise was far from confident that the marriage she'd so warmly supported would succeed. "I have good news from Niny. Castiglione writes me often, he really is a good egg. God grant them happiness and keep them from ending it [their marriage], as I'm afraid they will."[59] "Niny wrote me today, and thank heavens she still seems quite content; of course, she would never tell or write me anything, but I hope to see for myself, and soon."[60] "Niny wrote just now and seems happy. Thank God. Castiglione, the poor child, really strikes me as a good little boy."[61]

Isabella had every reason to be worried. After less than a month of conjugal life, Virginia was already recording the first quarrels with her husband in her diary. "I bickered with Francesco," she wrote on January 28; and again on February 3: "Verasis lost his temper"; and on February 13: "After dinner, in my bedroom, Verasis said he wanted to separate, then came around to make peace."[62]

The diary the countess kept in these early years—a diary that, unfortunately, we have only in fragments—is less remarkable for its puerility (as is generally claimed) than for its disaffection. With absolute detachment, not betraying the least emotion, the young wife records the events that punctuate her days. Not a word about the wedding night, or how she feels about her husband, or her new life in Piedmont. Or about fights or tears or loneliness. Her choice of clothes and her first extramarital affairs seem to her of equal importance. She confines herself to jotting down facts, sometimes indulging in a few brief descriptions, but never going any further.

What seems clear, though, is that even during the first marital spats Virginia is by no means intimidated by a husband ten years her senior and is more than ready to assert her own authority. She shows herself capable of calibrating her behavior to a degree he finds disorienting. Coldness, detachment, and estrangement deprive her interlocutor of any hope of breaking through the solid wall of indifference she had built around herself. In the years to come, she would make systematic use of this strategy with the many men in her life, but for the moment the punishment was reserved solely for her spouse, who was not living up to expectations. After putting her on a pedestal, swearing to obey her every desire, and declaring himself willing to sacrifice anything for her happiness, her love slave had promptly cast off the mask and begun acting like a master. In Turin, she hadn't found her dreamed-of freedom but a life planned down to the smallest details. Castiglione had changed into a nagging pedagogue and treated her like a little girl who needed to be educated, cajoled, and bribed with expensive little gifts. In essence, he believed himself entitled to exercise an authority over his wife which she was not willing to grant anyone. Virginia's beauty had given her a strong sense of her superiority. Ever since she was a child she'd been accustomed to subjecting all and sundry to her whims. So she used superficial conventions to keep her husband at arm's length, defying a claim to marital intimacy which she felt was an undue imposition. Her stubborn refusal to comply with Francesco's request to address him as *tu*[63]—a refusal that figured among Francesco's complaints to his father-in-law—clearly demonstrates her desire not to permit any intimacy between them.

Virginia's increasingly explicit rebellion against married life forced Castiglione to come to terms with the fact that his young wife, of whom he was so proud, could lure him into arguments and make him lose his temper. "When she gets something into her head," he confided to his father-in-law, "there is no way of talking her out of it." And the worst of it was that Virginia—self-contained as she was—remained an enigma to him: "Anyway, you know her character, and you know that, in her relations with others, she is always rather cold."[64] Though he tried to make excuses for her ("She is still a few months shy of seventeen, but I am certain that, once her judgment matures, she will be practically perfect"), repeating time and time again that "a proper appreciation of the things of this world [will] show her the path to be followed and make her see that between husband and wife duties are reciprocal,"[65] the poor man soon realized that his wife was not only armed with an implacable will but found it entertaining to go head to head with him, and to humiliate him with her indifference. Weak and in love, but also impulsive and hot-tempered, Francesco reacted by flying into rages as terrible as they were useless. Once the dust had settled, he was always the one to apologize.

The count was not the only one to pay the price for his wife's personality. Virginia took advantage of the new distance between them to liberate herself from her mother, with whom she'd always had a combative relationship. She was well aware that Isabella would do anything for her and considered her happiness "a consolation for all of her sorrows,"[66] but precisely because her mother knew her like no one else—and was capable of deciphering her moods, her whims, her silences—Virginia made it a priority to get out from under her thumb the moment she was married. She signaled this quite clearly when Isabella paid her a visit in early June—an affectionate undertaking that could have not gone worse.[67] Virginia sidestepped her mother's insistent demands by using her husband as a shield and treating her like an intruder, and the marquise, after venting her indignation, stormed out. It was the same thing all over again after the birth of her grandson, when the marquise eagerly rushed off to Turin only to be received "like a perfect stranger" and allowed to see her daughter for no more than an hour a day.[68]

But Isabella understood that the only way not to endanger the emotional bond with her difficult child, who appeared to expect the world on a platter, was to be patient. And though she knew that it was an impossible request, she never stopped asking her to "love me as I love you."[69] Despite Virginia's mood swings and the anxiety they caused her, the marquise continued to write letters in which family events, financial anxieties, and worries about her husband's health were interspersed with gossip about Florence and fashion. But what she liked most of all was to receive news of her daughter's health—to know that she was happy and in high spirits, to applaud her successes, and to remind her, as often as possible, that she'd been lucky enough to find "an uncommon husband,"[70] a husband "whose only defect [was] that he was too good,"[71] a "poor dear" whom, she advised her daughter, she shouldn't "make cry."[72] It didn't matter that Virginia paid no attention and remembered her only when it suited her. Isabella kept on. When her daughter begged her to stop meddling in her private affairs, she replied that she didn't mean to meddle and reminded her that she could always count on her.[73] On the other hand, the marquise had no qualms about taking out her fouler moods on her son-in-law, sternly warning him not to interfere in her relationship with her daughter.[74]

Things were very different between Virginia and her father. While her mother—with her directness, impulsiveness, and "coarseness"[75]—seemed to her to lack distinction, her father—with his elegance, moderation, and perfect familiarity with the ways of the world—filled her with admiration. In his detachment, the marquis was a role model for Virginia, and their affinities of temperament would turn out to be of crucial importance. Both of them—as her father repeated more than once—had "iron wills,"[76] thought highly of themselves, and were determined to prove that they were equal to their ambitions. But they were both also moody, prone to hypochondria, and helpless in the face of depression.[77]

This father, who was so similar to her but almost always kept his distance, had been the first man Virginia set out to conquer. From her earliest childhood, she'd sent him letters in perfect *fille modèle* style, informing him of her progress in Italian as well as in the other languages she was learning. On the cusp of adolescence, she'd even made an imperious declaration of love: "My dear papa, how I long to see you again, I'm sure you'll be happy to see how I've grown and what a beautifull girl I've made [*sic*]. Mama says that now you have to think about finding me a husband and getting ready a good dowry.

That is what Mama says, but what I say is that I want to spend some time with you, so come quickly."[78] Virginia went on craving her father's respect and admiration for a long time. As an adult, when she had some influence in high places, Virginia would even make herself indispensable to the marquis's diplomatic ambitions, turning her father's more than problematic career into a personal crusade.

At the start of her campaign of conquests, however, the great seductress was held in check by the first man she loved and whose love she wanted in return. Walled up in his egotism as he was, he could never have given her the proof of affection, consideration, and recognition that she yearned for. Even as he made use of his daughter's influence, the marquis, though his methods were not entirely orthodox, would never stop playing the part of the noble father. He avoided facing Virginia head-on but instead attempted a kind of cautious arbitration among the warring elements that made enemies of her mother, her husband, and finally her son, constantly preaching the same old principles of respectability, decorum, and prudence which she'd long ago abandoned. A letter from the summer of 1854 shows how different Virginia's dealings with her father were from the unreserved tone she used with her husband and her mother. With him, *la petite fille modèle* could still manage a smile; for him, she reserved the best version of herself. When she learned she was pregnant, she delivered the news to her mother, giving her husband, who was out of his mind with joy, the pleasure of informing his father-in-law. Not long after, however, she decided she would mention the event directly to her father, playfully placing him at the center of it. "As you learned from Francesco's letter, I believe I have a *picchinicchi* on the way, who will make a grandfather of you . . . and you will have a grandchild who will love and delight you, and when you have the spleen he will help you through it."[79] But her high spirits were to prove short-lived. She would be the first to succumb to the spleen. The child on the way would in fact consign her, with no hope of escape, to a husband she no longer had any reason to love and to a life that she already found dull. Over the months that followed, her diary reveals symptoms—physical ailments, fits of weeping, melancholy, a sense of isolation—of a depressive crisis from which Virginia would reemerge firmly determined to make a party of herself alone. On March 29, 1855, an explosion of happiness—telegrams, letters, presents—greeted the birth of little Giorgio Verasis di Castiglione (whom his parents immediately called Georges). But that day also marked the birth of a new Countess of Castiglione—a woman resolved on heeding no one and nothing but her own ever-changing needs.

Her first act of liberation was to take a lover. Three months after giving birth, Virginia spread her arms for Ambrogio Doria, a handsome Genoese official whom she'd known since childhood and who, having relocated to Turin as aide-de-camp to His Royal Highness the Duke of Genoa, had become the Count of Castiglione's closest friend. On the morning of June 29—taking advantage of Francesco's absence—Ambrogio declared his passion to Virginia. In response, Virginia led him into her bedroom, undressed in front of him, and wearing only "her white dressing gown"[80] yielded to his kisses and caresses; she put off giving herself to him completely until a few days later. This encounter with Ambrogio also marked her first use of a rudimentary code in her diary, which she was to go on using to record the different degrees of intimacy she'd granted her suitors—a code in which *b* likely stood for kisses, *bx* for embraces and intimate caresses, *f* for full sexual intercourse.[81]

If Virginia's diary gives us no more than a very faint sketch of that first adulterous scene, Ambrogio's letters ("I love you madly...! There is nothing in the world I wouldn't do for you—you have every right to demand it of me and even to abuse your rights";[82] "I love you as no one has ever loved you, or will ever love you"[83]) are quite unambiguous. They confirmed, for Virginia, her regality, and wreaked vengeance on a husband who'd taken her off the pedestal where he'd placed her two years earlier and dared to treat her like an ordinary wife. But precisely because the whole amorous venture was intended to confirm her powers of seduction, it required constant confirmation. During that same summer of 1855, she returned to La Spezia with little Giorgio (nurse and maid in tow) and wasted no time; she was determined to turn the heads of Ambrogio's two younger brothers, Andrea and Marcello Doria, even as she continued to keep up an ardent correspondence with Ambrogio. When she went back to Turin after the bathing season, she resumed her relationship with him but, now that the enchantment of the beginning was behind them, she turned quickly frigid, showing him a degree of indifference that until then she'd reserved solely for her husband. Francesco, for his part, unable to cope with the worsening of their marital crisis, veered between pathetic paternalism ("A crumb of tenderness bestowed from time to time is the best way for a wife to get whatever she may desire"[84]) and impossible requests ("Try to stock up on amiability and good humor for my return"[85]), none of which had any effect whatsoever.

But it wouldn't be long before the prospect of an affair worthy of her ambitions changed Virginia's state of mind.

# Turin
## 1854–1856

VIRGINIA'S MARRIAGE to the Count of Castiglione was problematic from the first, but her debut in Turin society went off without a hitch. She'd been preceded by her reputation as a beauty, and everyone was on pins and needles to find out whether this reputation was deserved. "Today the curiosity-seekers of Turin are in a tizzy over the arrival of the bride Castiglioni [*sic*]," Margherita di Collegno noted in her diary (and so we gather that critics were already lying in wait). "Lorenzo Litta[1] is going into a frenzy, almost a fury, because this bride—who was lucky enough to have been born and raised in Tuscany—pretended not to be able to speak anything but French. She behaves like a petty little girl."[2] Yet such misgivings did not prevent the very young countess from passing every test with flying colors. With her perfect self-control and absolute naturalness, she earned the admiration of an aristocratic society that was not at all inclined to indulgence. "The Turin debut of the Countess of Castion [Castiglione in the Piedmontese dialect] was astonishing. Everyone rushed to see her, crowded round her as if at the theater, and went into raptures. In short, it was a memorable event," Costanza d'Azeglio wrote to her son Emanuele.[3] Duke Borea d'Olmo, grand master of ceremonies at the court, would later recall that a horde of guests at one of the balls at the royal palace climbed up onto chairs in order to watch her come in.[4] Massimo d'Azeglio was proud of his protégée's success:

> The bride appeared on the horizon with everyone craning their necks to see. They found her just as beautiful as promised—which is no small thing. She was polite to everyone, as no one was expecting since some of them had predicted the opposite. I am convinced that all will turn out well and that I shall be able to congratulate myself on having been the lucky promoter of this marriage.[5]

But what did the young woman from Florence make of this new city where she'd come to live—a city that must have struck her as very different from the city of her birth?

There was no trace of letting things go, nor the faintest shadow of lighthearted Tuscan irreverence, in the habits and customs of the Piedmontese aristocracy, which for centuries had been distinguished by their loyalty to the House of Savoy and their bravery on the battlefield (the deaths at the Battle of Novara were the most recent proof of this). Proud of their antiquity, protective of their traditions, loyal to the Church's power and precepts, the nobility expected their men to adhere strictly to convention, an education "incomplete in certain respects" but "strict,"[6] and demanded irreproachable conduct from their women. It was the nobility's duty to hold the keys to society, and no intrusions of any kind could be tolerated. Cultured and knowledgeable as the Marquise d'Azeglio was, had she not confessed that she didn't know the first thing about the bourgeoisie?[7] The court was both polestar and benchmark for the major families of Turin, who hewed to an anachronistic protocol that never failed to astonish foreign diplomats.[8] The Savoy nobility, though provincial and conservative, enjoyed relations with the cream of Europe's aristocratic crop, and the young brides who arrived from beyond the Alps inevitably brought with them some shreds of education better suited to modern times. Naturally, Napoleonic rule had also left its mark on military organization and dress, strengthening ties with the French elite. But life at court was not immune to departures from decorum. While Victor Emmanuel II's mother and wife—both Habsburg princesses—graciously submitted to the strict dictates of etiquette and presided affably at receptions and balls, the king himself did not hide his annoyance at the constraints imposed on him.[9] A brusque and impatient man, whenever he was forced to be present at official banquets, he never so much as unfolded his napkin, and he refused to eat, or dance.[10]

But if at court the king could still lay down the law, when it came to the government of his country he was forced to consider the limits imposed on him by the constitution. In addition to the conservative stronghold of the Turin nobility, there was an entrepreneurial bourgeoisie dedicated to commerce, finance, and agriculture, as well as the Turin of the university and the progressive newspapers, whose main point of reference was not court but parliament. Both were crying out for modernization, embracing the ideas of the many patriots who'd found safe haven in the kingdom of Sardinia when a wave of repression had crashed over Italy after the failed revolutionary uprisings of 1848. From the southerners Bertrando Spaventa and Francesco de Sanctis to the northerners Marco Minghetti and Carlo Farini; from the Sicilian Giuseppe La Farina to the Lombards Cesare Correnti, Cesare Cantù, and Niccolò Tommaseo (a veteran of the

Venetian insurrection), philosophers, writers, and intellectuals from all over the peninsula were helping to promulgate, even in Piedmont, "the new Romantic culture of Italian nationalism," laying "the groundwork for the imminent and decisive struggle for national unity."[11]

Victor Emmanuel II felt no sympathy for liberal ideas, and his father—with whom he'd never been close—had not involved him in the decision to go to war with Austria. In 1849, the disastrous outcome of the first war of independence, combined with the defeat at Novara, had caused Charles Albert to abdicate and put Victor Emmanuel prematurely on the throne. At twenty-eight, with no political experience under his belt, he had begun his reign in an atmosphere of tragedy. The new ruler didn't look kindly on his father's political project—for which the country was now paying such a painful price—but whether from a sense of honor or dynastic pride or political realism, he retained the statute granted by his father and eventually turned over the presidency of the council to a man he trusted.[12] It would in fact be the liberal Massimo d'Azeglio who, with balance and prudence, steered Victor Emmanuel's reign through one of its most dramatic periods. D'Azeglio—a sincere patriot—was reluctant to plot revenge and put a plan for unification into action. He was convinced that in the long term Italy had to go it alone and achieve autonomy through a confederation of states governed by their respective legitimate rulers. However, in accordance with the statute, he initiated a policy of reform aimed at curbing the power of the Church, promoting the laicization of the state, and reducing the privileges of the nobles. At the same time he heightened the prestige of the monarchy, constructing the myth of an "honorable king" around Victor Emmanuel II.

Camillo Benso di Cavour—d'Azeglio's successor, who came in

with the center-left government[13]—was the man who convinced Victor Emmanuel that Italian independence represented a valuable opportunity for the kingdom of Savoy, whose future was far from certain. As a result of the House of Savoy's policy of endless expansion and its unscrupulous alliances with France and Austria—the two great powers between which the territory served as a divide—the ancient duchy had gradually expanded its territory through annexation and trade until it acquired the status of "kingdom,"[14] but its lack of homogeneity "exposed it to the risk of disintegration, if not worse, were there to be any major continental conflict,"[15] and its political fragility was evident to many.

"This little kingdom," said Margherita Trotti Bentivoglio, the Milanese wife of the Piedmontese patriot Giacinto Provana di Collegno,

> consists of four provinces that hold no feelings in common. There is Sardinia, civilized only in its center and under the rule of the priests. There is Genoa, which feels toward Piedmont precisely as Lombardy does toward Austria . . . It was hoped that the Genoese merchants would send us useful commercial members but all they've sent are arsonists, brutes, democrats, and a renegade priest [the Sardinian canon Giorgio Asproni]. Savoy, on the other hand, goes to the other extreme: more than half of its members are ultra-conservative . . . Piedmont is the only healthy part of the monarchy—but Piedmont has no political consciousness.[16]

Victor Emmanuel was quick to perceive the advantages that might accrue to his dynasty by adopting an Italian policy. And Cavour was determined to make the Piedmontese fully "conscious."

In order to gain strength and cohesion, the state's territory needed to be expanded further by driving the Austrians out of Lombardy and Venice and creating a kingdom of northern Italy, not in the name of the House of Savoy's old "artichoke policy" (expanding leaf by leaf)[17] but in the interests of an ideal of liberty and independence shared by everyone on the peninsula. Cavour, unlike d'Azeglio, was convinced that to cast off the Austrian yoke they needed the support of Britain and France. In May 1853, at the start of the Crimean War, when England and France helped the Ottoman Empire thwart Russia's expansionist aims, Cavour saw an opportunity to give Piedmont a seat at the table with the major powers. At the time Victor Emmanuel couldn't wait to wipe away "the stain of Novara," restoring to "the Sardinian army the prestige that ennobles material power,"[18] and in early 1855, after a long period fluctuating between hope and uncertainty,[19] the kingdom of Sardinia finally formed an alliance with the English and the French. On March 4 it declared war on Russia and at the end of April sent to the Crimea an expeditionary force of eighteen thousand men under the command of the minister of war, General Alfonso La Marmora.

In the midst of this intense political and diplomatic activity—in a very tense climate[20]—Virginia took her first steps into Turin society. On January 25, 1854, sporting a red and silver dress, she made her official entrance into the court on her husband's arm. But it was Massimo d'Azeglio who, once again, played the role of tutelary spirit. "He introduced the king to me, and I spoke with him," she notes in her diary,[21] revealing no trace of emotion about this important event, and furthermore reversing the meaning of the ceremony, seeing that *she* was the one who had to be introduced to the sovereign and not the other way around. D'Azeglio rejoiced over the soirée's success—"The Oldoini bride has been enthroned in Turin society with maximum applause"[22]—and observed that the Piedmont air had loosened his protégée's tongue.[23] Virginia didn't seem surprised to attract so much attention. Nor did she marvel that Victor Emmanuel was interested in conversing with her or that, "riding on horseback and dressed like a murderer,"[24] he escorted the carriage that brought her and Countess Carolina Vimercati home from the Palazzina di Caccia of Stupinigi in Turin. The Count of Castiglione meanwhile bragged to his father-in-law about his wife's dazzling success during their stay at the Castello d'Agliè, where they were the invited guests of the Duke and Duchess of Genoa.[25] And so—introduced by Francesco and her in-laws Clemente and Maria di Castiglione into Turin's beau monde—the countess befriended their friends and showed herself, at least when she wasn't confined to her husband's company, cheerful, witty, and full of fun.

Virginia now felt fully involved in the life of the court, as she would later demonstrate in her sincere grief over the death of Queen Maria Adelaide on January 20, 1855, and in her respect for the grief of her husband,[26] who, being engaged in the sovereign's service, took part in all of the many funeral rites. Back from the burial in Superga on the evening of the 24th, Francesco was greeted with unusual kindness by his wife. "He came into my bedroom in tears," she records in her diary.

> He cried like a baby over fresh-picked violets taken from a bouquet thrown to the queen—and over a dried pansy plucked from a garland that had been placed on the queen's tomb, where she lay and will lie forever. He gave me that pansy—a precious gift I greatly cherished . . . Then he undressed and went to bed at eight. I warmed up his bed

> and gave him tea, and he fell asleep . . . I came to my bedroom to write these lines. Thinking of the poor queen, I shed many tears.[27]

To be sure, the tears and the mortuary violets were standbys of romantic sentimentalism, but she was probably sincere. Her husband's family traditions, as well as his personal choices, bound him closely to the royal house, and Virginia too had been brought up to respect the monarchy. After all, her father was a high-ranking functionary of the kingdom of Sardinia and her mother close with Massimo d'Azeglio and a friend of the Count of Cavour, who was, besides, the Count of Castiglione's cousin.[28]

Increased enforcement of the Siccardi laws, which sanctioned the separation of Church and state, had made people's blood boil—particularly the law presented by Minister Rattazzi which suppressed and confiscated the possessions of religious orders that did not perform charitable or educational activities. In early 1855, some even saw the terrible series of deaths befalling the royal family[29] as a divine warning. And yet Victor Emmanuel—Cavour had him over a barrel—decided to go on enforcing the laws, thereby inviting papal excommunication. Certainly Virginia grasped the political significance of the provision, which constituted an implicit challenge to philopapist Austrian absolutism, and the significance of the military convention concluded with England and France. Though the birth of her son and, more than that, the amorous merry-go-round with the Doria brothers were keeping her busy, these things were of crucial importance to her friends and relatives, and above all to her diplomat father. The taking of Sevastopol on August 16—in which the Piedmontese contingent had participated, proving their mettle in the Battle of the Chernaya—would soon secure Russia's surrender.

Cavour's gamble had paid off. The small Savoyard kingdom could now hope for the gratitude of England and France, but with the European political situation changing so rapidly, nothing promised to be easy. It was therefore decided, while waiting for peace, to sound out the allies' intentions while at the same time raising Piedmont's international profile. At the end of November, with d'Azeglio, Cavour, and a select group of members of the royal house, Victor Emmanuel II paid official visits to France and England. In both Paris and London, he was the object of countless comments—regarding his bizarre physical appearance, his blunt manners, his freedom of language—which, ultimately, worked in his favor. Victor Emmanuel's nonchalance after all went hand in hand with his unwavering consciousness of the respect due his rank; the only conventions that held any water for him were those inherent in his condition as a sovereign. A member of the oldest reigning dynasty in Europe, he expected to be received in France with the same honors bestowed a few months earlier on Queen Victoria, regardless of the size of his kingdom. And Napoleon III—eager to win the sympathies of legitimate sovereigns and kick dust over the fact that he'd secured the crown by means of a coup d'état—indulged him. "With his usual elegance and tact," Fleury, the emperor's grand equerry, later recalled, "he did not fail to offer a worthy welcome to the heir to a neighboring throne . . . and made it clear what great importance he attached to Victor Emmanuel's visit."[30]

On November 23, Victor Emmanuel arrived by train at the Gare de Lyon, emblazoned for the occasion with his monogram and the word *Traktir*.[31] He was welcomed there by Prince Napoleon, the emperor's cousin, then climbed into a big gilded carriage escorted by Marshal Magnan, Colonel Fleury, and a contingent of the

Cent-Suisses. On the way to the Tuileries, the procession crossed the quais, where soldiers were lined up on both sides. "In the glittering uniform of a hussar, tall, with his bizarre face,"[32] the king maintained his most martial manner, but there was a surprise in store for him which he never could have predicted. The Count of Reiset had been so bold as to teach the emperor the Piedmontese anthem, "and when the incomparable musicians of the military band struck up the fanfare of the House of Savoy followed by the anthem, cheers burst out on every side and his emotions were written plainly on his face. Much as he tried to hide it behind his long mustache, his kind, round, bulging eyes were not as dry as he would have liked."[33] As he made his rounds, Victor Emmanuel needed no special encouragement to indulge in his bawdy ways, collecting salacious anecdotes about women and diplomatic gaffes, though he never forgot the purpose of his journey.

And since it had become clear that while the British government was inclined to sympathize with the sovereign of a constitutionalist and anticlerical kingdom, it was not about to entertain Piedmont's hopes of tangible compensation for its participation in the Crimea,[34] Victor Emmanuel and Cavour pinned their hopes on France. The emperor had in fact insisted that, when he returned from London, the king stay for a few extra days in Paris, in spite of the fact that, to Victor Emmanuel's annoyance, he made no effort to conceal that he preferred to talk politics with the king's minister. Indeed, it was to Cavour that, during the last supper at the Tuileries, on December 8, Napoleon III said point-blank: "Write to Walewski in confidence and tell him what you think I can do for Piedmont and for Italy."[35] As Rosario Romeo has observed, "explicating the meaning" of this phrase "and translating its potential into action would be the work for which Cavour would go down in history."[36] His first request was for the Sardinian government to be allowed to participate fully in the Congress of Paris—where two months later the major European powers would discuss the terms of the peace treaty—and to raise the Italian question.

Even before their promotional trip, however, Victor Emmanuel and Cavour, determined to leave no stone unturned when it came to the furtherment of the patriotic cause, had agreed to ask the Castiglione beauty for her help. Yet—contrary to what has repeatedly been claimed—it was neither Cavour nor the king who induced Virginia to make the trip to France.

In early spring, shortly after the birth of his son, the Count of Castiglione had announced to his father-in-law that he planned to take his wife to Paris for at least four or five months. He was hoping to arrive in time to show her the grand exposition scheduled to open on May 15.[37] He had also instructed his lawyers to settle some of his debts with the sale of a few properties in Piedmont, and such a trip would spare him the embarrassment of being in Turin when the sale took place.[38] On the other hand he was forced to take on more debt to cover the expense of the journey.[39] The king and the prime minister, having learned of the imprudent count's plans for a sojourn in Paris, thought they might put his wife's resources to work in the interests of the state. For Virginia's great beauty was not only indubitably good publicity for the country's image; she would also find every door open to her, allowing her to report to Turin what was being said in high places on the Italian question. Besides being beautiful, she was intelligent, she spoke several languages, and in Paris she could rely on important connections who'd known her since she was a child: her maternal grandfather had been the trusted lawyer of Napoleon III's father, and it was not out of the question to think the emperor himself had laid eyes on her when she was still a girl. In Florence, Virginia had been acquainted with Princess Mathilde, and her family was very close with the Poniatowski clan, which was just then putting down roots in the French capital. Just the year before, in 1854, Napoleon III had brought Prince Giuseppe to Paris and made him a senator. The enchanting Maria Anna di Ricci, too, was a Poniatowski child—the second wife of Count Walewski, who that very year had been made foreign minister. Even the representative of the Sardinian kingdom in Paris, Marquis Salvatore Pes di Villamarina, was an old friend of the Oldoinis', and the years of his tenure with the dukes of Lorraine[40] had coincided with Virginia's adolescence. The question remains whether Cavour and Victor Emmanuel had good reason to bank on the countess's easy ways in the erotic domain. But the latter would not hesitate to find out for himself. Bare-bones as they are, the diary entries speak volumes.

In early November 1855—when the preparations for the Paris expedition scheduled for the start of 1856 were in full swing—Count Enrico Martini di Cigala, Castiglione's maternal uncle and the king's aide-de-camp, began paying the young couple quite a number of visits. On the evening of Thursday, November 13, taking advantage of the fact that Francesco had gone to Milan, he sat with his niece for a long time and told her that the king was going to pay her a visit the following evening. Virginia donned a black velvet dress for the occasion and ordered the servant to shut the front door, leaving only the garden door open. Under cover of darkness, after the sun had gone down, Victor Emmanuel walked through the garden and joined her in the drawing room, where he stayed for two hours. "The king spoke of this and that, of his misfortunes, his worries, the war," writes Virginia. Even before Victor Emmanuel's return from his state visits to France and England, a man called Brémontier came several times to "copy out the alphabet"—the secret code for communicating with Cavour. The sovereign came to see her again the same day, and on the evening of the 15th Cavour paid a visit of his own. On the 16th—"wrapped in a black cloak and wearing a red hat"—the countess went to the royal palace to say goodbye to Victor Emmanuel, met him in the Hall of Arms, and talked with him about "the pope, Centurioni,[41] and François." That was when the king gave her the mysterious "Floron"[42] he had brought back from London. On the 17th, her last day in Turin (Francesco had by then already left for Genoa), Virginia finished packing amidst a flurry of visits. In the afternoon Marcello Doria, with whom she was still carrying on, came to call, and she made love with him on the floor. Then, while she was busy closing the last of her trunks, the king's aide-de-camp, the Count of Persano, announced that "the king was waiting outside!" Evidently he wished to say goodbye to her one last time. Virginia, keeping her cool, took her time doing her hair, put on the black velvet dress again, dismissed all the servants, and gave Persano the key to the garden. When, after a long conversation, she walked the king back to the garden, he forced himself on her. In confiding the sovereign's assault to her diary, Virginia again refrains from commentary, considering it normal behavior that happens every day. "I went to the toilet to fix myself up. Finished up the trunks with Antonio, whom I gave 20 francs; wrote some letters. By 12 I was all done and I went to sleep."[43]

Yet in light of her behavior in the days that followed, we may well suspect that Virginia's imperturbability was only apparent and that the emotions of the past weeks had altered her self-image. Up to that point, she'd been satisfied with the admiration she aroused wherever she showed her face, and like other young wives of her class she had consoled herself for her marital disappointment by taking a lover. Now, though—gambling on her intelligence and capacity for seduction—she was being asked to put herself at the service of her country and invested with a task that exempted her from respecting the moral regulations and social conventions that held women captive. She was also learning to navigate the ruthlessness of politics and the brutality of power, for which her body was a commodity to be disposed of at will. She needed only to draw her own conclusions and, casting off all qualms, feel free to make love how, when, and with whomever she pleased.

Leaving Turin behind her, Virginia went to visit her mother in Florence, where she gave herself to Count Lao Bentivoglio—a friend of her parents' whom she'd known since childhood.[44] After hallowing the holiday by bestowing her favors, she left him heartbroken and moved on to Genoa, where her husband was waiting for her, ready to embark for Marseille. In Genoa, she also saw Ambrogio Doria, who'd come to say goodbye despite the coldness she'd shown him of late. They hadn't seen each other for nearly three weeks, and even if at the moment of parting she seemed "emotional," Ambrogio realized he was dealing with a very different person from the "Bisisi" he'd once known: "The day you left Genoa you looked rather tired; I was surprised to find you so changed in such a short time."[45] He was not wrong. But the change went much deeper than he could imagine.

# Paris

## 1856–1857

THE COUNT OF CAVOUR wasn't the only one wondering about Napoleon III's foreign policy. All the chancelleries of Europe were speculating on it too. The emperor's domestic policy had, in the meantime, become plain to see. Ever since December 2, 1852—a year to the day after the coup d'état that transformed him from a president-prince into an emperor—Louis Napoleon Bonaparte had been attempting to secure the support of both the populace and the elite, promising stability and order, and trying to meet two common and nearly irreconcilable demands: fidelity to the Revolution and nostalgia for the monarchy and the Napoleonic era. He'd made an effort to satisfy the former by promoting modernization, industrialization, and the revival of the liberal economy, appealing to the business world, and attempting to improve the atrocious living conditions of the urban plebs.[1] As for the latter, Napoleon III had wanted to legitimize the new imperial regime by returning to the monarchical glories of the ancien régime, aiming to mesmerize his contemporaries with a splendor that brooked no comparison and "to write the regime into history, since apart from the revolutionary experiment and the Second Republic, France had always been ruled by a monarch surrounded by a court."[2] The Paris that welcomed the Castigliones in early 1856 was the perfect illustration of the emperor's "democratic Caesarism."[3] The capital, which now numbered more than a million inhabitants, was the very picture of modernity, with its transportation network, gas lighting (electricity was not far behind), and department stores, as well as its plethora of theaters and public places. Two years earlier Haussmann had initiated the pharaonic project of "beautifying Paris, making it politically secure, and enhancing its economic development."[4] Théophile Gautier—unlike his contemporary Baudelaire—seemed to have no regrets: "The royal palace is not the only place to have been beautified: the entire city is getting a breath of fresh air, becoming healthier and cleaner, being given a bath of civilization. Out with the foul-smelling alleys; out with the rotten slums where poverty is paired with disease, and, too often, vice as well."[5] From the windows of the elegant rented apartment in—heartening homonymy—rue de Castiglione, Virginia could see the treetops of the Tuileries Garden, where imperial power was staged in all its splendor. Ceremonies and celebrations had of course always been favorable opportunities for monarchical propaganda. The emperor's marriage to Eugénie de Montijo, Countess of Teba, celebrated at Notre-Dame in 1853; the spectacular reception given Queen Victoria; and the success of the Paris Exposition had already demonstrated the new regime's ability to promote an image commensurate with its ambitions. But there was, in this wide-ranging "promotional" strategy, such a marked predilection for balls that the term *fête impériale* quickly became synonymous with the Second Empire. What better occasion could there be for the emperor to invite and receive with equal grace representatives of the nobility, public officials, politicians, bankers, notables of the upper middle class, unscrupulous speculators, and the unpresentable envoys of the nouveau riche? The solemnity of the etiquette—modeled on that of the First Empire[6]—and the display of luxury were not, however, intended only for the guests (who were given the impression that they were enjoying an exclusive privilege); the newspapers, too, were unfailingly asked to report on court receptions, allowing a much larger public to participate from a distance; to become acquainted with the protocol; to memorize the names of the most prominent participants; and to keep abreast of the latest fashions.

And nothing thrilled readers so much as news about the court and the young and comely empress. For the guests, the balls provided an opportunity to approach the emperor, speak to him, and make requests, given that outside of these official social events the emperor and empress led a retired life. But Napoleon III, too, took advantage of these gatherings to strike up informal acquaintanceships, hatch secret plans, and facilitate under-the-table deals.

The absurdity of these grandiose pretensions, for a court that owed its existence to a coup d'état, was not lost on the regime's detractors. The Goncourt brothers—those nostalgic exegetes of the usages and customs of eighteenth-century Versailles—called it "a cobbled- and slapped-together court made up of new names and freshly usurped titles, a topsy-turvy parade-ground court... higgledy-piggledy and without hierarchy, where all one need do is show up to find a place, and often an important one."[7]

The upstart-in-chief was the emperor himself, who'd made his parvenu status "a banner and a title of honor."[8] As long ago as 1820, when he was a boy of twelve, his mother Hortense had prepared him for the possibility of his future reign, drilling it into him that his titles were of recent vintage and that "the role of the Bonapartes was to be a friend to all, to play the part of mediators and conciliators."[9] In the course of his eventful life, Louis never forgot his mother's lessons and always pursued a sovereignty "more charismatic than legitimate—democratic as well as populist."[10] And so, when finally he ascended the throne and announced his marriage to a Spanish noblewoman with no royal ancestors, he could proudly proclaim, "before all of Europe, the condition of upstart—a glorious title if it is achieved thanks to the freely given vote of a great people."[11] The experiment underway in the Tuileries entailed equipping this new form of monarchy, born of universal (obviously male-only) suffrage, with a protocol commensurate with the past but also consonant with the needs of the present, and both Napoleon III and his wife conducted themselves with this objective in mind. As the first authentic professionals of the modern promotion of power, they did all they could to ensure their success, promulgating the image of a young and elegant court intent on high times and dancing.

At the Tuileries there were eight balls, large and small, scheduled regularly from January to May. The large ones had three to four thousand attendees and required gala dress for women and *grand habit*—black tailcoat, knee-length trousers, and black silk socks—or a dress uniform for men. The guests entered via the grand staircase of the Tuileries' central pavilion and stood in the Galerie de la Paix while the imperial couple went through their ritual greeting of the diplomatic corps in the Throne Room; they were then conveyed into the immense Salle des Maréchaux, where, accompanied by a solemn march, the emperor made his entrance, giving his arm to the empress, who bowed three times before the assembly. Customarily, the emperor and empress were the ones to open the ball with a quadrille danced beside the guests of honor. And at eleven the buffet was served in the Galerie de Diane. Shortly after midnight the sovereigns retired to their quarters, while the guests went on dancing till dawn. The "small dances" were much more restricted but nevertheless governed by strict etiquette. To allow the distinguished guests greater freedom and fun, Eugénie made a habit of receiving them in her rooms on Mondays and using the Salon Bleu for the dances. But that wasn't all. As Princess Metternich, the Austrian ambassador's wife, would later recall,[12] there were also "several quite enchanting masquerade balls" at the Tuileries. Men who didn't wish to don a costume were allowed to wear cloaks "*alla Veneziana*"—a kind of short *tabarro*, of whatever color they preferred, cinched under the collar with a cord[13]—while the women could let their imaginations run wild. "Diverting as these balls were, of a luxury and elegance beyond compare, Their Majesties preferred the dances held at the ministries and embassies, where masks were allowed—where dominos were mixed in with the costumes, and where the atmosphere was much more lively."[14] While they often allowed the identity of their wearers to be surmised—the emperor's gait, for example, was distinctive enough to give him away—the masks allowed them to strike up conversations, use the informal, and become the object of jokes and amusing misapprehensions.

The appetite for disguise promoted by these institutions was completely in keeping with the eclecticism of the era. Disoriented after so many changes of regime—the First Empire, the Restoration, the bourgeois monarchy of Louis Philippe, the Second Republic—the France of the Second Empire abandoned the idea of forging its own style and made miscellaneous use of styles associated with great historical eras. "Having become superfluous due to historical circumstances," as Henri Bouchot observed, "the imperial regime [appeared to rely] on the past to cobble together a rather sketchy and ragtag identity."[15] With the help of skilled laborers, architects, sculptors, and painters, they compensated for this lack of originality by inaugurating an aesthetic of fakery which was destined to thrive. To please the nostalgic patrons of earlier eras—as well as the nouveau riche eager to equip themselves with houses and furnishings befitting the position they'd achieved—there was a systematic imitation of every style under the sun. While Napoleon III, adopting the cultural policy of Louis Philippe, went on inventorying France's monumental patrimony and financed Viollet-le-Duc's restorations, artistic production took its cues not only from ancient Rome, the Middle Ages, and the Renaissance but also from the Grand Siècle and the eighteenth century, pandering to the fluctuating tastes of a heterogeneous society predisposed to identifying with its own purchasing power. In deference to the bourgeoisie's demand for comfortable homes complete with every convenience and conducive to domestic intimacy, decorators gave further proof of eclecticism by appropriating the new idea of comfort derived from England. Whatever artistic style was chosen, whether in the empress's rooms at the Tuileries or in the homes of Parisians *à la page*, there were invariably enormous upholstered sofas and tufted armchairs from across the Channel—emblems of aspirational "coziness" in a society that could never get enough ostentation.

Even fashions hewed to the new criteria, becoming the subject of methodical reflection for major writers. For Balzac and Baudelaire, as for Barbey d'Aurevilly, Théophile Gautier, and Mérimée, the interest in clothes, accessories, makeup, and artifice assumed different forms and meanings, but for all of them dress—not unlike literature—was an artistic process that "adorned" nature,[16] abstracting man from his animality. In 1830—the year that the French Bourbons fell—Balzac published in installments, in the newspaper *La Mode*, an unfinished *Treatise on Elegant Living*. A theorist at heart, Balzac gave elegance—which is "in some ways the metaphysics of things"—philosophical status. Through all its endless renewals, he says, elegance remains loyal to the "immutable principles that should govern the outward manifestation of our thoughts."[17] In daily practice, though, fashion remained the prerogative of the weaker sex. Eternal minors subject to male authority and moral imperatives, the women of the wealthy classes were nevertheless free to decorate the spaces they lived in, choose their leisure activities, and dress, arrange their hair, makeup, and jewelry according to their moods, inclinations, and whims. And the empire's balls—its masquerades above all—were perfect occasions for challenging convention and freely indulging one's fantasies. It should therefore come as no surprise that Virginia made ample use of the *fête impériale* when carrying out her political mission. It is in fact by proceeding from one ball to the next, and from one disguise to the next, that we can best trace her triumphal march.

She made her debut at Princess Mathilde's palace, one of the great theaters of Parisian high society, where the emperor's cousin kept the aristocratic tradition of French *esprit* alive. Born in Trieste and raised in exile in Florence and Rome, Mathilde was the daughter of Jérôme Bonaparte, former king of Westphalia, and Catherina of Württemberg. After separating from her husband, the Russian plutocrat Anatoly Demidov, Mathilde was the first of the Bonapartes to obtain permission from Louis Philippe to return to France. Intelligent, strong-willed, and determined to "invent" her own destiny, the princess lived on—a guardian of the Napoleonic era with a sincere interest in art and literature who was interested chiefly in securing a prestigious role (the only such role possible for a woman) in the cultural sphere. Her primary accomplice in this pursuit would be her lover, whom she brought with her from Florence and with whom she kept up an official relationship for more than twenty years: Alfred-Émilien O'Hara van Nieuwerkerke, "a top-notch bachelor, handsome, tall, strapping, with gentle eyes and an even gentler voice,"[18] who'd enjoyed some success as a sculptor and, toward the tail end of the July Monarchy, had gotten to know everyone in Parisian artistic circles in the role of Mathilde's messenger. Louis Napoleon's surprise arrival in Paris in September 1848—and his election as president of the republic on December 10—had invested the princess's patronage with new political significance. The two cousins hadn't seen each other since the days of their youthful engagement (which went awry after Louis's failed coup d'état at Strasbourg in 1836—followed by his exile in America), but time and distance had not erased the memory of the feelings that bound them. Added to this was the admiration Mathilde had always felt for Queen Hortense—who had a special place in her cousin's heart. Not only did Louis, who'd spent most of his life in exile or prison and had no experience in Parisian society, benefit from Mathilde's network of friends and acquaintances; he was also able to count on her financial help for his presidential campaign. No sooner was he installed in the Élysée than he asked her to perform the duties of hostess, which she performed with authority and elegance. Still beautiful, "with a kind and friendly face, French manners, and Italian vivacity, she conversed with wit and grace, never putting on princessly airs but always ready to play the princess if she wished and when necessary."[19]

Her conduct, in short, excited respect from every quarter. Mathilde went on to finance the coup d'état of December 2, 1851, and when he became emperor her cousin had shown his gratitude by giving her the title "Her Imperial Highness," endowing her with a large appanage, and granting her the use of the beautiful Hôtel de Bragance on the rue de Courcelles. Meanwhile Nieuwerkerke, who'd been appointed director general of national museums as early as 1849, raked in praise until, eventually, he was made superintendent of fine arts. By the time Virginia arrived in Paris, Mathilde had already been forced to make way for Eugénie, but she continued to play an important role at the Tuileries, both because of her connections with European aristocracies—particularly her close connections with the Russian imperial family—and because of her ties with famous French artists.[20] This is not even to mention her salon on the rue de Courcelles, which operated under the aegis of Sainte-Beuve and was well on its way to becoming *the* showcase for French literary life. Political convictions and obvious ironies aside—no one was unaware that the salon was backed by the emperor, so that Mathilde and Nieuwerkerke formed a sort of "two-headed ministry of arts and letters"[21]—major French writers from Gautier to Flaubert, from the Goncourt brothers to Taine and Renan, and even the young Proust, would all fall under the real or mythologized spell of Her Imperial Highness, who, in the tradition of the grandes dames of yore, painted, wrote, and conversed gracefully, all the while doing her utmost, with the most charming warmth, to secure these young men the recognition they deserved. Sainte-Beuve would honor her with the sobriquet "Notre-Dame des Arts."

But there was one political cause Mathilde openly supported and was always ready to defend: the Italian question. Deeply connected to the Bel Paese—which had offered the Bonapartes refuge during their long years of exile—she recognized its inhabitants' right to reclaim their national identity and free themselves from foreign oppression. Defying French Catholic opinion, she was merciless when it came to the obscurantist policy of the papal government. Her house was always open to Italians who found themselves in Paris. Marquis Pes di Villamarina, representative of the Sardinian kingdom, and acquaintances from Florence—Poniatowski above all—could count on a particularly warm welcome from the princess.

Napoleon Jérôme Bonaparte, who became, with the advent of the empire, Prince Napoleon *tout court*, likewise loved Italy and was a staunch supporter of the patriotic movement. Anyway, King Jérôme's third son had made anticlericalism his banner: "Clericalism, for him, meant exploiting religion for political purposes, allying oneself with dynasties hostile to his family, and standing in opposition to modern ideas of liberty."[22] Support for the Italian national cause was one of the very few commitments to which the prince remained loyal in a life defined by contradictions and pure chance. Though he felt a fraternal affection for his cousin Louis, who, once he'd risen to power, had not been stingy with honors, appanages, and prestigious posts, Plon-Plon—as he'd been called in the family since childhood—"did not resign himself to being merely 'the other Bonaparte boy'"[23] and made this clear by brazenly revolting against the politics of the empire. Cultured, and gifted with uncommon intelligence and remarkable oratorical skill, the prince considered himself the true heir of Napoleon the Great's political legacy and pitted, against the authoritarian populism of Napoleon "the Little," a left-wing, Jacobin-style Bonapartism.[24] Besides, he had no qualms about playing up his impressive physical resemblance to his illustrious uncle, thereby fueling the widespread rumors about the legitimacy of his cousin's origins. He was, however, moody and impatient—and incapable of pursuing a long-term political project; he was content to make trouble for Napoleon III as often as he could. "The strange thing," his friend Émile Ollivier recalls,

> was how he ended up taking on the manners and flaws of someone with abominable ambition though he wasn't actually ambitious in the least. He was restless rather than enterprising; impetuous, but without follow-through; incapable of keeping still, as would have been necessary, and considering the course of events. He was always in too much of a hurry and lost heart if his goal seemed to shrink further out of reach. He was, basically, an unrealistic man... He burned up all his energy talking. After having, as was his wont, burned up the carpet pacing his study from end to end, irritated by those who urged him to carry out his proud resolutions, he would suddenly jettison the whole subject and take off on some trip or other.[25]

The prince would, in fact, attempt to forget the frustrations of his subordinate role in an endless series of trips and sumptuous hedonism. An unrepentant libertine, he was, nevertheless, capable of strong passions: Once he'd stolen the affections of the great actress Rachel from Napoleon III, he had a residence in perfect Pompeian style designed in her honor on avenue Montaigne—a place destined to leave its mark.[26] But not even this venture was devoid of polemical intent since, by choosing that style, "Prince Napoleon was distancing himself from the taste of the imperial court, which at that time was gripped by the glories of the eighteenth century, and presenting himself as an heir to the style of the First Empire."[27] In perpetual conflict with his imperial cousin, unkind to Eugénie, and arrogant with crowned heads and in fact anyone in power, Plon-Plon was impeccably courteous in society, and like Princess Mathilde's salon, the Palais-Royal, which Napoleon III had given him and his father as an appanage, stood at the center of Parisian social and cultural life. The prince, as Virginia would soon discover, was destined to play a crucial role in the relations between Piedmont and France.[28]

Indeed it was on the rue de Courcelles, on January 9, 1856—preceded by an advertising campaign expertly orchestrated by the Italian beau monde[29]—that the Countess and Count of Castiglione attended the first major ball of the Paris season. For the occasion Virginia sported an extraordinary hairdo (the first of many) that showed off her magnificent golden-brown locks. "She had pink feathers in her hair, which was pouffed above her temples. The rest was pulled back in two pendent ringlets. She looked like a marquise from another era, combed *à l'oiseau royal*,"[30] as the Count of Reiset recalled.[31] The warm welcome that Princess Mathilde reserved for the young couple made Virginia the center of attention, and everyone in attendance was quick to acknowledge that her beauty did not disappoint. But the highlight of the evening was the arrival of the emperor, who came alone because Eugénie, very far along in her pregnancy, could no longer leave the Tuileries.

Napoleon III was by then nearly fifty years old, and certainly no one would have called him handsome. According to Ernest Barthez, his son's doctor, the emperor had a quite unusual physique: broad and slumped shoulders, a long and massive torso, and short legs. His head, too, was an odd shape, and his sharp face, with its high and balding brow, made him look older than he was. His small, light-blue, somewhat veiled eyes had a "laughing and benevolent expression," which sometimes took on an expression that was "rather empty, atonic, and decidedly strange."[32] His eyes were "so dull and opaque" that, to the Austrian diplomat Apponyi, they appeared to "wander here and there without ever fixing on anything," making him seem "fraudulent but at the same time mild and harmless" in a way that inspired "pity rather than envy."[33] His lordly manners (which, as Princess Metternich was anxious to emphasize, had nothing of the upstart about them) were tempered by an affable naturalness that made him beloved by everyone who had a chance to get to know him well.[34] Even Queen Victoria, who received him in London during a state visit in 1855, painted an enthusiastic portrait of him to Augusta of Prussia:

> The emperor is a remarkable, an unusual man; on all occasions both publicly and in private, when he was quite alone with us, his manner was dignified, decorous, tactful and unbelievably calm. One would imagine that he had been educated as a crown prince. His manners have something which in English we call "fascinating."[35]

What did Virginia think when she first met the man on whom the future of her country depended—and whom it was imperative she like? Certainly Napoleon III did not impress her with his prowess, considering she later gave him the nickname "the Old Man." Nor do we have any idea what they said to each other when Princess Mathilde made the introductions. Perhaps—who knows—the sovereign recalled his sojourns in Florence and graciously asked for news of old Lamporecchi . . . According to Reiset, Virginia was intimidated and "couldn't find words to reply to the emperor, who went away with an unfavorable impression and, after taking his leave, commented, 'She is beautiful, but she seems lacking in *esprit*.'"[36] She would soon give him an opportunity to change his mind.

As she noted in the diary she'd resumed keeping in Paris, Virginia met him for the second time on the evening of January 26. Invited with her husband and Prince Poniatowski to the ball given at the Palais-Royal by King Jérôme and his son Prince Napoleon, the countess had insisted on showing up late and so arrived just as the emperor was leaving. Crossing paths with her on the palace stairs, the sovereign let out a "You're coming very late, madame,"[37] to which she replied with remarkable nonchalance: "It is you, sire, who are leaving very early."[38]

That same night, Virginia made the acquaintance of Count Charles de Morny, a key figure in the regime who wielded far greater behind-the-scenes power than that bestowed on him by the title of president of the legislative corps. Not only had he organized the December 2 coup d'état and ensured its success, but as the product of the clandestine relationship between Queen Hortense and the Count of Flahaut he was the emperor's half-brother. Napoleon discovered this only after his mother's death and found it deeply disturbing, since this child of adultery represented an indelible stain on the reputation of a woman to whom he had devoted a genuine cult and, worse, risked lending support to rumors about the dubious legitimacy of his own birth. No wonder, then, that the emperor reacted to the news by hiding behind the most stringent restraint, urging Morny, too, to keep it a secret. Disappointed by the absence of official recognition, the count had made up for it by choosing a hydrangea with the motto TACE SED MEMENTO as his crest and hanging portraits of Queen Hortense in plain view on the walls of his drawing room, alongside portraits of his father, the Count of Flahaut, who'd in fact been the natural-born son of Talleyrand, the man Morny had decided to take as a model. The famous diplomat's grandson had inherited his ambition, his political savvy, his cynicism and ability to seduce, his elegance, his inscrutability, his sangfroid, and his passion for money and women. After making a fortune under Louis Philippe, Morny played the Bonapartist card and organized every last detail of his half-brother's takeover, turning up the necessary funds and even being so bold as to have his adversaries arrested and order soldiers to open fire on crowds of protestors. It was also Morny who organized the triumphal plebiscite of December 21 and 22, which extended Bonaparte's presidential term for another ten years, not neglecting to ensure that he himself would reap the greatest benefit.

Virginia was introduced to Morny by Giuseppe Poniatowski, whose son Stanislao was about to marry the daughter of Morny's lover, the fabulously wealthy Fanny Le Hon. Virginia and the regime's secret strategist were a match made in heaven, and no sooner was she back in her house on the rue Castiglione than she jotted down in her diary: "I stayed in the salon to chat with Beppino [Poniatowski] and Morny."[39] So far she'd been cavorting on friendly territory, but three days later, when she was invited to the "grand ball" at the Tuileries, it was trial by fire. On the evening of January 29—announced in a stentorian voice by the person in charge of protocol—the Castiglione couple made their entrance into the Galerie de la Paix, crossing it under the gaze of a throng of onlookers to reach the Salle des Maréchaux, where the imperial couple waited. By virtue of what magnetism—beautiful though she was—did an eighteen-year-old from Italy, dressed in a homemade silver-blue evening gown, manage to attract such attention? Why were people in Paris, as they had been in Turin, prepared to stand on top of chairs to admire her?[40] The most likely answer is that the capricious, spoiled, unstable little provincial was a born actress, and the Tuileries' extraordinary scenography of gold, lights, and mirrors, with that exceptional audience in attendance, provided the stage she needed to discover her deepest vocation and become permanently persuaded of her own talent.

From that moment on, Virginia would prove herself capable of playing a vast repertoire of roles, even if haughty Venus, descending from Olympus for one brief, dazzling appearance, would long remain her favorite. And if she commanded the stage with the lucidity of a professional actress, narcissism is likely to have been of the essence. A generation after her, the no less beautiful and no less narcissistic Countess Greffulhe helps us understand the total satisfaction Virginia felt at her every public appearance: "I believe that there is no enjoyment in the world comparable to that of a woman who senses she is the focus of everyone's attention and draws life and energy from it."[41]

Virginia crossed the Salle des Maréchaux with regal calm and, having made the obligatory curtsy to the emperor and empress, went to sit down at a table in the gaming room "to chat with Beppino, Morny, and Villamarina." When Napoleon III came to join her, she showed not a glimmer of surprise: "The emperor came over to speak to me. Then everyone looked and flocked around me, I laughed, at 2 I left..."[42] The scene was destined to be repeated over the days that followed: "Saturday, February 2. At 9 I went to the *petit bal* at the Tuileries and stayed until 2; spoke to the emperor who gave me some oranges... Tuesday, February 5—I went to the Le Hon ball and spoke to the emperor in a mask..."[43] In less than a month Virginia had managed to capture the attention of Napoleon III and conquer the imperial court and the salons of Paris. "Clearly," Henri de Pène noted in *Nord*, "the queen of the season is that incomparable beauty from Italy, the Countess of Castiglione. "L'Italiana in Parigi": this is the title of a symphony admiringly intoned from morning to night and from night to morning. People wage war to proffer the finest praise of her profile, her hair, her eyes, and—the clearest consecration of her royalty—she has even gained some enemies."[44]

Cavour, who arrived in Paris on February 16 to take part in the congress that was to restore peace after the Crimean War, could therefore note that "the cousin with the beautiful eyes"[45] had proved to be an invaluable collaborator. During his stay, the count would see Virginia often—not only in political society, where he made a point of mixing, but also on the rue de Castiglione and at the Italian legation. We can find traces of their meetings in Virginia's diaries,[46] and Cavour's correspondence is not lacking in allusions. If, on February 21, Virginia wrote that she'd gone "with powdered hair, adorned with pearls and feathers,"[47] to the great concert that the emperor put on for the diplomatic corps, Cavour, the following day, would write in turn to the foreign minister Luigi Cibrario, "I warn you that I have enlisted the lovely Countess of Castiglione in the diplomatic corps, inviting her to *coqueter* [*sic*] and seduce, when necessary, the emperor... She discreetly began playing her part at the concert at the Tuilerie [*sic*] yesterday."[48] In the face of such blatant pragmatism, Cibrario felt it incumbent upon him—after all, she was still his friend's wife—to express his approval in a guarded fashion: "Magnificent idea to use the Grace for purposes of diplomacy. It is an extraordinary moment. Best to employ every weapon at our disposal."[49] That same day the count saw fit to tell the minister of the interior, Urbano Rattazzi, the same thing.[50] Obviously, he didn't consider the information irrelevant. He abstained, however, from mentioning that the price agreed with his cousin, if she succeeded, was a prestigious diplomatic assignment for the marquis Oldoini.[51] In addition to writing to her directly,[52] Cavour also mentioned Virginia in letters to Victor Emmanuel. Wishing to share the burden of responsibility for Oldoini's appointment with the king, the count made no attempt to conceal his opinion of the marquis: "I delivered the letter from V.M. to Nini. My lovely cousin is sulking because I cannot recommend that V.M. give her imbecilic father a position beyond his capabilities."[53] As expected, the king answered him shortly after, urging him to be indulgent.[54] The two men agreed, however, about deploying Virginia's attractions as they pleased, and not only in regard to the emperor: "I am on excellent terms with the Russian plenipotentiaries. To bring them over to our side, I introduced Orloff to Nini last night. If only she would *coqueter* a bit with him, we'd be off to the races."[55]

While Cavour was keen to win political sympathies wherever he went, he was also well aware that the only country from which Piedmont could expect to receive concrete assistance was France. The congress that started on February 25, in the grandiose halls of the new foreign ministry on the quai d'Orsay, and concluded on April 14 signaled Napoleon III's political triumph. In the eyes of the emperor the time was right to call the structure of European power into question and reaffirm—following the breakup of the absolutist front, which came with the end of the Austro–Russian alliance—France's political centrality on the continent. This was an explicit retaliation against the decisions made at the Congress of Vienna and marked "the first concerted legal step in undoing the work done by those who had defeated Napoleon I."[56] The question of the autonomy of nations—a question that would attract the attention of all of Europe—was indeed destined to redraw the European map. Cavour was well aware that, in the long term, Italy would reap the rewards of this change in French foreign policy, but he was yet to figure out whether and to what extent the emperor was, in the short term, willing to support Turin's demands.

The first signs were promising. The French foreign minister, Count Walewski, assured Cavour that the subalpine legation would be admitted to the congress on equal terms. On February 21, the count was invited to a dinner party at the Tuileries where the Austrian plenipotentiaries were not present, and the following day he received a visit from Dr. Conneau, Napoleon's personal physician and friend since youth, who informed him that he'd been authorized to serve as an intermediary for any secret information that the Sardinian government deemed useful to communicate to the sovereign. The historian and diplomat Imbert de Saint-Amand—who in 1856 was working under Walewski for the ministry of foreign affairs—would later observe that the understanding between the emperor and Cavour was rooted in the many things they had in common:

> Both advocates of free trade and the principle of nationality, they pursued their goals doggedly. Both trusted much more in the power of the press than in that of the tribune. Directors of the first order, they excelled in the art of managing and influencing public opinion; they employed secret agents, and official agendas were always accompanied by hidden ones. They had a genius for conspiracy and the temperaments of gamblers. Without the Count of Cavour,

Napoleon III could not have lifted a finger against Austria, and vice versa.[57]

And so a parallel diplomacy began, which allowed the emperor and the Italian statesman to sound out each other's intentions in an unofficial capacity, or rather to indicate to the other the margin for maneuver. Cavour's immediate objectives were three: the revocation of the seizure, decreed by the Austrian government, of the assets of the Lombard patriot refugees in Piedmont; an expansion of the territory of the kingdom; and the withdrawal of Austrian troops from the Italian peninsula outside of the Lombardo-Venetian kingdom. The emperor, for his part—though he made no secret of his misgivings—continued to make clear he was a possibilist and left the Savoyard minister the task of weaving his diplomatic web within the congress.

But in this parallel diplomacy, what function did Cavour intend to assign Virginia? When the count wrote to her, "*Réussissez, ma cousine, par les moyens qu'il vous plaira, mais réussissez*,"[58] what else could he have meant except that she must succeed in establishing a means of communication between the emperor and the Savoyard government? Even if it was highly unlikely that the young countess, by becoming the sovereign's lover, could exercise any real political influence over him, she could at least probe his intentions, gain valuable information, and convey confidential messages. It is no coincidence that the Paris postmaster was asked to deliver the letters addressed to her to Count Puliga, secretary of the Sardinian legation.[59]

Two cryptic notes handwritten by Nigra, Cavour's trusty secretary—which fortunately survived the destruction of all papers relating to the countess's "mission"—appear to confirm that this was indeed her role. If in the first ("Dear Countess, I have a very important message for you, but I can't give it to you until tomorrow at half past seven, at my house. Make yourself blond, blond as a field of wheat. *It's mandatory.* Do we understand each other?"[60]), we can sense only the urgency of transmitting confidential information and safely assume that Virginia's hair color is a coded message of some kind, the second ("Remember to pull the worm out of the Old Man's nose about the speech. The speech will be before tomorrow's council meeting"[61]) is much clearer and has Cavour written all over it. Indeed, Nigra Italianized the French idiomatic phrase *tirer les vers du nez*—meaning to get information out of someone—which Cavour had used right around the same time regarding a delicate conversation with Baron Rothschild.[62] And the Old Man in question could only be the emperor, whom Virginia, as we know, had given that unlovable nickname.

For the time being, though, Napoleon III had other priorities. When the Italian question came up, he was far from bullish, though he left some faint hope for the future. Cavour needed to go back to Turin with tangible results, however. The congress, for him, was a bust. The only recognition he'd gained for his little subalpine kingdom had been the recognition implicit in his having a seat at the table with the other great powers, on the condition that he didn't stick in his oar and spoke only at the end, once the treaty was concluded. After Lord Clarendon, Great Britain's Foreign Secretary, lambasted papal policies in the legations and the obscurantism of the Bourbon government in Naples—provoking the furious opposition of the Austrian foreign minister, the Count of Buol-Schauenstein—Cavour presented a memorandum on the necessity of reexamining the Italian situation. When, finally, it was his turn to speak, he confined himself to making a formal protest against the Austrian presence in the papal states and reaffirmed the urgent need for substantial reform in these states, which had already been called for by France and England. As for the kingdom of the Two Sicilies, Ferdinand II's policies not only discredited the monarchical institution but "gave strength to the revolutionary party and posed a genuine threat to Italy."[63]

Cavour returned to Turin disappointed at not having achieved a single one of his pre-agreed objectives, but his triumphal welcome home made him realize he'd won a much more important victory. "Everyone could see that he had made major progress in Paris: he had taken the Italian question upon himself and upon the kingdom of Sardinia, and he had made it a European question, implicating the diplomacies of all the great continental powers."[64] From that moment forward, for the liberal-democratic wing of the national movement—from the subalpine parliamentary Left to Garibaldi and Manin—the possibility of constructing a national Italian movement combining popular forces with the military power of the constitutional monarchy of Savoy seemed a real possibility. The next step was to declare war on Austria, but in order to do so negotiations with Napoleon III first had to be resumed.

Meanwhile, in Paris, Virginia went on with her mission, obtaining the first substantive confirmation of the work she'd already put in: In May 1856, Oldoini was appointed first secretary of the embassy in Saint Petersburg. He gave all the credit to his daughter.

"My dear papa," she replied with professional pride, "thank you for your lovely letter, which gave me great pleasure by notifying me of the event toward which I'd been working for quite some time.I am glad to have managed, at least in this case, to change minds! And to please you, no?"[65] And she did not fail to send letters to Cavour and the king, thanking them for the "various kindnesses" they had shown her father.[66]

If Virginia had every right to be satisfied with how far she'd come in a matter of months, she was also keenly aware that there was no time to lose. She'd managed to attract the emperor's attention, piquing his curiosity and establishing a privileged relationship with him, but it was now imperative that he crystallize his voluble desires and make her his lover on a permanent basis. The moment could not have been more propitious. The empress, who, on March 15, had given birth to the heir to the throne, was recovering from a difficult labor and, absorbed as she was in the joys of motherhood, had relinquished control over her husband's *petites distractions*. In any case, at least since he'd married, Napoleon III had not had a mistress *en titre*.

Virginia was managing to transform her every appearance into an out-and-out event regularly reported in the papers,[67] changing the style and color of her hair and designing spectacular evening gowns tailored by dozens of seamstresses working under her direction. As the journalist Henri de Pène observed, her haughty attitude and air of defiance, combined with her beauty, couldn't help but elicit some criticism even at this early stage. By the end of May, Mérimée, who'd taken an immediate dislike to the countess, mocked her hairstyle: "At the last Saint-Cloud ball, Madame de Castiglione had powder all over the front of her head and her chignon was glistening with bandoline.[68] She looked as if she'd fallen into a sack of flour."[69] And yet the writer was forced to admit that the Italian was "more than a little insolent and perfectly beautiful, therefore a very fashionable type."[70] Even Princess Metternich paid homage to her beauty, drawing a justly famous portrait in prose:

> I confess I was stunned by this miracle of beauty! She wore a white tulle dress covered with long-stemmed roses, and her magnificent hair was arranged in big tresses like a crown on her head. She had the figure of a nymph. Her neck, her shoulders, her arms, her hands—she didn't put on her gloves but held them in her hand—seemed sculpted in pink marble! She looked so much like an ancient statue that her décolletage, though excessive, did not seem indecent at all! And her face did not disappoint: delectably oval, with an incomparably fresh complexion, the eyes a dark, velvety green, and eyebrows that seemed drawn by a miniaturist's brush, a little nose like Roxelana's; impish yet perfectly straight, pearly teeth. In short, she was Venus come down from Mount Olympus! I have never seen such beauty and never will again.[71]

That an admirer of feminine charm such as the emperor couldn't avoid becoming intimate with the charms of the Italian countess was a conviction so widespread that, by the end of May, the Britain's Foreign Secretary asked the ambassador of the Sardinian kingdom for confirmation. "Lord Clarendon," Emanuele d'Azeglio wrote to Cavour, "was in high spirits and immediately began discussing whether the beautiful Virginia was the emperor's lover or not. He was leaning toward *yes*."[72] Before they could be sure, they had to wait another month. On June 27, while the court was at Saint-Cloud, the empress invited Virginia to an evening *en plein air* in honor of the Grand Duchess of Baden, the sovereign's cousin, at Villeneuve-l'Étang, a château surrounded by a vast park with a romantic constellation of ponds. Virginia donned a transparent white muslin dress and a hat with white marabou feathers for the occasion. As Stéphanie Tascher de la Pagerie—the daughter of the empress's grand master of ceremonies—would observe, "to resist the provocation of this "*toilette d'apparition*" one had to "call upon every inch of one's virtue."[73] The emperor apparently must have missed an inch. He beckoned Castiglione to join him on one of the boats rigged up for guests along the shores of a pond lit with countless colored lanterns. It was a full-scale *Embarquement pour Cythère*. Taking up the oars, the sovereign headed for the little island in the middle of the pond and, upon landing, vanished with his lady into the thick undergrowth. When the couple returned to the shore, everyone noted that Virginia looked a little "rumpled," and the empress betrayed a certain irritation.[74] When the English ambassador Lord Cowley later gave the Earl of Clarendon his account of the evening, he observed:

> The liberties Sa Majesté took with Castiglione scandalized all of Paris . . . From what I was told, the poor empress was in a deplorable condition—seized by a fit of fever, she started dancing, but being quite weak she took a bad fall. It was a full-blown orgy, the men danced with their hats on. It's all very sad and damaging to the emperor from a political point of view without doing him any good, to be sure, either morally or physically.[75]

And so, eleven days after what she'd described as the most beautiful day of her life (the day of her son's grandiose baptism in Notre-Dame cathedral), in the same place where she'd spent her honeymoon three years earlier, the empress suffered her first marital humiliation.

Eugénie de Montijo was a romantic young woman who loved her husband and had married him in no doubt that she was loved in return. It was not a marriage dictated by reasons of state but by feelings of a personal nature, rooted in bourgeois values. The daughter of a great Spanish aristocrat who'd sided with France during the First Empire and a half-Scottish mother, she'd been educated, along with her older sister María Francisca (known as Paca), at the Institute of the Sacred Heart in Paris. While Paca secured the best of the Spanish matches—the Duke of Alba—Eugénie seemed in no hurry to find a husband. A girl with many interests, independent, an expert equestrian, she was seeking a kindred spirit and was not going to compromise. When in 1849 Louis Napoleon Bonaparte, then president of the republic, began to woo her, she was recovering from a romantic disappointment and made it clear that, as a devout Catholic, the only proposition she was willing to entertain "would go by way of the altar." But she did allow herself to be courted. Her choice, though considered, was nonetheless heartfelt. Eugénie admired the intelligence, courage, and tenacity that Louis Napoleon, alone among his family members, had shown in taking up the great emperor's political mantle, and she was quick to recognize herself in his ideals. "We belonged to the same generation of exalted people," she would later recall. "There was, in both of our natures, something of the romanticism of 1830 and the utopianism of 1848. We dreamed of doing our utmost for the happiness of the people, and of improving the lot of the workers."[76] She was gratified by her husband's desire to have her beside him in his days of triumph and promised him a conjugal love that combined pride, moral support, and respect with sincere affection. The emperor, once he'd come to power, renounced his bachelor life, breaking things off with the beautiful but royally unacceptable Miss Howard, a rich courtesan with whom he'd had a long and passionate affair. When he tried and failed to marry the princess of a reigning house, he made up his mind to marry the woman he loved. Anyway, marrying for love could only make him more appealing to the people. He was a sensual man, and physical desire was one of the things that induced him to marry the otherwise impregnable Mademoiselle de Montijo, but it certainly wasn't the only reason. Twenty-two years older than Eugénie, and severely scarred by imprisonment and exile, Louis Napoleon was in love with her youth, her spontaneity and enthusiasm, and he admired her idealism, moral intransigence, and sense of honor. Above all he was proud of her beauty. "The empress," recalled Amélie Bouvet de la Maisonneuve, who entered her service as a reader,

> was rather tall. She had symmetrical features and a profile like an ancient medallion, with something inexpressible—such a special, almost uncommon charm that she couldn't be compared to any other woman . . . [Her] eyes were a vivid dark blue bathed in shadow, but full of wit, energy, tenderness—eyes like hers are alone enough to make a face memorable . . . Veins were visible through her delicate complexion, bringing to mind the blue blood of the ancient Spanish nobility. The nape of her neck was long, delicate—perfect. Her shoulders, chest, and arms would have suited the most beautiful statues.[77]

As a married man, the emperor rediscovered, in the private quarters of the Tuileries, the intimate enchantment of an exquisitely feminine domesticity—an atmosphere that transported him back in time to the little court of women that his mother, Hortense, presided over in her exile at Arenenberg. His sexual expectations, however, were likely disappointed: physical love was no more than a conjugal duty for Eugénie, who, after the birth of her son, would confide to a friend that she found it a "filthy thing."[78]

On the other hand, the young empress helped her husband greatly in the effort to confer dignity and prestige on a court lacking in legitimacy and snubbed by the old French aristocracy, who remained loyal to one or another branch of the Bourbons.

Eugénie was a smart, spirited woman, well aware of what was at stake politically. She soon applied herself to mustering resources on which the imperial couple could rely: the nobility born fifty years earlier on the battlefields of the First Empire and the new French society whose blazon was wealth. She trained for her public appearances, taking lessons in deportment from the famous actress Rachel. Drawing on expertise and experience did help her make courtly etiquette less cold and solemnity less solemn, and it made the Tuileries a showcase for French luxury and fashion—but it never allowed her to rise to the sort of inimitable style that had always been the hallmark of an authentic sovereign.

To realize the truth of this, one need look no further than Winterhalter's famous picture of her, painted two years after her marriage. Her ladies-in-waiting, arrayed in a circle around her, wear huge tiered dresses that open like flowers. Trivially pretty and almost interchangeable, they look like they're posing for a fashion magazine. Mérimée said they "seemed like a bunch of seamstresses cut loose from the Bal Mabille,"[79] and seven years later they couldn't have seemed much more distinguished if Lord Malmesbury, the English Foreign Secretary, was so bold as to say, "Apart from Madame Alewska, the empress's ladies-in-waiting are decidedly vulgar."[80] The only things setting Eugénie apart from her ladies-in-waiting in that bucolic "conversation piece" in the Watteau style are her elevated position at the center of the group, the honeysuckle crown, and the little bouquet she holds like a scepter. Though the sovereign was fully aware that her beauty was of a far superior quality than that depicted, the painting, exhibited in the royal château at Fontainebleau, nevertheless constituted her calling card. All things considered, the empress was a woman of her time, and as a staunch feminist was determined to stay true to herself. Thus she allowed herself to be portrayed with dreamy, romantic expressions, dressed as an odalisque languidly lying on a couch—poses that were not exactly regal but that emphasized the perfection of her neck and arms in keeping with the aesthetic canons of the era. Called upon to dictate fashions, she'd unwisely chosen Marie Antoinette as her model, forgetting what a passion for clothes had cost the unhappy queen. And if for Nancy Mitford one of l'Autrichienne's greatest faults was an absolute lack of good taste,[81] it must be said that l'Espagnole did not abound in it either, what with her caricatured reinterpretations of eighteenth-century fashions that insisted on immense crinolines made even more incongruous by embroidery, ruffles, fringes, ribbons, and trim of all kinds. Her aesthetic diktat would coincide with the favored first decade of the Second Empire, after which Eugénie would wisely decide to yield the scepter to another figure, that of the great dressmaker before whose authority she bowed: in 1864, Charles Frederick Worth, who had settled in Paris only two years earlier, would be appointed official supplier to the empress, and inaugurate the era of haute couture, destined to survive all changes of regime.

It is little wonder, then, that the public affront at Villeneuve-l'Étang took Eugénie by surprise, wounding her dignity as both a wife and a sovereign. How could the husband she so admired, a man she was so fond of, prove so incapable of controlling his own libido and cause such a scandal? Eugénie was too proud to suffer in silence, and from that day on she never stopped subjecting her recidivist spouse to terrible scenes and threats of separation. The emperor would later deliver an eloquent response to Prince Napoleon, who advised him to hush his wife up the hard way: "For pity's sake! If I so much as dared to threaten her, Eugénie wouldn't hesitate to throw open a window at the Tuileries and cry bloody murder."[82] Eventually the empress would resign herself to her husband's adventures, merely demanding that he respect convention—more out of maternal love than marital abnegation. Bent on ensuring the dynastic future of her only son, whose birth had almost cost her her life,[83] she would continue to oversee the splendors of the *fête impériale* even as she broadened her sphere of influence, taking an increasing interest in the country's political, economic, and social problems. "After the birth of the imperial prince, and especially after the first symptoms of the illness that would prove fatal to Napoleon, she understood that she had to prepare herself to manage the interregnum."[84] Her husband, who respected and trusted her judgment, was the first to encourage her leap into politics. And it was this encouragement that allowed their relationship to survive the death of marital intimacy.

But of all Napoleon III's mistresses, the Countess of Castiglione was the most difficult for Eugénie to bear—and not only because she was the mistress with whom Eugénie was compelled to compare herself.

As shameless as she was beautiful, the Italian had a taste for provocation, and her every move, punctually reported by the papers, was a potential source of embarrassment for the emperor. Equally alarming was her reputation as a secret agent for a country virtually teeming with terrorists and spies. Eugénie, though she did not forswear her conjugal grievances, adopted an imperturbable demeanor in public and only rarely let her feelings be known. She did not object to Virginia's presence at court receptions and greeted her with polite indifference, but she had her watched and was kept abreast of every secret meeting—day, time, place—between her imprudent husband and the dangerous Florentine. According to the English ambassador, the emperor would even meet Virginia in his study and had no qualms about giving her precedence over diplomatic requests for an audience.[85] As early as the spring of 1856, the police already had her under observation.[86]

We are in no position to know what the person directly concerned thought of this extraordinary adventure she was having at the tender age of nineteen. Since we have neither her correspondence with the emperor nor the diary she kept during this time in her life, we must limit ourselves to seeing her, as Nicole G. Albert has so brilliantly done,[87] through the eyes of contemporary journalists and memoirists. The journalists focused on her sensational appearances, describing in great detail the clothing and hairstyles that established her reputation as a "*vedette*"; the memoirists are for the most part in agreement that her beauty was indivisible from her hostility. Indeed, Virginia seems to have been the supreme practitioner of what, in those same exact years, Baudelaire called "the aristocratic pleasure of making oneself disagreeable." To Mérimée, who, trying to embarrass her, had asked if she practiced "androlatry," she'd retorted, "playing up the look of scorn she always wore on her marvelous face, 'I wasn't aware that there were men worth idolizing.'"[88]

Let us consider the judgments of five witnesses who observed her closely. Imbert de Saint-Amand, her unhappy lover, succinctly noted that the countess did not give too much of herself.[89] The Count of Fleury, one of the emperor's most loyal subjects and a man devoted to Eugénie, was much more explicit: "A female Narcissus who worshipped her own beauty, devoid of tenderness and sweetness, gracelessly ambitious, and nonsensically scornful, she soon revolted the man she'd wished to put under her spell."[90] For Madame Carette, a reader and later lady-in-waiting at the empress's palace, "Madame de Castiglione was conclusively, timelessly beautiful, but incredibly there was, despite the grace pervading every inch of her, an absence of charm. Her gorgeous face was always posed in an expression of haughtiness and harshness that reminded one of those divinities the ancients sought to propitiate with sacrifices."[91] And Princess Metternich, after dutifully celebrating the Italian's beauty, concluded, stingingly, "The Countess of Castiglione was lacking in one essential thing—charm! She seemed so constantly aware of her own triumphal beauty, so totally absorbed by it, that if one looked at her too closely it started to get on one's nerves."[92]

Guizot, who'd met Virginia at a friend's house in 1857, levels a similar judgment. He found her "truly beautiful, worthy of the court of Louis XV, a Venus of the era of Madame Pompadour," but with a "vain, selfish, harsh, cold" air.[93]

This "expression of sovereign disdain for all humanity"[94] was no more and no less than evidence of Virginia's idea of herself. At a reception once, when he saw her looking bored, Morny urged her to smile. "And why on earth would I do that? He who smiles lays down his arms," she retorted with a shrug. But Morny insisted: "What are you thinking about then?" "I am thinking how sovereign I am, and how much I despise," said Virginia curtly. She received in reply a simple "Brrr."[95] Twenty-some years later, when the Second Empire was but a distant memory, she would reaffirm her superiority over her rivals by writing at the bottom of a photograph of herself from that long-ago era: "In birth I equal them. In beauty I surpass them. In spirit I judge them."[96]

How to account for such arrogance? Had her Parisian triumph turned her adolescent narcissism into total certainty about her matchless superiority? Or was it the inversion of a provincial girl's inferiority complex vis-à-vis a society that, for centuries, had been setting the standard for worldliness and elegance? Did the countess merely see the Tuileries court as a site of competition where she had more titles to win? Or were these the first symptoms of a dangerous mythomania? Whatever the case, she wasn't about to let anything stand in her way.

The year 1856 ended triumphantly, with an invitation to Compiègne—an invitation Virginia had "moved heaven and earth"[97] to get. That same year, in the royal mansion eight miles from Paris where Joséphine Beauharnais had settled after her divorce and Napoleon III had declared his love to Eugénie, a cycle of receptions began that would remain, for more than a decade, the most exclusive and sought-after social events on the court calendar.

The Compiègne *séries*, as these events came to be known, had been thought up by Napoleon III and was overseen by the empress. They allowed the sovereigns to extend invitations to their splendid country residence "not only to the great officers of the Crown and the civilian and military officers with their wives"[98] but to the cream of the European aristocratic crop. They also allowed them to become acquainted with some of the most prominent members of the French elite, including scientists, writers, musicians, and artists of note.

Every week, from mid-October until early December, the imperial couple welcomed about sixty guests, handpicked for their importance and social prestige. The *séries* were by turns "serious," "elegant," "diplomatic," "military," or "artistic." The guests had a special train and a procession of carriages at their disposal. Princess Metternich nicely recalls the commotion in the courtyard of the palace cluttered with the hundreds of huge trunks that contained the ladies' wardrobes: "It was a sight unlike any other, as if all of Paris had moved in . . . The courtyard swarmed with manservants and maids shouting at the tops of their lungs trying to find their masters' trunks in that bedlam!"[99]

Despite such "bedlam," the organization of the *séries* was as impeccable as the accommodations were sumptuous. Guests were kept entertained with walks through the woods, theatrical novelties put on by companies up from Paris, board games, and, inevitably, a spectacular hunting party, followed by the ceremony (immortalized by Émile Zola) of the *curée*: that is, the doling out of scraps from the kill to the dogs, which took place by torchlight. The days were organized around luncheon, five o'clock tea, and dinner in the grand style, which was served in the great gallery of the château by "twenty majordomos in blue uniforms with metal buttons and swords, as well as fifty powdered footmen in grand livery with gold chevrons, all silent as automatons."[100] Yet for all the empress's efforts, there was no shortage of dull moments. "The evenings, which lasted until half past one, were a weak point," Princess Metternich noted. But when there was dancing or they "played charades, put on tableaux [vivants] or comedies, then there was real fun to be had,"[101] and the most fashionable writers, from Mérimée to Théophile Gautier and Feuillet de Conches, were called upon to contribute.

Arriving at Compiègne with her husband on Monday, October 27, for the *série élégante*—and equipped with a wardrobe commensurate with the occasion—the countess of course made headlines. One evening during a theatrical performance she left the hall, claiming illness, and when the emperor left his box not long after, never to return, not one of the spectators—least of all Eugénie and, presumably, Francesco—could have wondered why. But her stay at this place also afforded the insolent beauty an opportunity to fathom the depths of the hostility surrounding her.[102] As another guest at Compiègne, Madame Baroche—the wife of the president of the *conseil d'état*—recalled in her diary, Virginia fell victim to a "doubly regrettable" accident. During a visit in the empress's retinue to the ruins of the Château de Pierrefonds—which Viollet-le-Duc was about to rebuild from the ground up—"as she was leaping from rock to rock, lighter than a fawn, she fell, exposing to view the most beautiful legs in the world. Unfortunately she broke a bone in her wrist. Her heart-rending cries, however, did not elicit the slightest compassion: 'What a pouter,' people said; 'she didn't hurt herself at all.' Yet, for once, the countess had every right to act as she did."[103] Much as he disliked her, the Count of Fleury felt obliged to "come to the aid of that miserable Ariadne, fallen victim to general indifference,"[104] and arranged for her to be taken back to the château.[105] Virginia returned to Paris with a fractured wrist, and for two months no more was heard of her.

Meanwhile in Florence, her family was profoundly concerned about her health. Not knowing the details of the accident, Marquise Oldoini wrote to ask whether she'd broken her wrist picking up her son; whether, as the rumor went, she had in fact been invited to Compiègne, and whether she'd enjoyed herself there.[106] In another letter a few days letter she added: "My thoughts now revolve exclusively around your broken arm, and I shall not rest until I know they have removed your orthopedic apparatus and you have recovered the use of your wrist. By God, I would go on the rampage if my masterpiece were to be ruined by such an accident."[107] Castiglione, for his part, wrote to his father-in-law that, despite the accident, his wife was in an optimistic mood,[108] and toward the end of the year, he said much the same: "Niny is doing much better, they have taken off her cast with starch and her arm has healed completely... As a precautionary measure, the doctor wants her to keep the arm in a sling for twelve to fifteen days, which will prevent her from going out into society, but, on the other hand, she can now go out for a ride in a carriage."[109]

Yet Virginia had not forgotten her "mission." In early January, she was reminded of it by the king himself in a dispatch sent via the Italian legation.[110] And the letter she sent to Napoleon III, probably in 1857, via his first chamberlain, Count Baciocchi, leaves no doubt:

> Sire, in order to get to paradise, eluding foreign snares, I find it best to turn directly to God, rather than go through the saints. I have been entrusted with a particular message, to be delivered to Your Majesty by a circuitous route, but I think it more useful to the country to go straight to the point, so I am begging you, sire, to give me a quarter of an hour of your time. Perhaps at Baciocchi's... or Your Majesty can meet me by chance, as has happened several times already, between the Champs de Mars and Saint-Cloud. I am always at your disposal (Fleury is the best *accompagnatore* for the occasion), or... if Your Majesty fears wagging tongues, though they seem, in our case, to have ceased wagging of late, he need merely invite me

> to dinner. Even those hostile to Italy can then be present at our conversation, at a distance. Without allowing myself to give advice, I beg the emperor to give me the audience and appeal to your kind feelings for my country and for your most devoted Countess of Castiglione.[111]

The letter shows us a Virginia well versed in an art of flattery rooted in the skillful use of hyperbole, but the mention—not without irony—of wagging tongues that have ceased to wag suggests that things were changing between them.

Virginia's first appearance in society after the Compiègne incident was at the masquerade ball organized by Count and Countess Walewski at the foreign ministry on February 17. Virginia devised a disguise that would again be noticed for its boldness, provoking endless commentary. Count Imbert de Saint-Amand, who had dressed up as a Louis XVI pageboy, conveys the shock of her theatrical appearance at the height of the festivities:

> A woman has stepped into the room, and immediately all eyes are on her. She is the fashionable beauty par excellence—the Countess of Castiglione... She is dressed as the Queen of Hearts, a symbolic costume, for it alludes to the numberless hearts the countess "hauls after her," as Racine would say. A crown of hearts glitters atop her head. Her marvelous hair is pouffed around her brow and cascades down her neck. Her skirts and bodice are wrapped in a chain of hearts. Her train is attached at the hip. It is an outfit out of a fairy tale.[112]

Never had Virginia worn a more daring ensemble. Besides contravening the rules of modesty—she wore no corset—it expressed "a clear, tangible protest against the crinoline" defended to the bitter end by the empress.[113] With his usual coarseness whenever the subject is womankind, Viel-Castel commented on the bulging perfection of her breasts and reported the no less crude laughter of another guest: "Careful, countess, before long the men's clothes will be too tight!" Protected by a domino, Napoleon III did not let his emotions show, but to Viel-Castel's mind every man present undoubtedly "shared a thought that none dared express: *I would like to be in the emperor's place*."[114] For her part, the empress—in a gypsy costume—noticed, on her rival's dress, a large heart sewn at the height of the groin and was apparently content to observe that it was "just a bit too low."[115]

Eugénie's quip, whether real or invented, was a sentence that could not be appealed, and it transformed the Queen of Hearts's triumph into a prelude to defeat. Intoxicated by the pleasure of defiance, Virginia hadn't realized that she'd gone too far. She'd seen fit to flout the rules of politeness, respectability, and good taste which marked the limits of freedom for women in the bourgeois century. In turning herself into a symbol of masculine desire, the beauty of beauties had become a source of embarrassment for the emperor—all the more so since, if the rumors were to be believed, he wasn't the only one to enjoy her favors. The countess's bold flaunting of their relationship was likewise unacceptable. Napoleon was fond of his wife, and he admired her; he was grateful for her commitment to raising their son and fulfilling her duties as a sovereign, and he wished to spare her the humiliation of a mistress *en titre*. Though he was not willing to swear off extramarital affairs, he was keen at least not to make them official. Thus, ten days after the soirée at the foreign ministry, the emperor-king issued the imprudent Italian a shot across the bow: She may have been the most beautiful women of the era, but she was not the only one.

On February 27, Princess Mathilde gave another masquerade ball. While the empress, with powdered hair and a diamond-studded black tulle gown, played the role of Night with "a melancholy grace," Castiglione dressed up as a Pompadour-style marquise. Rumor had it that the countess had asked Mathilde if one could wear the same costume twice and received a wry reply: "Do as you wish, madame, but remember that, at my house, people do dress."[116] Virginia, taking this into account, opted for a crinoline grown adorned with a riot of lace, jewels, and fresh-picked flowers that would please the fashion pages.[117] Countess Walewska meanwhile had once again dressed as Diana the huntress, just as she had at the ministry ball, with "a quiver over her shoulder and a diamond tiara on her brow," but in her case the novelty lay in the fact that this time she was visibly "the object of imperial favor."[118]

It is hard to say whether Virginia was alarmed by this, for there is no doubt that the erotic sway she held over the emperor remained unassailable. At a ball given by the banker Fould in early March, as a response to the "quips provoked by her Queen of Hearts costume," she appeared "dressed as a Norman peasant girl covered up to her chin," as if to proclaim that, even clothed head to toe, she was still the most beautiful. At around two o'clock in the morning, she was seen talking excitedly to a masked companion when Count Bacciocchi, superintendent of "His Majesty's pleasures," suddenly appeared, followed by "a personage in a domino readily recognizable by his gait. Scolded by the lady for his untimely arrival—'Excuse me, but I said ten *past* two'—he offered his arm to the lovely Norman; the couple disappeared behind a door that led into a suite of rooms;

and, at last, solitude reigned. At about three o'clock the emperor dined with his face uncovered; he was in high spirits . . . It was evident that His Majesty had deigned to allow himself a bit of fun."[119]

It was equally evident that Virginia had no intention of taking a step back and exchanging her starring role for a supporting one. Others would make that decision for her.

# The Assassination Attempt
## 1857–1858

On the night of April 6, 1857, as he emerged unescorted from a house on avenue Montaigne, the emperor narrowly escaped an assassination attempt. It was by no means the first since he'd taken power, and it would not be the last,[1] but it was the first time he'd been attacked before or after a romantic assignation. And though the journalists were ordered not to report on it, there was no way of preventing the muffled circulation of rumors calling Castiglione into question. It was no secret that, since the previous fall,[2] the countess had been living at 24 avenue Montaigne. Clearly, Napoleon III had been taking advantage of her husband's absence to pay her a visit.

Afterward, the emperor had climbed into his carriage. When three armed men appeared, trying to block it, the coachman sent the horses into a gallop and ran them down. This trio of would-be assassins was led, according to the prosecution, by Paolo Tibaldi, a Mazzinian implicated in many matters of espionage whom Cavour probably also had in his employ. Arrested and found guilty, Tibaldi would be deported to Devil's Island—the horrific penal colony that Napoleon III had established in French Guiana—but it was still unclear who the instigators of the ambush were. After all, the Savoy government had no reason to eliminate the man whose support it was trying to secure. It may well have been a Mazzinian initiative, but there were also those who suspected a French secret service operation[3] conducted with Eugénie's blessing. "The empress's party was no stranger to this sort of carefully orchestrated, melodramatic mise en scène," Ferdinand Bac—who was in a position to know such things—later wrote of the attempt.[4] "Eugénie had her 'conjugal police,' directed by subordinates and fueled by familial favors." Perhaps, frightened by the possible consequences of her husband's reckless behavior, the empress had decided to put an end to it by encouraging a faux assassination attempt, which would make Castiglione look like a dangerous spy. Princess Mathilde had no doubts: "She went to the police for help. At the Tuileries they don't think twice about stashing dressmakers' dummies in the stairwells and calling them *conspirators*."[5] Twenty-some years later, Virginia herself would tell the Duke of Chartres that she'd been the victim of the Spanish woman's machinations, and that if it hadn't been for Costantino Nigra she would have "gone and burned out her brains."[6]

We cannot be sure what happened to Virginia after the attack either. Was she interrogated by the police and then escorted to the border? Or was it simply suggested that she leave the capital for some length of time?

She herself must have been ready for a change of scene when she accepted an invitation to visit the lovely London mansion of Lord and Lady Holland.[7] To judge by a letter from the minister of the Sardinian legation to Her Britannic Majesty, her arrival did not go unnoticed.

"My dear count," Emanuele d'Azeglio wrote to Cavour on July 10,

"Madame de Castiglione will be spending a few days at Holland House, and certainly her presence will prove a tremendous waste of time for everyone in her vicinity." D'Azeglio also boasted of having managed the twofold feat of wangling his demanding compatriot an invitation to the court ball and of entrusting her presentation to the wife of the Duke of Persigny, who was then Napoleon III's ambassador in London—thereby avoiding the risk of a refusal, which, for the Sardinian legation, would have constituted "a rather embarrassing snub." Irony aside, the diplomat was forced to observe that the countess didn't need him to wangle her the most prestigious invitations: "Apparently everyone at Buckingham Palace has been curious to see the celebrity of the moment, and all went smoothly. She received the invitation, the queen and the Duke of Cambridge came and talked with her over supper, and it was all done *decorosamente* . . . At Lady Waldegrave's house she aroused admiration all around, and this evening she will be going to Apponyi's and says she is leaving soon."[8]

That she was now a celebrity the whole world wished to meet—and that her London success was making up for the slander she'd suffered—she herself makes clear, with a healthy dose of self-mockery, in a letter addressed to her increasingly close friend Poniatowski. Her target of the moment was Prince Napoleon (perhaps guilty of having turned his back on her in the weeks following the assassination attempt), who was also in London.

> Prince Napoleon is scared to death of running into me and tomorrow Palmerston [the prime minister] wants me to lunch with him, but I don't think I'll go. Yesterday Prince N. called on Azeglio to ask, "*Est-ce que Madame C. est toujours içi? Et c'est vrai qu'elle va dans le monde?*" "*Mais il paraît puisque on l'y a vue et dans le grand monde!*"

> "*Ah c'est bien extraordinaire et j'en suis très étonné!!!*" ["Is it true that Madame C. is still here? And is it true that she is out in society?" "But it seems as if everyone has seen her out and about, and in the highest society imaginable." "Ah, that is extremely strange and I am quite astonished!"] Tomorrow to drive him mad I'm going to Aumale's where I've been invited by the duchess from four to midnight. Not bad, no?[9]

As we shall see, Virginia would make good use of her visit to Twickenham—the residential district on the outskirts of London where Louis Philippe's fourth-born son had settled into exile. While the Duke of Aumale showed himself susceptible to her beauty, she was struck by the romantic aura surrounding that handsome, cultivated, courageous, patriotic prince who'd been condemned to live in idleness a far cry from his country. The result of this mutual admiration was a bond that would endure for at least two decades. In the spring of 1866, for example, Virginia would find quite suitable words to offer her condolences upon the death of the prince's mother, Queen Maria Amalia: "I understand enough of your sorrow, monsieur, that I would not even try to mitigate it, but great sorrows suit great souls . . . and yours, Prince, will tell Your Majesty that your task is to comfort those who might falter before the will of God, to which every Christian must yield without argument or rancor."[10] And three years later she would pick up the pen again, to mourn the prince's well-beloved wife.[11]

Of course they also talked politics, and out of regard for the prince's patriotism, Virginia did not hesitate to declare herself more French than Italian.[12]

Introducing Virginia into London's *grand monde* was therefore principally the work of the Hollands, who had reserved the most festive welcome imaginable for their "darling beauty." Upon arriving at Holland House on July 1, Virginia had found, in the room set aside for her, a beautiful dressing mirror engraved with her initials, along with a pretentious homage in verse composed by Lord Holland.[13] Meanwhile, Lady Mary was denying the accusations of immorality that swirled about her guest with an "If it were true, she would not be here."[14] And when she was told that the French emperor had a portrait of the countess on display in his private living quarters,[15] she declared it a fitting tribute to her beauty. She herself wished to do as he did and commissioned a portrait from George Frederic Watts, an established painter whom she and her husband had been patronizing ever since their days in Florence. But Watts, trained in Tuscany in the cult of the Italian Renaissance, failed to inspire Virginia's confidence, and faced with the model's constant interference—which included rather extensive criticism of his work—he decided to abandon the commission. "In the end I found her unbridled need for flattery disgusting," he wrote to his wife, "and realizing I would never succeed in ingratiating myself with the countess, I prefer to abandon the project entirely."[16] Unfinished though it is, Watts's portrait is the only depiction of the countess in her youth of unquestionable artistic value, and the only depiction that can hold a candle to her own famous photograph album.

Portrayed half-length, the maiden staring at us with her big clear eyes has the transcendent beauty of Renaissance Madonnas and saints. Her small mouth, which seems about to break into the faintest of smiles, recalls the smile of Raphael's *Joanna of Aragon*. Her pale, perfectly oval face is framed by coppery brown hair, and the bareness of her shoulders is emphasized by the darkness of the background.

If the purity of her features and her expression of virginal reserve make her seem inaccessible, the whiteness of her skin magnetizes the gaze and is as good as an erotic provocation. If the countess herself did not care for the portrait, it was perhaps because of this subtle ambiguity—the very essence of Virginia's charm.

The first to ponder this painting was Robert de Montesquiou,[17] who asked the same question he would ask about the Countess Greffulhe: Why, the *professeur de beauté* wondered, had these two women who devoted themselves to the cult of their own image preferred to entrust their legacy to photography rather than resort to the great portrait painters of their times—Ingres and Richard for Castiglione, Whistler and Boldini for Greffulhe? Montesquiou came to the conclusion that, "torn between the desire to give rise to masterpieces and the fear, at once childish and megalomaniacal, that these masterpieces would equal or surpass the original, challenging it to a contest of beauty and lastingness," the *Beauté Italienne* had given in to her fear, "and so annihilated, in one fell swoop, the marvelous paintings and admirable statues that she might have inspired in contemporary artists, both painters and sculptors."[18]

Perhaps, though, Virginia was simply jealously guarding her ownership of her beauty, determined to be in complete control of it. She wouldn't stand for being pierced and put under glass like a lovely lifeless butterfly; she was going to show herself off in the fullness of life, in all the richness of her expressive range, in all the different parts she'd chosen to play one after the other. And only photography could immortalize her "forever different and identical to herself."[19] Which is why, in Paris, she took to frequenting the Mayer & Pierson photography studio on Boulevard des Capucines, where she posed with the hairstyles, gowns, and jewelry she wore at the receptions and balls that marked her ascent. She would go on doing so even after she came back from London, despite the numerous unknowns hanging over her head.

The first unknown was the price to be paid for her freedom, since, on the eve of her departure for England, she'd entered into a separation agreement with her husband. The initiative had been taken by the count, who, though he'd contemplated the possibility of separation almost from the start, had pulled out all the stops trying to save the marriage. In Paris, intent on leading a quiet life, the count had resigned himself to his wife's haute-monde frenzy and reckless spending, doing everything within his power to remain calm, though a jocular note in which he pledges to keep his outbursts under control[20] suggests that quarrels were frequent. In the early days Francesco had always escorted Virginia to society gatherings—if Fleury can be believed, at the great receptions she "let her husband take her over to a secluded corner where she would allow herself to be admired like a holy body"[21]—and he probably would have settled up with living in the shadow of his extremely beautiful wife, of whom he was so proud, had she shown him even a modicum of the respect that he'd stubbornly gone on believing he would, eventually, obtain. Was he really unaware that she was blatantly betraying him in league with the whole Italian legation? Was he a husband out of farce, as people tended to believe,[22] or simply a gentleman incapable of imagining that his wife could fail to live up to moral principles he himself took for granted? Was it a matter of credulity, acquiescence, or, more likely, blindness? Unaware that he was in a detestable position with both hands tied, he behaved as though he were still an aristocrat on a pleasure trip to Paris. He kept up with political events, visited museums, socialized in diplomatic circles and with his many French and Italian friends, and took part in elegant hunting parties.[23] And while Virginia had put an end to all marital intimacy and was leading an increasingly independent existence, Francesco seemed to take no notice. The letters he wrote to her during a trip to Piedmont in August of that crucial year of 1856 show him plainly unaware of the famous boat excursion that had taken place just two months earlier. The bittersweet irony and uncharacteristic liberty of language in his saying that he knows full well that the "very dear capricious creature," "the dear and capricious Nicchia," is indifferent to his scribblings but that she shouldn't "give even her husband the cold shoulder" lest she put him "in a foul mood,"[24] are interspersed with a paternalism that is, to say the least, misplaced. Thanking her for a longer than usual letter that had reached him while he was visiting Costigliole, he says that she could have been more affectionate but that a man must "be content with *what he can get*." As for him, his greatest wish is that there should "never be a cloud" between them, though he can't help but point out: "When, unfortunately, a storm breaks out, the fault does not always lie with me but a little bit with you too, because you treat me *too coldly* and are unwilling to accept that a modicum of tenderness every now and then is the best way for a wife to get everything she wants out of her husband." Aside from these complaints the letter, with its prolix catalog of practical information, seems thoroughly suffused with domestic normality. Costigliole was looking forward to seeing "its chatelaine" the following summer; her brothers-in-law sent her the warmest greetings and promised to visit her in Paris; and he bade farewell with a request for her to give "Georges hugs from Papa" and to "be cheerful and pious, and, if it is possible, love me as much as, for you will never love me more than, I love you."[25]

The letter that her husband, who'd just arrived in Turin on official business, sent her four months later, at the end of January 1857, was a horse of a different color. It must have alarmed Virginia more than a little. And not only because Francesco declared himself "very, very vexed" not to have heard from her, but because he told her that the king, with whom he'd had a long private conversation, wanted them to end their Parisian sojourn and go back to Piedmont in the spring. The sovereign had been so kind as to tell him he hoped they would spend the summer in Costigliole so that he might have an excuse to take a walk there from Pollenzo.[26]

Back in Paris, bolstered up by kingly authority, Francesco had announced to his wife that the time had come to pack their bags. Which she'd flatly refused to do. At the height of her success—certain that she now had the emperor in her grasp and subject to delusions of omnipotence—Virginia was too busy attending to the details of her outfits for the upcoming February masquerades to waste time on her husband, and she said she was ready to bring their life together to an end. On March 27, 1857, while his wife was dressing up as an eighteenth-century lady to show herself off at Princess Mathilde's, the count wrote to Prince Poniatowski announcing the separation as a fait accompli, and saying he intended to go back home on the first of June.[27] Not wanting to leave his moody, barely twenty-year-old bride alone in a foreign metropolis with the added responsibility of a three-year-old son, he intended to bring her with him and return her to her family. The trouble was how.

The assassination attempt had precipitated the situation. We do not know where Francesco was on the night of the ambush or whether he'd heard about it ahead of time. Certainly Virginia was shocked. She had quickly realized that the unfortunate event would pose a radical challenge to her relationship with the emperor and that it was vital she not abandon the field. Come what may, she needed to remain in Paris to defend her position. The count, finding her adamant, attempted to assert his authority by writing an imperious letter: "I am telling you that we shall leave Paris in early May, I have just told Madame Devaun that by the 11th we will vacate the apartment . . . I wanted to inform you of my decision so that you can make whatever arrangements you see fit to make in preparation for our departure."[28]

Presumably Virginia did not take this injunction seriously, since at the end of May they were both still in Paris, at each other's throats. Unable to stand up to his wife, Castiglione changed his strategy, saying he was willing to abandon the idea of separation if Virginia promised to change her attitude. "You will try to modify your ideas, adjusting them to the condition of a wife and a mother. You will do your best not to treat me with that indifference I find so hurtful, and in all domestic matters *you will consult me before you act*." If not, there was nothing left for them to do but go their separate ways. Attached to the letter was a sheet to be signed with the conditions of an "amicable" separation.[29] In truth, there was very little amicable about it, since it entailed entrusting their son to the count, who "would put an end to all relations, both in person and by mail, with the countess, starting the very moment she decided to leave son and husband."[30]

In addition to wielding his legally conferred authority as paterfamilias to inflict a punitive separation agreement on his rebellious wife, Castiglione felt compelled to justify it with a long and detailed series of accusations—among them "her refusal to fulfill her marital duties under the pretext that she no longer wishes to become pregnant"—which, in the end, was no more than an admission of weakness.[31]

In June the couple came to an arrangement and agreed to sign the document. Breaking the news to Marquise Oldoini in a sorrowful letter, the count resumed the poise of a perfect gentleman: "I am deeply saddened by this, especially when I think of Niny's future, but God is my witness that I have done everything to avoid this sad outcome, and that she will be the one who will, when she looks back on it, have many things to reproach herself for."[32] Proving himself blind yet again to what was going on right under his nose, he expressed his gratitude to Prince Poniatowski—"goodness personified"—who had agreed to act as a mediator between husband and wife. Thanks to Poniatowski's mediation, in fact, Virginia had been allowed to stay in Paris, while Francesco planned to return to Italy on July 1 with little Giorgio. But the count did not want to leave Paris before the arrival of Marquis Oldoini—who, having been informed of the situation, was on his way—so that he would "at least have the consolation of leaving Virginia in her father's hands."[33] For her part the marquise, well aware of her daughter's character, advocated a policy of prudent realism, advising her husband "not to influence Niny's plans in any way whatsoever, it being too delicate a matter not to attract reproach . . ."[34]

Virginia had capitulated to the humiliating and oppressive agreement devised by Castiglione for at least two reasons. First, she was in a hurry to get rid of her husband so as to be able to devote herself to winning back the emperor; second, she knew that Castiglione, despite his warlike declarations, was still hoping for a reconciliation and that she could still convince him to reverse his decision. Hadn't she already persuaded him to let little Giorgio come with her to

London rather than go back to Turin with his father? But the certainty of triumphing over her husband wasn't enough for Virginia. Only the emperor could ensure her economic independence; the very possibility of continuing to carry out the mission entrusted to her by Victor Emmanuel II and Cavour depended on the strength of her relationship with him—and Virginia had no intention of abandoning this mission.

In Paris the young conspirator had discovered not only the enormous power that her beauty gave her and the possibility of putting that power at the service of an exhilarating cause; she had also developed a genuine passion for politics. For the first time, narcissism had given way to an interest that called on her intelligence, analytical capacity, and clear-eyed judgment. It was an interest she would continue to demonstrate through the many political upheavals to come. "She spent hours discussing . . . the foundations of a new Europe, the re-founding of states . . ." wrote Karl Philipp Bach—Jérôme Bonaparte's illegitimate son, who led a quiet life in Baden, where he often visited with Virginia. "She envisioned a great unified Italy, destined to resume its leading role in a reestablishment of the Roman empire, with the help of French Latinity . . . But she was well aware that her grand plans and the hopes they inspired threatened to founder because of the vacillations of imperial policy."[35]

At the time of the assassination attempt on avenue Montaigne, however, the fate of Italy was still in the hands of the inscrutable Napoleon III, who was also being kept under strict surveillance by both his wife and the Countess Walewska. In an effort to dispose of Virginia, Eugénie had in fact entrusted another Florentine with satisfying her husband's extramarital needs—and it was a shrewd choice, for the new favorite would prove both tactful and discreet.

Fourteen years older than Virginia and endowed with "wit, beauty, simplicity, brio, and elegance," Maria Anna Zanobi di Ricci "was all things attractive and fascinating in one person."[36] In Florence in 1846 she'd married the Polish count Alexandre Colonna-Walewski, who, as the offspring of Napoleon I's affair with Maria Walewska, had chosen France as his second homeland, serving first in the army and then as a diplomat. A selfish libertine down on his luck, Walewski had revealed himself to be a lousy husband, but that hadn't prevented the young countess from doing everything she could to further his career. Ever since Napoleon III had appointed him minister of foreign affairs in May 1855, Maria Anna had flawlessly fulfilled the role of mistress of the house, balancing out her husband's haughtiness with grace and courtesy, and organizing receptions that soon made the foreign ministry one of the epicenters of the *fête impériale*. Once she became Napoleon III's mistress—Viel-Castel spoke of it as a certainty in September 1857[37]—the beautiful countess would revive the financial fortunes of the family, remaining friendly with Eugénie and concealing the scandal of her position behind a veil of modesty and respect for convention.

Though Maria Anna's manners were the polar opposite of Virginia's, the two Florentines were both equally ruthless and determined. But the older and more experienced woman soon put an end to the younger one's efforts to make herself the center of attention. All kinds of circumstantial evidence suggest that, in the months after the assassination attempt, Virginia started seeing the emperor again, but her place at the Tuileries was now firmly occupied by a rival whose constant presence at the court was justified by her position as the wife of the minister of foreign affairs. Nor could Walewska be said to lack erotic attractions if, on the imperial train bound for

Compiègne, Napoleon III felt compelled to make love to her in a compartment that shared a wall with the empress's.[38] Though it was again at Compiègne that Virginia, invited to the castle around this same time, would celebrate her final triumph by luring the tireless monarch into bed—an exploit destined to remain emblazoned in her memory seeing that, forty years later, she included among her testamentary provisions that of being buried with the "Compiègne nightgown, 1857."

Virginia still exerted a strong attraction on the emperor, but she had made too many blunders to edge out her fierce new rival. The most serious of them was her indiscretion: she had done nothing to hide their affair, alluding to the very expensive gifts Napoleon had given her—including what would become a legendary necklace with five rows of black and white pearls—and commenting on his modest amatory prowess. An indiscretion all the more unforgivable in the eyes of someone like the emperor, who worshipped secrecy and was constantly having to deal with his wife's jealousy. Determined to put an end to the relationship, which was becoming more and more awkward, Napoleon gave Poniatowski the thankless task of bidding the overly loquacious Italian his polite but firm farewell.

Virginia had not lacked prudence solely with the sovereign. She'd also enjoyed flirting with the old baron James de Rothschild and driving his son Gustave out of his mind. It seems the thick police file compiled by Prefect Piétri at Eugénie's request contained records not just of large loans received by the young Rothschild but also of the confidences in which the Italian had indulged in the banker's bed—confidences concerning business plans as well as the emperor's sexual habits.[39] What's more, Virginia had brazenly flirted with the Count of Nieuwerkerke,[40] strolling with him on the rooftops of the Louvre in the dead of the night and thereby alienating Princess Mathilde, her friend, who had defended her after the ambush on avenue Montaigne. Unreliable as they often are, the malignancies that Viel-Castel records about Virginia suggest her impudence, her exhibitionism, and her lust for money. The rumor put into circulation by Prince Napoleon that Lord Hertford—"a monster, one of those men who stand at the edge of the abyss, their excesses disclosing the worst instincts of humanity"[41]—had shelled out a million to spend a night with her and subject her "to all the trials of the most refined libertinism"[42] makes it clear that the haughty countess's reputation was by then at its nadir.

To make matters worse, early the next year another assassination attempt overshadowed the one on avenue Montaigne and compounded Virginia's problems. On the evening of February 14, 1858, three bombs were thrown at the carriage taking Napoleon III and Eugénie to the Opéra. The imperial couple were miraculously spared, but the explosion resulted in carnage, leaving eight dead and one hundred and fifty wounded in the vicinity. Of the four attackers—all Italian patriots—the best known was Felice Orsini, who had dedicated his life to conspiracy.[43] The attack reverberated not only through France but through all of Europe:

> The old rumors about the power of the sects began circulating again, and it was said that this new attack was an offshoot of the old death sentence leveled against Louis Napoleon, an apostate member of the Carbonari whom not even the imperial crown could protect. Bombs were now taking the place of daggers, but the murderous instincts of Italian conspirators had not changed. This was the thought in conservative circles as well as in moderate ones.[44]

Piedmont was the first to suffer the political backlash of the drama. The emperor accused the kingdom of Sardinia of offering refuge to anarchists throughout the peninsula; of not exercising sufficient control; of permitting the publication of incendiary writings. And he threatened to rethink his pro-Italian intentions. Composed with Cavour's help, the response that Victor Emmanuel entrusted to his personal envoy, General Della Rocca, was not devoid of pride:

> Tell him ... that this is no way to treat a faithful ally; that I have never tolerated violence from any quarter; that I follow the ever stainless path of honor, and that for this honor I answer only to God and my people. That for eight hundred and fifty years we have walked this path with our heads held high, and that no one will ever make me lower mine, and that I desire nothing more than to be his friend withal.[45]

But Napoleon III's determination to tip the European balance in France's favor was too strong for him to be swayed by the assassination attempts. In fact, the sovereign would reap the benefits of Felice Orsini's noble self-defense, which was destined to command the respect of many. The letter that the Italian patriot addressed to the emperor before going to the guillotine echoed Cavour's warning to the Congress of Paris: "Until Italy is independent, European peace, and your own peace, will be no more than an illusion. Your Majesty cannot spurn the last avowal of a patriot bound for the scaffold: Liberate my homeland, and the blessings of twenty-five million citizens will follow you everywhere and for all time to come."[46] Not only did the emperor allow this missive to be read aloud in court by

Orsini's lawyer, he ordered its publication in *Le Moniteur*—the official newspaper of the empire—making clear his intention to support the nationalist cause.

Unbeknownst to Walewski, who had always been hostile to pro-Savoy policy,[47] Napoleon initiated personal diplomacy with Turin through Dr. Conneau, while Cavour decided to send Costantino Nigra, the young secretary of whom he once said: "I am as sure of him as of myself."[48] After months of negotiation, Napoleon finally asked Cavour to join him in the greatest secrecy at the spa in Plombières. During this meeting, which took place on July 24, 1858, a plan destined to revolutionize the political order of the Bel Paese was mapped out. The emperor committed to joining Piedmont in its war against Austria with the following objectives in mind: The kingdom of Sardinia would take Lombardy, the Veneto, and Rome; Tuscany and the papal legations would be governed by the Duchy of Parma; Latium and Rome would remain with the pope; if Ferdinand II decided to abdicate, the kingdom of the Two Sicilies would go to Lucien Murat (the son of Napoleon the Great's sister). In return, and with reference to so-called "natural frontiers," the emperor demanded the cession of Savoy and Nice, and said he hoped to strengthen ties between the imperial and Savoy families by marrying Prince Napoleon to Princess Clotilde, the fifteen-year-old daughter of Victor Emmanuel. The emperor also said, however, that there would have to be an Austrian provocation before war was declared.

The meeting at Plombières proved decisive. Five months later, the treaty of alliance and mutual defense between France and the kingdom of Sardinia was signed by both sovereigns, and on January 30, 1859, Prince Napoleon led Clotilde to the altar.

Whether or not she was aware of the complex negotiations between Paris and Turin, and whatever her relations with the emperor, Virginia was forced to acknowledge that confidential information would now be passing through different channels. Her mission was over. Not that this would prevent her from keeping a close eye on the political situation, drawing on her vast network of lovers, friends, and acquaintances to her own exclusive advantage.

Relations with her husband were meanwhile deteriorating. In July a letter from Francesco asked about the "dreadful system of promissory notes" whose management he'd been foolish enough to entrust her with and that had led to his ruin. He forgave her for the harm she'd done him—and for "the miserable existence" to which her feckless behavior had condemned him—but he did not spare her one final unpleasant warning: "The day will come when your fatal beauty fades; there will not be so many flatterers, and you will see things more clearly; then, perhaps, you will understand how ignominiously you betrayed the vow you took before God and for four years neglected your conjugal duties, making me the unhappiest of men."[49]

As far as Virginia was concerned, there were no other options; the future loomed as uncertainly as ever, and with no support and no money she was forced to return to Italy. She first went to La Spezia—and while he was still busy making his way to Plombières, Cavour proposed that his niece Giuseppina Alfieri di Sostegno accompany him, as soon as she was back in Italy, "to pay Niny a visit."[50] The riot of scents and colors of the "beautiful gulf," and the sea-bathing so essential to her health, must have brought her some comfort, but they did not rid her of her worries.

On November 14, Castiglione wrote to his father-in-law that

Virginia was back in Turin and would stay with him until Christmas. In the meantime, he would be moving in to his brother's house, where his son would come pay him a visit. The couple had in fact just finally arrived—with the help of Prince Poniatowski and Count Cigala—at a separation by mutual agreement. The count could only repeat to his father-in-law what he'd already written to Marquise Oldoini: "God is my witness that my heart is broken and that *for four years* I have done everything I can to avoid this, resigning myself to an impossible existence."[51] After failing to get his daughter to come to her senses—"Don't do anything rash, my dear"[52]—by enumerating the risks of a separation, the marquis appealed to his son-in-law's discretion so as to avoid an unnecessary scandal. Castiglione, who was in Paris to hash things out with Poniatowski, wrote to his father-in-law, swearing on his honor that he had "nothing to rebuke the countess for on the plane of moral behavior."[53] Oldoini, immensely relieved, immediately passed this information on to his wife.

Virginia was fully aware that her only protection was her husband's need to preserve the family's dignity, at least outwardly. And so she managed to gain custody of her son, though for a limited period of time, in exchange for a life lived under guard. But since she was determined to defend at any cost the sliver of freedom that remained to her (after one last attempt at Paris[54]), in early 1859 she resigned herself to moving with Giorgio into an isolated house on the heights of the Turinese hill of San Vito, overlooking the Po River—a house ironically called Villa Gloria.

# Villa Gloria
## 1859

So far, we have told the Countess of Castiglione's story almost exclusively through the eyes of others; the few fragments of her diary that have come down to us are no more than crude catalogs of facts, and her letters to her parents and husband never depart from a rather wary reticence. The first to question her character and behavior were her family members, followed soon thereafter by the high society people who met her in Turin and Paris. At a very early age, Virginia had learned to display a consummate actress's self-mastery whenever she appeared in public. That she was the center of attention is indisputable. Innumerable newspaper articles and other contemporary accounts document the uproar provoked by her spectacular public appearances as well as the myriad rumors swirling about her exploits with the emperor. Yet, for everyone, the Countess of Castiglione has remained a genuine enigma. And she surely would have remained an enigma for us, too, had it not been for the letters she wrote to Giuseppe Poniatowski between 1858 and 1863—the most crucial years of her life. Read sequentially, these letters—almost two thousand pages of them—become something like a monologue in which the young woman tells her own story without apology.

On the one hand there is her hope for a different sort of life, her desire for freedom, and her thirst for revenge. On the other hand there are her fears and ailments, her suspicions and resentments, and her endless, nagging need for cash. But the red thread in this correspondence is the affection that binds her to Poniatowski, her urge to share everything with him. "There is no affection in the world like ours,"[1] she reminds him at one point. And it is this covenant of sincerity—"we told each other we would tell each other everything"—that allows her to step out of character and finally be . . . herself. Or almost.

Who, then, was the man to whom Virginia—conquering her diffidence and emotional frigidity—declared, "*À tort ou à raison*, I love you, and my affection shall never fail"?

As a child, Joseph Poniatowski had learned how to make do with his irregular status. His father gave him his first lessons in taking things as they came and never hesitating to seize whatever opportunities life threw at him. Like other members of the Polish royal family, General Stanisław Poniatowski had taken the path of exile after his uncle renounced the crown. In Rome, where he'd initially settled, he enjoyed the pope's benevolence until a scandalous affair with Cassandra Luci—a cobbler's daughter,[2] and married to boot, who bore him five children—led to a move to Florence. The far more tolerant Leopold II, Grand Duke of Tuscany, welcomed him eagerly into his circle of intimates, allowing him to legitimize his progeny, giving him the title of Duke of Monterotondo, and providing him with the means necessary to lead the life of a wealthy gentleman. An opera enthusiast and organizer of festivals and concerts, Poniatowski was quick to encourage the strong musical aptitudes of his third-born son, Joseph. The child thus benefited from lessons with excellent teachers and became a singer and a conductor. He also tried his hand at composing, and in late 1838, in Lord Rowland Standish's private theater, he staged his first opera, *Giovanni da Procida*, playing the tenor part himself, with his brother Carlo and his sister-in-law Elisa in supporting roles. Over the next decade he would compose no fewer than seven operas, which were performed in several Italian cities. Despite his success, after his father's death he was forced to put away his musical career and take up a diplomatic one in order to support his wife and son. Leopold II soon put his adaptability and taste for adventure to good use.

In November 1848, when the revolutionary winds were again prevailing on the peninsula, Leopold II made him minister plenipotentiary, first to the French republic and later to London, "to become acquainted and ascertain the position of both governments . . . with regard to independence and Italian unification."[3]

Equipped with an illustrious name—plus the added value of the title "prince," granted by the duke—astute, attractive, and at ease in every social circle, Poniatowski fulfilled his mission brilliantly and, four years later, was awarded the office of chamberlain. After Louis Napoleon's coup d'état, the musician-diplomat returned to Paris, where Poland (a country in which he'd never set foot) gave him an unexpected gift. As a tribute to his ancestor Józef Antoni Poniatowski, Napoleon's heroic marshal, the new emperor offered him French citizenship and made him a senator. Warmly welcomed at the Tuileries, the prince laid the groundwork for his sister Isabella's daughter, the beautiful Maria Anna Walewska (who, as we have seen, was destined to become the emperor's mistress). Paris—in addition to being a land of plenty, where with a bit of luck and cunning one could make a fortune—was also the capital of the arts, and it wasn't long before Joseph, who'd begun composing again, had his work performed at the Opéra.

Virginia had known him since she was a babe in arms and regarded him a member of the family: Poniatowski had long been her mother's official chaperone, and the prince's son—only two years older than Virginia—had been her playmate and called her "*ma petite soeur*."[4] In fact, it was Poniatowski, who showed a special fondness for the little Oldoini, who was credited with the pet name "Nicchia"—an abbreviation of the diminutive Virginicchia but also Tuscan for *conchiglia* (seashell)[5]—which had become her second first name. Joseph's brother Charles had even stood as her witness on her wedding day. But when two years later she and Joseph met again, the nature of the relationship between the countess and the prince had changed.

He had immediately placed himself at Virginia's disposal, recognizing her liaison with Napoleon as a valuable opportunity to ingratiate himself with the ruler and infiltrate the upper echelons of power. And Virginia, for her part, had found a perfect accomplice in this old family friend. They were both individualistic, intolerant of rules, in love with success, power, and money—but while the prince made no secret of it, she had to dissimulate, hiding behind a haughtiness that established an unbridgeable gap between her and others. It wasn't merely Poniatowski's unscrupulousness, or his cheerful cynicism, or his dashingness that enthralled her; she also appreciated his profound artistic vocation, which gave him access to a higher dimension of existence, to which she, however confusedly, aspired. In 1862, recalling one evening when she'd sat watching him play piano, almost transfigured by happiness, she would confess, "If I'd been able to foresee the inner joy and *l'oubli du monde extérieur* [forgetfulness of the exterior world] that I experienced in that moment, you can be sure I would have committed all manner of infamy to obtain it."

Probably, during her solitary days at Villa Gloria, Virginia realized how important Poniatowski had become to her life. He was the only person who knew all her secrets, and the only one with whom she could revel in total honesty without any fear of judgment. But above all—and now more than ever—she needed his advice and assistance if she was going to escape from this trap in Turin, where she found herself at the mercy of her husband's and family's extortionate manipulations. To fill the solitude, she wrote to him endlessly. Indeed each page of this correspondence (written in a large, vigorous handwriting that reflects feverish need) is bursting at the seams. The need for the thread that bound them not to be broken; to give and get news; to make plans; to be comforted; to cry out in anger and despair. With the exception of a few brief fragments, the prince's answers have been lost,[6] but Virginia's letters alone are enough for us to understand how intimate their bond really was. If in her correspondence with her father, husband, and lovers she always chooses to write in French and never veers from the formal *vous*, in her correspondence with Poniatowski she resorts to the vernacular Italian of her childhood with a sense of spelling and syntax that is, to say the least, approximate, and the formal *lei* tends to stray into *tu*. It is not exactly clear when Nicchia and Il Vecio—as he called himself—became lovers,[7] though Virginia certainly gave herself to her friend before returning to France in the fall of 1860. But while it added a more complicit and spicier tone to their letters, physical intimacy did not, in her eyes, constitute an important change in their relationship. Sex for Virginia was not a significant factor in and of itself and could be employed with equal nonchalance for political and monetary purposes and for emotional or even recreational reasons. In any case Il Veccio very likely made the first move. He was just past forty, sensual, and exuberant, and he never wearied of collecting mistresses of all kinds, though his sexual experience with Nicchia had a shattering effect on him and would be emblazoned in his memory "for eternity."[8] For her, however, indulging the Old Man's "ardent" desire was just another way of cementing their bond.[9]

That the prince had been her mother's lover for many years didn't seem to displease Virginia, or cause her any remorse—a word that anyway wasn't in her vocabulary. She'd never gotten along very well with "the Marquise"—as she insisted on calling her—and since her return to Italy their differing views had grown even more different. Which was exactly why the prince was sometimes the best person to come to her aid in family quarrels. Virginia would brutally ask him to "muzzle" his old mistress.

In the spring of 1859, Piedmont wasn't the only one preparing an Italian war of independence; from her hermitage in the hills of Turin, the Countess Verasis di Castiglione was on an all-out crusade to win her own. Her first objective was not to go back to living with her husband; her second to secure the means to avoid doing so. The count's bankruptcy due to debts racked up in Paris threatened to devour her dowry, which wasn't enough for her to lead a decent life anyway—especially since in Turin "every door was closed to [her]." The Castiglione family had quarantined her in order to ward off gossip; Victor Emmanuel had done nothing to stop her being excluded from court receptions; and Cavour, though saddened by

Nini's "troubles,"[10] had more pressing concerns. "Think of it," Virginia writes to Il Vecio, "here I am, alone like a bitch. Everybody, without exception, has *tourné le dos* [turned their back] and left me high and dry." And in a letter written a little later she underlined the point: "And here I am, cast out into the world unhoused and unroofed and uncarriaged, twenty-two years old, and never have I had a single good day." But she ruled out the possibility of going back to Florence, where she would find herself back under the jurisdiction of her parents, leading a "broken and defiled" life. She hoped rather to return to Paris as soon as possible, though first she had to obtain the emperor's approval and the necessary guarantees that she could do so "with [her] head held high." As for money, it was essential to stay in touch with banker friends so that she would know in advance which stocks to speculate on, as she'd done in Paris. None of these objectives could have been achieved without the help of Poniatowski, who, after the considerable loans he'd given Castiglione, became the cessionary of all the count's assets[11] and was able, by dealing with the demands of all the many creditors, to protect the interests of Virginia, who'd meanwhile shrewdly requested separation of property.[12] It was Poniatowski, along with General Cigala—and with Marquis Oldoini's blessing—who took charge of the separation negotiations between the couple; and it was also Poniatowski—already Virginia's business partner for a while now—who conducted the financial transactions in Paris which she dictated from afar. Above all, only Poniatowski was in a position to sound out Napoleon III and determine how Virginia could best get back into his good graces. The important thing, she maintained, was to act quickly: "I don't imagine he thinks about me anymore, but I think he must not be allowed to forget. If he does think about me, we have to strike while the iron is hot, and I'm relying on you to be on the lookout for any opportunity to do so." There was no time to waste on the business side of things either. "If I don't do something this year, I'm dead and buried for life," she wrote, not mincing her words.

Bringing all of this together—and speeding it up—was the imminent prospect of war.

# Baby

"My dear Mina, I am again very sorry that Mina is so ill. I hope Mina will soon be well and come out with me to take a little air, goodbye from Georges Verasis."[1] Written in capital letters, in the hesitant handwriting of a child who has only recently learned to manipulate pen and paper, the first of the letters that Giorgio Verasis addressed to his mother announces the two major themes of their relationship: his concern for the health of the woman he will always call Mina, never Mama, and the pain caused by her distance.

The second letter introduces the leitmotif of hope disappointed: "I have been waiting for Mina all day. I am sorry that Mina is not come. I hope Mina is well and I send Mina kisses. I hope to see Mina tomorrow, Lo Fü."[2] A transliteration of the Chinese word for "love," Lo Fü is the nickname—probably given to him by his mother[3]—Giorgio uses to sign all of his childhood correspondence.

The third letter, drafted in Dieppe on elegant stationery (with a coat of arms and a debossed name quite at odds with the child's halting handwriting) presumably dates from the summer of 1863. It shows us an eight-year-old boy who already knows that to curry favor with his mother he must court her, like the men he'd seen swarming around her ever since he could remember:

> My most dear dear Mina, I am very sorry that Mina is not yet come back and I wish very very much to see Mina . . . I send Mina this poem with many kisses: Although from Mina I am separated, / My heart is always with dear Mina. / My love and gratitude to Mina is always / Where Mina is and dwells.[4]

Desperate for her attention, Giorgio intuited that such courtship was the best way to get into the good graces of a mother who had no qualms about subjecting him to the same moody and capricious treatment she doled out to her lovers.

Marquis Oldoini had hoped the child would fill "the need for serious and profound affection" inherent in his daughter's "character."[5] But Virginia seems to have been too immature and self-centered for it to make much difference. She had neither the time nor the resources to summon maternal feelings for that "Picchinicchi" whose birth she described in her diary without a word of affection.[6] Not that this kept her from considering this unloved child her exclusive property. But hadn't the congratulatory telegrams from the family, the gifts, the endless festivities leading up to the "grandiose" baptism of March 22, 1855—at which she'd received her parents and friends while "lying on a chaise longue"[7]—not been more than enough confirmation that she herself was the true protagonist of the event? Castiglione's reaction was quite different. The letter he sent his father-in-law "the moment that Divine Providence, in its goodness, deigned to answer my most ardent prayers,"[8] reveals his sense of responsibility and his profound emotion at becoming a father, a consolation for the loss of his first son. The name Giorgio—which was chosen solemnly—was the name of "the first count of Costigliole," a friend of Emanuele Filiberto of Savoy's, "who was governor of Casale and distinguished himself in battle."[9] For the time being, however, the little one was called "Baby," or, in view of his imperious demands, "Captain Baby." But though in these early days Castiglione's gratitude at having become the father of such "a magnificent child"[10] led him to indulge his wife's whims more than usual, their differing attitudes toward their son would soon lead to irresolvable conflict.

In the first written list of accusations that the count, even before he left Paris, leveled against his wife with separation in mind, is "her lack of affection for her son,"[11] and in May 1857, when he returned to Turin, Castiglione had no misgivings about claiming his right to retain custody of Giorgio. To Virginia, who'd just put the emperor's brush-off behind her, this challenge to her maternal rights must have seemed an intolerable affront, as did the conditions for gaining custody of Baby, and she therefore held out against her husband's quite reasonable demands with insolent insistence. No doubt Little Giorgio quickly realized he'd become the object of chronic dispute. Whereas his father, in deference to family tradition, wanted him to have a military education in keeping with the values of the Savoy nobility, his mother meant to make him a gentlemen, complete with all the credentials he would need to shine on the international stage, be it in politics and diplomacy or in the world of business. In essence Virginia's ambition was for her son to be free to openly cultivate the passions that she could pursue only vicariously, working behind the scenes and at risk to her freedom, her reputation, and even her health.

This surrogate ambition would lead her to put endless demands on the child despite the fact that, as time wore on and she became distracted by other concerns, she would sometimes forget he existed.

Giorgio, though, never forgot his mother and the two blissful years he'd spent in symbiosis with her at Villa Gloria—when it could be said of Virginia that "no woman ever loved a child with so much tenderness and devotion."[12]

On her return from Paris in December 1858, Virginia finally showed some interest in her adoring Picchinicchi, who lightened the burden of solitude in the Turin hills. When he went to visit her for the first time, Count Henry d'Ideville found her lying on a sofa with Giorgio playing right beside her. The boy struck him as the perfect reflection of his mother's beauty. "He is the most enchanting and delightful creature imaginable, with those blond curls framing his face, his bare arms and shoulders, his big, sweet, astonished-looking eyes. He looks a great deal like his mother, but his gaze is gentler or, rather, less severe."[13] Count d'Ideville was also struck by Virginia's personal involvement in his education. "With commendable talent, she has been giving her son lessons in English, French, and German—languages that he is mastering as well as his native tongue."[14] She demanded among other things that Giorgio always write to her in English. Proud of the child's beauty, Virginia had used him as an accessory to her own self-aggrandizing even back in Paris. She had portraits taken of him very early on, at a time when "no baby was so often and so well photographed,"[15] until she had at least a hundred. The first photograph of Baby at the age of one, proudly displayed by his nurse beside his self-satisfied mother, is also one of the first pictures of Virginia that Pierson ever took. And as her son grew to resemble her more and more, she enjoyed emphasizing this resemblance, edging into sexual ambiguity through a subtle game of mirrors. An oil portrait shows him at the age of three, unequivocally dressed as a girl in a precious lace dress with velvet trim which leaves his shoulders uncovered, and a very elaborate curly coiffure.[16] In a photograph from the same period the hairstyle is identical, and again he is dressed in feminine clothes. (Not coincidentally, in correspondence with her friend Estancelin, she jestingly called him "Georgette.") Two impressive portraits from 1861 attest to just how splendidly the child served his mother's narcissism. In both photographs, the countess—wrapped in a black silk cloak hovering like a halo over an immense crinoline, with a little black tricorn tipped down over her brow, topped by a huge white feather—takes center stage. In the first, her gaze is directed toward Giorgio, who, seated on a stool, dressed as a girl in a hat like his mother's, has his head lowered, staring at the ground. In the second, the countess's back is turned to her son, and having climbed onto the stool where he'd been sitting in the previous shot, she now towers over him in all her majesty, making him look even smaller than he is. Bareheaded, with his chubby face fully lit, Giorgio has clearly been called back to his duties as a pageboy, and staring somewhat sullenly at the lens, he holds the outermost edge of his mother's majestic train in his left hand. But if Baby in these photographs is no more than an ornamental appendage in the choreography Virginia devised to highlight her own beauty, in the photographs taken a couple of years later, when he was seven or eight, he figures as her "miniaturized avatar" and "the faithful reflection of his mother."[17] These are disturbing images, to say the least—somewhere between Lewis Carroll's pictures of girls and the little *travestis* meant to stimulate pedophilic fantasies. In the first, Giorgio is framed in profile, with his long hair gathered in a soft bun decorated with a floral clip and his bare shoulders emerging from a dark velvet cloth. In the second, he is an enchanting nymphet, the index finger of his left hand just barely touching his chin as he stares mischievously into the lens. A cascade of dark golden hair, through which we see a single snow-white arm, masks the nudity of his torso, while a velvet cloth conceals his lower half. Virginia had even decided to immortalize him with the same asymmetrical hairstyle she herself had sported at one of the balls at Saint-Cloud, when she divided her splendid hair—her pride and joy—by curling half of it into a pyramid and powdering it white, leaving the other half blond and sleek, hanging down against her face. But if Virginia's taste for extravagance and masquerade, when applied to her son, revealed the contradictory and unstable character of her relationship with him, a photograph that Pierson took a few years later leaves us in no doubt about the nature of their relationship. *The Kiss* is one of the rare portraits in which mother and son interact. Giorgio—who is now thirteen and has finally been allowed to cut his hair—is standing tall before his mother, preparing to kiss her hand. The scene suggests not so much a gesture of filial deference as a religious rite. In a long white gown that contrasts with the black mass of Virginia's dress, the handsome teenager looks like an altar boy about to receive communion, and his ecstatic gaze seems to promise unconditional devotion. It is one of the last images we have of him, and it sheds a retrospective light on the cult he dedicated to his mother from earliest childhood.

But now back to Villa Gloria, where the young Castiglione was enjoying his mother's attention.

# The War of Independence
## 1859–1860

The war declared on April 29, 1859—the war that had underpinned Virginia's mission in France—presented her with two major opportunities. For one, it gave her a chance to solve her economic problems, since, as she reminded Poniatowski, who'd been through it in 1848, "revolutions are the time to makes one's fortune." For another, it offered her an excuse to reestablish direct contact with the emperor.

On January 10, 1859, putting his trust in the Plombières agreements, Victor Emmanuel had reopened the work of the subalpine government with a warlike speech declaring Piedmont's intention to put an end to Austria's occupation of the peninsula. Napoleon III himself had suggested the crucial passage—"we are not insensible to the cry of grief which reaches us from many parts of Italy"[1]—but over the following months, faced with international mobilization to avert yet another European war and England's offer to host yet another peace conference, the emperor appeared to grow more hesitant. While thousands of volunteers flooded into Piedmont, Victor Emmanuel and Cavour recalled many conscripts into the military and issued a new loan whose purpose was all too clear to the markets and chancelleries. But it was in Vienna, in fact, that the will to war prevailed. On April 21, Austria, weary of provocations, finally took the initiative and gave Piedmont an ultimatum: immediate disarmament and disbandment of the volunteer corps, or war. They had three days to respond. And so the Austrian government took responsibility for aggression in the eyes of Europe, and the second Italian war of independence began.

While they waited for their allies the French to arrive, the Piedmontese got ready to delay, for as long as possible, the advance of the Austrian army, which had twice as many men and stood arrayed in battle gear on the Lombard side of the Ticino. They were afraid that the enemy would immediately set their sights on Turin, which was impossible to defend. But instead, with the risk of an insurrection in Lombardy and Veneto at his back, wavering and bogged down by torrential rains, the commander-in-chief of the Austrian forces, Ferenc Gyulay, moved slowly, wasting precious time. When Napoleon III landed in Genoa on May 12 with three army corps and two more on their way from the Susa Valley, there had still been no direct confrontation. According to the treaty, the emperor had supreme command of the Franco-Italian forces, while Victor Emmanuel, flanked by General La Marmora, was in charge of the Savoy army. From the earliest Franco-Sardinian victories at Montebello and Palestro, the contrast between the Italian sovereign's recklessness and the emperor's cautiousness and disconcerting slowness became clear. Even after the victory at Magenta and the subsequent liberation of Milan, where the two allies entered in triumph on June 6, Napoleon III went on squandering every opportunity to alter the course of the conflict for good and all. Even after the ultimate victory at Solferino, which cost the French army as many as 1,622 dead and

8,530 wounded,[2] he made no effort to pursue the enemy. In fact, from the time the war began, the sovereign had been preoccupied by retaining consensus at home while dreading complications on the Rhine. By repeatedly defeating Austria and so asserting French hegemony, he achieved the goal he'd set for himself. His allies would not realize this until a month later, on July 7, when out of the blue the emperor told Victor Emmanuel that he intended to end the war. On July 11, at Villafranca, the French sovereign signed an armistice with Emperor Franz Joseph that, in a resounding contravention of the Plombières agreement, left Veneto under Austrian rule.

When the war broke out, while her husband fled his creditors by leaving for the front,[3] Virginia stayed in Turin. Though the city was in danger of falling into enemy hands, she was not afraid.[4] Her mother, relatives, and friends had urged her to take refuge in the safer city of Genoa, where the emperor had landed. But this news alone was enough to dissuade her: "Everyone will say that's why I'm there, and I'd be cooped up in a room, not even looking out of the window. No, I'm absolutely not going to go there. It's time to get moving, not get people talking." These were not mere words on the countess's part. And Villa Gloria would prove to be an excellent position from which to do battle.

While Cavour was kept in the dark about the progress of the war by Victor Emmanuel, who, to ward off interference, limited communications from the front as much as possible, Virginia managed to stay abreast of the goings-on in the Piedmontese and French armies thanks to two top-grade sources. The first was Count Enrico Martini di Cigala, Victor Emmanuel's aide-de-camp and her husband's maternal uncle, on whose collusion Virginia had known she could rely ever since he'd helped facilitate her secret meetings with the king before her mission in Paris. Cigala made no secret of his affection for this enchanting and all too reviled niece. He even sided with her in her dispute with Castiglione. Virginia reciprocated by allowing him a tiny bit of intimacy, and the coarse colonel must have lost his mind: How else can we explain his offering, in defiance of military ethics, to keep her unfailingly informed about the progress of the war without wondering what use his niece—"a little crazy but a good egg deep down"[5]—would make of such confidential information? There are a full sixty-seven letters from "Barba Cigala," as he signed himself—the Piedmontese *barba* meaning "uncle"—to Virginia, and together they provide a detailed chronicle of the conflict. In turn, beating the official bulletins to the punch, the beautiful recluse passed the news on to Charles-Adolphe Huteau, her trusted man in Paris, so that he could tell his banker friends, who used it to play the stock market.[6]

Cigala wrote in haste, trying in vain to boil down the day's military operations into a few pages of prose. His style leaves something to be desired, and his sentimental glosses are witheringly banal.[7] He resorts to barracks language[8] when expressing his indignation at the brazenness of Victor Emmanuel—"il Farfo" (the fool)—who'd been joined by his longtime mistress Rosa Vercellana,[9] and he is sarcastic about both the Piedmontese sovereign's boasts and the icy indifference of the Frenchman—"il Bullo" (the bully)—to the thousands of dead soldiers. But Barba was a pure-bred soldier, ready to "sacrifice everything for military honor"[10] and be killed for his king, and it is precisely the absence of rhetoric in his chronicle that allows us to perceive, among the strategical errors and organizational shortcomings of the commanders, an emotional and living testimony to the decisive role played by the Savoyard army[11] in the war that would change Italy's destiny.

Curiously, among the letters from Cigala now preserved in the Turin State Archives, the one containing an account of the decisive battle of Palestro is missing. This was the battle in which the Piedmontese army held its own and triumphed over the Austrians, allowing the French army to cross the Sesia and march toward Milan. Since there is no way Cigala failed to write about this battle, it has been assumed that Virginia, knowing its importance, sent the letter on to Cavour. But the facts tell a different story. After the way she'd been treated, she no longer felt duty bound to give her illustrious cousin any information whatsoever and was operating with only her own interests in mind; thus it was not to Cavour that she forwarded this letter but to Poniatowski (among whose papers it can still be found today),[12] most likely wanting to let him know not so much that the Piedmontese army had fought honorably at Palestro, or that the allies had been forced to acknowledge that Piedmontese soldiers were equal to French ones, as that the emperor, according to Cigala, had asked Victor Emmanuel how she was doing. Moreover, when passing this tidbit on to his aide-de-camp, the king—who liked poking fun at him over his fondness for Virginia—had spitefully added that when the emperor talked about her he appeared to be "in heat."

This language would undoubtedly have horrified Virginia's second informant, the chivalrous Prince de La Tour d'Auvergne, who, ever since he'd arrived in Turin as Napoleon III's minister plenipotentiary, had been courting her in the most respectful manner imaginable. The diplomat had shown "great desire" and she "dread,"[13] but the advantages of a relationship with him were so glaring that she could not refuse him. Out of gratitude, the prince had given her permission to make use of his personal diplomatic courier, enabling her to send letters to her correspondents in Paris care of Huteau quickly and safe from prying eyes. He also kept her abreast of what was going on with the French commanders, as well as the political situation in Turin and the tenor of Cavour's relations with Victor Emmanuel and the emperor. As Virginia put it: "What a gift, no?"

What La Tour d'Auvergne could not imagine was that his "dear beloved angel" intended to start playing another game with the French emperor.

In truth, flattering though it was, the news that two sovereigns on the battlefield had found time to talk about her also outraged Virginia. Not that this stopped her from taking advantage of it. "As you will see from Barba's letter," she wrote to Poniatowski,

> yesterday, for the first time, he asked about me... that Pig King is always trying to get back at Cigala... who would never say a bad word about me and God only knows how the other man replied. In brief, I've written to find out. But as usual my poor shoulder will have to bear another burden. He is jealous and [?][14] convinced, as he told me at the Tuileries, that I was the king's *maîtresse*. He must have asked, finally, to find out the truth, not realizing that with the king there is no need for ruse to make him talk, even about things that *aren't real* and *never were*. He opens his mouth to everyone and anyone, and you can be sure he'll have him believing it too! The two of them may have confessed all to each other, but if *he* [the emperor] has done this to me again (about the king, I don't care) he will pay for it. I am waiting to hear whether the king has been lying as usual, in which case I'll have the Prince of Carignano take care of him. The prince likes me very much and knows the king... That's all I'll say. But *à qui la faute* [who's to blame]?

Fortunately, it wasn't long before a "very *charming, affectionate*" letter from the Old Man came to reassure her. She wasted no time sending Poniatowski an "unexpurgated copy": "My heart is at ease, but my curiosity is extreme. I am worried—not a word about your situation, your health! Why *four* lines? You can remedy this, and soon—and make me happy."

Napoleon's message was promising, but Virginia needed Poniatowski's advice.

> How can I reply? *Un peu, beaucoup, passionnément, ou rien de tout* [a little, a lot, passionately, or nothing at all]*???* How to reply, too, to the prospect of going there: he asks when and why I would not come. And he repeats the question at the end. So he is entertaining the idea of my coming back to Paris.

And recovering all her boldness, the beautiful schemer adds: "I am convinced he would do anything for me but I think that if he saw me . . . he would perhaps do *something*. *C'est une bonne occasion* [It is a good opportunity] and mustn't be missed, because if I let him get away, I won't catch him again."

As in the libertine novels of the previous century, Virginia, with Poniatowski's help, began weaving a web of words—seductive, admiring words—designed to ensnare a cunning prey, and wary too, considering he'd been ensnared by both of them before. But times had changed. Unlike the Marquise of Merteuil and the Viscount Valmont, the two accomplices were not practicing libertinage as a higher art of living; they were, rather, using it to secure the material conditions necessary to assert themselves in a money-based society.

And when in private they took off their masks, their strategies and language were the strategies and language of the brothel.

Since May 12—the day that Napoleon III landed in Genoa—Virginia had been waiting for a "good opportunity," but the situation was in flux. After receiving assurances from the emperor that they would soon be seeing each other again, she heard nothing more and was on pins and needles. Meanwhile, Cigala, sure that she was already aware of the fact, brought her a dispatch from Cavour telling her that the emperor had been "*un peu blessé* [slightly injured]," and she feared the worst. More than anything, though, she was indignant at not having been informed of this either by the not very "*charitable*" Poniatowski or by her "*inhuman*" lover. "Did they not perhaps imagine," she wrote to Il Vecio,

> that I might find out in some embarrassing way and make the discovery myself, or in any case *suffer*? No? You don't even have a heart anymore? . . . What does all this mean? I beg you to *please find out by taking this letter to the Old Man* and telling him whatever you can on my behalf, if you can still find words *à mon profit* [to my advantage], which I cannot write because I resent *everyone* too much to put on a show.

As for the show of "heart," her next letter leaves us in no doubt about Virginia's feelings toward her august lover. As far as she was concerned, the emperor was simply a promissory note in imminent danger of expiration.

> I see in the papers that the Old Man is confined to bed and faring very badly and isn't coming. Damn!!! If he croaks, we're f——. That's

why we need to hurry, as I keep saying. There's no time like the present. Tomorrow *news*. As for me, say *angry, hurt,* whatever you want, and try to find out if he really isn't coming. Go right away on my behalf and say I'm not writing so as not to bother him. But if you deem it seemly, here are a couple of lines; if not, burn them.

We might well imagine that the contingent "couple of lines" she'd written the emperor were in fact quite affectionate, seeing that on May 26 the emperor replied to her:

A bad fall from a carriage almost cost me my life, but I have already almost made a full recovery. My quite seriously injured right hand still struggles to wield the pen. Had it not been for this unfortunate accident I could have taken part in the campaign—and I had promised to see you again! What pleasure it would have given me, *mon amie*, to see you once more! But this pleasure has been denied me. *Perhaps there is another greater one in store?* Thank you for your beautiful letter. Trust in my devotion to you and tell me all about what is happening with you, chapter and verse. Farewell once more. Yours, N.

Determined not to make the same mistakes again, Virginia anxiously sought Poniatowski's advice:

What *am I to do*? Nothing is too little, something is too much. And then, how am I to comport myself? (1) look as though I don't give a f——, act cheerful and never talk about it? (2) look sad and *in love* and speak in innuendoes? (3) play the Victim? But to pull it off it has to be seen and it has to be convincing.

Il Vecio's reply, which for once we have, is explicit: "If you find a way to see him I think you should do so. I would stick to (2) and (3): sad, emotional, helpless. Nicchia has no need of my advice for anything further. Once his heart is softened, the rest will come naturally."[15]

In letter after letter, the petticoat Clausewitz kept running through every possible scenario—like a true thespian preparing to play every part. After receiving a "curt and unkind" letter from the emperor, she knew she had to correct course:

> Now I understand that stubborn old man. He took it badly that I talked so much about him in my letter, but you didn't tell me that I needed to act like a lover and I did. I can play the gossip and I can play modest. I know how to cry on command and laugh on command but in this case I don't know what to do anymore and without instructions I'm going to commit *bêtises*.

She never tired of submitting new epistolary strategies to Poniatowski—strategies that she was the first to mock:

> But don't laugh at these love letters of mine or you'll make me lose the plot. The Old Man has to be kept *warm* and for that he has to be kept near the fire. If he gets too far from it he'll get cold, cold—icy like every other satisfied heart.
>
> We must strike before he croaks and you, using my excuse, must see him, serenade him, insist until he says: "But what can be done?" And then advise him . . .

Virginia not only wanted to ensnare the emperor again; she also gave some thought to what strategies might help her friend procure an important post. "If for now there's nothing in Paris," Poniatowski wrote to her, "I would move heaven and earth to get a foot in the *stirrup*—and then just keep right on riding right behind him. It seemed I was in Cavour's good books, but I don't know anything anymore."[16] According to Virginia, taking advantage of French sympathy for the Italian cause, the prince ought to "offer whatever services he could render as an Italian." And Virginia insisted on the term "offer," since "the cursed *principality*" kept Poniatowski from "asking." She would handle any requests, in any case, but they had to act quickly because—as she prophesied in her picturesque Italian—"we must profit from this moment of free rein and sympathy for Italian revolution . . . a moment that will not come again, and we must do so much more quickly than you may think." The countess had no confidence in either the emperor's physical condition or the political stability of his empire, and she was fully aware of the risks he was running by getting involved with Italy at all. As for Prince Napoleon's views on the Tuscan throne, Virginia summed up the situation, as she was wont to do with Il Vecio, with the words of an aria: "And if Plon-Plon were to say, like Maria Padilla,[17] 'This crown is mine,' then there would be an even bigger mess even faster and Saint Helena will be a hop, skip, and a jump away."

Within a month the Armistice of Villafranca proved her right, but Virginia was not about to dawdle. On June 8, the emperor entered Milan greeted by a frenzied crowd, and Virginia, by writing to Poniatowski that "today I'm so giddy I feel like going out and celebrating," hinted that she might make a trip to the Lombard capital too.[18] As she kept reiterating to Il Vecio, it was a critical moment for both of them, and she didn't want to pass it up. But we can't be sure whether she put her plan into action. (Lord Malmesbury also wondered—the same Lord Malmesbury who "found, in all that eventful excitement, time to ask Sir James [Hudson][19] if Contessa Nicchia [was] in the camp!"[20])

If we can judge by a long letter Virginia wrote to Poniatowski[21] about her ploys to secure him a prominent post, the meeting with the emperor did take place, since she clearly spoke to him without a go-between. Although the content of this letter is highly cryptic, it contains references to a Franco-Italian diplomatic assignment for Poniatowski related to the future political order of the peninsula, with an eye to both countries' political and economic interests—an assignment that would require a considerable investment of money as well as the assistance of Ignace Bauer, the Rothschilds' representative in Turin.[22] The product, perhaps, of Virginia's fertile imagination—and founded on Poniatowski's dual nationality and diplomatic experience—the plan met with the disapproval of the "Foul Master" (Victor Emmanuel), while the "very good" Old Man, once "serenaded" by Virginia, was all for it. We can only assume that the discussion took place in Milan, where a council of war had been held on the morning of the 9th. Virginia was clearly adept at maneuvering behind the scenes if she managed to induce two sovereigns, who'd come together to make crucial strategic decisions of the utmost urgency, to deal with a matter that was certainly not a priority just to please her. Indeed, after the Armistice of Villafranca, Napoleon is said to have instructed Poniatowski to follow up with the Count of Reiset on the political situation in Tuscany and to propagandize in favor of the Lorraines so as to avert the risk of a coalition with the kingdom of Sardinia. It is no coincidence that the Count of Viel-Castel, at odds with imperial policy, leveled a succinctly severe judgment against both men: "As for the emperor's maneuvers to persuade the Italians to effectuate a restoration of the dukes—you have to laugh not to cry! . . . Naturally, he sent two agents, but which agents? Reiset and Poniatowski! I rest my case."[23]

In any case, with the crude realism that by now we recognize as her stock-in-trade, Virginia announced to Il Vecio that the emperor was "in a fever of emotion." Perhaps, she added, "the glorification of wounded soldiers" had "given him an itch" that he needed her "to scratch." But the opportunity did not arise. Virginia had hoped to see him again in Turin, but Napoleon wasted no time leaving the capital of Piedmont, which, forgetting the many French soldiers who'd died for the Italian cause, had given him a glacial welcome—borne of indignation at the Villafranca betrayal. Maximus d'Azeglio marveled:

> If two months ago the problem had been posed—How can one go to Italy with 200 t[housand] men, spend half a billion, win four battles, give the Italians back one of the most beautiful provinces, and go home showered with curses and derided by public opinion?—it would have been declared insoluble. But no! Events have demonstrated its truth.[24]

# An Unhappy Lover
## 1857–1862

"YOU NEVER WANTED our destinies to cross,"[1] Henri de La Tour d'Auvergne, one of the men who fell madly in love with the countess, reminded her sadly, at the end of their relationship. Yet who more than he could have made her live—after her failed youthful marriage and her dead-end affair with Napoleon III—an authentic love story?

As we have seen, Virginia had nailed down the prince's devotion for eminently practical reasons. Relegated to Villa Gloria but intent on regaining the emperor's favor, she found Napoleon III's envoy a valuable informant on war matters. But La Tour d'Auvergne had all the qualities that might have aroused the countess's interest for other reasons too. He had an illustrious name and a notable fortune; a career diplomat, widowed only a few months earlier, at thirty-five years of age, he'd already had important postings, and by sending him to Turin to prepare for his intervention on behalf of the Italian cause, the emperor had entrusted him with a crucial diplomatic mission. Moreover, he was "one of the most seductive and amiable men one could ever hope to meet . . . a munificent gentleman, and the very image of elegance and courtesy."[2] But Virginia only briefly let him feel that he might be loved, giving rise to a passion destined to survive the death of his illusions by many years.

With his intense and determined gaze, his wide and sensual face, his black eyes, black hair, and powerful build, the prince looked the part he was destined to play, and he was immediately moved by the beautiful recluse's melancholy existence. Though he'd been on a mission in Florence at the time, he was undoubtedly aware of her sensational affair with the emperor and the rumors of her clandestine relationship with Victor Emmanuel. This alone would have been good reason for him to take a professional interest in her, but soon a deeper feeling made him throw caution to the wind and begin paying frequent visits to Villa Gloria. Virginia always treated him affably, but she remained deaf to his declarations of love: "What I feel for you is tender friendship. Anything else is out of the question, it would be folly on our part—a failure on mine . . . Do not deprive me of your sweet affection, it is such a comfort to me." For as long as he went on seeing her, the prince would, however much it pained him, comply with her orders. Having shown herself beyond compare in triumph, Virginia did not intend to be outdone in adversity, and in her isolation at Villa Gloria she was busy reinventing herself as a tragic heroine, enriching her repertoire with a role she would play more and more as the years went by. Knowing that La Tour d'Auvergne belonged to a profoundly religious family and was the grandchild of a powerful cardinal, she decided a comparison with the Madonna did not seem malapropos: "I have a heart, I do, even if I try to hide it. From birth it has had to conceal the cruel wounds inflicted on it, but it is nonetheless as *great*, *good*, and *tender* as the heart of the Holy Virgin . . ."[3] Having set the record straight and established appropriately dramatic premises, Virginia was in a position to encourage her worshipper to persevere in his hopes. "Too bad you aren't here today," she wrote to him between visits,

> I would have been so good. Do you need to be consoled? I am in the mood for tender consolation . . . But to open my heart to you is folly . . . Forget my words, and never dare remind me of the yielding of an instant, or this moment of weakness either![4]

Who knows how long she would have gone on stringing him along if, in early May, Napoleon III's arrival in Genoa had induced her to yield: the French diplomat's passion was too valuable a card. On June 18, she gave him a small green-and-blue seal as a token of her love,[5] and he, in a letter from Genoa—now the headquarters of the French army—could at last celebrate a "day of happiness in [his] life" when his heart was at ease. There was nothing his "beloved friend" could not ask of him. "I will be at your disposal wherever and whenever you wish. All you have to do is let me know. All I ask is that you be as kind as you can be, as far as circumstances allow."[6]

The prince never tired of remembering what those moments of grace meant to him. "How quickly time passed for me last night, my dear angel! I was with you for a good five hours and never realized. It seemed but an instant. Yet we did not speak; but I was close to you, I could see you, I could kiss you, I felt you were mine and I could not have been happier." This happiness filled him "with confidence in the future" and led him to ask, anxiously, if he'd managed to give her "a bit of pleasure."[7] His hopes were justified if after a night of love he could write, "Are you tired? You shuddered so much. I'm not at all tired myself and have never felt happier."[8]

But it was a happiness constantly undercut by his lover's behavior.

After going to bed with him, Virginia immediately reestablished her distance, and, not content to take refuge behind physical ailments, mood swings, and excuses of all kinds, she humiliated her lover using a technique she'd already perfected to her husband's detriment. Unlike Castiglione, though, La Tour d'Auvergne was capable of self-control and, as befitted his profession, was shrewdly capable of steering clear of conflict. In his letters, lessons of style—"Why do you hurt me and say unpleasant things to me? You need only reply reasonably instead of with your heart"[9]—alternate with a lenience dictated by love: "Yesterday you were really so bad to me, my beloved angel, and yet my feelings for you were as sweet and tender as ever; but sometimes you like to turn into a little tyrant, an almost barbaric despot, and trample on other people's feelings."

Soon the prince also ventured a diagnosis of her tempestuous behavior. What drove her to deny her emotions was a sense of pride, but a misguided sense, because "to love does not mean to be humiliated; you can say it without shame to the one who loves you. You, however, if you were in love, would not say it to the one you loved. And I cannot wrap my head around that." He said this not for his own sake but for hers, "for the sake of your future happiness," about which he cared deeply—more than anything else.[10]

Though he knew their relationship was hanging by a thread, the prince did all he could to make it more romantic. Virginia's scandalous reputation and embarrassing marital situation didn't stop him from introducing her to his mother. Widowed for many years, Princesse Laurence de La Tour d'Auvergne was an iron-fisted grand dame who'd worked hard to make the careers of her three sons, one of whom was now an ambassador, the other a prince of the Church, and the third a soldier. After his wife's death, her firstborn had entrusted her with her grandson Godefroy's upbringing, and she'd dutifully moved to Turin. She was very forbearing with her son and soon acquiesced to meeting Virginia. It went splendidly, and a friendship was born.

La Tour d'Auvergne devoted every free moment to his beloved. Keeping her abreast of all his affairs ("you are me"[11]); asking after her health and domestic problems; taking a fond interest in little Giorgio, he believed that such tactful and delicate devotion might help strengthen a relationship that was continually imperiled by her whims. He knew she didn't love him as he would have preferred to be loved, but that didn't deter him from his passion, which grew more violent by the day. Unfortunately, however, the moment of parting drew near.

In November 1859, the Treaty of Zurich officially ended the second war of independence and, with it, La Tour d'Auvergne's diplomatic mission in the Savoy capital. French priorities now turned to improving relations with Prussia, and Napoleon III rewarded the prince's diplomatic talents by sending him to Berlin.

Convinced (as was Walewski) that entering the war with Austria to support Savoy's ambitions had been a serious political mistake; allergic to Victor Emmanuel's coarseness; and on bad terms with Cavour,[12] the prince should have been glad to be coming to the end of a mission grown more and more thankless. But the news of his prestigious new post—which of course meant parting from Virginia—struck him like a death sentence: "Until the final moment comes, my dear friend, I intend to hold to good habits. I am therefore sending you a cake, the last, alas, and I shall see you tonight at eight o'clock, and I shall see to it that I don't leave your side for twenty-four hours. My head and heart are in tatters."[13]

On January 23, 1860, at 9:30 a.m., the prince said goodbye to Virginia "without hardly having the courage even to look at [her]," he found it all so heartbreaking.[14] And soon distance made him a slave of love. It grew daily more clear to him that he could not live without her, and the passage of time, far from calming his desires, only exacerbated them. "My every thought," he wrote from Berlin months later, "can be summed up as follows: I want to see you, I need to see you. But for that to happen you need to help, and to help you need to want to see me at least a little."[15] Certainly, he could map out plans, ask her to go to Berlin or let him join her incognito in Turin, Genoa, Paris, Dieppe, or some other spa town, but was Virginia really willing to indulge his desires? The prince was the first to doubt it.

While he went on writing long, diary-like letters day after day, she responded to him only sporadically and, worse still, didn't bother to spare him any humiliation. Fiercely protective of her own independence, she planned a trip to Paris without telling him beforehand. "You arrange your little side business on your own," the prince noted bitterly; "I can see you don't need anyone after all. All the better for you and all the worse for me."[16] But over and above that, Virginia intended to keep their relationship strictly secret. As a precaution, they wrote to each other through the Parisian intermediary Huteau, and she, unable to have her letters sent back to her, demanded that her lover burn them immediately after reading them.[17] But the worst was that, just a month after he left, she dealt him a shocking blow by demanding that he treat her "as a stranger" and refrain from "tenderness."

Determined to hold on until the bitter end, the prince was willing to swallow these insults if it meant keeping the possibility for dialogue open. God only knew what he suffered and went on suffering to comply with "the obligation" she imposed on him, whose rationale he could not fathom. If they'd been together, he certainly wouldn't have resigned himself to it, but as things stood he had no choice: "I'm unhappy, but I'm not complaining." She had always known that their relationship wouldn't last, and for that he could hardly blame her: "It is all my fault; clearly you did not consider me worthy of you."[18] Yet "coldness," "indifference," and "vexations" weren't enough to drive her from his mind. How could he break free from a physical desire that gave him no peace and, even when he wrote to her, forced him to stop, so overwhelmed did he become by emotion? A "good" letter was enough to rekindle the prince's hopes. "You can make me happy anytime you wish," he writes at one point—"make me mad with happiness!"[19] For her part, once she'd established her distance and made it clear that she considered the affair over, she might take an affable tone, or share a bit of gossip, or go back to confiding the physical and financial problems that plagued her, or even ask him for help, all depending on her mood and interests of the moment—giving him the illusion their relationship was still up and running.

Ignorant of a truth that Virginia had confided only to Poniatowski, La Tour d'Auvergne tried to account for his lover's behavior in the light of her many physical and psychological ailments. Virginia was only twenty-three years old, but in her melancholy life alone with her son at Villa Gloria she spent most of her time in bed, afflicted by a thousand physical ailments, in a city that she did not like and that did not like her. Was it perhaps this state of perpetual infirmity, aggravated by depression, that made her intolerant of any emotional demands? But then why did she continue to confide her unhappiness to a lover she wanted to keep at a distance? "It hurts my heart to hear the reasons for your despondency and sadness," the prince wrote to her, mournfully acknowledging that he couldn't help and reminding her that "*if* you had had sufficient affection for me, perhaps I might have helped you take a less solemn view of life's sorrows."[20]

From the first, La Tour d'Auvergne had said he cared more about her happiness than his own, and even now, when he was not indulging in recriminations, he went on telling her so. Why didn't she join him in Berlin? "I would look after you like a precious little treasure! I would force you to see yourself the way you used to see yourself, not for *me* who loves you and would love you anyway... but for your own sake."[21]

Perhaps, if both of them kept writing to each other—always swinging between one mood and another, unfailingly contradicting what they'd claimed a few letters or even a few lines earlier—it was simply because they needed each other.

A slave to his passion, La Tour d'Auvergne could resign himself to the fact that he was not loved, but he could not break away from his beloved for good. For him, to see her was to feel alive.[22] His desire for her gave him no peace. He found the idea of making love with another woman intolerable.[23] Thus he strove to heed her frequent pleas for "discretion" and brought up every subject capable of eliciting the interest of his correspondent. He told her about the rituals of the Prussian court; he gave her news of the diplomatic community in Berlin (the Italian guests above all); he asked her about his successors in Turin; and naturally he didn't fail to toss in a little bit about politics. He had to admit that the aftermath of the Villafranca treaty made it clear that the strategic project Napoleon

III had sent him to Turin to pursue had failed. Instead of confederating, Italy had begun a process of unification that threatened the autonomy of the papal states and put the balance of Europe back into question, forcing the emperor to distance himself from Victor Emmanuel. The prince's noble nonchalance could not conceal his disappointment. "If I watch my language," he wrote to her in late February 1860, "it's only because I'm writing to the most beautiful, the most adorable of the Piedmontese," though he could not refrain from observing, "You will need more than two months, even with Mr. Nigra, to make Italy. In Turin they should keep in mind that it takes much less time to unmake than to make."[24] And a month later he repeated that, "appearances and hopes notwithstanding," the future of Italy was "more than precarious."[25]

These were short-lived diversions, however, for the thought of Virginia invariably began to obsess him once more. Depending on the tenor of her replies and how long he'd waited for them, the prince would veer from *vous* to *tu*, and from the blackest despair—"Your silence and indifference has so disheartened me that I no longer know how to think or write"—to a revival of hope: "But then you must have missed me a little, if you say that *nothing has changed for you, except that I am absent*... I enjoyed that sentence so much, it almost makes me believe that you love me too."[26] For a moment, perhaps, he even managed to delude himself: "However vague your assurances may be, my heart gobbles them up gratefully."[27] And hadn't Virginia "solemnly" promised him[28] that they would spend a few days together over the summer? While he waited to see her again, he sought refuge in memories. "Only in the past can I find some joy,"[29] he confessed, and he conjured that past with propitiatory rites which he recounted in detail to his beloved. When he was alone, he would open his desk drawer and take out the two little portraits she'd sent him as gifts; he would admire them, ask them questions, and cover them with kisses. In the long, lonely nights, he let his memories lull him until he slipped away into an illusory world in which his "adored angel" came to him with open arms, lending herself to his every desire. That being the case, he never stopped thinking of her and longing for her even during the day, and while he waited to see her again, he looked forward to the joy of feeling her "dear little mouth" on his, and vowed to share with her a little of the happiness he felt: "I would kiss you everywhere, not forgetting a single one of your secret *nooks* that I love so much."[30]

The more intoxicating his erotic dreams became, the more painful it was for him to be roused from them. Virginia, still unwell, stubbornly refused to seek treatment and, deaf to his pleas, told him she was in no position to makes plans. He despaired: "I cannot bear the thought that at your age, with friends all around on whom you can entirely rely, you are abandoning yourself to such despondency."[31] And he urged her to fight: "You have more strength and energy in the well of your soul than anyone I know."[32] Virginia absolutely had to shake herself off, "pluck up her courage," and go away, at least for a few weeks, "anywhere,"[33] as long as it was far from Villa Gloria, where she was interring her youth.

It required a great deal of perseverance, however, to keep up hope for a better future, and he, too, was "short on health, strength, and courage."[34] He couldn't eat or sleep and was always feverish and exhausted until he lost all interest in everything. He couldn't even summon the strength to tell his mother that his son, little Godefroy, had received an inheritance of one million francs from his great-uncle the cardinal.[35] His survival, as he kept repeating in letter after letter, depended entirely on her, and he asked her, "in the absence of other feelings," to grant him "a little pity."[36]

Pity for others had never been Virginia's strong suit, and the central worry around which all her other worries revolved was, at that time, her own uncertain future. She found herself in a scenario in which La Tour d'Auvergne represented, for lack of anything better, certainty: he was proof of her power over men. But the irritating sexual tribute she was forced to pay made her treat her victim even more ferociously. Her strategy of domination was divided into three key phases. The first consisted in keeping her distance—and to this end Virginia refused, as she had with her husband, to call the prince by his name.[37] In the second she went from coldness to offense: "You're well aware that I like it when you call me a fool, an idiot, an imbecile," the prince groveled, "but I wish that, when we were far apart, you would also throw in a few words of sweetness."[38] But no matter how much he lavished on her—attention, gifts, money—she never laid down her arms, never showed him any gratitude, and even blamed him for her troubles.[39] In the third phase—the most effective of all—she made herself inaccessible. And yet this cruelty did not quell the scorned lover's ardor. For two more years, despite the distance between them, La Tour d'Auvergne was still at her mercy. As he was forced to admit: "There isn't a feeling in the world that you haven't managed to inspire in me."[40]

These letters from the distinguished, though enslaved, French diplomat filled Virginia—in spite of the bad luck bearing down on her—with a sense of omnipotence. She went on and on asking him for confirmation of her power, and only after she'd set her sights on reconquering Paris did she drop him for good.

# In Pursuit of the Emperor

## 1860

WITH THE WAR at an end and Napoleon out of Italy, Virginia had to rely on Poniatowski's good offices to keep the sovereign from forgetting her. But the news from Paris was far from reassuring. When she learned that Walewska had firmly established herself at the Tuileries as his official mistress, the countess was overcome with rage. She felt like the victim of a plot hatched by "two vipers." To "rescue" her husband from Virginia's influence, the empress had replaced her with that "tubercular flirt" Maria Anna, who, as one might expect, had turned out to be a real "bitch." It would not be long, however, before Eugénie realized her mistake, for "the Riccis are more perfidious than the devil himself." As for the Old Man, she prophesied: "Poor fellow, one of these days he'll pay dearly for his glory and his throne—he'll pay with his skin, and that will be the expiation of his sins." And to her friend Poniatowski, who preached "perseverance, courage, and patience," she replied: "As words all three are beautiful, but for the first I'd need your help, and you wouldn't let me get away with the second or give me the *means* for the third, since if one can't eat one can't live." She went back to pestering the prince to mention her to the emperor because she couldn't give up;

she refused to believe the game had really been lost. Week after week, she hammered away at him with the same questions: What was he doing? What was on his mind? What was he saying? And why wouldn't the prince confront him? No matter how many times Poniatowski repeated that this was impossible, since for at least two years now the emperor hadn't granted him more than a hello,[1] she did not let up. Again she insisted that he at least sound out his "dear niece," but even here the way was barred. Both the new favorite and the empress knew that he'd acted as a messenger for her in the past, and they weren't about to let this happen again.[2]

Virginia could not accept the reality of the situation. Bewildered by anger, jealousy, and her desire for revenge, she was lost in a jumble of obsessive thoughts. Why hadn't the Old Man replied to her "beautiful" letter? Why had he stopped writing to her altogether? Of course "Maria will make him lose his head (and he will lose it, for his penance, with a tramp)"; "And he sees her *where, how, when?*"; "Is she down on the bed or the *fauteuil*?" Virginia could easily visualize the armchairs and divans on which the emperor consummated his lightning-quick passions, since some months earlier she'd written to Il Vecio that she wanted to "get back onto that sofa."[3] It was not, however, her ex-friend's erotic exploits that sent her into a rage; it was her financial exploits, now that Maria Anna—perpetually short of cash as she was—could pay off her husband's debts thanks to those million-dollar speculations to which Virginia no longer had access. To "beat" her rival, all she needed was for the emperor to set eyes on her, even for a moment. But that wasn't the end of it: "Oh Christ, he *needs* to fall into my clutches again! It would be funny to make love to him now that I'm experienced and not a cretin." And this time she would know better than to talk to him about Italy!

But Virginia was in such dire straits that she had no time to waste on pointless rants. Thanks to the intervention of the elderly Prince Jérôme-Napoleon, Poniatowski had finally managed to obtain a private audience with the emperor, which, however, went nowhere,[4] and not long after, the countess received a letter in which she was implored to refrain from returning to Paris. The time had come to negotiate.

After sending Poniatowski the original of the Old Man's message and urging him to lock it in the iron safe in his study,[5] the countess began to mull over how she might induce her imperial lover to discharge her with enough severance pay to last. She needed to hint at the problem, but discreetly, while the prince baldly confronted the emperor. It had to be a coordinated attack, and as usual Virginia went over the maneuvers in detail, in letter after letter.

First she responded to the Old Man with "a nice letter—because it's better to sweet-talk him and play Spartan," letting the prince decide whether to send it. She had written it to preserve her dignity, "since one doesn't have to look as if one came from Peretola [a small village near Florence] to want to make them *pay*." She had no intention of coming off as a vulgar beggar. It was imperative that Poniatowski make clear to the emperor that the money troubles in which she was embroiled were by no means her fault. On the contrary, "the *folies* she had committed during her three years in Paris for his sake" had driven her husband to bankruptcy, and the compensation offered by the sovereign—a mere six thousand francs—was unacceptable. How could he think of leaving someone like her "in poverty and shame"? The prince also needed to insist that she would no longer accept her old appanage and "that it was impossible her for to accept anything in the future unless it were without her knowledge." The emperor needed to be frightened with all the gossip and chatter unleashed, even in Turin, when she and her husband separated. "Nobody here now hesitates to say, 'Is it true she's a P.?'[6] Castiglione has been patient because he has been told he needs to be, but now he has sent her to the paymaster [perhaps Victor Emmanuel]." Virginia wasn't above making use of her husband's embarrassing situation (that "poor man," "condemned to such an odious role"). And she even suggested, with extraordinary audacity, that the messenger hint at the potential risk represented by the letters the emperor had written to her, which she had religiously preserved . . . Cornered, the Old Man would at last ask what he could do for the poor afflicted woman, and it was up to Poniatowski to tell him in no uncertain terms: He needed to provide her with enough capital to overcome the difficulties in which, having sacrificed her reputation, she found herself, and he needed to help her gain genuine independence through advantageous financial dealings.

This second request—the most important to Virginia—risked going unheeded since Napoleon had already declared that he no longer wished to "give out confidential information, to avoid making the whole country chatter."[7] All the evidence leads us to believe, however, that in the end the emperor met his ex-lover's demands. We don't know whether he resigned himself to giving her the cash directly, but the correspondence with Poniatowski makes it clear that Virginia had privileged contacts in the world of finance. And she couldn't have been too hard up if, in 1860, planning a return to France, she could afford to rent a furnished apartment on rue Marivaux, in the heart of Paris; a house on rue Nicolo, in the elegant residential suburb of Passy; and a seaside villa in Dieppe.[8]

But her return to Paris was to become the subject of new and no less difficult negotiations. Though the emperor told her that her presence in the capital would be a fresh source of disagreeable gossip, Virginia paid no heed, and in the spring of 1860 she paid a brief visit to check on her financial affairs. She made the rounds with the utmost discretion. "I tried to seem neither sick nor healthy, neither happy nor distressed"—but she found herself unwelcome and was forced to ask Poniatowski to intervene once more, concocting yet another epistolary stratagem. Knowing full well how dangerous letters could be, Virginia had always asked for hers to be sent back with an RSVP [please return] and was confident Il Vecio would burn the letters she sent him. Clearly not so confident that Napoleon would do the same, she planned to write to him by means of a third party, entrusting the prince with a letter to the emperor and requesting that he let him read but not retain it.

Although the letter itself is no longer among Poniatowski's papers, the accompanying note does not mince words:

> Here then is what I have in my *head*—not in my heart—*mais c'est le seul moyen pratique* [but it's the only *practical* way of going about it] and we just have to scream into our pillows. I'm quite vexed and would chop off a finger not to have to hold out my hand, but I hope you'll try to give it some serious thought and that you'll understand the necessity of taking the bold step mentioned in the other letter... which you only have to show him and then take back immediately. Let's not dwell on what may come of it, good or bad, but it's now or never. I'm leaving, fine, *mais ce n'est pas la question* [but that isn't what's important]. Whether I go or stay, my life is still on the line.

The fundamental problem, the emperor needed to be reminded, was a problem of money, and she was willing to entertain the possibility of staying in Turin only if she could live off investments in her own name, but since she was dependent on a husband who loathed her for leading him around by the nose and ruining him, this was out of the question. And what gave the Old Man the right to give her orders? Obviously he hadn't realized the Italians no longer needed him. "He has to get it through his head things have changed. This June is for us (you will say *us* because, in or out, I am always a part of it) what *last May* was for him, but with the difference that here there would be a scandal." As it happened, that very June Garibaldi was liberating Sicily and preparing to march on Naples, making a decisive contribution to the unification of the country, which Napoleon III had so vocally opposed. Virginia, too, had made her contribution and paid a very high price, but, whatever her reputation, she was proud to be the citizen of a free nation, and was in no mood to be pushed around. She didn't see how the Old Man could stop her from going to Paris, and indeed he ought to watch what he said.

Poniatowski urged her to adopt a less bellicose tone, but she wouldn't hear it:

> I'll tell you again that I'd rather be bad than good. If one doesn't get anything out of it, what's the purpose of abasing oneself? If I'm going to triumph, he must understand he can't toy with a woman with impunity. And it doesn't take much to be *sur son passage* [underfoot] and always in his way... He'd rue the day—the cretin. Then, you'll say, what good will it do? It will satisfy my desire—and I've never desired anything more.

Virginia certainly didn't lack for pluck. Shut away in Villa Gloria, she lay waiting to go back to Paris "like a queen with [her] head held high and make everybody pay." She kept fighting for survival. Her war was not yet over.

She was ill constantly, and the variety of her ailments—fevers, migraines, conjunctivitis, bronchitis, stones, hernias, abscesses, gynecological problems—makes it impossible to attribute them exclusively to hypochondria: "I am thin and pale and weak as a kitten. I'm covered with pimples. I can't stay in bed or on my feet. In short, I'm really completely f——," she wrote as early as autumn 1859.[9] Or again: "I'm so ugly I'm fit to throw in the toilet." And her material conditions put her to the test: "I'm cold, I'm hungry, and I'll be even hungrier in two months. I don't know what there will be to eat."

She sometimes wondered whether all this—"All this at twenty!" —had a meaning: "And why must I fight? And for what reason, and for what? There is no reason, it's pointless and will do no one any good. Ah Vecio, it's time for me to call it a day." But she wanted to exit the stage like a tragic heroine, and in case she was short on time, she asked the prince to inscribe one word on her tomb: FATALITÉ. Her correspondent scolded her to no purpose, counseling calm. When the situation demanded it, Virginia could be merciless with herself:

> I am sorry to have made you lose sleep, but I didn't suspect my letter could still have such an effect on you, and what was so sad about it? My death? *Hallelujah!* And *miserere*! A consolation for everyone except you and some poor devil who'll shed a tear and say *poor thing*. What have I to do with this world?

For the first time, Virginia asked herself a question that would occur to her more and more often in her later years. But the indomitable energy that allowed her to take up her solitary struggle again, day after day, was already as good as an answer. Virginia was fighting to win a new life free of masters, and to be free herself to decide what shape to give this life. Though "*Sempre libera degg'io*" from *La Traviata* is not among the arias quoted in her correspondence, nothing is more significant than this reference to her decision—which cost her dearly—not to go back to living with her husband: "The only thing in this world I've never regretted, but am glad about, is the separation that they [her parents] dreaded and that you [Poniatowski] didn't much like either. Never ever has a shadow of regret so much as flitted through my mind, except the regret that I didn't do it four years ago."

In Paris, thanks in part to her position as the emperor's mistress, Virginia had learned the rules of financial speculation—a game of chance played behind the scenes of society life where fortunes were made and unmade from one day to the next. Played furiously by bankers, industrialists, politicians, and members of high society, successful speculation required timely information, lightning speed, intuition, audacity, and maximum secrecy. Never in history had money been so important. Never had it been written and talked about so much.[10] We cannot be sure whether Virginia read *La Maison Nucingen*, which was published when she was still a baby—a story in which Balzac describes the French world of high finance—but as an adult she had firsthand experience of it. Besides cultivating the friendship of the banker James de Rothschild (the model for the Baron of Nucingen), who, regaining the prominent position he'd enjoyed under Louis Philippe, was soon to triumph over the Pereire brothers and seize control of the Parisian financial world, Virginia had also struck up an acquaintance with Achille Fould, Napoleon III's all-powerful financial advisor, as well as with various businessmen in the orbit of the Tuileries. The adventurous countess's innate secrecy, cunning, and audacity proved strong points in the dangerous game she had to play to pave her way toward freedom.

Business matters occupy a prominent place in her letters to Poniatowski. For hundreds of pages, with feverish anxiety, in a telegraphic style that brooks no conjunctions, Virginia discusses purchases and sales, companies that issue shares, high-yielding government bonds, interests, dividends, and promissory notes come due. Missed opportunities and bad investments seem more common than profits, but every now and then there is a "stroke of good fortune" to lift her spirits.

It should be noted that, in this joint undertaking, Virginia was the one at the helm. She researched the transactions, proposed them to her correspondent, gave directions, pressured and empowered him. And so the relationship between the two accomplices was reversed. Il Vecio was now relying on the good offices of Nicchia. The prince—who'd always taken life lightly, relying on his luck—was, like his friend, in desperate need of money, but he delegated the task of obtaining it to her. In the dark about these goings-on, Marquise Oldoini—who knew Poniatowski well—joked to Virginia about his "marvelous speculations."[11] For her part, Virginia never stopped exhorting him: "You must see, speak, listen, and then decide on a course of action, *otherwise you'll get wrinkles on your face* and you can say goodbye to the whole kit and caboodle, you won't pocket a pretty penny, and I hardly have two to rub together." But the prince took his time and remained "cheerful." Virginia railed against him:

> And what are you thinking? You come and go and *sing* and play and *dance* and tell me nothing. You transform yourself into an *artist* and

> a *diplomat* and you don't want *que je crie gare* [me to worry]! . . . Do you think I'm down here eating and drinking and sleeping? Don't you know I'm in bed day and night worse off than Saint Philomena?

In fact, in addition to fulfilling his assignment—an assignment she'd procured for him—as the emperor's emissary in Tuscany, Poniatowski was extremely busy with music. In 1859 he published an essay titled "Le Progrès de la musique dramatique," the next year he staged his four-act opera *Pierre de Médicis* in Paris, and in 1861 his one-act comic opera *Au travers du mur* premiered. Still, the state of his finances kept creeping closer to catastrophe.[12]

But Virginia, who could be so vengeful when it came to her lovers, had limitless indulgence for Il Vecio and was always eager to help him and his family:

> If I fall, you fall too, and your whole family, *puisque je suis l'ancre salutaire* [since I am the lifeline]. As long as there's enough for me, there will be enough for you. *L'un ne vivra pas si l'autre meurt* [One won't live if the other dies] . . . Two souls like ours can't be separated, don't you *feel* it? *Malgré tout, toutes et tous* [Come what may].

She'd first given proof of this by taking the prince's side after her husband's bankruptcy. In fact, the count had been unable to repay Poniatowski the enormous loan he'd taken out during his Parisian sojourn, which nearly proved fatal to the prince, who was up to his neck in debt. The result was a dispute of which Virginia and Francesco's letters, read in tandem, provide a detailed account.

On returning to Italy, the count had hoped to be able to pay off his many debts[13] by selling the Turin palazzo and the majority of his properties—excluding his most beloved, the Castello di Costigliole. Unfortunately, political precariousness and the prospect of war had paralyzed the Piedmontese real estate market, causing prices to plummet. Thus Castiglione had decided to cede all his assets to his friend Poniatowski with the understanding that the prince would recover what he was owed, repay the other creditors, and find a way to salvage what could be salvaged for little Giorgio. But preoccupied as he was with other concerns in Paris, the prince had entrusted the liquidation of the assets to a certain Mr. Tesio, one of his trusted associates, who turned out to be a first-class fraud. He sold off the furnishings of the Castello di Costigliole, as well as the livestock and agricultural equipment—thus lowering the value of the property—and pocketed the proceeds. The news had alarmed the count's creditors, and the count, feeling morally responsible and preparing to leave for the front, had put the business in the hands of lawyers. On June 20, 1859, in the middle of the war, all of Castiglione's creditors were summoned to the law firm of Giovanni Battista Cassinis and Luigi Borsarelli di Rifreddo "to be informed of the state of affairs" and possibly "to assume administration of the assets."

Virginia, summoned as a creditor, immediately grasped that this initiative, besides challenging the legality of the transfer to Poniatowski—thereby depriving Poniatowski of the possibility of dealing with her own financial emergencies—might postpone the collection of her dowry arrears until who knew when.

"These scoundrels," she wrote to Il Vecio,

> have nothing more pressing to do than send me the same memo they sent to all the *creditors*... They didn't even bother to warn me they were going to take this step (which they wash their hands of like

> Pontius Pilate—hands they put all over our money since they're the ones who'll gobble it up) . . . damned swine . . . I assume that they've sent the memo to you too by now, so that you can send someone with *power of attorney* for the *28th without fail.*

Alarmed by Il Vecio's inertia, Virginia leapt back into the fray: "I hope you understand that they're not joking around and you need to send a representative or they'll take everything. And you can't say *I'll do it tomorrow* because whoever finishes last ends up twiddling his thumbs and *I don't want that.*" She hoped that the missed opportunity would prompt him to take the situation in hand: "And to think that perhaps all of this could have been avoided! Let's look a little toward the future, since so far we've been sound asleep!"

Evidently the prince preferred to remain sound asleep. Three months later, a long and very ceremonious letter from Baron Borsarelli, a lawyer at the Court of Cassation, forced him into a corner. Either he could revoke Tesio's power of attorney or the Count of Castiglione had no choice but to sue him for having failed to keep his commitments. So Poniatowski dropped Tesio and resigned himself to receivership.

For Virginia—eager to recoup her annuity and hoping to secure an extra under-the-table payout with the sale of her husband's properties—it was a major blow. Though she dedicated herself full-time to her financial dealings, she lived in fear they would not produce the desired results, and the thought of bidding farewell to even the modest interests of her dowry terrified her. "I'm sick all over again. I can see everything I've built crumbling to the ground," she wrote to Il Vecio, returning repeatedly, in letter after letter, to her overriding need for economic tranquillity: "I just need a little. But reliable and steady, because this life is *impossible* for me alone with so many worries and the fear that I won't have enough for dinner tomorrow." And again: "If I don't have anything of my own, neither here there nor anywhere, how am I supposed to go on? The only thing left is the Po." And not without irony, she added: "*I prefer the Seine.*" An obsessive leitmotif: "I just need a little, but reliable and steady," she writes again later, even alluding to the possibility of being forced to sell *herself*...

But practical concerns weren't the only thing preying on Virginia's mind. Quite unusual feelings surface in her letters from this period—guilt, for example, and fear of other people's judgment. When in order to make some money her husband decides to sell off the lovely family furniture, the silver, and the china, she rebels: "It's a mortification I don't want to face... because it's a stain I can't bear, to have ruined a man and a little boy for the sake of my pleasures and then abandoned them." She'd always replied to the accusation that she was the cause of her husband's financial catastrophe with characteristic impudence, saying if only the count had followed her advice (liquidating a portion of his assets to pay off his debts and hanging on to the rest), he would have avoided the whole situation. But the thought that the prince might suffer the same fate terrifies her. "Believe me, my Beppino, you have to do something or else you're f—— and I'll be paying for everyone... The thought makes my blood run cold. Sometimes I just feel like screaming."

Her husband's decision to make "the great sacrifice of the castle," since the palace and lands turned out to be unsalable, also shook her to the core. "Imagine, everyone around here crying bloody murder and attacking Prince Poniatowski who is selling off a house that has been in the family for eight hundred years... They will all say it's my fault, and he, he's dying of *chagrin* [sorrow] and sick and torturing himself over it. You know how much it means to him." And she thought, too, about her son, who might one day come to her and say: "You lived well, while you cast me into disgrace and let me die of hunger."

To shut everyone up with a spectacular *beau geste*, Virginia even considered buying the castle herself, which was being sold "for a pittance," using her dowry and counting on a good deal. "If I could buy it and *keep it* of course, it would be a victory for us. If fortune smiles on us, we could give it back, or if *obliged* to keep it, it would still be a victory in this country to have salvaged for a son the house sold by his father." Though supported by Barba Cigala and made known to the count, this plan fell through. But for once Virginia was forced to admit that her husband's disgrace and the accusations of the "world" were not nothing to her: "The doors have closed and will not reopen." But these were mere moments of weakness in a war she was waging against the world, on every front.

Well aware of the power she exercised over men, she didn't scruple to wield it. And she had the same scorn for all of them: emperors, kings, ambassadors, and bankers alike. Ever since she was a little girl, she'd learned to dissimulate and not be entrapped by feelings—not, like the famous marquise in *Les Liaisons dangereuses*, to avenge her sex, but to prevent people who loved her from exercising any power whatsoever over her. For some time now, she had been keeping her distance from her parents, who were guilty of criticizing her life choices. "It's always better to be away from them," she wrote to Poniatowski; "they're all *au guet* [raring] to lay hands on me the first chance they get and I want to be free." These were also the first symptoms of a persecution mania that would grow more pronounced with the passage of the years. She was convinced that everyone was plotting against her, and above all Marquise Oldoini, who encouraged her husband and nephew—in turn encouraged by Carlo Poniatowski, who blamed Virginia for leading the prince to rack and ruin. "We must be united in offense and defense alike, and arm ourselves ... *envers et contre tous* [against all comers]," she wrote to the prince, "because they want to drive a wedge between us and they will manage it if you're *nice* even just once. Such is the web they've woven! It's strange the way they've teamed up against me—the proof is that anyone who has anything to do with me, anyone who wishes me well and speaks reason, becomes a villain in their eyes."

One wonders what it was about Poniatowski that made Virginia trust him so implicitly, given that he acted like a pimp, encouraged her to prostitute herself, slept with her when the opportunity arose, and, as if that weren't enough, asked her to solve his financial problems. Who "laid hands on her" more than he did? And why did she let him?

Was it her own individuality that led her to see the prince as a soul mate—to choose him as a companion and guide in her new life full of unknowns? Of course, if becoming a monarch's lover had been a source of pride for European noblewomen for centuries, ceasing to be one, in an age of hypocritical moralism, had become the worst shame imaginable, and it was only natural that she should ask for help from someone who'd long shown unconditional support. But this is only part of the story. The letters also reveal a different and surprising side of Virginia, conveying the full range of emotions inherent in her relationship with Il Vecio.

Abstracting herself from the romantic sentimentalism that prevailed in her era, the Countess of Castiglione seems instead to keep faith with the libertine spirit of the previous century, which regarded love as a transitory whim. She was always careful to emphasize that what she felt for her friend was not "love (stupidity), but loads and loads of affection." Why, then, does the word *love* keep flowing from her pen? And how could it be kept at bay? One expedient was to refer to it in the conditional, employing various rhetorical devices: "Thanks for your letter, but you don't have to be too nice, otherwise I'll fall in love with you." "It's worse than being *amoureux* [in love] when you start trembling the moment you hear a carriage and quavering as soon as you see a letter... I suppose it's the same for you."

To let him know how she feels, Virginia falls back on quotations from the arias they both love: "All I can say is that you will never be less to me than what I wrote that night and cannot repeat without singing *I puritani*."[14] And she uses the duet in Verdi's *Luisa Miller*, "*Andrem, raminghi e poveri, dove il destin ci porta* [We will go roaming and poor, wherever destiny carries us]," to reaffirm that nothing will ever come between them.

Out of love, Virginia was generous, as she continually demonstrated by putting her credit at the service of Il Vecio's ambitions and going into debt for him. As we shall see, she will put herself personally on the line by asking Laffitte the banker—with whom she had a relationship—for a loan of 150,000 francs to extricate her friend from one of his many monetary quandaries, a loan that was never to be repaid.

Out of love, the woman who had bent men to her will as a matter of course became attentive and cautious. She was afraid of "annoying" Il Vecio with her interminable letters and nagging questions and long lists of decisions to be made. She tactfully recommended he abstain from rash judgments and circumspectly warned him that his reputation as a "jaunty fellow, capable of anything and good for nothing," stood in the way of his ambitions. And she never stopped bucking him up: "Knock on every door with no scruples or false modesty for fear they won't open. Don't be thrown."

Out of love, finally, she lost her temper: "But for God's sake not even a word after a month apart? Naturally you don't give a damn about women, but Nicchia deserves *des égards* [a little respect] and demands affection—I won't go so far as to say love." And she threw tantrums, too: "Don't treat me so badly for Christ's sake! Perhaps it's a misunderstanding *on your part* or a lack of understanding *on mine*, you know, and since you don't know, I will tell you: When Bisisi gets angry, she says no, but in her heart it's yes, always, and she would give her whole soul."

When necessary she knew how to steer clear of quarrels—"For the time being, I don't want to start a fight or take you to task, but permit me to tell you that you are dead wrong to treat Nicchia so harshly"—and when she protested about the slowness of his replies, missed rendezvous, and lapses, she did so in an affectionate tone. He had his head buried "in a sack of [musical] notes" and so forgot to send her birthday wishes; and for his birthday, since she had no money, she sent him "a little lock of hair to make a ring."

She didn't demand an exclusive relationship; she wasn't jealous or possessive; she asked only that she be able to depend on him. "You're well aware that I let you do *whatever* you want without turning a hair, but I don't like to see you so absent and detached from my affairs." In a letter written on her twenty-third birthday, she announced her intention to "settle down physically and morally," specifying: "Morally speaking, *you* are necessary and, wherever I may find myself, this will always be the only surefire remedy for lifting my spirits and keeping them up (I mean it)."

Virginia needed his good cheer and placidity because she was never not anxious. "Nothing does me so much good as spending a little time with you." She needed his indestructible optimism to regain some self-confidence: "Here without Il Vecio, I'm lost . . . and moreover I'm good for nothing, I'm at my wits' end! Everything's so dreary!" His passion for music and love of life were indispensable for her to rediscover the pleasures of the spirit and senses. And Il Vecio answered her with ardent words: "I hold you to my heart with the noblest and loftiest feelings, because I love your soul no less than your body. I am forever yours."[15]

Virginia preferred to avoid the subject of feelings and speak instead of necessity—as when, for example, she had a rather traumatic experience. One day in 1863 she went to visit her uncle Cencio[16] Lamporecchi in Pietrasanta, who, afflicted as he was by a serious nervous illness, did not recognize her. Virginia found this deeply disturbing. To think that "one day Il Vecio might be like this and not recognize Nicchia! That he might address her as *lei* and be indifferent to her being there or not!" She felt like dying, and she appealed to the Blessed Virgin and all the saints that he be spared such tribulation, since without Il Vecio she would no longer be able to recognize herself.

They saw each other in Turin, Florence, La Spezia, and La Vigna—the prince's country seat—when he returned to Italy for work or family reasons. And each time it was a fête. Virginia anxiously begged him to visit, asking for dates and itineraries, even planning the details and prearranging a place where they could make love. In preparation for a week at La Vigna, she laid out the details: "Business during the day, *une partie des soirées en amitié. Il ne reste donc que les nuits pour l'amour* [part of the evenings for friendship. And after that, the nights for love]." And if the visit was a short one, she wished that there would be "*place pour le bonheur* [room for happiness]." In sexual matters, she remained succinct, limiting herself to paraphrases or coded terms, like "Lisetta"—a part of the body?—or a no less mysterious "occupation of eau de cologne," but when she was more explicit, she threw respectability to the winds: "I'm waiting for you, but not for you on top of me, other than for a kiss on the mouth." Even with Il Vecio, sex remained merely an accessory. She reminds him of this in a letter in which she calls him to order:

> A new one. *He says* that *you said* here that *you f—— me*... As you can imagine, I didn't let myself get upset and replied, "Whoever *repeats* that is a *liar*, whoever *made it up* is a liar, and *whoever* said it is a liar."... No clue as yet as to *whoever it is* who claims to have gotten it out of you, but I said, "It isn't true, I don't believe it. P. loves me too much to come out with a slur like that." Some people smiled... Amen. I shall say no more. That's that. But if you want to do me some good, tell me that you have never said anything like it and we shall speak no more of it.

In the end, she would cease to have faith even in Il Vecio—but that would take another few years. Meanwhile she cast around for a new accomplice.

# A Libertine Friendship

"TONIGHT FOR DINNER half past seven . . . and after that???????"[1]

Written in pencil on a sheet of paper with an elegant heraldic monogram composed of two intertwined Vs, for Virginia Verasis—a monogram that also appeared on many of the objects she used daily—the countess's message is undated, but the question marks regarding the epilogue to the evening are an eloquent expression of the erotic complicity that cemented her forty-year relationship with General Louis Estancelin. It was precisely the absence of romantic misunderstandings that protected this deep and lasting friendship from the capricious mood swings and prohibitions Virginia otherwise lavished upon her lovers. The general didn't need to love her to want to see her, to chat, to enjoy her company—and he expected the same of Virginia. And since, for once, the cruel beauty lent herself blithely to the game, one wonders whether the sexual drudgery she engaged in to keep her adulators under her thumb was really *always* incompatible with pleasure . . . In the numerous letters we still have from Estancelin, we can entertain ourselves looking for an answer.[2]

The countess and the general had met in the summer of 1857 at Twickenham, where they were both guests of the Duke of Aumale, the fourth son of Louis Philippe, who'd chosen England as his place of exile. Virginia was then twenty years old and at the height of her beauty and celebrity. Estancelin was thirty-four, a man known for his imposing appearance, sly expression (half-hidden behind his dark mustache), and independent thinking. Descended from ancient Norman stock and a career military man, he had known Louis Philippe's children since his adolescence, and his loyalty to the Orléanist cause had certainly not waned following the revolution of 1848. Virginia for her part was passionate about political and royal highnesses and had probably imagined the Norman gentleman could act as her intermediary and sound out the Duke of Aumale's intentions. She invited him to come see her back in France.

Estancelin would allow almost three years to go by before taking her up on the invitation, but he never forgot the radiant vision of the girl in a straw hat adorned with a big yellow ribbon or the adorable blond child who played at her feet. During a stay in Dieppe, hearing that Virginia was there too,[3] he decided to try his luck and wrote to her as forthrightly as anyone ever had: "Will you agree to meet me? And when?"[4] After that first visit, it was Virginia who wrote him a note, which flattered him. "To think that you, so spoiled and admired, should pay such amiable attention to me, whom you barely know!"[5] he replied. And so they got into the habit of writing and meeting in both Dieppe and Paris. The result was a friendship that was at first platonic but free from societal constraints, and marked by a sincerity and trust so unusual for Virginia that it even led her to shed her reticence and confess to Estancelin her political ambitions, her financial plans, and the tactical reasons governing her choice of lovers, one after the other. "The Norman,"[6] as she called him, listened with interest and sympathy, placing his solid common sense and vast experience of life at her disposal. The responsibilities of a husband and father had never stopped him from enjoying his freedom[7]—from loving many women and letting himself be loved by them—and he soon expressed his desire to give her tangible proof of his admiration. She had indulged him in Dieppe, waiting for him naked and covered in jewelry from head to foot—her marvelous arms laden with bracelets. Flabbergasted by this numinous vision worthy of Gustave Moreau, the Norman had beat a retreat, but the comic effect of this fiasco had strengthened their bond and led to a long string of encounters "sans bracelets."

A great connoisseur of the female soul, Estancelin uncovered Virginia's personality without ever being sidetracked by her claim to be "the greatest woman of all time, past present and future"[8] and still less by her declarations of sincerity. "You are a women, a woman par excellence, and an Italian to boot!" he wrote to her, venturing an initial diagnosis: "You are sincere . . . on a whim, but more than anything you're moody, strange at times, independent in your judgments perhaps, but in your affections? And then, are you capable of them? I have my doubts."[9] All the same—grateful for the intimacy he'd been granted—he was also quick to acknowledge her good qualities: "You are intelligent, and you are much wittier and subtler than I would have expected, less capricious than anticipated, more straightforward and better company than I would have guessed."[10] After all, what right did he have to complain? Hadn't she given him all that he asked of her?[11] But the problem was convincing his friend to play the game of pleasure with him, which was no easy task. In fact, willing though she was to give in to his desires, Virginia made it clear she didn't share them, and had a good time provoking Estancelin's masculine self-regard. She told him over and over that she was "made of marble,"[12] and when they made love, her silence did not express, as he would have liked to believe, "the mute eloquence" of pleasure,[13] but a total lack of sensation. Not wishing to admit defeat, Estancelin kept putting her to the test. She had thrown down the gauntlet, and he took it up not only every time they saw each other but also from afar. Adopting the strategies deployed in libertine novels, he attempted to awaken Virginia's desires with letters of disconcerting boldness.

Unlike *Lettre à la présidente*,[14] written two decades earlier by Théophile Gautier to the beautiful Madame Sabatier (Baudelaire's "*ange plein de gaieté*," whom Auguste Clésinger had sculpted nude in the ecstasy of orgasm),[15] which was meant to be read and commented on in a courtesan's salon, the letters addressed to Virginia were a private game, cloaked in secrecy. But we might wonder whether Estancelin would have dared to write such letters to a woman of his own milieu, and whether the free language encouraged by his Italian friend was the singular prerogative of a relationship beyond convention or, rather, the sort of license one permits oneself in the course of a sexual affair.

When Virginia made fun of him for his amorous exploits, inviting him "to come sleep on [her] knees and rest from battles waged with others," the general replied that, if he was tired, it was with good reason, because it meant "that he had fought with ardor." It would have been unforgivable to be tired if she had written to him "My darling, I am waiting for you with feverish impatience..." But this was not at all the case with Virginia, who was always offering and then withholding herself. It was time for her to leave off with her "I am indisposed... Stop harassing me... Don't insist... etc. etc. etc."[16] The Norman would try to explain to her what she was missing in a three-part lesson, and he began by sending her a composition in which he described an experience common to many adolescents who first discovered the pleasures of the senses in the arms of a schoolmate.

But, Estancelin asked, can the "girl of marble comprehend the girl of fire?"[17]

Titled "Souvenir du couvent," the letter in question describes an intimate game played by two boarders, or perhaps two young lay sisters, in the darkness of a dormitory. We watch as the more experienced one takes the initiative while her companion is sound asleep. But is she really asleep when, after letting herself be expertly explored by her hand, she too springs into action?

> She tried to enlace her legs with mine, we were pressed right up against each other, we had never been so close, she kissed me and I kissed her back, not violent caresses but the *lightest* of touches, the kind that make you *throb*, and you know the way you feel in those moments... I wanted to take the lead and yet... I caressed her and felt titillated... It took all my strength to stop from slipping my head down between her thighs, I was waiting for her to start, and I gave myself over to it completely... her leg kept rubbing upward against mine... I opened my thighs, and when I felt her touching my hair... my sex... I trembled with pleasure, I shuddered... oh darling, what spasms... what fiery desires... you have seen me excited but never as excited as that... I feel... on fire... the slightest motion fills me with intoxication... infinite pleasure... we were in each other's arms like that for at least twenty minutes... then, as usual, my flower fell asleep (or feigned it)... I was far from doing the same... I wanted to give her pleasure, one last time, and for the orgasm to rouse her...

Thus was the challenge issued by the *fille de feu* to the *femme de marbre*, who probably felt satisfied to have her under her spell:

> I run my hand softly down her thigh, little by little, stroking her, I inch closer and closer... this time she doesn't flutter a lash... I feel her hair... I linger there while she goes on sleeping... I touch her sex, all swollen and burning hot... I sense her emotion in the trembling of her thighs, and my heart is still in my throat too... her sex is small and doesn't have much hair, but it's so soft... I feel her harden... her little button stiffening and pulsing... Then, with one finger, slowly, I stroke it... more and more boldly... Without a word she went on feigning sleep, letting me do what I did... I seemed to feel my thighs opening... I squeezed her leg between mine as hard as I could... I was flooded with pleasure... She just let me do it, her hand didn't come anywhere near me, I went on masturbating her for more than a quarter of an hour...

Yet, despite this long amorous sparring match and a few promising indications, the challenger was forced to ask herself: "But was she enjoying it or not? I couldn't be sure... She quivered in her sleep and murmured softly, "Oh! Huu???" So, not taking a moment to gloat and "not daring to wake her," she turned her attention back to her own pleasure: "I wanted to take her hand to masturbate myself... but the way she was lying kept me from getting hold of it, so I threw caution to the wind and, while I went on touching her, I opened her thighs and with my other hand I touched myself, I was so excited that I came almost immediately..." And when the beautiful dreamer had finally opened her eyes with "the most innocent expression in the world," her bedmate couldn't stop herself from laughing. "What are you laughing at?" she asked in amazement. "At your adorable little weaknesses," her friend shot back. "You wicked thing, why do you laugh? Because I'm still not as good as you? But one day I will be..." "Yes, but that day has not yet come..."[18]

In sending Virginia such an audacious text, Estancelin clearly counted on her complicity, especially since he persevered in his provocation and—we move on now to the second lesson—even dared to insert himself into the scene.

In a letter probably sent from his Château de Baromesnil, the Norman thanked Virginia for sending him a photograph of herself as a New Year's gift and told her of the "effect produced" by her gift:

> At first I *innocently* admired the beautiful contours, the elegant shapes... but suddenly, noticing the position of the fingers and the hand, a memory swept over me. I felt a serpent of fire shuddering, elongating, standing up straight, and tense, rigid, hard... It rose its haughty head... I was alone... I locked the door, sank into a big armchair, and then your delicate fingers, without bracelets... Conjuring a sweet illusion, I closed my eyes, feeling a delectable motion, which made me hotter and hotter by the second, at the touch of a memory, at the caresses of a beloved hand... I surrendered myself to pleasure and was flooded with it! This morning I put your gift next to me in bed, and for an hour I felt your caresses and went wild with you.[19]

Having laid the groundwork, Estancelin decided the moment had finally come to give Virginia a real lesson in *ars amatoria* and told her in explicit detail about an erotic encounter he'd had with a very passionate woman.

> I put my arm around her waist... My hand goes in between the folds of her dressing gown and caresses her breast, which stiffens and swells beneath my fingers... an *arm without bracelets* responds to a caress, and it too squeezes between us, and a sweet warm hand feels a serpent standing up straight, rigid and hard, raising its haughty head, and sets it free... Under her fingers the buttons give way one after the other... My hands slide in between her burning thighs... I arrive at the cave of love... Her legs are spread, her thighs parted... I feel myself penetrating her, my lips glued to hers, all I can say is oh darling I feel so good! I feel so good!... And what about me? the woman of fire replies...[20]

With this third letter, the general believed he'd done what he had set out to do. Now he passed the baton to the woman of marble, hoping his letters had warmed her slightly. "To want or not to want? To be or not to be?"[21]

Made of marble or fire, unfeeling or indifferent, simulating or sincere, Virginia seemed to appreciate this erotic game with Estancelin. In her friend's expert arms she was probably able to find the sexual gratification most suited to her, and he, in turn, made a display of virility that impressed his fellow men. And weren't the admiration and desire that, despite distance and the passage of time, the Norman never ceased to express perhaps the ideal mirror for her own narcissism? "The most perfect work of creation," he wrote to her, "is a woman in the full splendor of her beauty: but the most seductive work of heaven, and perhaps... of the spirit of malice? is the woman who combines physical attractiveness with the gifts of the heart and the charm of intelligence. I shall leave for Dieppe tomorrow evening to go see her. I arrive at nine o'clock at the Hôtel

Royal, and I will be hers whenever she wishes; to tell her how much . . . and then we'll see! I thank you and remain your humble servant."[22]

At any rate, come what may, Estancelin would remain Virginia's friend, never ceasing to admire "her beauty, her rare intelligence, her loyal friendship."[23] And the very fact that—unlike so many others—he never lost his head for her only makes his judgment more valuable.[24]

# A Stranger in Her Own Land
## 1859–1861

While Virginia was looking for a way and means to return to Paris, the Oldoinis were anxiously wondering what other surprises their volatile daughter still had in store for them. And though the marquise, now resigned to her daughter's ungovernability, maintained a prudent distance, the marquis, who was not unaware of Virginia's "resistance to advice,"[1] continued to play the part of the noble father from his post in Saint Petersburg. He urged her to look after herself; reminded her—citing experience and the affinity between them—that the moral life affects the body; and implored her to take it easy. He had held out some hope that Nini would reconcile with her husband, and on hearing the news of their legal separation, which took effect on July 18, 1859, he expressed his sincere regret, reminding her of the duties that would come with her new condition:

> It is up to you, if not to justify yourself, at least to show that you are not completely at fault, and with all my authority and my affection I expect you to offer proof of this, and if you have been a faithful wife and a good mother, you must now continue to be a respectable

and respected woman, for your new condition brings with it a thousand problems, and to solve them you will need to rely entirely on your tact.[2]

This was hypocritical counsel, considering Oldoini could by no means be ignorant of his daughter's amorous exploits. Was the letter meant to serve as a reminder of the conventions necessary to life in society? Certainly, the marquis was well aware of her privileged connections to power; for years and years, he would go on asking her to help him with transfers and his rise through the ranks.[3] Virginia always tried to satisfy these requests. She put a great deal of stock in her father's opinion, and even in the midst of her Paris mission she had made it a point of pride to obtain him a posting as first secretary in Saint Petersburg. Wasn't coming to his aid also a way to make up for disappointing him? And perhaps by managing to fulfill her father's ambitions, she was also able to confirm that she could still rely on some paternal credit.

With the war over, Virginia intended to do everything in her power to escape from her isolation and regain her will to live—especially now that Cavour, though without any further clarification, had told her that both he and the king looked favorably on her return to France.[4]

The Armistice of Villafranca and the preliminaries of peace signed on July 11 by Napoleon III and Franz Joseph provided for the cession of Lombardy to France, then by the latter to Piedmont, but nothing was decided about the situation in central Italy, which was fast becoming a powder keg. In Tuscany, as in the Emilian duchies and the papal legations, insurrections had ousted sovereigns and installed provisional governments, pending unification with Piedmont. Austria and France, albeit for quite different reasons, intended to place those sovereigns back on their thrones. To solve this thorny problem and avoid another armed conflict, it was again decided to resort to the weapons of international diplomacy: the major powers would be brought together for a peace conference. The Piedmontese legation was, of course, led by Cavour, and Marquis Oldoini was avid to take part. If this was out of the question, he still wished to leave Saint Petersburg as soon as possible, he wrote to his daughter, and be assigned to another legation, preferably in Spain, and with a higher rank.[5]

This was far from an easy task, and Virginia decided to turn to Costantino Nigra, who was home from Paris on a month's leave. Conscious of the complexity of the political situation and the difficulties facing the La Marmora government formed after Cavour's resignation, Nigra warned her that her father's expectations were excessive, and that leaving Saint Petersburg was risky. However, after rekindling the spark of their old Parisian connivances, the two friends had a fine time cooking up a little scheme. It was a pleasant diversion for both of them. She needed a break from her isolation, and he himself was grappling with an unhappy marital situation.

To avoid attracting attention, they met each evening outside the gate of Villa Gloria, not far from Nigra's in-laws' house, where he was on his way to dine.[6] After telling her she would need all her powers of seduction and explaining what she should say, the diplomat directed her to the ministry of foreign affairs. And that was how Virginia, regaining all her former boldness and verve, came to tell her father about her conversation with "an old fool"—presumably the foreign minister, Giuseppe Dabormida—whose name she didn't mention out of caution:

> Now I can go become a nun like Nigra says: I climbed the stairs of the ministry twice but wasn't able to seduce this old man, though I had primped myself up as suggested by my friend who was there with me. First, he replied *by looking* at the ground (and then left). Then he put the register in front of me in which Oldoini was *seventh* on the list. There's no way, and from his point of view he's in the right, he has to be fair. Everyone before you is less well placed, and none of them enjoys your past and future advantages. We ought to create new positions because there are more men than positions, and find a way to place the first three, then we could stop and take a breath and perhaps who knows. In brief, there is nothing to be *done*. Moral of the story: (1) *Minister won't even discuss it.* (2) *Chargé d'affaires impossible.* (3) *Congress: not within my purview.*
>
> It took *me and all the clothes on my back* to get these fine replies out of an old fool. And beautiful as I am, the visit cost me 100 francs (for a new hat). *My friend couldn't believe it* and said, "Get thee to a nunnery."

After reviewing the options available to the marquis, Virginia suggests that her father wait for the political situation to stabilize and speaks of the congress like a secret agent: "It's Papa Camillo who's going, and this depends on just *two* horses: Imperiale [Napoleon III] and Mongolo [Czar Alexander III]." But she knew how to take these horses by the reins and would soon write to her "cousin, for *give and take* was the only way to get anything out of him." If Cavour did not reply, she would go visit him at Leri—the country house where the count was getting ready to resume leadership of the government. Virginia was already gloating to Poniatowski about "the great trick she'd pulled off" when she had no choice but to tell her father that Cavour had given her "an unambiguous refusal," "saying that a man like Marquis Oldoini cannot go and copy dispatches written by Nigra."[7] Evidently, in this instance, collaborating with his "cousin with the beautiful eyes" was not important enough to make him clutter up the delegation with a diplomat he didn't respect. Furious, she said: "This reply was unacceptable, but I intend to make him pay for it the first chance I get, and perhaps it won't be long." But while Virginia ruminated on her revenge, she couldn't ignore her failure: "I raised hell and nothing came of it. Chance perhaps will do better than I... The Friend [Nigra] counsels patience but I am out of patience."[8] She did, however, hear some consoling news from her collaborators. The "old fool" had told them: "I said no to everything, but I kept my eyes pinned to the ground; if I'd dared lift them to gaze upon that marvel, I would have collapsed right there and then."[9] Virginia's beauty remained a formidable weapon.

In December, after coming to a political and economic agreement with England, Napoleon III again floated the idea of "resolving the Italian problem" with a confederation that would also include most of the papal dominion. By doing so he thought he could return to the initial spirit of his alliance with the kingdom of Sardinia and so put himself in a position to discuss ceding Nice and Savoy to France."[10] But the emperor's new political position—unacceptable to both Austria and the pope—nullified any possibility of reaching a diplomatic agreement, and on January 7, 1860, an exultant Virginia wrote to her father: "*Le congrès donc biffé! J'en suis bien aise, n'ayant pu rien faire* [So the conference has been canceled! I'm quite happy about it, since I wasn't able to do a thing]." Her letter—twenty-four pages long—paints a picture of the new political situation: the emperor's change of course and new desire to replace "the princes with the prince [Napoleon]"; the perilous position of her no longer indispensable "dear cousin," whom the congress would have put back on top; the weakness of the government; diplomatic maneuvers; the departure of La Tour d'Auvergne, "likewise routed by the cancelation of the congress and obliged to go straight to Berlin"; the arrival, in his place, of the Baron of Talleyrand, a "lowlife" who didn't care for the marquis. In essence, all "the news heard in the *offices* and therefore not to be repeated in salons."[11]

Adopting the telegraphic style and hermetic language[12] of business letters, Virginia shows herself perfectly capable of keeping her father informed of intricate political events and grasping their implications, and she persuades him to keep his post in Saint Petersburg and settle for a leave of absence, but she also has no choice but to tell him about her latest dispute with her husband.

Separation had forced Virginia and Francesco to face the prickly problem of who would get custody of their son. Castiglione said that he was willing to let her retain custody until the boy reached the age of ten, on condition that she agreed to stay in Italy. But it was clear to everyone that Virginia meant to settle in France. She'd left her furniture and personal effects in Paris and had already spent a few days there in the spring. "If Nina wants to keep her son outside of Italy," a dejected Marquise Oldoini writes to her husband,

> there will be no reasoning with Castiglione because he is too determined to have him at least in the same country so as to be able to see him as he pleases . . . And you'll agree it's difficult to know how to reply when he tells me, "I don't have anything left in the world except this little boy and they want to take him away from me too." What can one say?

And since Virginia had told her she didn't want her advice, Isabella passes a piece of advice on to her husband: "Hear her out, but if she really loves this boy she needs to make some kind of sacrifice."[13] Not to mention that, without her son, she would find herself further compromised in the eyes of society, "since to be alone in the world is an even more spurious position."[14]

Her father scolded her, but Virginia wouldn't listen to reason. "I will not ask anyone's permission, and I will go where my health and finances allow... When one has the courage to remain shut away without seeing a living soul for *four years—someone like me—at my age*, for no reason, *that is more than enough*. The count has no right to expect me to go on living like this." As approximate as ever in her totting up of time (she had been at Villa Gloria for less than two years), the young woman could not forget the "Cinderella" treatment meted out by the Castiglione family, who barred her from court—a court to which she belonged in her own right, having first gone there as a newlywed, still almost a child. "I don't like society, of course, I don't want to be part of it, but on the other hand if I disappear completely that would do me harm, I *intend* to make an appearance from time to time, and I don't need to assure you that I will do so with full respect for propriety."[15]

As usual, Virginia was defensive and dealt in blame, but finding herself "a stranger in [her] own land"[16] she felt she had no choice but to leave. Her father retreated, recommending the diplomatic skills of Prince Poniatowski and General Cigala. For once, reckless Francesco and shrewd Niny concurred: They asked Il Vecio and Barba to help them come to an agreement. The negotiations regarding the Castigliones' assets, like the negotiations regarding their separation, dragged on, prolonging the Oldoinis' agony, but Virginia had already turned over a new leaf. In early September, she and her son went to Dieppe. She'd pacified her husband by telling him it was only a holiday,[17] but she had been careful not to inform her parents, who were less likely to believe her. "They tell me you are in Dieppe," her mother wrote, saying she was sorry to have learned this from a third party and hoped that the trip would do her health some good.[18] Virginia had been prescribed a visit to this elegant town overlooking the sea by the illustrious alienist Dr. Blanche[19]—whose patients included many famous writers and artists, among them Guy de Maupassant, Gérard de Nerval, and Fromental Halévy—and she made the beautiful eighteenth-century villa she'd rented on rue du Faubourg de la Barre not just a refuge where she could be cured of her illnesses and fits of depression but also a strategic site to keep up profitable social relationships and receive her lovers of the moment without attracting attention. We can't be sure whether she took advantage of that first visit to see Prince de La Tour d'Auvergne again, but Poniatowski almost certainly joined her; their correspondence contains more than one reference to their tête-à-têtes in Dieppe. But we can be completely sure that at the end of the bathing season, instead of returning to Italy, Virginia took the road to Paris.

In the French capital, as she'd written to Il Vecio, there was room for everyone, and all could pass unnoticed at their pleasure. Even for the countess, this turned out to be true. On November 18, Viel-Castel noted in his diary: "Madame Castiglione has been in Paris for two months, but no one is talking about her as of yet."[20] But this had not been her plan.

She had wanted to take advantage of her newfound freedom to live as she pleased—admired, honored, and courted—her hair, her clothes, her jewelry, and her spectacular public appearances all very much a matter of discussion. She had wanted—as she had told the Old Man—to return to the scene with her head held high, like a queen, crowning her triumph at the Tuileries, and humiliating her rivals once and for all. This dose of reality disturbed Virginia's mythomania, but it didn't keep her from seeing that her plans for revenge required caution, discretion, and patience. She had to find a way to make everyone forget the embarrassments of her past. She adopted the same strategy that had taken her to the Villa Gloria, choosing a quiet residential neighborhood—in this case Passy, on the outskirts of Paris—where she rented a villa.

She saw Dr. Blanche, who lived with his family in Auteuil, in a house not far from hers. And in Passy she befriended the influential Laborde sisters, who lived on rue Raynouard. Valentine Laborde had married Gabriel Delessert—the former prefect of Paris under Louis Philippe, and the scion of a powerful banking family—and had formerly been the mistress of Mérimée and, later, Maxime Du Camp. A prominent figure in Parisian society and a personal friend of Empress Eugénie's, Madame Delessert ran an important liberal salon popular with politicians and writers, and she was assisted in her duties as hostess by her daughter, Cécile, Countess of Nadaillac, and her son, Édouard, a talented painter and photographer instantly smitten with the charms of his beautiful neighbor. Édouard Odier—the husband of Valentine's sister—was also a painter. Thirty years her senior, Madame Delessert treated Virginia, whom she found "as good as she was beautiful," with motherly indulgence.[21] She was also a supporter of the Italian cause, as can be inferred from the letter of condolence she sent Virginia after Cavour's death in 1861.[22] It was thanks to the Delesserts that Virginia earned the esteem of Adolphe Thiers, the journalist and historian of the Revolution, twice president of the council under Louis Philippe, and leader of the parliamentary opposition to the imperial regime.

But her life was not free of humiliation. More than once the countess was treated as an unwelcome guest and had her "honor offended." Clotilde—Victor Emmanuel II's virtuous daughter, who'd married Prince Napoleon—avoided her like the plague. And Princess Mathilde had stopped answering her letters or sticking up for her.[23] Writing to her mother, Virginia played the part of an anchorite, weary of worldly vanities. This worried Isabella: "I was very sorry to read that at your age you consider amusements unsuitable for you, I hope you will change your mind." When she learned that the reality of the situation was rather different, she gave her daughter a gentle scolding:

> But my dear, do you really think it would displease me to know that you dined at the princess's house or with other respectable people? Or that in your drawing room you receive *gens comme il faut*, that you are sociable, and that everyone loves you as you have always been loved? No my dear, what would displease me is to know that you are isolated from the world like a sinner, that you see no one, that everyone says: She is an *extravagante* [eccentric]. In this world, if you don't wish to make tongues wag, you have to do the same as everyone else.[24]

As always, it was only with Poniatowski that Virginia took off her mask, congratulating herself for having chosen the path most likely to get her back on her feet: "But what a retreat! Everyone wants me to come and I do . . . The Rothschilds *fine*, the *Thiers* ditto, and I've even made a conquest of old Laffitte, who's coming to see me today! But I've taken off my veil!" And that wasn't all:

> Madame [Eugénie] almost wants to see me, and the new bride [Countess Walewska] has already almost had a fit. But if you talk to him, tell him to take heart... that I'm minding my own business, that he shouldn't think I have *plans*, I'm no good anymore, that I don't give a damn about society, and that I ask him nothing—only that I not see him and that he leave me alone.

The only person who wasn't saying a word, Virginia observed, was "him," the emperor, and it was time to bring him out into the open:

> Now as for the Old Man! What to do with him? I think it would be better to see him or at least write to him that I am here and that I'll look for him *en passant*, or else play innocent and give him, by way of reply, that big *sore* head you like, and let him be the one to say *je voudrais la voir* [I want to see her]. I am now in a position to receive him without anyone butting in, and it isn't such a bad thing that I've kept him in the dark and the cold.

The "big *sore* head" was undoubtedly the splendid photographic portrait in which, with her chin melancholically resting on her hand and one arm against the frame of an enormous window, Virginia gazes off into the distance. After returning to Paris, she'd had Pierson photograph her dressed as Béatrix,[25] the heroine of Ernest Legouvé's eponymous play, staged at the Odéon on March 25, 1861. Played by the great Italian actress Adelaide Ristori—much admired by Virginia—Béatrix sacrificed herself out of love for a prince who'd been forced to give her up for political reasons. There was nothing better than this portrait, which the emperor had not yet seen, to remind him of her incomparable beauty and the sorrow to which his abandonment had condemned her!

It was time for "this eternal story of payments" to have a happy ending.

> It must be *him* giving me something, not me getting something out of him. And so—what can I tell you? It will be an aberration, as Barba says, but I, the poor one, am not about to do what I'm expected to do. I don't think it's right, and it isn't the sort of thing I'm made for, and I've found that in this world it's stupid not to try to live in the least horrible way possible.

Virginia's hold on the ruler must still in fact have been quite strong. Shortly after her arrival, she wrote triumphantly to Poniatowski:

> You say I don't do anything! You see that I have gotten going without delay, and that since yesterday I've already seen the Old Man, softened him up, decided on a course of action, and made arrangements to see him here tomorrow morning at 10 o'clock on the dot. I know that's early but *il le faut* [so it must be] for Nicchia, he wanted to see you here *pour délibérer ce qu'on peut faire de cet homme* [to discuss what can be done with this man] because that's the story I cooked up for him and that it's up to you to *grossir* [flesh out].

"Cet homme" was none other than the Count of Castiglione, who'd been transformed from a victim into an executioner. In taking over the negotiation (up to then conducted on her behalf by the prince) for payments from the emperor, Virginia had turned the tables. Her problem now was not the stain on her reputation but rather her bullying husband, who had taken his revenge by leaving her penniless and threatening to take away her son—her sole reason for living. As Virginia reported to Poniatowski, the Old Man had fallen right into the trap. He'd begun by cautiously observing, "There must be some way to hush him up, maybe with money, I don't know..." To which she'd promptly retorted, "Yes, but I don't have money, so how do I do that?" And so she finally induced the emperor into making the exact proposal the two accomplices had been working toward for months: "I will talk it over with Poniatowski and see what can be done."

Virginia had clear ideas about what came next. The prince was to present himself at the Tuileries and read the Old Man excerpts from letters in which the count claimed custody of his son and lashed out at his wife. Then he was to show him receipts for the loans made to Castiglione, proving that Poniatowski himself was not, as the count maintained, a thief who had seized his fortune with the help of his adulterous wife. In short, they had to "sing him several antiphons. Say I didn't even want to mention it to him and that you said you didn't want so much responsibility and that you encouraged me to share it with him."

The emperor went back to paying her occasional visits, and she stuck to playing the role of sorrowful mother. To the not at all extraordinary accusation that she was "the mistress of the Duke of Aumale as well as others," she had the effrontery to reply, "I will indeed have to become such a woman, partly to make ends meet and partly to keep myself in a daze, for *if they take my child there is nothing left for me but that* or the convent." Was she still pretending to be in love when the Old Man came to see her after nightfall, while she counted the minutes, like a prostitute before the money changes hands? Of course she wasn't really keen to detain him since, by "sending for him and *sending him back* in the same fashion," Poniatowski could show up at her door just an hour later. But for the emperor, too, it must be said, the sexual enticements of the beautiful Italian had lost their luster. She was no longer the flesh-and-blood corollary of those exhilarating days when he'd planned to make Italy the trump card of his European policy. Instead, she reminded him of a serious error of judgment for which he was continuing to pay the price. Perhaps, united in defeat, for the first time the former lovers had sincere feelings for each other: "I don't know whether I told or wrote you that the other day in Paris I saw the Old Man, who came to me drooping and miserable.[26] He was so down in the mouth I felt sorry for him. He wept over my *lot*, which he finds *déplorable*, and over my untenable position—but what can be done?"

Virginia now knew what could be done, but so far she had kept it to herself. If the Old Man did not provide her with enough income to maintain the standard of living to which she believed herself entitled and merely handed her over to the bankers, she would make him change his mind, employing every means at her disposal. In the meantime, in the spring of 1861, she returned to Italy with the firm intention of staying there as briefly as she could.

# The Burglarized Banker

"I AM NEITHER your lover nor your banker. You do not treat me like a friend. So what am I? I prefer not to answer the question,"[1] Charles Laffitte wrote to the Countess of Castiglione at a critical juncture in their relationship. His irritation was justified, for it was only out of fondness and friendship that the banker had lent her the 150,000 francs whose repayment he was now requesting in vain. She'd been careful not to tell him that the large sum had been spent saving her friend Poniatowski from bankruptcy—no one would give him credit anymore—or that he had no intention of repaying it. But this was not to be the only debt Virginia owed Laffitte. Not long after, Laffitte wrote to ask her for "the few hundred thousand francs" he'd lent her with "the utmost solicitude many years ago" and which he now urgently needed.[2] Written over the course of a decade (1862–1872), Laffitte's letters and Virginia's sporadic replies are further confirmation, if confirmation was needed, of the countess's obsession with money. As will be recalled, even before her exile in Turin she'd thrown herself into the world of finance, attempting to secure her financial independence and to prove, to herself and to others, what she was capable of. On her first trip to Paris she'd become acquainted with the Rothschilds, at this point her bankers, and with Delessert. Now, in 1862, she boasted of having "made a conquest"[3] of Charles Laffitte, a prominent figure in the capital's financial and social worlds.

Following the death of their patriarch, Jacques, a powerful banker and minister to Louis Philippe, the Ferrère-Laffitte family was experiencing a new golden age under the Second Empire. They had helped finance Napoleon III's coup d'état; Jacques's niece had married the minister of the interior, the Duke of Persigny; and various family members occupied key positions in business and finance. The son of one of Jacques's brothers—awarded the title of count in 1843—Charles Laffitte combined political commitments, as deputy of the département of Eure, with financial and entrepreneurial commitments. And he was never one to shirk worldly pursuits. He owned a well-established racing stable and was among the founding members of the exclusive Jockey Club. A portly man with thick white hair and conspicuous whiskers, the banker was pushing sixty—an "old man," for Virginia[4]—and could not be called handsome, though his intelligence, his civility, and his great stores of energy were certainly attractive. Separated for many years, Laffitte divided his time between his house on avenue Matignon in Paris and the splendid property of Le Val Fleuri in the Parc des Maisons. Even after she married the Marquis of Galliffet, his daughter Georgina had gone on living with him. A lady-in-waiting to the empress, beautiful, and extremely sophisticated, she would never have won any contest of virtue. The banker may have been thirty-four years older than Virginia, but he was far from oblivious of her charms—and she had more than one reason to be charming. Though Laffitte's bank[5] couldn't hold a candle to the Rothschilds', the financier's entrepreneurial strength in railroads was incontestable. As early as 1855, in the king's retinue in Paris, Cavour had met with him to initiate agreements that would allow the Victor Emmanuel company—which Laffitte had created two years earlier—to beat out the Rothschilds and extend the railroad network, ensuring "rapid, direct, and continuous international communication between France, western Switzerland, and Italy."[6]

Since the 1830s, a veritable "railroad mania"[7] had taken hold of French society. Trains were changing the very nature of travel and offered new profit possibilities for large and small shareholders alike. It was inevitable that Virginia—who was not unaware of Laffitte's business relations with the Italian government—saw him as a source of valuable information for her stock-market speculations. At the end of 1863,[8] the banker gave her detailed instructions to put the "people of Turin" in contact with one of his envoys, encouraging her to write to the king to ask if he could buy a thousand railroad shares that had just been issued.[9]

Her money troubles being what they were, Virginia was not shy about welcoming Laffitte into her bed, and he did, truly, love her. A chivalrous feeling of devotion[10] prompted him to take care of her when, after emerging from her exile at Villa Gloria, the young mother struggled to get back on her feet in Paris. "I loved you because you were ill, dejected, outcast, and afraid," he would remind her years later, by which time their relationship was in crisis, but "now things have changed, you have gone back into society and are once again the Beauty everybody is courting... I have done my part."[11]

Probably it had always been clear to the banker that he didn't represent a permanent solution for Virginia and couldn't aspire to an exclusive relationship. He was content with a discreet but steady association. Their affair was affectionate, and little George was not disregarded. The two of them made a habit of seeing each other at her place in Passy or, more rarely, at Laffitte's house when his daughter and son-in-law were away.[12] Occasionally they even met in Dieppe. They wrote to each other often, alternating between English and French, sharing news and scheduling their next rendezvous. He called her his "Dearest Beauty," and she gave him the nickname "48," after the street number of his bank on the rue Basse-du-Rempart.

It must be said, however, that her return to the social scene, the complicated management of new clandestine relationships, and the ongoing financial difficulties she faced as she waited for the wheel of fortune turn in her favor (finding herself regularly disappointed at its failure to do so), had certainly neither softened Virginia's heart nor her attitude toward men: Laffitte was no exception, especially once the large sums of money he asked her to repay made him an object of her resentment.

In business as in love, there was nothing off-limits to her and nothing she wasn't owed. The countess did not respond to requests, ignored entreaties, and if she really felt compelled to come out and say what she meant, veered between aggression and abuse. Realizing she was financially obligated on several fronts, Laffitte had advanced her many thousands of francs, after which he was transformed into a scrounger and forced to tell her, day in and day out, that the debt was too large, his bank was going through hard times, and, in short, he needed the money back as soon as possible. If she was unable to fulfill her commitment, she certainly had no shortage of other friends—the Rothschilds, for starters—to whom she could turn. What really embittered him was Virginia's defiant attitude and willingness to hurt him. She made it clear she had other relationships,[13] and when he asked her to extricate herself out of respect for the feelings that bound them, she replied, "Let's leave the heart to the imbeciles." This was something Laffitte simply could not tolerate:

> I have not yet recovered from seeing you on Friday. It left me with a sort of sadness and robbed me of any residue of illusion. You are right: Let's leave the heart to the imbeciles and try to be practical. So please, once more, put an end to this unpleasant affair, which was to last only twenty-four hours, then a week. Give orders to your agent, or whomever you see fit, to pay into my account the sum in question... If you attribute any delicacy of spirit to me, you should understand how painful it is for me to see my behavior repaid with aggression and reproaches, when I know that I deserve nothing but feelings of gratitude and affection.[14]

And since he had heard secondhand that Virginia was not merely mocking his devotion but had had the bad taste to indulge in derogatory remarks in the presence of others, the banker appeared determined to put an end to a relationship that had run its course:

> My days are over and my presence at Passy is no longer required. I no longer delude myself that there was a time when you loved me... I have the feeling I am in your way. It may have taken me too long to realize it, but you will pardon me if, until today, I could hardly believe in such a reward for three years of devotion.

He could not but act accordingly: "Don't worry, I will no longer be in your way. Your name shall not pass my lips. From here on out I prefer to be dead as far as you're concerned, as you have been... dead to all the world." In the bitterness of parting, he could only wish that she might "replace my lost affection with one as sincere, as disinterested, and as lasting as mine."[15]

Virginia had not meant to break things off, however, and ran for cover:

> The bad storm which appeared in the sky has influenced your nerves; I suppose this is the only excuse I can find to your foolish letter to which I ought not reply. I thought long and hard before doing so . . . Because you are angry with others you take it out on me for no reason? Would you ask me to apologize for being too good and trusting? For having retained, in spite of everything, the most affectionate feelings toward you, which I have always proclaimed urbi et orbi?

In short, the real guilty party was Laffitte, who'd allowed himself to be swayed against "his best friend"—a title she was not about to give up.[16]

But he was too attached to Virginia, and had too much sense, to give their affair such a ridiculously dramatic cast. The season of love was past and gone, and he could only sigh. In a letter he explained why, having arrived in Dieppe without any word from the countess, he hadn't tried to see her. "Ever since the frost covered my heart," he wrote, "it no longer races but, though the ardor is undiminished, dawdles. You have offended both me and my feelings for you."[17] But frost would have turned to ice if Laffitte had known all the duplicity his Dearest Beauty was engaged in behind his back.

Having realized she could no longer rely on Laffitte's unlimited indulgence, Virginia was forced to acknowledge that without the banker she would lose, among other things, the privilege of buying shares related to his financial transactions in a timely fashion—for example, the one even then in progress, regarding beds for the army[18]—which would sink her deeper into debt. She therefore sought advice from one of Laffitte's close associates, Louis Le Provost, whom the banker had introduced to her at the start of their relationship, and whom she'd soon made her own, using him to obtain information about financial activities that her lover had not seen fit to pass on to her.

Marshaling all the tactics she had mastered, Virginia bewitched him with her beauty, melted his heart with her melancholy, moved him to pity with her financial worries, and finally involved him in a matter about which a subordinate should have remained entirely ignorant. By doing this she made him "her staunchly devoted servant," as he wrote at the end of every one of his letters. But when Le Provost was so reckless as to break a lance in defense of the countess, his patron put him in his place, curtly reminding him that it was none of his business.[19] But by now his devotion was proving invaluable. Understanding he could never play the role of her lover, he carved out a place for himself as her advisor.

When, for example, the banker sent her his sorrowful farewell missive, Le Provost provided Virginia with a meticulous list of directions for her to follow down to the smallest detail. In writing to Laffitte, she must express astonishment and sorrow and above all sad dismay at the cruelty of attacking a friend where Laffitte knew it would hurt her most. And, revealing an unmistakable taste for melodrama, the clerk concluded:

> Close with a heartfelt sentence more or less as follows: 'Although your cruel conduct has wounded me deeply, my friendship for you has

> not diminished—never, in fact, could I, nor would I, forget the devotion you have proven to me time and time again. Come, touch my hand, which is loyal and worthy, and above all assure me that the black cloud that has temporarily obscured your heart has lifted for good.[20]

Though it wasn't easy to coax Virginia to moderate her tone, once he understood the context, Le Provost must have managed to dissuade her from sending the banker an overdramatic letter full of righteous indignation and gloomy pessimism like the one she'd written a few months earlier, in a convulsive script that conveyed her state of exaltation:

> You are turned *mad* or perhaps I have turned imbecilic myself; in any case I still think I'm clearheaded enough to tell you you're wrong, wrong to claim that you're coming to Dieppe for me, wrong to take advantage of this to say unpleasant things to me that you don't mean, wrong because you know I don't deserve this. You are well aware that I am frank, loyal, honest, and you cannot doubt my feelings for you, which are those of a friend.[21]

It was indeed in the name of this friendship—so unjustly called into question—that Virginia asked Laffitte to rescue her from the terrible situation in which she found herself: "I am counting on your help to solve the dilemma of whether I should throw in with God or the devil."[22]

And so Le Provost advised her to take a more dispassionate tone. Better to make a less violent, but subtly blackmailing, appeal to his emotions, asking for the kind of protection that he had been so eager to offer in the past, and that she continued to hold dear.

> Woe is me if, when promising help and friendship to a soul in distress, you did not have the firm intention of offering her precious support! I admit I have no right to doubt your friendship. Precisely because I have faith in this friendship, I say to you: Come, let us talk face-to-face. How can a poor derelict, a prisoner of sadness and loneliness, do without your advice?[23]

For Le Provost, the most effective expedient remained to lure the banker to Virginia's house—what man wouldn't have done anything within his power to obtain this privilege?[24]—and, ineluctably, into her bed.

The two accomplices' strategy did not, however, achieve the desired results; the banker refused to return to Passy and went on demanding his due. By now Laffitte knew his Dearest Beauty too well to be entrapped by her words, intimidated by her anger, or moved by her tears, and he was done with being a laughingstock. But then—a stroke of genius—Le Provost counseled the countess to play one last card: Knowing how fond he was of little Giorgio, she had to make Laffitte believe, in the most melodramatic way possible, that she, reduced to poverty, found herself forced to separate from her son:

> Perhaps it's already too late, but if I were you I would give it one last try and at noon, when you gave me the sign, I would come in the carriage with the child. Laffitte will come down. And you will say: I am being separated from what I love most in the world—because of money—they are taking away half of myself... But I don't want this beloved creature to leave—leave Paris—without you being able to hug him one last time. Not even someone with a heart of stone

> could be impervious to such a display of emotion. So you must try. Dress however you like and take the first cab. Come. It must be done. The ploy will work, and in any case you will prove you have a virtuous heart.[25]

Virginia heeded Le Provost's advice but scornfully rejected the mise en scène cooked up by his imagination (tinged by serialized novels). "In this world, everyone must play the part that suits her best. I can be a perfect artiste, but the role of comedienne doesn't suit me at all. I must remain myself and derive what little I can from it."[26] She elected to appeal to the banker's emotions, and this time she hit the mark. Laffitte received her letter in Compiègne and hastened to reply that he felt her pain and would gladly pay for Giorgio to continue his studies in Paris so that she would not have to be parted from him.[27]

That was not at all what Virginia had expected. She'd been hoping for financial assistance for herself, not her son. Though Laffitte was undoubtedly being generous, he had avoided falling into the trap and, tired of asking for repayment of the loan, announced his intention to put the matter into a lawyer's hands. Virginia was as unaccommodating as ever. She was riled by the letters sent to her care of the Rothschild bank[28] and avoided seeing the other party, using her ailments as an excuse. "There is no point telling her to come if, for health reasons, this is physically impossible for her. Please, then, make an announcement abovedeck and below that, as soon as she is able to go out and climb all your stairs and brave the cold that reigns at your door, she will come." And to leave no doubt about her state of mind, the countess, in the first person now, took a combative tone: "There's no need to send people asking about me: I won't say a word . . . So leave me alone, all of you. Mr. Georges has also been ill in the hospital for eight days and I will end up in a madhouse if this goes on."[29]

As the years passed, Virginia's increasingly incomprehensible handwriting gave her correspondents a run for their money. ("The only word I managed to decipher in your letter is *jaw*. Not quite enough to be able to answer you," Laffitte protested. "Why don't you learn to write properly?"[30]) She therefore deemed it best to use "Mr. Georges" as an amanuensis for her business letters. One wonders how a teenager might feel, transcribing the letters of a mother hounded by creditors. It was also Giorgio's job to inform Laffitte that Mina was hoping to see him as soon as possible to exchange New Year's gifts. In doing so the fledgling secretary appealed to the indulgence his mother's friend felt for him and urged him "not to forget her gift." The dispute between Virginia and her old lover would drag on for years, but the legal proceedings and her ultimate victory would not prevent Laffitte—even after he'd definitively distanced himself from Virginia—from staying on friendly terms with her. There is no point wondering whether—or how much—his passion for his Dearest Beauty had made him suffer. As Le Provost wrote to her (he, meanwhile, had had the good taste to change masters and, with Virginia's help,[31] entered the service of the Rothschilds): "Who could ever fathom the ways of Providence, or the heart of a banker?"[32]

# A Son in Contention
## 1861

On her return to Turin in the early months of 1861, Virginia found Italy a very different country from the one she had left less than a year earlier. With the exception of Lazio and Triveneto, every part of the peninsula had voiced, by plebiscite, its desire to join the Savoy kingdom, and on March 17 Victor Emmanuel II officially proclaimed the birth of the Italian state. The "Pig King" had the wind at his back, and the time had come to "serenade" the man who would one day declare himself her "Miserable Master." Too many things now depended on his goodwill for her to find fault with the narrow-mindedness, greed, and barracks manners of the man who'd just assumed the title King of Italy for himself and his heirs. Determined though she was to spend most of the year in France, Virginia remained an Italian citizen with vested interests in Liguria, and she had a title to defend. She needed to recover her rightful place at court and reestablish a stable relationship with the sovereign. The time had come, too, to claim the reward for her contribution to the national cause five years earlier, so devastating for her marriage and reputation. Her first victory in this regard was to secure, thanks to Cavour's good offices,[1] an apartment in the royal palace, which put her in an ideal position to reawaken the sovereign's sexual appetites. It would not have been difficult for her to do.

For quite different reasons, the Count of Castiglione had also obtained an apartment in the royal palace. "His Majesty the King," he wrote to his father-in-law, "in order to give me a special token of his benevolence, has appointed me an honorary officer and signed a decree according to which I am at his disposal for any orders he deems appropriate to give me, either directly or through the minister of the household."[2] This new role as private secretary to the sovereign, with a salary that allowed him to live "honorably," put him in an advantageous position when it came to custody of his son. And yet, continuing to display the same astonishing naiveté with which he'd confronted the twofold drama of financial and marital failure, the count elected to rely on the mediation of Uncle Cigala and Poniatowski, who had been the guarantors of the amicable separation of 1859. The separation agreement, as we have seen, envisioned the mother retaining custody of the child as long as she provided for his maintenance and remained in Italy so that he could pursue his education; otherwise the count would regain custody and place Giorgio in a military school. But with Poniatowski's disastrous liquidation of his assets, as well as the request for the separation of assets made by his wife, the situation had grown more contentious. It didn't take long for the count to stop rejoicing at the fact that Virginia could rely on the "advice of two good friends" like Poniatowski and Cigala.[3] For their part, Il Vecio and Barba both would have been glad to forgo reprising their role as mediators in this final act of separation between the Verasis spouses.

As for Marquise Oldoini, she decided not to take a stand because, as she wrote to her husband with characteristic bluntness, she wasn't sure what to hope for. She knew a reconciliation was out of the question—"it's impossible for her to put up with his annoyingness or for him to put up with her extravagance"[4]—and custody of her grandson seemed to her a sort of wild card:

> Niny would like him back ... and if Castiglione sends him back so much the better, if he doesn't send him back I don't want to have forced the count only to be reproached for whatever happens to him in that little steamroller's hands. Let that clown Beppino take charge, I, for my part, I repeat, abide by your policy, even though this will lead me to suffer Niny's wrath, but do as you like, I've had just about enough of it.[5]

So Oldoini let Poniatowski take care of the problem. In his role as paterfamilias, the marquis had no wish to jeopardize his authority by intervening in a matter whose outcome was unknown, especially since he made it a rule of to steer clear of any conflict with his daughter. But Poniatowski—faced with two increasingly recalcitrant spouses—forced him to get involved, asking him to use his sway over his son-in-law to talk him out of this nonsense about military school. No one, the marquis replied, wanted Giorgio to remain with his mother more than he, and clearly Castiglione would throw in the towel if Virginia could be persuaded "to take up residence with her son in Italy, whence she could be entirely free to take her trips to Paris whenever she pleased, leaving the boy with a tutor and, occasionally, taking him along." Knowing full well the idea was unrealizable, he displayed a far-fetched optimism:

> I don't think Niny truly wants to abandon everything, everyone, launch herself into the fray, and forget that she is a mother and daughter. *No*, dear Beppino, let's not give into our fears just yet. I know that Niny is a good girl, and that it's just the anger of the moment that fills her with such villainous feelings.[6]

Virginia had no intention of heeding her father's advice, but she didn't wish to butt heads with him either. She cared what he thought, and she knew which arguments would give a virtuous cast to her decision to return to France, which she was determined to do at any cost. As she would remind him in a very long letter written after yet another fight with her husband, she had made up her mind to settle in Paris for the good of little Giorgio. She wanted to spare him a coarse and backward military education, which would clip his wings for good, turning "*ce bijoux d'enfant, cette merveille d'homme*, [this jewel of a child, this marvel of a man]," whom she was so carefully molding, into a soldier in Saluzzo with a café owner for a wife and 82 francs a month. For this same reason, as she'd already said in the course of their exhausting negotiations, if her husband opted for military school she was determined never to see the child again and to break off relations with the whole family. What she wanted to secure for her son—not in ultra-provincial Turin but in the most cosmopolitan and brilliant capital of Europe—was an education worthy of a gentleman, which would allow him "to become a great statesman, to travel the world with a respectable position, to marry a millionaire princess, and—beautiful, intelligent, with a brilliant future before him—to lead a existence happy, grateful, useful life."[7] Virginia was well aware that her father, who valued elegance above all, would not fail to share her hopes for Giorgio: she wanted for him the destiny that she would have liked for herself—a destiny that, notwithstanding her beauty, her intelligence, and her knowledge of the world, the era had denied her.

Even as Virginia went on expressing her desire for her son to have a decent education, she confessed to Poniatowski that she didn't really want to take care of Baby. She had resigned herself to it for the time being, but she intended to place him in a boarding school in Paris "in order to make him an educated and knowledgeable *man* and, as soon as he grows up, not to have him around, to be free, and to spend a third of what I'm spending now." In any case, though, it was imperative to get the child back, for everyone in Italy was vying to spoil him rotten ("he is already getting spoiled, and soon he won't give a damn about anything or anyone"), thus nullifying the education she'd given him. "I have been telling *everyone* that if this little boy goes on this way, around all these people, he will become an *indomitable devil*, wicked and *perfectly ignorant*, because I have given him a *taste* for study and didn't *force* him to work, as those vipers say." Her conclusion was not, by any means, a model of delicacy: "If they give him back to me I'll take him back to save him and if not I won't give a damn." In reality Virginia was not one to give up *anything* she believed belonged to her, let alone her son, and so she went on prodding Poniatowski—sometimes exhorting him to "sweet-talk" her husband, or to threaten him, or to tug at his heartstrings by reminding him how the absence of her son had made her suffer. And she put just as much pressure on Barba.

On April 28, 1861—after an arduous eight-month mission in Egypt and Syria—the Count of Castiglione returned home to Turin to find several varieties of unpleasantness awaiting him. For starters—as he wrote to Poniatowski—his wife had taken advantage of his absence to go back to Paris with their son in tow. Then there were the sales of Costigliole and the house in Turin, which "caused him to shed not a few tears." Ignoring the pre-agreed stipulations, Poniatowski had also sold some family heirlooms and the chapel attached to the castle to the new owner, thus depriving the count of the right to "go and pray at his parents' tomb." Faced with such dire humiliations, Francesco took issue with the primary progenitor of his misfortunes: "The countess, who is aware of my devotion to my relations, and who has not seen fit to the make the slightest sacrifice for the name she still retains, might have asked you to heed at least this one stipulation." As if this weren't enough, Virginia had requested and obtained the separation of her dowry, leaving the count entitled only to alimony. "Knowing how things had gone, she might have acted differently and avoided inflicting this additional humiliation on me in the courts, but the countess wished to be true to herself to the last." She should not be surprised when, availing himself of his rights, Francesco requested a legal separation—synonymous with scandal and as good as an accusation of his spouse—and custody of Giorgio. "I have nothing left to leave to my son," he acknowledged bitterly, "but I will share the crust of bread I earn by working round-the-clock, and at least he will see how much affection I have for him and not be poisoned against me by his mother."[8]

Poniatowski immediately communicated the contents of this letter to Virginia, who laid out the steps they should take—that is, "in curt, clear, precise language," to confront the count with his choices: "(1) peace (2) war (3) conditions and advantages of peace (4) disadvantages and futility of war (5) details of the two cases."[9]

Biddable Poniatowski communicated with the count and Cigala precisely as she wished him to, permitting himself just one liberty:

Virginia had advised him not to respond "using too many words," which might make it seem more "a letter of apology than an ultimatum," but the proposal the prince sent to Francesco care of Cigala was subtle in its blackmail: "If the count requests legal separation and wishes to regain custody of Giorgio, he commits an act of hostility against the countess, which she does not deserve, given the care and perfect education she is providing her son and her unimpeachable conduct. Such harshness will be painful to her, but if it comes to pass she will be relieved of any responsibility and will think only of herself." (And since Cigala and Castiglione knew that Virginia was capable of anything, they could be sure this was not an idle threat.) If on the other hand the husband gave up the idea of a legal separation and left his son where he was, the wife "was willing to make sacrifices in his favor, regarding the available capital on hand as well as the fruits of her dowry, not as alimony... but because it was never her intention to take everything for herself and give nothing to her husband." And why should a child be taken from a mother who had the means to provide him with a good education and ensure him a little capital?[10]

Castiglione, meanwhile, frightened by the irreversibility of the separation, had already begun to take a softer tone. "The fault is mine, I now realize, I was not able to make the countess respect me as I should have." And he put forward two new proposals. The first—a "friendly settlement"—even entertained the possibility of attempting to live together again: "If perhaps the countess, *once she has recovered*, would wish to come live with me in Milan, I would still be willing to welcome her, but on the condition that she comes to us with a firm intention, with what little we have, and without saying unpleasant things to me." The second, more extreme proposal involved legal action: Castiglione could request that his wife be compelled by law to move back beneath the marital roof. If she refused, he would have the right to seize the interest from her dowry and take back the child.[11]

Poniatowski's reply took the discussion back to square one. Now that the separation of the dowry had protected Virginia from any claims the count might make, she was prepared to cede part of it to him in exchange for custody of their son. Furthermore, knowing he was "besieged by creditors," she was willing to pay him ten thousand francs and, if fortune smiled on him and his stock-market speculations, she asked nothing more than a share of the spoils. As Virginia well knew, Castiglione had made it a point of honor to repay every last one of his creditors and could not refuse an amount that would have silenced even the most bothersome of them.

Aware that, yet again, his hands were tied, Francesco despondently proceeded with the negotiations, taking solace in the hope—which Poniatowski carefully rekindled—of a possible reconciliation. "As for the proposal to come and live in Milan with you, she is seriously considering it," the prince wrote, deviously.[12] "She implores me to thank you and tell you that if she doesn't accept straight away it's only because she's ill, and for the moment she needs peace and quiet." And of course he took the opportunity to remind him of poor Niny's irreproachable conduct, tucked away as she was in a "little house in Passy, without luxuries or even comforts," almost always in bed, almost always alone.[13] But not even the Count of Castiglione could protest at the news that, on June 17, Virginia had emerged from her hermitage to attend the funeral ceremonies of the Count of Cavour at the Church of Sainte Marie-Madeleine.[14] He had in fact died in Turin eleven days earlier at the age of only fifty-one—that stubborn visionary who had changed the destiny of Italy, but whose work, as George Sand once wrote to him, extended well beyond the bounds of the peninsula and was, for all those who loved liberty, "the life-or-death question of our age."[15]

With him disappeared the only man who had ever filled "the cousin with the beautiful eyes" with awe.

# Waiting for the Maternal Kiss

## 1861–1865

After his interval of bliss at Villa Gloria, Giorgio found himself increasingly excluded from the maternal paradise. Obsessed with regaining her place in Parisian society, beset by financial problems, grappling with new lovers she needed to keep at bay, and often ill, Virginia no longer had time to look after her son and so delegated the task to Lina Rauch, a young German governess who was "half man" and worth "two whole men."[1] Though stern and not given to effusions, Mademoiselle Rauch was a kind-hearted person and immediately grasped that the best way to protect Giorgio was to get him used to complying with the injunctions of a mother who always wanted the last word not only on her son's education but on his social life.[2] In the isolated house in Passy, the boy was not permitted to disturb her when she was unwell or receiving visitors, and without friends his own age or anything to do but study, he lived in anticipation of the few moments she was willing to grant him. Even if they were often harbingers of outbursts and punishments, those few moments were nevertheless proof that Mina remembered him. He had such a desperate need for attention that he even denounced himself for his own failings,[3] though he knew doing so would elicit nothing from his mother but anger.

As early as September 1861, when Virginia was fighting for custody, Marquise Oldoini—who had been living with her grandson at La Spezia—was distressed to observe the neurotically perverse power Virginia had over him:

> But this exasperating creature, with her constant pouting, dazzles him and even while he's here she finds ways to afflict him, with very tender letters that make him cry, but I'll make sure he laughs while he's here, and he adores me more than words can say. It's fine for him to study and be obedient, but goodness me, a child needs a bit of glee, a bit of sun . . . I think Beppino and Castiglione are plotting to get him back to Niny and of course I'm happy about that for her . . . but I wish she would torment him less.[4]

When she saw, with regret, that Virginia was far from softening her behavior and in fact becoming more and more severe with Baby as time went by, Isabella exploited the fear of death that overwhelmed him whenever he fell ill to persuade her daughter to change her ways: "It isn't good for a child to have such sad thoughts, try to cheer him up instead, life is already hard enough when you're an adult, try to make his childhood easier, let him be free and easy, have fun, and don't torment him with so much study and shouting at him over nothing."[5]

Virginia herself speaks of her son's anguish in a letter to Poniatowski: "Baby is freezing to death and has scarlet fever which is running its course. He was delirious and in his delirium he said: '*Oui j'obéirai parce que Mina m'a appris qu'il faut obéir mais je mourrai, je suis sûr, vous verrez* [Yes I will obey because Mina taught me that I must obey, but I will die, I'm sure of it, you'll see].'" But she didn't find this moving so much as irritating—because it was all "the marquise's fault" for pitting her son against her. "As soon as he's better, I'll give her a piece of my mind, I can't be bothered with these sorts of theatrics."[6]

Lo Fü's letters to his mother from three different holidays in Dieppe between 1861 and 1865 tell us the heartbreaking story of a child who, year after year, vainly renewed his request for love. Always waiting for a response that was always slow in coming, Giorgio invokes the benevolence of the maternal divinity, following all the procedures laid down by religious worship: adoration, submission, acts of contrition for sins committed, petitions for her to hear his pleas. In the autumn of 1861, after his stay with his grandmother at La Spezia, the child went with Virginia to Dieppe, where he was sad to see that he made no one happy. His mother was always cross, and Mademoiselle Rauch never stopped scolding him.[7] And when he learned that his divinity was about to go to Paris, leaving him alone with his governess, he became intractable. As he himself explained to his mother,[8] the pain of abandonment made him lose his temper, but this admission did not make Virginia lenient. On the contrary, her son's mea culpas and good intentions struck her as insincere and sent her into out-and-out rages. "Mr. Georges ought to stop writing to me," she ordered in a moment of exasperation,

> because I'm tired of reading all the time: Mina, I've been bad, I don't dare write to Mina, I'm afraid of displeasing Mina . . . It's ridiculous. Afraid of what now? I am well aware that his conduct is unworthy . . .

> He is right to be afraid because he will be punished, and punished harshly.[9]

Because of this fear, which Virginia stubbornly refused to understand, Giorgio got into the habit of lying to her, suffering her wrath again and again. After which the young culprit was all the more ready to acknowledge his wrongdoing. As he wrote to his grandfather, he made a promise to himself not to anger his mother because she spent "a lot of money" so that he could be "a good child."[10] Mademoiselle Rauch, unlike Virginia, became increasingly certain that Giorgio's behavioral problems and emotional extremes had a pathological cause, and she felt duty bound to confide in Marquis Oldoini: "Though he has every intention of being a well-behaved child, he often loses control; but his contrition, which is invariably sincere and immediate, makes him suffer so much he is sometimes ill for hours. This cannot go on."[11] In September 1864—relegated to the French seaside resort with no one but Mademoiselle Rauch for company, with no playmates or distractions other than homework and the occasional walk on the beach—Giorgio lived in anticipation of his mother's arrival. "I hope every moment Mina will come, but as Mina is not yet come I send Mina this letter. It rains dreadfully and I annoy myself."[12] The sadness of being so far away from her was exacerbated by his chronic fear of being forgotten: "Now that Mina's birthday is come I wish Mina much happiness . . . I would be happy to pass this day with Mina, who full of pleasure will surely forget that Lo Fü without news and separated from Mina is unhappy."[13] But Virginia seemed indifferent to her son's suffering. Mademoiselle Rauch felt obliged to confront her directly:

> To be frank, I am not at all happy with the way the Lady Countess is acting, she is well aware that Mr. Georges is distressed not to receive any letters from her, so why make a child suffer who is so emotional? I say the same thing in every letter. Endeavor to maintain the affection of your son, you can neither hate him nor abandon him, therefore you must love him . . . I beg the countess to please write to us, but kind letters, not the sort that make a person's hair stand on end or give you indigestion.[14]

Giorgio's anticipation of an affectionate gesture from his mother reaches a fever pitch in the letters sent from May to July 1865. His desperate sense of need and his fear of abandonment are as overwhelming as ever, but Lo Fü now expresses them in a more articulate way, constantly repeating vows to obey her, protests of loyal devotion, and tender wishes, as well as sending her affectionate little gifts. At the age of ten, Giorgio had already learned how to deal with his mother's despotic volatility.

Dispatched to Dieppe to recover from a serious bout of whooping cough,[15] he sends Virginia a report on his physical condition, explains the doctor's prescriptions, tells her about his walks on the beach, and insistently asks after her own health. He keeps her informed of the letters he is writing to his father and grandparents and of the letters he receives in return, and he asks her permission for even the most uncomplicated matters. Often forced indoors by bad weather, he tries to stave off boredom by seeking out the company of Dr. Blanche's children and grandchildren, who are on holiday in the house next door. His detailed account of a dinner with the Blanches and his two nannies is that of a miniature man of the house, eager to make a good impression. Already well aware of his mother's financial difficulties, he is careful not to spend too much,[16] since when they run out of money it's up to him to tell Mina. He also turns out to be precociously attuned to social connections. He tells his mother about seeing Le Provost, Laffitte's associate who also has a house next door to theirs; remembers the names of everyone who sends her greetings; and even tells her about one of Prince Napoleon's brief visits to the town.[17]

To convey his love for Mina, the little boy resorted to the language of flowers, sending roses, pansies, and wildflowers whose colorful silhouettes can still be seen on the paper.[18] Fortunately he had no idea that his idol was turning these tender tributes over to her lovers.[19] Giorgio decorated his pages with rather beautiful drawings and even planned to give her a little bird he'd picked up during a walk. And, again and again, his craving to be with his mother rises to the surface: "I will not be a soldier because I would not stay without seeing Mina often."[20]

He tried to be courageous, but he was a child tormented by longing. When the postman didn't bring Virginia's long-awaited letter, he would sulk[21] or burst into tears,[22] and when, *rara avis*, a letter from her arrived, his gratitude was outsized. Meanwhile the long sojourn in Dieppe weighed on him more each day; he feared he'd never see his mother again, even in Paris, and if he had to "stay alone in that boring house in Passy," he said, he would surely die.[23] This frantic anticipation of his mother's arrival, which was continually postponed for health reasons, grew worse with time. "The sorrowful Lo Fü"[24] counted the days[25] until he would see her again. He wrote to her in his childish English: "I hope that Mina will come today. It is so long time that I am not with Mina";[26] "The days pass very slowly and I would be very happy to be with Mina";[27] "I am waiting Mina with great impatience."[28] When Mina gave him detailed instructions on how to get the house ready for her, he was overwhelmed with joy, sure the big moment was at hand,[29] and the ensuing disappointment proved all the more cruel: "As Mina had written to me that Mina would come this week, I went yesterday to the station hoping to see Mina on the train. When I heard the railway whistle, my heart beated but I was very sorry not to find Mina."[30] Once more Lo Fü began to count the days, and at the end of his next letter he noted: "It is two big months I am alone."[31]

Back in Paris, Giorgio found his mother less affectionate than ever. As the fretful marquise told her husband, her daughter's letters indicated a worrying "moral and physical condition"—the consequence, according to the marquise, of "her imbroglios."[32] Chronically in need of money; besieged by creditors; unable, even in dreams, to pay back her friend Charles Laffitte his two enormous loans, Virginia disburdened herself. According to their separation agreement, her husband claimed custody of their son, who was just another trouble to her, after all.

And so, at the end of 1865, the child left for Italy, escorted by Mademoiselle Rauch. He went to live with his father in Florence, where the Count of Castiglione had settled the previous year, following Victor Emmanuel there, now that the city was the capital of the kingdom of Italy. Marquise Oldoini had gone to stay with her son-in-law, too, hoping to give her grandson an affectionate welcome. That Giorgio was emotional, frail, and in a very poor state of health was immediately apparent. When he fell ill in April, the marquise—who was looking after him while his father was away—did not conceal her worries from her husband:

> Giorgio has fallen ill again, and more seriously, because he has very high fevers, for the moment he is doing fine, but the doctors say that his chest is very weak, and to be honest I had never seen him naked, and he is very thin. The doctors repeated to Castiglione that the boy was malnourished as a child and now studies too much. This only enrages Castiglione more than ever, and when he had the fever he swore he was going to burn all the books and never let him out of his sight ever again.[33]

The focus of the family's accusations was conspicuous by her absence. The countess hadn't written to her mother in months—not even bothering to reply to the telegram in which she gave her news of her son's health.[34] She no longer wrote to Giorgio either, though when he left Paris she'd promised to write him every Sunday.[35] Months would go by without Giorgio receiving a line from his mother. All the while he sent her long letters in the form of a diary, letting her know everything he saw and did.[36] Her unkindness hurt him, but again and again he told her how he longed to be with her. And when Mina did make up her mind to answer ("receiving a million would not have made him happier"[37]), he was overwhelmed by nostalgia, ready to make any sacrifice for her sake, starting with his gratitude to his father—anything just to be with her and, "as in the good old days," wish her good morning and have her give him "a kiss before bed."[38] In June 1866, on the eve of Italy's new war against Austria,[39] he wasn't shy about saying how glad he was that his father might be going off to the front. If he did, perhaps his mother would summon him back to Paris.[40]

For Proust at thirteen there was no greater misfortune than to be "separated from Mama."[41] The eleven-year-old Giorgio was in no less of an agony and, like Proust, made the memory of her nightly kiss a symbol of paradise lost. The child could hardly have imagined that, less than a year later, another loss would plunge him into even deeper despair.

# A Man's Ambitions

## 1861–1866

In the fall of 1861, Virginia arrived back in Paris, a letter from her husband hard on her heels. He complained that he had not yet received a reply to the latest of his proposals for reconciliation. At first the deserting spouse had thought to mollify her husband by thanking him for his offer while reminding him that an "amicable" separation was the best solution; that way, they could "live in peace" and "do well by" their child in sparing him from his parents' quarrels. After all, the count was making no great sacrifice by giving up a wife who was "unsuitable" for him, nor was she making any great sacrifice by abdicating "a position" that she in no way regretted giving up. "I think for myself,"[1] she concluded, her tone undiplomatic. Perhaps that is why she had put off replying to his latest proposal, feeling her departure from Turin was eloquent enough. Francesco now told her that all his predictions had come true: He had warned her about the dangers of getting mixed up in speculation and they'd gone bankrupt; he had warned her that Manzella, one of the countess's many fixers, was a scoundrel, and he'd betrayed them; he had told Poniatowski that the attorney Tesio was untrustworthy, and Tesio had robbed them blind. She ought to stop deluding herself. "Your wretched fate ordains *us* to be poor, and we must resign ourselves to it."[2]

But Virginia could not bear to be contradicted, and speculation and investments didn't just represent the hope of easy money. She found them irresistibly attractive. The back-and-forth between the worlds of politics and business excited her, and she was always convinced that she knew the right ventures to pursue. Like all gamblers, she loved risk, and there was no loss or gain large enough to make her leave the table. But afraid as she was all her life of going broke she would compulsively accumulate government stocks, pensions, annuities, interests, and jewels—forever convinced that she was on the brink of ruin. She would inform Poniatowski of all her investments, dividends, losses, and maturity dates with maniacal meticulousness, and yet persistently avoided forming an accurate picture of her financial situation.

She had no doubt, however, that her true stock in trade was her beauty, and having lost any possibility of putting it to use with the emperor, she resigned herself to considering various promising new investors. She started with two bankers: Charles Laffitte, whom we have already met, and Ignace Bauer. These parallel relationships forced her to keep a close eye on her datebook to avoid overlaps or awkward surprises. Secretive and unforthcoming by nature, she was now determined not to make mistakes of the kind that had lost her Napoleon III's favor; she observed the utmost discretion and demanded the same of her lovers. Despite having three different boudoirs—the Passy house, the Paris apartment on rue Marivaux,[3] and the villa in Dieppe—she clearly had some difficulty juggling matters, especially since the relationships with two bankers did not rule out others with Il Vecio, with General Estancelin, or fleeting encounters. Who knows? Perhaps Virginia, like Ninon de Lenclos two centuries before her, classified the men to whom she gave herself variously as "payers," "whims," or "lovers." Would it be accurate, then, for us to dub her a "courtesan"? From a bourgeois moral point of view, no doubt, but on a social level, the term is dead wrong. Unlike the notorious *grandes horizontales* of the era, Virginia came from a high-ranking family, and her husband was a member of the most ancient nobility. Furthermore, there were other women—Princess Mathilde, for starters—who lived apart from their husbands and maintained long-term romantic relationships without anybody batting an eye. In the aristocratic world, libertine morality continued to retain its rights, however discreetly. Julie Careau recalled with indignation that before the Revolution, when as a courtesan she lived on the margins of society, the beau monde was not in the least scandalized by an upper-class lady brazenly trading in favors.

In reality, what was disturbing about the Countess of Castiglione —much more so than her nonchalant attitude toward romance— was her "scandalous extravagance,"[4] her restlessness, and her mysterious, itinerant existence. She was always appearing and then disappearing, always traveling—so much so that they nicknamed her "the valise of mystery"[5]—and in fact, in the catalog of the auction of her archives at Drouot, we find no less than four laissez-passers issued by Victor Emmanuel between 1860 and 1864, which allowed her to travel anywhere in Europe.[6] She shied away from public places, left the house in a veil, and rejected the first rule of high society, which required ladies of rank to reciprocate invitations and receive people at home, perhaps even hosting a salon. But she would have loathed the equally codified customs of the demi-monde, with its assignations, and vulgar luxury, and subservience to male pleasure.

And if, flummoxed by the insolent way she bore "the burden of beauty," the bilious Count of Viel-Castel called her "a courtesan like the Aspasias,"[7] there were several other haute-monde ladies—the Countess Walewska, the Duchess of Persigny, and the Marquise of Galliffet among them—about whom he might have ventured a similar opinion. If anything Virginia's behavior was in keeping with her reputation as a spy,[8] and she seemed less a courtesan than an adventuress, who "loved only her ambitions": politics, business, power. "Man's ambitions,"[9] as Ferdinand Bac would astutely observe. Didn't Émile Zola brilliantly portray her as an enigmatic Italian adventuress some fifteen years later in *Son Excellence Eugène Rougon*?[10] In that novel, the countess appears as a beautiful and pugnacious modern-day Clorinda[11] intent on hatching political conspiracies, daunting men with a whip in one hand and a folder of secret documents in the other—a folder from which she won't be separated for a second.

Virginia knew her reputation was under suspicion, and that was precisely why she was in such a hurry to be readmitted to the Tuileries. The biggest obstacle was obviously the empress's veto, but once she'd swallowed her pride the defeated rival could depend on her friend Nigra, who had returned to Paris in August 1861 as minister plenipotentiary of the king of Italy. Years earlier, when he'd come as Cavour's spokesman, the young diplomat had gotten into Eugénie's good graces, and he may well have put in a good word for Virginia, since in February 1862 Marquise Oldoini was delighted to learn that her daughter had visited the empress and been welcomed with the utmost kindness.[12] Around the same time—thanks to the good offices of Poniatowski and Cigala—Virginia also prevailed in her quarrel with her husband. Francesco gave in to signing an "accommodation" that allowed her to "keep her child with her until he reaches the age of ten," at which point he would be "handed over irrevocably to the count."[13] When Virginia told her father how the negotiations had turned out, she declared that her "*affaires d'argent*" would soon be mended; she'd "brought off a masterstroke" guaranteed to provide her with "a few years' peace."[14] But the news from her family was far from happy. In Saint Petersburg, Marquis Oldoini was going through one of his periodic depressive crises, made worse by the difficulties of managing a patrimonial estate so overburdened by mortgages as to be less and less profitable. His affectionate and supportive wife did her best to comfort him: "I'm sorry that you get so agitated and nervous about all this ... Alas I used to sigh and brood too, but these days I take things more calmly and I advise you to do the same so as not to ruin your health."[15] Then in March 1862, the marquis was compelled to return to Florence when the elder Lamporecchi's health took a turn for the worse. For Isabella, who was very close to her grandfather, it was an ordeal. But while Castiglione—a model son-in-law to the end—said he was "heartbroken" not to be able to "rush to the man's bedside to attest to his enormous affection for him,"[16] Virginia, in Paris, said that she herself was too ill to travel, though she asked her father to send her the "fatal news" by telegraph, and also to remind her "of the rules to follow for mourning, for even if in truth the heart knows no rules, the world observes them, and we must comply, especially in Italy, so I would like to be informed."[17]

For Virginia the death of this ninety-year-old patriarch (about whom she would never stop bragging) represented a break with the world of her childhood and hastened the disintegration of the Lamporecchi clan—a clan already pretty well eroded by its members' money troubles and mental disorders. Isabella did what she could to avoid making her daughter feel estranged from it all, confiding her worries and feelings. Two days after her father's death, she told Virginia[18] how the old man had been optimistic to the end; he was even convinced he was doing better and went on reworking a poem, "Il Bonaparte," which he'd submitted to his friend Tabarrini's judgment just the year before.[19] She also told her that, against the advice of her family and Virginia herself, she'd refused to tell her father that he was about to die. Had she done so, the elder Lamporecchi would certainly have given her a special gift, but she'd always let herself be "swindled" when her own interests were involved, and she advised her daughter not to follow her example[20]—a piece of advice that Niny surely didn't need.

A letter from her husband, which came a couple of weeks after her grandfather's death, was not the sort of thing to lift a person's spirits either. On the day after his birthday, Francesco took stock of his life, which made Virginia think about her own as well:

> Yesterday I turned thirty-six, four more years and then forty, and that's how life goes: You spend half of it doing foolish things and the other half regretting them . . . I am very disappointed to hear that your health is still poor, *if I were the doctor* I would heal you in an instant, because above all it's a question of your morale, which suffers from the impossible life you've been leading these last five years, and I also see that you absolutely need some sort of diversion. *You would need only to* want to change your way of life, which is wasting you away little by little, and take up a less luxurious, more serene existence, but whether we like it or not we must follow our destiny, and

> you will never choose to heed my advice because *I am your husband*, though if the knot that binds us were to be magically undone, I am convinced you would find no better friend than me . . . What I wish for you with all my heart is that you recover completely and find, *wherever you decide to live*, happiness and tranquillity.[21]

But Virginia seemed not even slightly inclined to seek out tranquillity. She returned to Turin in the spring for a brief visit to finish carving up her husband's assets with a meticulous inventory of furniture, paintings, antique weapons, books, silver, carpets, linen, and household goods in hand. Judging by a note from Count Federico di Castellengo, Victor Emmanuel's grand equerry, her stay in Turin also allowed her to take up with the king again.[22] Having finished with the carving, she decided to take a holiday for a few weeks in London, at the height of the season, and from there,[23] hearing that Poniatowski was about to leave for China, she traveled back to Paris to say goodbye. The prince had not hidden his "boundless joy,"[24] and when the time came to go their separate ways, she gave herself to him, body and soul. Poniatowski was quite emotional:

> want you to know that I am not an ungrateful man, and that the evening of July 15, 1862, will remain fixed in my memory for all eternity. The event was already extraordinary enough by itself; there is only one Nicchia in the world, but I've never seen her as pretty and *cheeky* and tender as on that occasion, and then, coming all the way from London, giving up all those *cocodes milords* to bid Il Vecio farewell, really, it was much too kind, and I would like to say thank you forever and ever.[25]

But for Virginia there was only the present. "I don't believe in love and count only on the love of the moment," she once wrote to an unknown correspondent.[26] In La Spezia during the bathing season that year, she won the hearts of several commanders and officers off the ships flooding in to the huge military arsenal, which was booming. We cannot be sure whether during that summer of 1862 she really had a *grand amour* with the frigate captain Guglielmo Acton,[27] which didn't prevent her from writing "I have given you my soul" to an anonymous "ironclad" man stationed in La Spezia.[28] It was likewise "with all his soul" that a Turin friend, who'd fetched up in La Spezia, kissed her "eyes and feet," expressing his eternal sorrow over the all too brief intimacy he'd been granted.[29] It was, perhaps, the last happy season of erotic games played for no other reason than confirming her own attractiveness.

Back in Paris, Virginia found herself grappling with the unresolved problem of her reputation and the imperative need to take advantage of the kindness the empress had shown her in private and so make her official return to the Tuileries. The first propitious occasion would be at Compiègne in October, when the imperial couple were going to welcome Maria Pia of Savoy, who would be passing through France after her wedding to the king of Portugal.[30] As an Italian, Virginia hoped to be invited—provided, as she wrote to Poniatowski, the young queen did not welcome her "with the grimace" that her sister Clotilde had given her. Virginia put her trust in Il Vecio, asking him to deliver the Prince of Carignano a letter in which she pleaded her case with the young queen of Portugal. Impressive for its cunning, as well as for in its insolence, it deserves to be quoted in full:

TO H. R. H. EUGENE OF SAVOY, PRINCE OF CARIGNANO

I beg you, my lord, to forgive me for another letter, which finds me troubling Your Highness yet again, and also for my excessive confidence, which, abusing your indulgence toward me, leads me to dare ask you for a rather delicate favor, as always in the best interests of my beloved son. After all, it is solely for him and his future, and also a little for the present of Count Verasis, whom it is best not to displease too much for the time being, since, to hear him tell it, my *unsociable* position compromises his own. If I have been attempting to keep my place at court, I have done so for the sole purpose of ensuring my son's entry into society. I myself have no interest in appearing there, but I must be able to do so from time to time. But Your Highness, attentive as you are to everything *said and done* by the beau monde, knows how little their judgments are worth, and he is not unaware of how they are always ready to draw arbitrary conclusions and massacre the innocent for a trifle, seeing unspeakable enormities where often there are nothing but quite ordinary events. On the other hand, as soon as they think they've caught a whiff of worldly glory, this same beau monde falls in line and places you on the altar.

At long last, she gets to the point:

It has been proposed that I go to Compiègne as the only Italian, and almost a member of the family, who would like to meet the Queen of Portugal. But will this queen deign to remember that she was a child with me—that she and I played under the gaze of her mother,

> who honored me with her affection? If I should expect a different sort of treatment, I confess—and I believe that Your Highness, with his customary discretion, will approve—I would prefer to leave Paris and go on a trip so as not to avoid letting it be known by all and sundry that I am unwanted by my own people, as well as to avoid the risk of receiving a welcome improper and inadequate to what a person in my position is entitled to expect.

In a nutshell, Virginia will appear at court, but only if she is given an adequate welcome. But there is an even more delicate topic that must be addressed, and it must be addressed head on:

> I feel compelled to tell you this, My Lord, since I believe that you will not have forgotten how Princess Clotilde, besides treating me coldly and refusing to have me in her home, also had the ungenerousness to say things about me that are, I hope, somewhat less pleasant than what she truly thinks. For this reason, I fear she will speak badly of me to her sister, who, meeting me at court, will not be able to refuse my presentation but may, nevertheless, take an insulting attitude toward me.
>
> Prince Napoleon will have the opportunity, if he so chooses, to inform Your Highness of the opinions of his wife. As for me, my lord, I ask you to do me the immense pleasure of telling the prince *and the prince alone* that the king's daughter is mistaken if she believes *that her father was something more to me than the husband of the poor queen* who attended my wedding and kept me in her circle, and it is equally false that my husband no longer wishes to hear a word about me… As for the queen, your niece, if Your Highness would like to do me a courtesy, you might give her a letter informing

her that she will see me in Paris and that if she were to show me a little kindness you would be grateful.

I ask your forgiveness once more, my lord, for sharing these trifles with you, but . . . why does Your Highness deign to take an interest in me? You get nothing out of it but annoyance, and my gratitude.

Virginia's cleverly constructed conclusion is rooted in her need to take back her rightful place in society with her head held high, and her obsequious tone—motivated by the fact that this letter must also serve as an "official" missive that Carignano can show his niece—is striking compared with the message Virginia sent to the prince in her role as a secret agent.[31] By insisting that it is only her sense of duty toward her son and husband that drives her to take this step, Virginia invalidates any possible personal criticism by casting aspersions, like a disenchanted moralist, on the ferocious frivolity of the beau monde, which attacks the innocent, only to change its opinion when given a sign from above. Having come around to the real reason for the letter—that is, her wish to appear at court, but only if she appears there in an appropriate manner—she refrains from making any allusion whatsoever to her scandalous relationship with the emperor, which is the first stroke of genius. The writer is an Italian addressing a member of the ruling house of her country, and the opinion of the French concerns her only insofar as it influences the judgments leveled by her "own people." The second stroke of genius consists in the circumlocution that elegantly denies Princess Clotilde's more than legitimate suspicions about her relationship with Victor Emmanuel: an indisputable fact that no one in Turin—and Prince di Carignano least of all—could doubt. But for Virginia the only truth that mattered was the truth dictated by the needs of the moment, and she was expert at finding arguments to validate it.

The invitation did not arrive, however, and she dealt with her disappointment by returning to her various schemes. Her correspondence with Il Vecio shows her busy with business appointments, commitments, and meetings, interspersed with a few brief holidays. "I'm off, and I'm not coming back. Travel to Dieppe: *Tuesday, September 14, 1862,* morning, midday train, arrive at 4," she commanded him, detailing the program to follow:

> Stay the night, all day Wednesday, same Thursday, then depart at eight in the evening. This exact schedule means no engagements between midday Tuesday and Thursday midnight exactly! Is that enough??? I hope that with this in mind, pleasures, duties, games, commitments, pastimes can be put aside for three days and I can obtain the honor of possessing His Polish Highness. Admit that I am a good little creature, a decent woman, an *honnête homme*!

A few days before the New Year, he is the one who writes to her: "If caution forbids us from celebrating the New Year in Passy, we will do it on rue Saint-Florentin.[32] If we cannot embrace on January 1, I at least want this piece of paper to bring you a little kiss... I'm thirsty for Nicchia."[33]

But these getaways were too short for her to forget the worries that gave her no peace: her ailments, her constant quest for business deals, her fear of going broke, the perpetual ferrying of jewels to and from *La Tante* ("Auntie"—or in other words, the pawnshop), the demands of her lovers, her husband's tedious attempts at reconciliation, the undue interference of her parents, the tantrums of a son who would not submit to the harsh discipline she'd developed to make him "a marvel," and above all the bitter realization that she'd lost the leading role she had played during the glorious two-year period of 1856–1857 and now had no choice but to put up a fight in order to keep from being ousted from the scene.

However, she had a marvelous expedient whenever she felt like bending life to her will and reaffirming that she was, indeed, royalty: she could go back and pose for Pierson.

During the years of imperial favor, the lens of the regime's official photographer had celebrated her triumph; now it allowed her to escape into a fictional world. No one has put it better than Pierre Apraxine: "In the quiet of the studio where the mirrors multiply her reflection, sheltered from the constraints of a reality she ignores or despises, the countess resumes her dialogue with Pierson. With him she dreams up scenarios in which her beauty is the only heroine, trying out role after role and pose after pose until its every last facet is revealed."[34] Between 1861 and 1867, Virginia was immortalized in approximately 170 different poses—a series of masterpieces destined to change the art of photographic portraiture.

# Back on the Scene
## 1863–1866

After the Compiègne disappointment, the Italian beauty had begun to fear the doors of the imperial palace were now barred to her forever when, on January 28, 1863, she received a note from Count Baciocchi, the emperor's first chamberlain, inviting her to the Tuileries for a masquerade ball that would take place in twelve days' time. Before accepting, Virginia asked Baciocchi if she should consider it a gesture of courtesy destined not to be repeated, for she did not intend to "intervene as a guarantor for the entertainment of the public."[1] Once she'd received some reassurance from the count, however, she started her preparations.

She selected an imaginative costume, which allowed her—in addition to wearing royal attire—to allude to her birth in Florence and recall the brief period when Tuscany, before being incorporated into the empire, had been, by Napoleon I's diktat, an independent kingdom under the regency of Maria Luisa de Borbón y Sajonia: a coded message, which the great emperor's grandson could interpret as he pleased.

On February 9, 1863, Virginia climbed the grand staircase of the Tuileries dressed as an imaginary Etruscan queen, with a black velvet peplum over a wide-skirted red-orange moiré dress and an immense ostrich-feather fan hanging at her side on a chain fastened to her belt. Her bare feet were clad in sandals. Her lovely hair formed an uncontainable cascade of golden-brown curls like serpents down her shoulders, swathing her in a bright halo made even brighter by the blackness of the peplum. She also sported a riot of jewels on gilded leather inspired by the Etruscans[2] and commissioned from Maison Mellerio; a tiara of openwork acanthus leaves over a Greek motif; and long golden triangular earrings with a Greek design and little amphorae pendants closely resembling the pendants on her necklace. This elemental and dramatic costume—designed by Virginia with the help of the famous singer Mario de Candia—reflected her passion for the theater and looked something like a freehand interpretation of Adelaide Ristori's costume in Legouvé's *Médée*.[3] We can assume that Poniatowski prompted Virginia to ask for help from de Candia—like her, a Florentine and an expert in stagecraft—and the influence of the mythological paintings of Eugène Delacroix and Gustave Moreau is crystal clear. But the overall conception was Virginia's, and it is even now striking in its modernity. We should not be surprised, then, if a contemporary aesthete like Montesquiou deemed it "rather ugly" and "shabbily diabolical."[4]

As usual, before stepping onto the scene escorted by Nigra, Castiglione waited until the party was in full swing. A diary fragment allows us to relive this *coup de théâtre* in her own words:

> Waited for an hour, found Nigra, entered the ball with him, met Mathilde [who] was going out, not greeted . . . As soon as I entered, crowd around me, impossible to stay longer than 5 minutes, the hall filled up, everyone enchanted, a powerful effect of simplicity in the

> midst of all those ladies dressed like flies, midges, and butterflies—like sprites in opera. Not a single pretty thing, and then they were all furious to see me so beautiful and admired and made pathetic faces! Everyone was laughing up their sleeves but no one dared say a word.

The first to compliment her was Count Walewski, who wasted no time inviting her to the masquerade ball he was throwing at his house on Saturday. Maria Anna, in a black domino, was there with her husband. Very probably the two Florentines hadn't crossed paths since Walewska took Virginia's place in the emperor's bed, but the "tubercular flirt" spoke to her old friend as if they'd just fallen out the day before, with a "Are you coming tomorrow? You're all right now?" To which Virginia replied coldly: "I don't know." Then she bumped into the owner of the house: "During the ball, main salon, ran into Emp. very embarrassed to talk to me, asked how I was, reacted with a distracted air to Etruscan queen costume, spoke of the news, another sovereign... He would have liked to talk more but they were all spying on us, said goodbye, and left. I was very calm."[5]

It was the triumphal return that Virginia had so long dreamed of. But there would be no time to rejoice. "Everywhere, everyone is talking about my costume, which is considered indecent! All those wicked women had the nerve to say I had nothing on underneath and was wearing the ancient moiré over my bare skin! The newspapers are full of horrible slanders, and it's a point of discussion in every salon."[6] Undoubtedly it was a slander, but it was also something worse: They were all insulting her by mistaking her for someone else.

The whirlwind of balls on the haut monde calendar had led to a confusion of places and dates, and though everyone agreed that Virginia's reappearance caused "a great sensation" and it was clear "she hadn't lost an atom of her beauty,"[7] many had confused her austere, even demure Etruscan queen costume with the much more daring Salammbô costume worn, with trendsetting timing,[8] by another beautiful foreigner, Madame Barbara "Barbe" Rimsky-Korsakov, and not even at the Tuileries but at a ball thrown around the same time by Countess Walewska. The unscrupulous Russian noblewoman was five years older than Virginia, had also arrived in Paris toward the end of the 1850s, and also had a brief relationship with the emperor. Her extraordinary costume was a creation of the great English tailor Charles Frederick Worth, who was then just beginning his sensational Parisian career. Despite his unfailing attendance at all the Tuileries balls, Mérimée himself committed the error. To the empress's mother, he reported:

> There is still talk of Madame de Castiglione's *coup de théâtre*, dressed as Salammbô with bare legs and toe rings and her hair loose over the loveliest shoulders in the world. It seems she has been proscribed from the Metternich salon, where they ought to be accustomed to extravagance, but I suppose that it is due more to her Piedmontese parentage than to her dearth of virtue.[9]

What crueler joke, for Virginia, than this misprision of balls, characters, and persons? She'd lost her uniqueness, and as had been so perfidiously whispered, however graceful it was, her costume was that of "a fallen queen." As if this weren't enough, an echo of the embarrassing misunderstanding had even reached Italy: "I'm still waiting to find out what this costume was: some say Salammbô, some Etruscan queen, some Eve. I would like to know the truth, so that I can shut everybody up,"[10] her mother wrote cautiously, while the count flew into a rage. Already infuriated to have found his wife's name in *Les femmes galantes des Napoléons*, a scandalous book published in 1862, he'd now read in *L'Italie* that Virginia had shown up half-naked at a dance. He was no longer willing, he wrote in an indignant letter, to play the part of "the compliant husband of the beautiful Countess of Castiglione"[11] and threatened to revoke her custody of their son.

While she waited for Pierson's photographs and Carrier-Belleuse's terracotta statuette to immortalize her costume and do it justice, Virginia went to war. She ordered the author of the article that had appeared in *L'Italie* to issue a retraction, and failing to obtain one turned to the minister of the interior, the Duke of Persigny, asking him to ban the paper. She did not hesitate to send a plea even to the empress, who promised to defend her from slander, as Virginia promptly reported her husband. "I would certainly prefer to know that you are in the good graces of the empress than in those of the emperor," Francesco shot back, "since horns tend to be worn with reluctance, even when they sprout from crowned heads."[12] Finally, after he challenged the editor of the paper to a duel, he managed to obtain the requested correction. "Now that this matter is settled," he wrote to his wife, "you will have to understand that I have no intention of living with two witnesses by my side and an arsenal at my belt just because you enjoy *making merry* in Paris and London."[13]

This letter was more than she was willing to allow. She immediately hurled back accusations at the sender, employing that tone of contemptuous superiority that never failed to wound her husband:

> I hope this evidence is sufficient to convince you of my innocence, and in any case I cannot be held answerable for anything. Indeed, I would be curious to know how you could entertain such an absurd idea, and yet you know me, and knowing me really I don't understand how you could . . . Besides being mistaken, you don't even show me the courtesy of sparing me some embarrassment and teaching one man a *lesson,* which would be sure to shut up, for good, all the other mouths still raring to bite.

She also accused him of treacherously disputing the terms of their agreement only a year after they agreed to these terms. To her husband's blackmail, Virginia responded with more blackmail, employing a strategy that was tried and true:

> I will tell you in no uncertain terms: Despite all my affection for my son, despite the fact that I care about his future and wish to remain on good terms with you, I will be forced, whether I like it or not, to give him up too—to enjoy the peace and quiet that my health absolutely demands.

Her nerves could no longer tolerate her husband's "baseless barbs" and "*Averno furies,*" and she was not going to apologize for this. If he persevered "in [his] senseless rage," she was reconciled to giving her son back to him, along with the name that was the cause of her unhappiness.[14] Francesco—not eager to deprive his son of his mother's affection or, for that matter, to sever the knot that still bound him to his wife, and vice versa—bowed his head once more and resigned himself.

But Virginia was far from ready to resign herself to the rude lies that had ruined her triumphant return to the Tuileries stage, and having retreated to Passy, she was busy meditating vague plans for revenge. Then, two months after the ball an unexpected visit from Mademoiselle Stéphanie Tascher de la Pagerie gave her a chance to silence all the tattle and prevail over the scandal with her head held high. The daughter of the grand master of ceremonies of the empress's household asked her to take part in a charity initiative to aid the orphans of the Oeuvre de Saint-Joseph, which was to be held over the course of three days in the Baroness of Meyendorff's sumptuous *hôtel particulier*. They were planning a series of tableaux vivants (a form of entertainment brought back into vogue by the empress) starring various members of high society. Certain that her presence would attract a good number of spectators keen to admire her legendary beauty, Mademoiselle de la Pagerie suggested that Virginia participate wearing the costume of the Etruscan queen, and so clear up the unfortunate error once and for all. Virginia agreed on the condition that she be allowed to perform on the final day, and that her chosen theme not be announced in advance.

News of her involvement had made the event a sellout: there was great curiosity to see the famous Countess of Castiglione in the flesh, and everyone was wondering what role she would play. She had asked for a cave as a backdrop, it was said; perhaps she would dress up as a druidic priestess. There was also a rumor that she would appear naked, taking inspiration from Ingres's *La Source*. In her diary, Mademoiselle de La Pagerie describes the scene, in which

Virginia announced her withdrawal from a society that did not deserve her:

> The curtain rises. Shock and disappointment are general. The *bella delle belle* [most beautiful of the beautiful], the long-awaited, the longed-for is there, in the cave, wearing a nun's costume that covers her from head to toe; above her head is a cardboard box with the words "Hermitage of Passy." Astonishment at the sight is so great that the spectators cannot contain a murmur of dismay: one man even whistles. At that point, the beauty runs off stage, knocking everything over in her hurry and ripping her dress; she climbs into the carriage and, before disappearing, in one breath, says: "What vile creatures."[15]

The photographs taken later in Pierson's studio show her dressed in a dark habit tied at the waist with a rope, her arms crossed beneath her breasts, her head and shoulders covered by a black cloak, and her forehead enveloped in a white wimple that frames her face, which is more menacingly beautiful than ever. In that triangular countenance, the classic perfection of her features imposes itself in all its purity, but her large, clear eyes stare harshly at the viewer, and there is not a shadow of a smile on her pursed lips. On the back of a photograph entitled "Soeur Élize" from the series *L'Ermite de Passy*, Robert de Montesquiou would have the emotional experience of reading an account of the event, written in his idol's own hand:

> This is an exact reproduction of my tableau vivant, three quarters of an hour spent motionless in front of an audience up in arms, shouts, whistles, apples, pears (or stones); all because for six months, according

> to Duchatel, I was *supposed* to be appearing naked as in Ingres's *La Source*. And so the poor and wounded were able to benefit, that evening, from a sum of between forty and fifty thousand francs, for a single appearance [?]—I alone [having] filled the theater at 300, 200, 100 francs per seat. It was hard standing still there with a stern expression, not batting an eye, and not even throwing Soeur Élize's rope out to that rude and vulgar audience so they could hang themselves![16]

In this melodramatic narrative, we cannot ignore the prima donna's pride, claiming as she does both her own attractiveness and the professional imperturbability required to stand up to the spectators' hostility until the bitter end. But once she was back in the shadows, Virginia found no peace. There must be a conspiracy, she thought—a diabolical conspiracy hatched against her by the jealousy, envy, and fear of mediocre people overwhelmed by her intellectual, moral, and aesthetic superiority, as well as by the ingratitude of those who'd used and then abandoned her, defenseless, to her fate. Debilitated by persecution mania, depression, and the physical exhaustion resulting from her poor health, she now truly took refuge in the Passy "hermitage," spending whole days in the dark, lying in bed under black silk sheets and gradually becoming convinced she'd been born under an unlucky star, crippled by resentments and suspicions, and armed only with an unalterable contempt for the human race. The anonymous letter she received in March 1864 certainly couldn't have made her feel any more at ease:

> Madame, you are, I suppose, a Christian.
>
> You believe in God, I hope, and in the immortality of the soul, I expect, and consequently in a life blessed or damned for eternity.

> What would you say, Madame, if out of one of the carriages that stop each day outside the door of your home, instead of one of those more or less handsome, more or less old, alas! but of course invariably rich gentleman, climbed . . . Death? And if he appeared in your boudoir or under the lustrous drapes of your bed, tell me: What would you say?
>
> Despite your devil-may-care attitude, you would tremble in every fiber of your being, wouldn't you? . . . And your whole past would come back to you: the betrayed husband; the adorable, neglected son, who will someday be ashamed of his mother; the wives, forgotten by their husbands when they lay in your arms; the fortunes squandered on outrageous luxury and preposterous clothes . . . Wouldn't such visions throw you into horrible anguish?
>
> It is always the right time to repent . . .
>
> Believe me, madame, I beg you, believe the advice of a friend, of *your only true* friend.[17]

Busy as she was with the problem of earthly survival, Virginia probably kept telling herself, like Tirso de Molina's Don Juan Tenorio, that "there was still time" to worry about the afterlife, and her initial reaction was to send the letter to a laboratory that specialized in chemical analysis to make sure the paper and ink weren't poisoned.[18] But when the results came back negative, she still wasn't reassured. She was terribly superstitious, and this image of Death who might come knocking at her door at any moment struck her like a curse. Written in beautiful calligraphy and refined French, the letter reinforced her belief that she was the victim of a conspiracy hatched in high places and constantly monitored by people who were aware of all her comings and goings.

The first to sense the worsening of Virginia's neurasthenia was Marquise Oldoini, who, in a letter written a few months earlier, covered her apprehensions in a tone of affectionate jest:

> Something's always hurting, isn't it? I'm sorry you've been sick and in pain. I've been in bed myself for 20 days and all I have left are my *ouches*. Let's hope that I improve and that you soon feel completely better because the old ought to be feeling not too shabby and the young ought to be feeling very well.

And since Virginia had informed her of her intention to remain in Dieppe indefinitely, her mother tried to talk her out of it. "It seems to me you might make somewhat better arrangements for the winter instead of counting the stars of Dieppe . . . dying of boredom . . . If you feel like making the trip, come here, or go to La Spezia, or some other warm-weather hideaway can be found." Immediately afterward, however, the marquise was careful to clarify, "I'm only saying, of course, that you should do whatever gives you the greatest pleasure"—signing the letter "Mother Ouch."[19] But to her husband Isabella confided her "affliction" over her daughter's health.

> Her physical health and the state of her *mind* both frighten me terribly. Today I received a poorly written letter from her in her own handwriting, and she tells me of her condition in such a way that it seems clear she is inordinately fond of her weaknesses. What can I say? If I had the energy and was certain I'd be welcome there I would take out a loan and go, but I don't have the energy and I'm not at all certain, and it would be better if I took out a loan and sent her money, since I am convinced, completely convinced, that the

majority of her strangeness and malaise is the result of her financial imbroglios.

She therefore begged her husband—who thanks to the joint efforts of his daughter, wife, and son-in-law had just been appointed resident minister in Baden—to go to Paris and see how Niny was really doing, but not breathe a word about her mother's worries, "because that would only make me seem more tiresome than I am."[20] In reality she was troubled by a much more distressing thought which, as her daughter became increasingly hostile, she finally confided to her husband: "Unfortunately I see my sad foreboding of the *family* illness is coming true—that is, an illness of the mind—and the most painful thing is that she is obsessed with malevolence."[21]

It was not only motherly indulgence but a tormenting sense of guilt that now led the marquise to endure, as far as possible, the impossible extravagances, the bullying, the rudeness, and the silences of her unfortunate daughter. She encouraged her husband to do the same. "Alas, it hurts my heart to think of these awful obsessions of hers as only sequelae of a physical illness unfortunately inherited from both of our families," she wrote in 1866, adding: "If we have done wrong she is not to blame."[22]

And Virginia herself, in light of her mother's precarious health—afflicted as she was by colic, tooth, eye, and bronchial problems—her father's frequent bouts of depression, and the progressive mental deterioration of two of her Lamporecchi uncles,[23] who had asked the marquise whether her ailments were not an inherited burden. Isabella hastened to reassure her. When she'd given birth to her, she was "*la femme la plus saine du monde*," and certainly the child had "neither bad humors nor bad blood in the family."[24]

Whatever the causes and nature of her illness, Virginia was determined to fight it. She was only twenty-five years old and her will to live was much stronger than her obscure ailment. She entrusted herself to the care of Dr. Blanche—whose clinic was in Passy, at the Hôtel de Lamballe, an elegant eighteenth-century mansion within walking distance of Virginia's home—but also to that of Dr. Arnal, who boasted the imperial couple among his patients and was said to know how to solve the problem of untimely pregnancies discreetly. We cannot be sure whether Virginia had recourse to him for this treatment as well,[25] but she certainly saw him often.[26] In her letters she is constantly making mention of dentists, osteopaths, and specialists of various kinds, but her daily habits couldn't have been less healthy: she spent whole days in bed and her diet, as her mother deplored, was unhealthy and disorderly in the extreme. This was partly due to constant turnover in her domestic staff, as was inevitable given her treatment of them. "I am convinced that you will always have bad servants because you are too demanding and/or mistreat them excessively for totally insignificant reasons," Poniatowski once wrote to her, reminding her of the case of the Duchesse Caumont de la Force, "who was impaled with a pitchfork by an ill-treated coachman."[27]

Yet Virginia managed to live with her ailments, wrench herself out of bed, get her affairs under control again, look beautiful and elegant in society, and attend the theater and opera. She visited the Rothschilds in Ferrières at their spectacular brand-new castle; she was a popular attraction for the guests invited by the Delesserts and Dr. Blanche;[28] and she was a regular visitor at the Thiers' home. She never stopped forging relationships useful to her needs, and yet she was always traveling and juggling a jumble of lovers. Her energy was feverish, and she tended to grow ever more tense, intolerant, suspicious, until abruptly it abandoned her, plunging her into a new period of blackness.

Her psychological recovery—after the scandal of the Etruscan queen, her quarrels with her husband, and the fiasco at Meyendorff's—was slow. When her father announced his intention to visit her in Paris, she fended him off with a vast array of excuses, even promising to pay a visit to Baden. At the last minute, however, she changed her plans. She had a servant write to say that she had to rush to the bedside of her son, who had fallen ill in Dieppe.[29]

Though she made no secret of her difficulties, Virginia also promised her mother—to whom, after a long pause in their correspondence, she'd started writing again—that she would visit her. Unlike her husband, Isabella put no limits on motherly compassion:

> I'm telling the truth when I say that that blessed daughter of ours has made me shed more than a few tears. Her letters are so scornful that, with the uterine disease, and the terrible blood of the Oldoini and Lamporecchi families, it makes me tremble. Now she writes that she is desperate up there, that she has nowhere to live, no servants, that she can't stay, that her affairs (or rather her debts) have not yet permitted her to leave, that she wants to come here soon but doesn't want the count to speak, write, come, take advantage of her, that his coming from Florence would drive her to despair and make her sick . . . And as for society, I am to tell everyone in advance that she doesn't wish to see anyone, or go anywhere, because she didn't bring clothes. Truly it hurt me to read this letter, but I answered it as best I could, I think. I started by telling her that if she needs it, she should borrow money from a banker and that I will try to get

> Papa to pay it back; that I promise not to let the count make a peep and if he does I'll kill him; that as for society, since not a soul comes to see her mother anymore, I don't think there will be anyone who will come to see her either. I really don't know what more to say. If I knew what to do I would do it, but unfortunately I know that there's no use doing anything.

In anticipation of the capital moving from Turin to Florence—an event due to occur in February 1865—the countess rented an apartment in her hometown, informing her mother only after everything was settled. Isabella confessed to her husband that she wasn't exactly eager for her daughter to arrive in Turin, though she'd often repeated that "with her health ruined, and since in that blessed city of Paris she has neither health nor money nor friends nor distractions, it would be a great thing for her to abandon her unhappy fixation with the place and come back and live somewhere close by. I don't mean in the same house (I have my own troubles), but at least in the same country, or in the same *state*."[30] Evidently there were still many things the marquise didn't know about her daughter—for example, her relationship with Victor Emmanuel, which was behind her sudden decision to relocate.

A few months later Virginia took advantage of her father's new position in Karlsruhe to forge new relationships. The Grand Duchy of Baden was, along with Prussia, the only German state that recognized the kingdom of Italy, and the marquis's mandate envisaged missions in the rest of Germany too. The small constitutional monarchy was one of the favored destinations of European sophistication not only because of the prestige of Grand Duke Frederick I and his wife, Louise of Prussia, but because of the spa town of Baden-Baden, and in the summer of 1865 Marquis Oldoini—"surrounded" as he was by royal highnesses[31]—was determined to give his all, and to do so he was counting on a boost from his famous daughter.[32]

Like a diva on tour, Virginia laid out her demands: a well-equipped bedroom, living room, and bathroom, three rooms to use as her wardrobe, and a personal maid.[33] But that wasn't all. She wished to attend every reception and not "stand at the door and watch"; otherwise, it was not worth "the bother."[34] These demands satisfied, however, she recovered all her grace, coquetry, and sparkle, and more than lived up to her reputation as an international *vedette*, charming the grand duke and duchess; securing the friendship of Augusta of Saxe-Weimar (the wife of Wilhelm I, King of Prussia); making the acquaintance of diplomats and politicians who were passing through town; and cherishing every word said about political equilibrium in a Europe undergoing rapid change. Virginia loved the familiar tone that reigned in the little court and was proud "of having the trust of a family related to the greatest names in Europe" with no fear of the disgraces that "afflicted" her in Paris.[35] Indeed, she took the opportunity to complain to the grand duchess about the slanderous rumors swirling around her. At teatime, on the veranda overlooking a swathe of the Black Forest's pines—ignoring the dismay of the ladies-in-waiting—Virginia explained how "men, when a woman wounds their vanity, always retaliate in some sordid way. You have not yet finished slamming the door in their faces and already they're telling every Tom, Dick, and Harry that they were the ones who left you so as not to fall into the clutches of a Messalina."[36]

But once this pleasant spa holiday was over, all the problems waiting for her in Paris came back to haunt her. Certainly the impending visit of the "martyr" Francesco, who was planning to visit his son, did not improve her mood. Isabella had advised her to greet him with a "*bravo* and talk to him about the weather and the rain,"[37] but the encounter was not likely to be friendly seeing that Giorgio had turned ten on March 29 and the count was demanding custody, on the basis of their agreement. Virginia had hoped her husband would change his mind, but knowing she could not win another custody battle, she let her son leave for Turin with his trusty governess. And her financial situation, too, must have been far from good if between March and July 1866 she was forced to take her jewelry to the pawnbroker four times.[38] Although she yielded to her husband's demands, she could not resist sending him another of her epistolary scoldings. Not only had the count, contravening all the duties of a gentleman, dared to check that she'd paid their son's insurance on time—how dare he have "the insolence" to question her word!—but he'd also threatened to let her see him only "if she behaved herself." It was time for Francesco to understand once and for all what it meant for her to be a mother: "I thank you for the grace you grant me, as to a woman condemned to death, but summoning all my courage, I would rather die than abjure my religion, because my child was that for me: a religion." She also reminded him, in language peppered with Rousseauisms, that such a violent act would be damaging to Giorgio: "You have torn him from his mother's arms, which he so needed, only to expose him to the falsehoods of a court and leave him forever in alien hands, since you are never with him. After all, I should have every right to oppose this education contrary to the laws of human nature, but I would rather let you lose yourself as well as him." Blinded by vanity, and hell-bent on imposing his authority as "master" whatever the cost, the count was forcing her to sever the last ties. "My son is lost to me," she wrote.

"I have offered him up, and my heart has put on mourning clothes... I therefore beg you not to come torment me anymore, for if necessary I am determined to take refuge in a distant land in order to end my days in peace... I want the world to consider me already dead, but until I really am dead my life deserves respect."[39]

After this, as we have already seen, Virginia stopped answering Giorgio's letters. Having escaped her control and passed into enemy hands, he too had come under suspicion and was accused of ingratitude.

But Virginia simply could not accept being dispossessed of the son she'd considered an appendage and an object of pride. She became fiercely resentful of her mother, who was guilty of taking care of the child. In June 1866, when Italy—this time allied with Prussia—again went to war with Austria, and Castiglione was on his way to the front, Virginia again went to war with everyone who had stabbed her in the back. Marquise Oldoini gave her husband a desolate account of the situation. "Niny is furious," she told him,

> she writes letters left and right railing against Castiglione's immorality; she says that Mlle Rauch is vermin and is making love to Huteau; that the count has taken away her secretary, who in parenthesis says he left because he couldn't stand it anymore. Finally after venting her fury against these two and the count, she writes to everyone wanting to know why, she says, I have abandoned her. It's quite clear she hates me.[40]

Domestic fury did not, however, keep Virginia from closely following the progress of the war, staying ahead of the news to the benefit of her stock-market speculations, which obsessed her more than ever. This is clear from a letter she wrote to Efisio Puliga, the secretary of the Italian legation in Berlin. Puliga, a dubious character to say the least, had for years profited from the protection of Virginia, who, per her usual tactics, did not confine herself to relationships with the upper echelons but also ensured the complicity of subordinates at every level: for the emperor, Baciocchi; for Victor Emmanuel, the Count of Castellengo; for Nigra, Costantino Ressmann;[41] for Laffitte, Le Provost; for everyday matters in the legations where Marquis Oldoini was struggling to make a career, Passera and Puliga. In this case, Pulic (as she'd rechristened Puliga), employed as he was in a crucial observation point like Berlin, was ideally positioned to get and give news. But initially the countess's expectations were disappointed, and she decided to put her faith in the Prince of Carignano instead. They'd been as thick as thieves for years, and now her friend Eugenio was proposing a transaction that would allow her to "tell everybody, except a few, to go straight to hell" and finally "enjoy herself."[42] But she was forced to recognize that, whatever she did, it would never be enough to give her the freedom she was fighting for so ferociously. Not so long as her stupid, inept husband, who hid his wrath behind formal courtesy, continued to have an incontestable authority—an authority conferred on him by an unjust law[43]—over her existence. Of course, the countess could have broken off all relations with the count and her son, and forsaken her country, but that would have come at a cost she wasn't willing to pay. Fate, however, had a surprise in store for her.

# Finally Free?
## 1867–1872

"Dear Countess, be of good cheer."[1] With these six words, on May 31, 1867, Costantino Nigra bore Virginia the "bitter tidings"[2] of the death of Count Francesco Verasis di Castiglione, who passed away on the afternoon of May 30 while riding beside the carriage of the Duke and Duchess d'Aosta[3] on the road from Turin to Stupinigi, where they were going to celebrate after their wedding.

Although his health had deteriorated of late, and he'd seemed tired from overwork, the count insisted on paying tribute to the newlyweds by taking part in the wedding procession. But as he rode he was stricken. He fell from his horse and rolled beneath the wheels of the carriage, where he died instantly. He was forty-one years old.

Just as when her grandfather had died, the news reached Virginia while she lay sick in bed. To insistent messages from Cigala and Marquise Oldoini, she replied that she would come as soon as she was able. But days passed, and she still hadn't made up her mind to leave. In order to ward off the Castiglione family's criticisms, she thought it best to send Clemente—who was eagerly awaiting his sister-in-law's arrival—a doctor's note.[4] Perhaps she wished to keep her distance from her husband's funeral, where her presence would have been a source of embarrassment for herself and others, or perhaps she was simply too upset to deal with the situation. But two weeks later she was still in Paris, writing to Marquis Oldoini to explain her inaction, which she intended to maintain:

> I am ill and in too much pain to write at any length, and anyway you can well imagine what I will not tell you . . . Know that, first of all, it was impossible for me to set out straightaway, I wanted to attend the funeral, believe me . . . But now that the day has passed there is no more reason to go except business which unfortunately is very easy to see to since there's nothing and the child will have to go to the college paid for by the king or, in the absence of others, by me.

After making it clear that the count had not left behind one red cent and repeating that her poor health, exacerbated by this "new shock," demanded "every courtesy," Virginia finally turned to the subject of her son, who was in Florence with his grandmother. As long as she was unable to reach him, she preferred that he be kept in the dark about the tragedy, giving him "a few more days' serenity." Then she herself would handle "the unpleasant task of telling him that he now has only a mother to rely upon." And since the marquis had written to her that, "in the face of a grave and a son, one must let bygones be bygones," and that, unless he'd always been wrong about her, he was confident she would devote herself to the child,[5] Virginia hastened to reassure him: "There is no need, as you say, to advise me in this regard—the ten years of my life I've sacrificed to him already stand as evidence."[6]

What Oldoini heard from his wife, however, was of an entirely different nature:

> Niny being always ill (without ever learning what the illness is), I have had neither telegrams nor letters from that witch of a daughter. Nor does she ask me for news of Giorgio. From Turin, Cigala, Clemente, and everyone else urges me to give Giorgio the news because it is no longer possible to carry on this way with no more letters from his father, who wrote to him often. It has been a prolonged torture for his son, and this morning Castellengo and I have decided we must tell him. Whatever God wills, so it shall be. But if she says we did wrong, I hope you will take my side, and tell her she is a *Bitch*. She has not written so much as a single line to me, who she'll have die tragically, like her husband.[7]

Meanwhile the boy went on writing to his father and was surprised that his father wasn't writing back. At last, Isabella told him the truth. "I will confess," she wrote afterward to Virginia, "that breaking the sad news to Giorgio was the most painful thing I have ever done in my life." After yielding to tears and grief, he felt better, but he was racked by the fear that his mother had stopped loving him, and her continuing silence made him more anxious than he already was. The marquise was trying to soothe him in every way she could think of, but Virginia needed to understand that the boy wanted some peace, and it wasn't right to deny him. The time had come to tell her daughter the truth: "You've kicked everything away. You no longer have a family or friends or even servants . . . Try to change your character, come back to yourself, and come back to your mother, if you still care about her."[8] From that point on, Marquise Oldoini kept Virginia at arm's length. No psychological blemish could justify her daughter's conduct, and all her pity went to her grandson, the victim of a neglectful mother. "I don't know whether I told you I did the right thing with Giorgio. People I don't even know have been writing from Paris, who hear I have a reputation as a good-hearted person, recommending I save the boy from a mother who tyrannizes and beats him. Poor Giorgio!!!" she confided to her husband.[9]

But Virginia's priorities were of a different order. The first thing she did on arriving in Turin was arrange to have her husband's last will and testament invalidated—a last will and testament in which the count made no mention of his wife and named Giorgio as his sole heir, entrusting Giorgio's guardianship to his brother Clemente. Once she'd reaffirmed her exclusive power over her son vis-à-vis the Castiglione family, Virginia then asserted her rights as a widow over the few possessions Francesco had salvaged from bankruptcy. Possessiveness, regardless of the object or its value, was always one of her distinguishing characteristics. What was hers was hers, and she would not so much as consider giving up either Baby or her husband's humblest personal effects. Even dead, and disgusting as he'd become to her, Francesco had never ceased to belong to the countess. "Still," she had written to him in one of the most turbulent phases of their separation,

> there is a bond between us—and more than one even—which you yourself have called *fatal* and said that you would *never have severed it*. There is, indeed, something fatal between us, which follows us everywhere, together or apart. It is inescapable . . . Believe me, this fatal bond will lead us ineluctably back to one another. It will lead

> us to act in concert, and lend each other a helping hand. When, inevitably, we meet again, you will be glad to find I am still yours.[10]

Her husband's premature death nullified her far-fetched prophecies, but this did not mean she was going to renounce the role of widow or the advantages she could obtain from it. In fact she hewed to the strictest rules of mourning, and not only in dress; she even had her writing paper bordered in black.

Francesco was right to define the bond between them as "fatal." He'd borne its wounds deep in his heart.[11] The victim of a conventional idea of marriage—and a man convinced that he needed to lead his adolescent wife by the hand—he didn't understand that he was dealing with a rebel who wouldn't tolerate any imposition and who thumbed her nose at his marital authority. After enduring the scandal of her affair with the emperor and the inevitable separation with dignified stoicism, he was forced to give up all his possessions to pay off debts contracted during their ill-starred sojourn in Paris. "If for a single moment," he wrote to Poniatowski, "I thought that a single one of my creditors might not get back every cent I owe him, I would blow my brains out this very evening, for when a gentleman cannot pay back what he owes in any other way, he must do so with the sacrifice of his own life." Castiglione understood he was a relic, in an era when money was the only law respected by men, but even so he refused to disregard the ethics of his caste. The second war of independence was a chance for redemption, allowing him to "fight for the glory" of his homeland and put his life at the service of the king—"glad if, in the future, the opportunity presents itself to lay down this life for him."[12]

"A dutiful man," as his wife described him,[13] the count had carried out his work as the king's private secretary with passion and competence, making himself indispensable as well as performing delicate missions abroad. Furthermore, as emerges from the inventory of personal effects—books, paintings, souvenirs, daguerreotypes—drawn up postmortem at his apartment in Florence, he was a man of many interests, passionate about photography, with an extensive knowledge of history and a keen awareness of the institutional and political problems weighing on the new kingdom of Italy. Why, then, after rebuilding his life, wasn't he strong enough to put an end to his miserable marital affair? Why did he instead go on proposing that Virginia move back in with him? Was it amorous obsession, or a sense of responsibility? He realized too late that she'd toyed with his goodwill and failed in her motherly duties; he decided too late to demand custody of his son and sever the "fatal bond" once and for all, and, in the will drawn up a year before his death, to entrust Giorgio to his brother. Knowing full well that on a legal level nothing could prevent a mother from regaining custody of her child, the Castiglione family had acted as interpreters of the deceased's last wishes, omitting his wife's name in the long epitaph chiseled on his tomb. When her husband died, Virginia was thirty years old and, despite the countless ailments that afflicted her, still beautiful; even if her complexion had lost some of its radiance, and her figure had become slightly heavier, the charm of youth had been replaced by the charm of a woman at the height of her sensual magnetism. But she was not unaware that she was running short on time, and she capitulated to playing the Victor Emmanuel II card. For five years now, she'd been using her stays in Italy as opportunities to galvanize the Savoyard sovereign with occasional sexual encounters, which had certainly not been without practical advantages, but the death of her husband prompted her to focus on establishing a steadier and more profitable relationship.

We do not know whether the count was aware of his wife's relations with the king, but, though delicacy was not one of his specialties, Victor Emmanuel was fond of "Castillon,"[14] and must have done what he could to spare him humiliation. But now nothing prevented Virginia from aspiring to a completely respectable official relationship with the sovereign—himself a widower—especially as the transfer of the capital to Florence protected her from the toxic environment in Turin and allowed her greater freedom of movement. She knew that Rosa Vercellana—become Countess of Mirafiori and Fontanafredda—and the children that Victor Emmanuel had with her were as good as family members, whom he would not be giving up. But this longtime mistress presented no obstacle for Virginia. How could she ever fear comparison with a boorish and prematurely aged peasant girl?

In any case, the countess had no illusions about the king of Italy's gallantry. When she was still extremely young she'd endured his sexual rapacity, and his lack of education, elegance, and manners were common knowledge. His unquestioned qualities—his dynastic pride, courage, ambition, quick reflexes, cunning, and psychological intuition—had their counterparts: arrogance, boastfulness, and jealousy of anyone who might put him in the shade. His unfaltering loyalty to the Savoyard monarchy did not prevent Costanza d'Azeglio from deploring the pernicious influence of the "*triste entourage*"—including Rosina and her acolytes—who encouraged the sovereign to indulge his worst habits: "Sometimes the poor king has lucid intervals and demonstrates good sense, which surprises everyone present. It's a shame he is surrounded by such unworthy people!

The good Lord would be doing us a very great favor if he helped him overcome his shameful passions and inspired him with sentiments worthier of the noble condition to which he has raised him. Foreigners find him disconcerting. They visit and talk with him and feel sympathy for him, but then they see him at work and are overcome with disgust."[15] But that wasn't all. "He had a selfish character. In all the years I spent in Turin I never saw him perform a single act of generosity," the Count of Reiset would write in his memoirs. "At most, on occasion, he might be generous toward his lovers, at least while his burning, if ephemeral, passion was still in play... He was a material man."[16]

Seeing that his passion for her was far from ephemeral, Virginia was determined to wring everything she could out of him.

At the time of her love affair with Napoleon III, the young countess had to prove herself equal to the splendor of the Tuileries and its solemn etiquette; she had to learn to use elegant flattery to obtain a nod of assent from the emperor in all his evasive courtesy. With a provincial and vulgar sovereign like Victor Emmanuel, there was no need to display such delicacy. It was necessary to arm oneself instead with courage. His sexual exploits were common knowledge, as Carlo Dossi recalls without any euphemism in *Note azzurre*:

> Victor Emmanuel was one of the most illustrious fuckers of the age. The section for women in his annual budget was about one and a half million per year... He had a virile member so thick and long that it tore apart even the largest women... The court doctor had a great deal of trouble reaccommodating the uteruses he displaced... When he copulated, this earthly Jupiter roared like a lion. He liked women to come to him naked in little shoes and stockings, and he

> would smoke Havana cigars and ogle them with pleasure while they danced all around him. But sooner or later the venereal urge would take hold, and he fucked them all. One evening he wrote Filippi, the naturalist, a note saying: "Please send a stuffed lion to my bedroom tonight." And the lion was sent to the court, destined for God knows what mysteries.[17]

The king may have had no scruples about behaving brutally and breaking his promises, but Virginia was ready to pay him back in kind. They both knew what they wanted, and if he aspired to enjoy her favors, he would need to treat her quite differently from maids and prostitutes. He would also have to get used to the idea that he needed to compensate her as she saw fit. The Countess of Castiglione could not possibly be satisfied with a modest widow's pension, and it was of the essence that the king take responsibility for the education of the count's son.

Some dispute had broken out over a set of silver that Virginia found in her husband's house. Countess Mary Casanova said it was hers. She'd even gone so far as to write to Marquis Oldoini,[18] claiming to have sold the silver to the Count of Castiglione, who had never paid her for it. Unfortunately, Virginia was in no position to return it since she'd already taken it to the pawnshop and had no money to redeem it, so she told Victor Emmanuel that it was up to him to pay his secretary's debts. When, after saying he would see to it, the king was slow to keep his promise, leaving her at the mercy of a furious Casanova, Virginia threatened never to set foot in Pitti Palace again and soon emerged victorious. "As I mentioned, here in Florence I've had all kinds of headaches involving money matters that concern His Majesty as well as Casanova," she told her father:

It all ended in one of the most terrible scenes ever seen between sovereign and subject, male and female, in the pouring rain, between lightning and thunder, with a *bolt of lightning* that *killed* one of the king's horses while His Majesty, in an open carriage, ordered the aide-de-camp to ring and bang at my door, which I refused to open. Other people—ministers and favorites, attachés and servants—had flocked en masse upon hearing that I'd made up my mind never to set foot in the palace again (never imagining that he would come in person) until a certain sum had been disbursed, *promised* by *the word of the king*, which *I had given on his behalf*—including to Casanova, for several dirty deals. When *finally* the lightning sent Baby flying to the ground, shattered the windows, and blinded everybody present, the king burst in and said: "Kings have the privilege of having the doors even of convents opened, but I would never have entered, no matter the weather, if it weren't to deliver this package that I wished to bring you personally to make certain you receive it. Now I don't intend to disturb you any further, and despite the storm I'm off, but I remind you that today, July 28, is the anniversary of my father's death, and it was at his funeral that I saw you for the first time in La Spezia fifteen years ago,[19] and just now I have braved being *struck by lightning* to obey you." And away he went, leaving everyone stunned by his tone, foreboding disaster. And so I opened the package, just in time to reply by handing a note to one of the members of his entourage who was still here. The financial statement he found on his desk when he got back was accompanied by a simple note written in my hand:

Missing Casanova
xxx
xxx (two or three names)

> A full-blown drama, plotted by a huddle of *scoundrels*...The king has someone come fetch Baby and tells him: "Go to your mother and explain to her that this time I won't enter by force, but if she would like to come here I will be happy to receive her; otherwise I am ready to come as soon as she wishes to explain this *error*, which I am ready to correct. She is right, I was mistaken." So I saw him for dinner that same day, with great fanfare.[20]

A dark and stormy night with the king at her feet, the befuddled villains, the triumphal return to the palace: the scene was too exhilarating for Virginia to resist enriching it with a few extra details, but she must have given a fairly faithful account. And the sovereign remembered correctly: He had seen her for the first time on July 28, 1853, while on holiday in La Spezia with his family. The beauty of the sixteen-year-old Virginia was forever engraved in his memory. During that same summer, the Count of Castiglione was also conquered, with all the consequences we have already seen.

This nocturnal visit had taken even the countess by surprise. The "Pig King" had miraculously been replaced by a gallant knight who, in the name of ancient amorous bondage, submitted to his lady's will. For a moment Virginia had allowed herself to hope. The Middle Ages were, after all, back in fashion, and the role the sovereign was offering her was well suited to her repertoire.

The next day, when he read the full list of outstanding accounts, the king reassured her with a brief but eloquent message: "Countess Nicchia, it will be taken care of immediately. Best wishes, Victor Emmanuel." And he sent her a photograph complete with dedication: "The Miserable Master kisses the hands of dearest Nicchia, July 28, 1867."[21] Having once more verified her bargaining power,

Nicchia soon made it plain that the elegance she had in store for him was far too good for a boorish satyr like him. A telegram sent in September 1867 reads: "Madame Countess Verasis, this evening you left me truly breathless with emotion. I offer you all my heartfelt compliments and wish you *éternelle continuation* [all the best forever], V.E."[22]

Virginia's incessant and invariably insistent requests took various forms, and if they weren't answered instantly she was always ready to play the part of the persecuted victim: "Despite everything I prayed for everyone in that church in La Spezia where fifteen years ago we prayed together. But now it seems to me that I need to pray for myself."[23] Having failed in her efforts to obtain the appanage of Villa Annalena, which was the former residence of Murat and Louis Philippe's son (hadn't Rosa Vercellana been entitled to the Medician villa of La Petraia?), she was forced to settle for a twelve-room apartment across from Pitti Palace. But when it came to money, "compromise" was not in her vocabulary. Not content with an annual pension of 12,000 francs,[24] she relied on the king's well-informed financial advice to augment it. Judging by the few fragmentary rough drafts of the coded letters she sent to her lover,[25] "Countess Nicchia" did not beat around the bush: "Your Majesty merely needs to tell your minister of finance that you wish a large share to be set aside and that you will give the name later. In any case, however the deal is done, by whatever means, bring in Nicchia right away. Miserable Master must tell Digny clearly straight off. This is the only chance to fix my finances."[26]

Not only was Virginia being kept up to date on the initiatives of the kingdom's new minister of finance, Count Luigi Guglielmo Cambray-Digny; she also maintained friendly relations with Filippo

Antonio Gualterio, who became minister of the interior in October 1867 and, three months later, minister of the royal household.[27] Meanwhile, she still kept in touch with the Rothschilds and informed the king that the French bankers were looking for reliable Italian interlocutors. "The only chance to fix my finances" was the legal monopoly on tobacco, stipulated by Cambray-Digny on July 25, 1868, and granted to the Società generale di credito mobiliare italiano—a company with a consortium of private investors. This was a colossal financial operation, involving the advance of 180 million lire meant to fill the nation's coffers but also to fuel speculation. Victor Emmanuel himself probably stood to gain something, considering he'd followed "the process of the law" with "unusual attention." The two provisions of 1866–1867 concerning the liquidation of the assets of religious communities likewise presented golden opportunities for investors and the state's finances. So in October of 1868, the king asked Countess Nicchia "to initiate discussions with Rothschild," who was soon at the government's disposal regarding the question of ecclesiastical assets.[28]

If Virginia—no stranger to the ties binding politics and business in imperial France—found it completely natural that Victor Emmanuel's favorite engaged in what we would today call insider trading, the Piedmontese ruling class and the public were not of the same opinion. The immense debt resulting from the last two wars of independence and the organization of the unitary state aggravated an already chronic financial crisis, and corruption grew rife. A scandal over contracts for the construction of the central-southern railroad followed almost immediately after the passing of the Cambray-Digny law, and soon rumors circulated "that the sovereign was also involved in the corrupt and suspiciously profitable assignment of the tobacco monopoly to private individuals."[29] Though this was far from the first time a king was accused of making free and easy use of public money to foot his private expenses, it was, even so, not the best moment to make demands. Yet in early 1869, while Virginia was in Paris, where she continued to go quite frequently, the Miserable Master wrote to her via the loyal Castellengo: "3250 [Cambray-Digny] is in talks with 3342 [Rothschild] for the cession of 3362 [ecclesiastical properties], it's a question of several million." She deemed it best to return to Italy "and take part in the talks," since "an opportunity to make a fortune like this doesn't come around every day."[30] By the time Virginia got back to Florence, however, she was furious to discover the negotiations were too far along for her to profit by offering her services as a go-between.[31]

Her imperious demands, delays, and mood swings put Victor Emmanuel's patience to the test. Heedless of the sovereign's obligations—beset as he was by the difficult financial and political situation, as well as the Roman question—she always insisted on being received without delay and mistreated the attendants responsible for informing her of the king's decisions. Victor Emmanuel did his best to appease her: "The ordnance [officer] will have the good fortune to see her again before the Miserable Master. I will arrive in Turin on Tuesday… At the feet of Nicchia, the Miserable Master."[32]

But Virginia did not soften her tone:

> Your Majesty said that I have been *treating him badly*! Not true. If they give the king misinformation, or if the Miserable Master takes things the wrong way, it isn't my fault. It's the fault of not being able to talk to each other when necessary and of being forced to always

> be employing *third parties* who are unintelligent or malevolent, not to mention ignorant of our affairs, as has happened this time too, and so everything has gone to hell and Nicchia, as usual, is left beaten and betrayed. After sweating blood for months putting together something supposed to do everyone good without costing anyone anything . . .[33]

And since, once his lover's wishes had been granted, the king usually ignored any further complaints (but Virginia was impossible to satisfy), she insisted:

> I don't ask to see the Miserable Master because the king claims I have treated him badly and he doesn't want to hear from me, when in fact *he* is the one who is treating Nicchia badly, very badly, not wanting to hear what she has to *say afterward* . . . ! But I don't want to argue about being right, I prefer to stay in Florence and not see him and see him go by *without so much as a glance* . . . But I have an *urgent need* to let him know things that *I can't* or *do not want* to say to a Mazolino, so I beg the king to ordain *Spinola*[34] to come hear them tomorrow first thing . . .
>
> My respectful homages to the king. Nicchia.[35]

Then, in October 1869, after a few particularly contentious months, something momentous occurred. The king, fallen seriously ill and thought to be at death's door, was overcome by pangs of conscience and asked the priest who'd come to administer him the last rites to unite him in marriage with Vercellana. For the second time—ten years after the first—Virginia saw her plans to become a sovereign's *maîtresse en titre* go up in smoke, and having no other cards to play, she tried to salvage what she could. At the end of the year—the king had meanwhile recovered—she wrote to him:

> I don't know what to wish the Miserable Master that would please him, since Nicchia doesn't have the gift of giving it to him!
>
> I am glad to send the king my respectful greetings, affection, thanks for the year *1868*, '69 *has been bad* from the first day to the last, which I ended in Florence; I will start 1870 in La Spezia in hopes that it will be more favorable for us and afterward I will go "where destiny takes me." If you want me, send for me.[36]

Victor Emmanuel replied, simply yet explicitly, "I want it,"[37] but by this time Virginia knew she was mounting a rearguard action.

The year 1870 promised to be decisive for both Italian politics and the House of Savoy, and Victor Emmanuel no longer had time for Nicchia's relentless demands. To complete the process of Italian unification, Rome—as Cavour had preached ten years earlier to the Subalpine Parliament—needed to become the country's capital. It was only a matter of waiting for the right moment. Up to then the greatest obstacle had been the veto of Napoleon III, who, threatened by a serious domestic crisis, could not alienate the Catholics. But at the outbreak of the Franco-Prussian War, Eugène Rouher's reckless declaration three years earlier beneath the vaults of the Legislative Assembly—"Italy will never take possession of Rome"[38]—gave Victor Emmanuel good reason not to go to his former ally's aid. And so, on September 20, 1870, immediately following the French defeat at Sedan, General Cadorna entered Rome through the breach in Porta Pia—which the French troops had abandoned—thereby annexing the papal state to the kingdom of Italy. The year ended in glory for the House of Savoy, with the investiture of Amedeo d'Aosta as king of Spain.

Virginia's balance sheet was less brilliant. In mid-December—unable to see the Vile Master—she told him she intended to ask Amedeo to look after young Castiglione, orphaned by a father who had died in his service, and at the same time she reminded Victor Emmanuel of his responsibilities:

> I am at a loss as to which saint to pray to; the patron of patience is exhausted, and the one of resignation is not on my calendar... I therefore petition, once more, *the ancient* Miserable Master to let me see him in these Spanish days. I have things to tell him which I hope and trust will disburden the old king of both a mother and a son, which a new king has a *sacred duty* to protect... The old one might have eased the harsh necessity in which we find ourselves and received blessings and *louanges* [hymns of praise] instead of fearing reproaches. I won't pelt you with them, don't worry, I will spare you my laments about the past, and I will endeavor to lift all future remorse from your head. You're not in for a drubbing... But from one sly fox to another, there's no need for phrases, however lovely. Hugs from here. You should come right away and let's make peace forever, Nicchia.[39]

Once again Virginia shows herself astute enough to tweak her tone to the occasion, and capable of wielding all kinds of rhetorical devices to coax her lover into listening to her: challenges and threats, irony and accusation, statements of complicity and hints of renewed intimacy.

But their reconciliation was destined to be short-lived. She would not let up with her requests—commissions on under-the-table deals, career advancements for the insatiable Marquis Oldoini,[40] guarantees for her son's future—and she couldn't bear to hear the word *no*.

She was especially unwilling to resign herself to one of the king's refusals. When she asked him to stop the expropriation of the Oldoini properties along the coast in La Spezia, Victor Emmanuel explained that these were necessary to the ongoing expansion of the military port and that there was nothing he could do even if he wished to. In this particular case, it must be said, Virginia was not driven solely by personal interest. Of course she was profoundly attached to the landscapes of her childhood and above all to the Cappuccini hill—the site of the family villa—which sloped down to the sea in a riot of vineyards, olive trees, and wild roses; she'd waged war with her parents wherever they'd been forced to sell even a small parcel of it. But her dream was to turn it into a protected oasis for all the inhabitants of La Spezia,[41] and she could not accept that one of the most beautiful stretches of the Ligurian coast should be destroyed in the name of progress, or that the king of Italy would condone such a massacre. Her idea of protecting the national landscape was, however, too ahead of its time to be taken under consideration.[42]

So it was with a certain bitterness that, soon after this failure to intervene, she sized up her relationship with the sovereign. Her first error had been to put stock in the feelings of a king:

> The feelings of kings! They exist only *au passé* [in the past], and can be read in the tales that innocent children learn by heart and, fortunately, forget as they grow up. Kings have no feeling for anything

> or anyone when they are not guided by those who have moral or material interests *à les entretenir bouillant* [to keep them interested] using a thousand stratagems that Nicchia has spurned and so is losing the game!

When she wrote these lines, was she also thinking of Napoleon III's broken promises? Her *j'accuse,* directed at the king of Italy, recalls the Duke of Morny's denouncements of the emperor of the French: "He is distrustful and ungrateful and loves no one except those who servilely adulate and obey."[43] Despite her intentions, Virginia did not spare the king her "laments about the past" and made the reasons for her "recriminations" clear:

> I say that if I hadn't come to Italy for you, I would not have lost Italy and France, which I am now going to lose due to my long absence, as well as what few things I have, about which I care *a great deal* (I am not a king). Furthermore, I lost a good position in society there and never found one here, and now I don't even have the Cappuccini resources to draw on. All things you don't want to hear about anymore because you feel sorry about it all.

Though the Miserable Master tried to brush her off, Virginia would not let up. "I want to see him and I will see him . . . I have nothing to feel bad about, very little to *explain,* and a great deal to *complain* about, and I don't wish to do that except to his face." And if her lover refused to grant her that "*dernière entrevue*" [last audience], she threatened—as she'd threatened before, in her time with the emperor—to confront him during one of his public appearances.

"After all, if the king doesn't wish to see me, since I wish to see him, I will see him. As for when, and how, and where, I will seek an occasion, and I will find it."[44] It wasn't easy to get rid of Virginia.

Yet—also in 1870—she may well have been rewarded with responsibilities she could be proud of. It is quite probable that she was used as a go-between in the unofficial negotiations between the Italian government and the Vatican, seeking a solution to the Roman question. After the king's excommunication and the pope's threat to abandon the eternal city, official diplomacy was flanked by a series of parallel initiatives discreetly measuring the room to maneuver and attempting to reach an agreement. The Countess of Castiglione had the necessary qualifications—not only because she'd already acquitted herself well as a secret agent but because she'd known Cardinal Giacomo Antonelli[45] since childhood. (Antonelli, the pope's secretary of state, was an old friend of the Oldoini family, and the marquise in particular; indeed, Virginia, lost in fantasies toward the end of her life, would include him on a list of hypothetical fathers.[46]) Antonelli was the key figure in the difficult political negotiations between the Italian government and the papacy, and he was the one who made arrangements with Cadorna so that the influx of Piedmontese troops would result in only minimal bloodshed.[47] It seems clear that, in return for her good offices, the pontiff gave Virginia a gemstone bracelet decorated with an image of the papal tiara.[48] When, alone with her memories, she found her last refuge in celebrating her own legend, that precious piece of jewelry would allow her to claim that not only had she created Italy, she had also saved the papacy by persuading Pius IX to remain in Rome. She had certainly not forgotten her cousin Cavour's wish: a free Church in a free state.[49]

# The Siege
## 1870–1872

But Virginia had more than one string to her bow. For a while now she'd been harboring a whole host of reservations about Napoleon III's political decisions and wondered how long his reign could last. In a lengthy letter to Adolphe Thiers written in the early months of 1870, she was skeptical about kicking off the new regime "with the same old emperor, trying to pass him off as a different man," and she criticized the formation of a new government—the first of the so-called "liberal Empire"[1]—made up half of Bonapartist ministers and half of center-left ministers, none of whom were ever going to listen to a word the other side said.[2] Still, the dramatic events that followed the defeat of Sedan—the emperor imprisoned, the empress in flight, the collapse of the empire—gave her a shock. "I have arrived dead tired, agonized, filled with worries, anxieties, fears, regrets,"[3] she wrote from Florence in the aftermath of the catastrophe. She loved France. It was her second homeland. And she was afraid the conditions for peace imposed by Prussia would prove unsustainable. Not a minor detail: she was also afraid for her house in Passy, which had been left unattended, and asked Thiers for help—not knowing that her old friend would soon need hers.

On October 12, when Paris had been under siege for twenty days, the old opponent of the imperial regime—he was now seventy-three years old—arrived in Florence as the representative of a government of national defense formed immediately after the defeat at Sedan. His mission was to obtain the support of the Italian government and an honorable armistice with Prussia. As might have been predicted, with the Roman question now settled, France had returned to neutrality, but Thiers, now negotiating with Bismarck, was relying on the countess's help. Talks had broken down when the Iron Chancellor had told the French foreign minister, Jules Favre, that one of the conditions for peace was the cession of Alsace and Lorraine.[4] Already kept informed by the dispatches that Nigra sent from Tours (where the diplomatic corps had been transferred,[5] along with the government delegation chaired by Adolphe Crémieux), Virginia was soon brought up to speed by a "dismayed" Visconti Venosta:

> The two clashed over *terms* and forms—one as a winner, the other as a loser—and to these immense difficulties they added the worst difficulty of all: that of being incapable of understanding one another. They went their separate ways in the worst possible manner: one striking terror into the heart of Paris, advising the whole city be torched; the other giving a formal order to attack indiscriminately and invade from every side whatever happened, with no regard for anything in their way![6]

Favre's lack of diplomatic preparation would prompt Albert Sorel, who was present at the talks, to imagine a school of international studies designed to avoid just such disasters—the École libre de sciences politiques, which opened its doors in February 1872, under the aegis of Hippolyte Taine, Ernest Renan, and François Guizot. But Virginia needed no special lessons in diplomatic strategy. She could, as always, rely on several sources of information. For what was going on in the Prussian headquarters in Versailles, she went to her old friend Count Brassier de Saint-Simon, the ambassador of the North German Confederation in Florence,[7]; and she was on friendly terms with Bismarck, whom she'd met several times in Paris[8] and Baden. Thiers would never forget Virginia's lightning-quick negotiation. "I remember well," he wrote to her two years later, "how committed you showed yourself in Florence, in those dramatic days for our poor France."[9]

After arriving in Florence on October 12, Thiers wasted no time paying his Italian friend a visit. She had meanwhile already told Victor Emmanuel that, since she was "very close" with the French visitor's wife, she intended to take charge of him during his stay in the capital.[10] Probably using Brassier de Saint-Simon as a messenger, Virginia sent Bismarck—who was then in Versailles—a request for him to meet with Thiers.[11] Having become convinced that any form of support from the Italian government was out of the question, Thiers headed back to France on October 18, but not before giving Virginia a code[12] to communicate with him and introducing her to the lawyer Léon Cléry (in Florence, as was Antoine Sénard, as a representative of the government of national defense), whom he told: "Put yourself completely at the disposal of Madame de Castiglione. She is the most loyal, devoted, and intelligent friend we could hope to have, and no one is in a better position to help us."[13] On October 22 Virginia received a coded telegram from Thiers: "I have arrived safe and sound. I will go first with baggage and then without baggage. I need to know the details."[14]

On October 31 Thiers met with Bismarck in Versailles, as Virginia was immediately informed by a note from the ambassador.[15] And by then—as we can gather from a copy of a dispatch with the letterhead of the Agenzia Stefani telegraph service—Virginia already knew that Thiers had met "with Bismarck for three hours" on October 30 and would meet with him again the next day.[16]

The two statesmen were trying to reach an agreement suspending hostilities and so allowing the French to hold regular elections and establish a legitimate government, without whose approval Bismarck considered it impossible to countenance a peace treaty. The talks went on until November 6, when Thiers was called back to Paris. The government of national defense had opted for resistance to the death, rallying around the republican Gambetta, who had by now become minister of war as well as minister of the interior. Virginia heard the news from her informants and immediately wrote to Thiers, deploring this turn of events, "because everything could have been, and still could be, worked out; but these gentlemen don't want that, and what's more they're determined to break off all communication, jeopardizing any hope of remedying the situation."[17]

"These gentlemen" were the republicans, against whom she ranted and raved; their government was irresponsible and was going to lead France to disaster. Written at speed and in pencil, in a messier script even than usual, her indictment doesn't even excuse Thiers, who'd pushed her into mediation attempts that proved absolutely pointless. In her urgency to get out her thoughts the countess neglected (as was her custom when writing to respectable correspondents) to have the letter neatly rewritten by her son, but then, in the end, she decided not to send it.

> Egotism is the greatest of nature's gifts because it makes us impassible and indifferent to any misfortune, to good and evil alike. It renders us imperturbable. Unfortunately I don't possess it; on the other hand, though, I do possess an instinct for *pity*. I offer, as proof of this, the deep sorrow I feel over the horrors of the war and all the attempts I have made at *your request* to communicate with the enemy side (which I would call the more reasonable side, and indeed at this point the only one with which I will try, if I can, to continue negotiating, doing everything I can to help it, since at least it doesn't betray you or leave you in the lurch). Pardon me for these expressions, addressed to those of you who've been driven mad by hatred and been blinded by danger to the point that you're now incapable of seeing the depths of the abyss yawning beneath the feet of every Frenchman and indeed the whole future of France—to the point that you can't even see its current weakness, which some of you are trying to convert into a false point of honor. Some of the men in power are taking advantage of the situation to break off negotiations willy-nilly, and in my opinion they are abusing their power—but this is merely my personal opinion, and I am merely a woman! And women count for nothing when we have no chance of making ourselves useful, nor of acting, nor, above all, of *succeeding*. As my cousin Cavour said: What *matters* is success. Whoever succeeds always does well, whatever the means.[18]

But Thiers had by no means thrown in the towel, nor did Virginia stop weaving her web in the shadows. The right words had to be found in order to plead the case of the vanquished—words that would appeal to the victor's political foresight: "Prussia has indisputably proved the honor of its military, or rather the superiority of its generals," she wrote to Bismarck,

> and all men of war will recognize it; there is no need to add a new leaf to this sad crown of glory, but diplomatic merit, in the form of a peace treaty, ought to be yours and to bear your signature.
>
> Approval and satisfaction will be universal . . . The world, which you have commanded to stop in its tracks, will begin moving again, and have the opportunity to mourn its dead.
>
> There are enough of them to make all of Europe wear black.
>
> Don't give rise to *hatred*, an implacable hatred, which, joining forces with revenge, would kill any chance of affection or love . . .
>
> You will say that I am talking like the heroine of a novel—no, I speak for the statesman that you shall be. But on reflection you will see that the victor ought to be a *discreet friend*, not a *demanding father*. As long as your back is covered, and the enemies are defeated and lying face down, all's well—but after? *Woe* to the victor!

Virginia herself was the one speaking like a "statesman," showing the Prussian minister the course he should follow. Probably the countess had talked over the contents of this letter with Thiers, and certainly she was aware of Bismarck's own desire to reach a peace agreement, but still, how can we be anything but astonished by the ease with which she sets out to impart lessons in high diplomacy and political morality to one of the greatest statesmen of the age? Her ability to make the powerful listen did not always come by way of the boudoir. "Think deeply, maturely, calmly," she writes later in the same letter,

> and you will find my reasoning accurate and even advantageous to both sides . . . They lost, and are lost: but it's up to you to yield; you must show a valiant largesse. Permit me to give you this piece of advice, and consider it a matter just between us . . .

Once the private nature of her enterprise had been clarified (Italy, she said, had nothing to do with it), Virginia could present herself as an intermediary above party ties, relaying the requests of the Parisians, who since the end of September had been caught in the vise of the Prussian army:

> Take one last step for the Parisians, since it has been agreed to spare Paris itself,[19] and go so far as to let them live; in exchange, I assure you of the effective and diligent cooperation of defense officials in the formation of a regular and stable government with which you can sign a treaty and so guarantee peace, which will come about, sooner or later.
>
> I know that the military authorities demand equivalent compensation, and I am not unaware that these are the laws of war and that Prussia has a legal right to demand these laws be respected. But everyone will be grateful if you would make an exception—justified by such extraordinary and historically unanticipated circumstances—in the case of a city like Paris. I ask you only not to say no, and to tell me what the material, non-military, compensations would be, as well as the safeguards you would be willing to accept, so that I can make one last attempt at reconciliation.
>
> Your kindness is beyond praise and your keen intelligence beyond any need of proof. You deserve only gratitude, and you can count on gratitude from Thiers, on behalf of France.[20]

Virginia used very different language when she wrote to Count Ressmann, Nigra's colleague at the Italian legation:

> This is what I say—the one Bismarck honors by choosing her as his interlocutor, the one who arranged the *entrevues* with Thiers, and if he couldn't take advantage of it, tough luck. The groundwork was laid and it was all *still possible*... I could perhaps still *renouer* [pick up the thread] but I would have to do it myself... if, after Tours, Thiers wants to go back there. I said if Nigra *avait été à sa place il aurait osé et réussi* [had been in his place he would have been bold and succeeded]. Cavour always said: *réussissez, on aura toujours bien fait* [succeed, and you will always have done well].

Indeed, an armistice *was* still possible, and Virginia was counting on Nigra's powers of persuasion to "*redresser les cerveaux égarés* [bring bewildered brains back to their senses]"—but it all had to be done behind the scenes:

> I warn you that Bismarck does not want to allow the intrusion *des neutres ni pression quelconque* [of neutral parties nor any pressure whatsoever]. He will let himself be flayed by me, to whatever extent one *can* flay a soldier from whom one can't get even the top layer of flesh since, as luck would have it, he is bomb-proof.

The fact remained that "if this is a *game* the French are playing—*se donner les airs de refuser pour céder après* [pretending to refuse now only to yield later]—*il sera trop tard et il sera partie perdue sans revanche possible* [it will be too late and the game will be lost with no possibility of a rematch]."[21] Yet again the countess demonstrated that she knew what she was talking about.

But the fate of France was, to be truthful, not the only thing on her mind. Directly after the outbreak of the war, she'd summoned her fifteen-year-old son back to Florence; he had been studying at a boarding school in Neuilly[22] and "made his way home from Paris amidst fire and flame,"[23] but there hadn't been time to have her things packed and shipped, and she was worried about her furnishings, her silverware, and other precious items and documents. For a hoarder like Virginia, the idea of all this falling into foreign hands must have been particularly intolerable. Furthermore, for obvious reasons, she was very anxious to recover the box with her bank bonds, private correspondence, and business letters. Some of her most ticklish papers were in a folder compiled by her stockbroker at the Rothschild bank—including the speculations she had made on the eve of the war[24]—and another folder of documents to do with Dr. Arnal, who, as we have seen, tended to her gynecological problems.

The number of letters, dispatches, telegrams, and laissez-passers that Virginia sent between September and October 1870[25]—at the height of the Franco-Prussian conflict—is astonishing. She appealed, with amazing fluency—and a tenacity that refused to yield, even when she knew she was asking the impossible—to half of Europe's most powerful people, from the Queen of Prussia to the English royals and the Rothschilds.

Her race against time began with the fall of the empire and the establishment of an emergency government no longer able to ensure civil order. As early as August 14, after the first French defeats, Virginia, with Victor Emmanuel's backing, wrote to her friend Nigra:

"I didn't want to bother you, but I need to speak to the Italian minister, and soon—so says the Master—unable as I am to approach the Germans or anyone else." The countess demanded that the Italian legation garrison her house in Passy, "placing it under the official protection of the Italian flag against Prussian incursions, as well as having the French forces defend against any attack by mobs trying to enter, loot, or burn it." Her requests didn't stop there. Nigra was asked to alert the French civil and military authorities and report her case to the prefect of police. Her instructions were peremptory: "If it were in real danger, it would be necessary to have everything removed except wardrobes and unexceptional furniture and placed in the storage rooms at the embassy and at the Rothschilds', where it is safer, but if then, as seems likely from here, their house is also in danger, then have all the crates sent to me in Turin."[26]

Three days later Nigra informs her that all of her orders have been carried out, but he observes, not without irony:

> So far it is allowable to hope that the plebs' shameful attempts will not throw the city into chaos. When it comes to bombs, the protections are the same for all and sundry, and the prefecture doesn't have any special ones for sale. There can, anyway, be no other protection than luck, and I wish no. 51 rue Nicolo, as well as its beautiful owner, the very best of it from the bottom of my heart.[27]

And on August 21, knowing her suspiciousness, Nigra sent her the reply from the prefect of police to "convince her" that he had not only "promised but acted on his promise." As for the eventualities feared by the "gracious countess," that of being robbed by the French was unlikely since "a large portion of the Parisian rabble had been conscripted and was therefore outside the city walls." And the second—looting by the enemy—was to be ruled out due to the "conduct of the Prussians in the conquered départements. They aspire too much to the title of 'heroes of civilization' to come torch and sack Paris and so go home with a reputation as murderers."[28] But Virginia was still not convinced. In the meantime, she decided to have all her personal effects, furniture, fittings, paintings, and silver sent to Italy. On September 8, as the Prussian army surrounded Paris and crossing France became impossible—"What a time! But now the moment has come to act, not talk"—she wrote to Thiers to obtain special authorization for the shipment of her crates as well as for police surveillance of her house in Passy.[29] Two days later, unable to reach Nigra (who'd gone with the government to Tours, where "he was intent on concealing the cabinet's reservations with the affability of his speeches"[30]), she sent a threatening letter to the Italian legation, which was guilty of not having immediately sent her the crates she'd arranged to store at the home of a police officer, her neighbor in Passy, who had subsequently vanished without a trace: "Please, investigate, find out and tell me what has become of him and of the keys, since the Italian Legation cannot leave the house of an Italian subject thus abandoned *à la merci du premier passant* [at the mercy of the first comer]." The legation officials still had time to get the crates safely to the storage room, and even if, understandably, they had "a great many other things to do," they could not have "the minister's [Nigra's] sin on their conscience" (that is, the sin of not notifying her in time). "You all thought I was *crazy* then because I wanted to *déménager* [clear out all my things]," she said indignantly, "and now here you all are acting like I'm a *criminal* for having left all my son's possessions so terribly exposed to the bombs and especially to the routine thievery of times like these—and to the needs of the government of the people, who, seeing a house filled with everything they require, will move in and make it their own." Let it be said to Nigra, and to every other minister, "friend or foe": This was an unacceptable attitude to take toward a woman and a boy. A detailed list followed: After bricking up the street windows of the house in Passy, retrieve the crates from the cellar, seal the front door, raise the Italian flag, report the residence to the ministry of foreign affairs as the dwelling place of an Italian subject and to the ministry of police as uninhabited.

While Paris was still besieged, and the French government—some of whose members remained in the capital while others took refuge first in Tours and, later, Bordeaux—was divided between supporters of peace and supporters of fighting to the death, and while the Prussians continued to prevail on the battlefields, Virginia didn't scruple to ask Thiers yet again—with greater tact and different arguments, naturally—to take care of her private problems.

> With all the great misfortunes currently befalling France, this is no time to tell you about all my little miseries, but I am familiar enough with the quickness of your wit to dare, without scruple or fear, to distract you from them for just a little while; I therefore ask you first to listen to what I say and then to help me obtain what I am asking for: protection.

If the Italian legation was foolish enough not to have dealings with the provisional government,[31] her house would become a target for French looters. But she dared to "ask for the support of the republic":

> I am merely a woman, in a private position; I am quite well known in France, where, due to certain family misfortunes that forced me to leave my country, I have lived for fifteen years—other than returning once a year to visit my parents. I could even have obtained French citizenship, but I haven't because of my son, who must remain Italian though he was educated in Paris, where he was attending boarding school until a month ago.

Clearly her reputation as a spy and a lover of Napoleon III's also exposed her to the republicans' reprisals, but with her usual ease Virginia revises the past to suit the needs of the present, claiming to have nothing to do with politics and to be interested in them only "because I happened to be present at some discussions between close friends." She elegantly glosses over her relationship with the emperor (of which Thiers cannot have been ignorant): "When I was young and beautiful I was at the Tuileries court but now it is water under the bridge, for ten years now I have lived the life of a recluse." And she reminds the French republicans that "we are in a free country: if a foreigner is pleased to frequent houses where she is welcomed with open arms, if she is held in high esteem by courts and royal families, she certainly can't be blamed! Consider my acquaintance with the exiled French princes."

Finally, tired of justifying herself, Virginia dons a cloak of pride. She would conduct herself with "the disgraced dynasty" as she had with the Orléans, and if she happened to meet members of the imperial family in private, she was certainly not going to snub them: "My character cannot tolerate *about-faces* like that—the result of small-minded sentiments and pretended shame. I don't want anything from anyone, and I will behave toward those who have been kind to me according to the dictates of courtesy and good manners."[32] A quite lovely explosion of pride—apart from the dubious declaration that she didn't want anything from anyone. Thiers's return to the scene would soon prove her wrong.

On January 26, Favre gave in and signed the armistice with Prussia, again proving that he was a terrible negotiator; the elections of February 8 confirmed the victory of the supporters of peace, and on February 17 Thiers was appointed head of the executive power—that is, of the state and the government. In no way daunted by the whirlwind of events that would determine the fate of France—or by the burden of responsibility fallen on the shoulders of her old friend—Virginia didn't hesitate to repeat her requests, politely reminding Thiers of all she had done for him. And for dramatic effect, she had no qualms about calling her now sixteen-year-old son a "child":

> Now that you are king, I must turn to you for a favor! But I am sure that your first favor will be for an old friend like me, whose feelings for you, your intelligence, and your family have been inalterable—no matter what everyone else said. I know your kind feelings for me and feel entitled to count on your protection, which I must invoke as I prepare to leave for Paris, which apparently is not yet prudent or easy for a woman alone with a child!

Meanwhile, having managed to get only one of her treasure chests shipped to Turin, "the most beautiful and most amiable countess" (as Thiers called her) asked him for a blank laissez-passer—like the one she'd obtained from the Prussians—so that as soon as the war was over she could send a trusted envoy to keep an eye on her interests. In fact, Virginia feared that the conditions of peace—signed at Versailles on February 26, with the cession of Alsace and Lorraine and an indemnity of five billion francs to be paid to Germany over the course of five years—would sow discontent in the capital, which was already alarmed by the relocation of the government and the National Assembly to Versailles. "It is up to you alone," she wrote to her friend, "to calm the troubled minds of Paris, helping them bear their sorrows in the salutary quiet of peace: there is no resignation more honorable."[33]

Once again, Virginia was right. On March 18 Paris rose up, disavowing the government, suppressing parliament, and inaugurating the Commune. Two months later Thiers resorted to force and ordered Marshal MacMahon to march on the capital, and, on May 28, the Commune ended in a terrible bloodbath. Virginia didn't even wait for Thiers to be elected president of the Third French Republic before appealing to him again. Rather than begin where she'd left off, however, she sought a means to congratulate her friend for the return to order—albeit an order achieved quite ruthlessly, at the cost of the lives of tens of thousands of citizens. With great tact, Virginia focused her flattery on the painful choices that her friend had been forced to make despite himself:

> My dear Viceroy,
>
> Should one congratulate you, blame you, admire you, or rather pity you?
>
> In truth I do not know where to begin in reminding you of my troubles in the tumult of your woes, your glories, your personal losses and public sorrows, and after your triumph. To better express my thoughts, I certainly cannot write better than you speak, and *I won't even attempt to console you.*

She was keen to establish her influence over Thiers and went on to recommend two people close to her heart. The first was Lao Bentivoglio. (Fifteen years earlier, the two had a fling that, for him, would be an "eternal, ineffable, powerful memory."[34]) Having put "the follies of youth" behind him, Bentivoglio, a Florentine related to the Poniatowskis, had gone to work as a diplomat under Napoleon III and made a modest career for himself in the Middle East. But now, two years after his retirement, he'd been dismissed from his position as consul general of France in Smyrna with no new posting in sight. Bentivoglio had no personal wealth and a wife and three sons to support. He had gone to his cousin Giuseppe Poniatowski and Virginia for help.[35] But the prince had left Paris when the empire fell. Only the protean Nicchia was in a position to intercede with the new government, and she acted without delay.

Calling Thiers's attention to the Bentivoglio case, Virginia did not limit herself to invoking the count's "selfless service" "in the most inhospitable lands" and "the misery and desolation" to which his unjust dismissal has condemned an entire family; with her usual acumen, she also brings up a subject to which the *petit président* could not be insensitive. Didn't the fate that loomed over Bentivoglio's children risk turning them into them rebels? "These innocent children, who are French and will no longer be able to either serve their country or return to Italy, since from their father they will certainly have inherited a French heart," were destined to come of age under the banners of bitterness and resentment. How could anyone be surprised if—"ruined, lost, uprooted, adrift, and alone"—they became "criminals like the ones who burned Paris and caused its ruin?" Virginia apparently had no doubt that the spirit of revolution was endemic in French society and that there were hard times ahead for the Third Republic. Seeing that Thiers's government had adopted "the banner of law and order," she took the liberty of appealing to her friend's "lively intelligence and humanity" to ask him "to ensure that Count Bentivoglio remains in his position or is transferred to an equivalent one."[36]

The other recommendation was of a more delicate nature: It concerned a man who'd held an important position under the empire. Virginia submitted the case of Baron Arthur-Léon Imbert de Saint Amand to Thiers's "personal goodwill." Saint-Amand was a writer and career diplomat who, showing "the unusual merit of wishing to remain, at first, loyal to his old protectors," had tendered his resignation—a risky decision given that, "though he had neither fortune nor career," the young gentleman was responsible for his mother and sister. Virginia therefore asked Thiers to ignore his "honorable and commendable error"[37] and reinstate the shortsighted diplomat. Was this request—made without the knowledge of the person in question—meant to heal a breach with a man whose heart she had broken?

Their affair, begun in the early days of 1869, had been short-lived, but it had profoundly affected the thirty-five-year-old writer. Before opening her arms to him, she delighted in giving him the usual icy welcome.

> It was that first day I crossed the threshold and entered your house—that house where I suffered so much... I entered trembling... You addressed me coldly: "What have you come here for?" But behind your indifference I could sense a hidden satisfaction. Then, giving me the portrait I now cover with kisses, you said, "This is for you"... And you bade me sit down beside you... And then, and then...

> tears blind my eyes . . . Oh! Your voice, your voice, how sweet it was when, as you held me close to your heart, you said "Be calm, be calm." Oh, I would shed blood, give up my whole life if necessary, to experience such a moment again!

In fact, Saint-Amand was too proud to put up with the treatment Virginia inflicted on her lovers. For a few sporadic moments of bliss—"you were so good, so kind last night"—one had to submit to her whims, suffer her betrayals, "abdicate one's own will and give up being oneself." On the other hand, although "bad, cruel, terrible," Virginia was at least unequivocal: "The thing that gives me the most joy in the world is my freedom . . . As for the hostile feelings that lurk beneath the disappointment caused by my attachment to another, they can do me no harm, for I brush them aside, just as I brush aside your reproaches."[38] Saint-Amand could not come to terms with such a state of affairs and eventually put an end to the relationship, but she, as always, saw no reason for a definitive break, preferring to keep all her ex-lovers securely tied to her chariot. In order to reel the unhappy Saint-Amand in again, she merely had to remind him of her own unhappiness. "Since you said you didn't want to see me anymore," she wrote in March 1869, "I have been staying away from you, depriving myself of my only pleasure, if I can call such an unusual and melancholic diversion, like the saddest music, pleasure."[39] And so it was as the "Muse of Melancholy" that he would celebrate her years later, in nostalgic poems.[40] Their relations were interrupted by the Franco-Prussian War and Virginia's return to Italy, but then, when she learned of the dire straits in which her old friend found himself, the ever-unpredictable countess had rushed to his defense. Prompted by a sincere impulse to help, her *beau geste* was also a way of getting back in contact with Saint-Amand and ensuring his gratitude, but for this, of course, he would need to be made aware of what she'd done. Accordingly, Virginia saw fit to send him her letter to Thiers, leaving him free to decide whether to forward it to its intended recipient. If Saint-Amand preferred not to make use of her services, he was asked to return the letter to Virginia "*without reproaches* or a shadow of *regret*"; she had only wished to give proof of her friendship by doing him a favor "without it being asked of her."[41] We do not know whether it was thanks to her recommendation[42] that Saint-Amand kept his job at the ministry, but Virginia's arrow certainly hit its mark and obtained the response she desired:

> He who loved you so dearly, who still loves you, who will never forget you, felt profound emotion at seeing your much-loved handwriting again. When the whole world had abandoned him, you remembered him. Bless you . . . I dare not hope ever to see you again. Perhaps you will refuse to grant me that bliss. Thy will be done! In any event I shall always love you . . . always.[43]

Yet when the opportunity arose to memorialize his admiration for Virginia in his writings about the court during the Second Empire, Saint-Amand painted a very brief, unsympathetic portrait, which highlighted only her beauty.[44] Pangs of love had given way to resentment. Virginia's *beau geste* left no trace.

# Mother and Daughter

Paris getting back to normal; the wish to finally be reunited with "[her] things";[1] the friendship of Thiers and the Rothschilds; the return of the Orléans family, whom she'd known for so long; curiosity about the rapidly evolving political situation—all of these were reasons for Virginia to move back to France. Her relationship with Victor Emmanuel had failed to produce the desired results, and it was increasingly difficult for her to find a receptive ear among the representatives of the Italian government. She was at home in Turin and Florence, but Roman society (in late January 1871, the court had moved there from Florence) was terra incognita. And the death of her mother would distance her from her past yet more.

For years, Marquise Oldoini's health had been failing. In January 1872, the situation took a definitive turn for the worse. Warned by Carlo Poniatowski that the end was near,[2] Virginia—who had been on the outs with her mother for some time—arrived in La Spezia with her son and never left her bedside. On February 6, a telegram from Giorgio informed his grandfather, who was in Lisbon, where he had been in charge of the Italian legation since 1868, that the marquise was asking to see him.[3] In reality, Isabella was in a state of confusion and nervous agitation, and no longer herself. On March 9, it would be her daughter who closed her eyelids.

The time had come for Virginia to come to grips with this antagonist, from whom she had tried to distance herself in every way possible ever since she was a teenager. Not only had her mother been guilty of excessive love—a love that involved delegating the task of being happy to her daughter—she'd had the unforgivable misfortune to be able to read her daughter like a book, which was intolerable for someone like Virginia, who made secrecy her watchword. Paradoxically, though, what drove the two women apart were their similarities.

From Isabella, Virginia inherited her intelligence, her unconventional ways of thinking, her caustic tongue, and her spirited independence, but she put these qualities to very different uses. Her mother had mustered them to deal courageously and equanimously with a life very unlike the one she'd hoped for: a vain and neurotic husband; a troubled family; an increasingly compromised financial situation. Having left the follies of youth behind her, she shouldered her responsibilities without ever giving up a sort of genteel hedonism, and without ever ceasing to worry about her loved ones. She had lived, in other words, in a manner her daughter had no intention of emulating. Armed with an unshakable faith in her own beauty and intellectual superiority, Virginia refused to let herself be trapped, like her mother, by duties, compromises, and sacrifices. She longed to be free to give her existence whatever shape suited her best. And knowing full well that she harbored ambitions irreconcilable with the spirit of sacrifice imposed on women by bourgeois morality, she chose to rely on her wits. Unlike Isabella, she was careful not to expose herself to criticism by saying what she thought or acting familiar or speaking Florentine dialect in public, and only with Poniatowski did she enjoy the luxury of being herself. Her father, as we have seen, offered Virginia a model of dissimulation, with his studied elegance and ceremonious, diplomatic tongue. Virginia sized up situations and fashioned whatever mask she thought would work best. The impressions she made might vary, but her aim was always the same: to awaken admiration, and to dominate so as not to be dominated. The first encumbering bond she severed without hesitation was her bond with her mother.

Mother and daughter were also entirely different in their way of confronting situations that were beyond repair. The disappointments and defeats of Virginia's life led her to take refuge in memory; her mother, by contrast, was able to resist the creeping darkness of the present. She was pained by her daughter's behavior and her son-in-law's death, and she worried about her grandson, at the mercy of his mother's eccentricities; about her beloved brother Sandro, impoverished by gambling debts; about her faraway husband, always restless and in need of more and more psychological support. But money problems, illnesses, and sorrows did not alter her character, cloud her clarity of judgment, or compromise her generosity. She played the arduous role of matriarch to the end, trying to hold on to the reins of her runaway family. And when she couldn't change the course of events, she found the right words to say to everyone.

When she sent New Year's greetings to her grandson, who'd lost his father only six months earlier, Isabella steeled herself and, though her own heart was broken, urged him to acceptance: "As for you my child, this last year was the cruelest of them all, no worse misfortune could have befallen you than losing your beloved father. I hope that God will make it up to you in future and take you under his wing." And knowing full well how harsh his mother was with him, she reminded him that, far away as they were, he was always dearly loved by his grandparents.[4]

A long-standing and ever-present concern was her husband's nervous instability and pathological restlessness. She knew how to placate him and, like her daughter, did what she could to indulge his whims, trying to help when he became obsessed with reassignment or leaves of absence. But when, after moving heaven and earth to obtain the Lisbon embassy, the marquis said he wished to return to La Spezia, Isabella forced him to face facts. She knew that her days were numbered, and she wanted to protect him from himself. Six months before her death, she was still begging him not to leave his "noble" state for the state of misery in which she found herself: "As long as you can, you should try to enjoy a comfortable and peaceful life. I don't mean to go on at you, but you know I have ten and owe twenty, so you can imagine how it is."[5] Sparing loved ones her own suffering was a consolation she had no wish to relinquish.

Marquis Oldoini took his wife's advice to heart—so much to heart, in fact, that he felt himself under no obligation to attend her funeral. But his selfishness didn't keep him from mourning her sincerely. "Your poor mother, who loved us so much!" he wrote to his daughter. "Now she is your guardian angel in heaven ... You may find it hard to credit how much, despite our separate lives, I miss her and feel abandoned."[6]

Of course her mother's death made its mark on Virginia too. But how? Was it respect for propriety or a sincere feeling of devotion that led her to rush to the marquise's bedside at the end of her life? Her mother's mental condition had not allowed for a reconciliation, but it had brought Virginia face-to-face with what she feared most:

the loss of self-control and the threat of dementia that hung over her family's head. "It is better for her to die, for the world and for herself; even if she were to recover, she would always be very, very ill," she wrote to Carlo Poniatowski. Her death "stunned" her and represented a loss for which, so she claimed, only God could console her.[7] She would play her part from start to finish—strewing the marquise's coffin with flowers, organizing a beautiful funeral ceremony, observing the strictest rules of mourning, and politely receiving the condolences of relatives and friends.

Whether she felt remorse for the pain she'd inflicted on her mother is a question not worth asking; she never showed any consideration for the people closest to her. But Isabella's death complicated her relationship with her father. Without the marquise as mediator, Virginia was forced to deal with Marquis Oldoini's selfishness, stubbornness, and nervousness—and vice versa. And since they both needed money, the properties in La Spezia were fated to become their first battleground.[8] For the moment, though, Virginia's primary objective was to settle back in Paris.

# The Third Republic

## 1872–1879

Early in the summer of 1872—when after an absence of almost three years Virginia returned to Paris—the French capital had just emerged from one of the most terrible periods in its history. The defeat at Sedan, as Benedetto Croce wrote, "seemed a new *finis Romae*."[1] The disastrous Treaty of Versailles, which entailed the loss of Alsace and Lorraine; the tragic conclusion of the Paris Commune; and, last but not least, the war debt of five billion francs to be paid over five years, imperiled the stability of the Third Republic and the new constitutional framework that France had erected at the end of the Second Empire. The blackened skeletons of the Tuileries Palace and the many buildings torched by the Communards still stood as daily reminders of the civil war that had just taken place. Yet despite political instability, economic recession, and social tensions, all of Paris's old attractions remained intact, and the city continued to lay down the law in matters of taste, arts, and fashion. This was where Virginia was determined to return, regaining the place she deserved.

At last she was reunited with all the furnishings, fittings, and precious objects for which she'd moved heaven and earth, but she no longer had the house in Passy—the lease had expired—and she was forced to put everything in storage in far-flung places. While she cast around for an apartment that suited her many needs, she took up residence in two furnished rooms in the Hôtel de l'Alma after contriving to stow her son with the Rothschilds on rue Laffitte. Then—as she wrote to her father—after two terrible summers spent "sweating it out in the sun of Italian cities busy with matters of all kinds," she headed for Dieppe.[2] In September, she had to go to Rome to contest the expropriations looming over the La Spezia properties, but she returned to France immediately afterward, declining her father's invitation to join him in Lisbon: "For the time being, I can't come, so many boring affairs to see to." Besides, she was still in deep mourning for her mother and didn't want to make an appearance in her "black and ugly woolen dress like the Cinderella of the legation." Even if she was reduced to showing off "remnants," "the daughter of Italy" wished them to be "beautiful and clean and not so lugubrious."[3]

The many boring affairs that awaited her in Paris were, as always, money problems. So far she'd managed not to pay back Charles Laffitte for the loans of a decade earlier. But now the banker, in dire financial straits, was threatening to take her to court. And Virginia could not count on any help from Poniatowski, for whose sake she'd incurred the debt in the first place. He'd settled in London after the fall of the empire, his health was not good, and he found himself in circumstances more reduced than ever, now that he only had his earnings as a musician.

It wasn't the first time the two former business partners had locked horns like this. In the past, outraged by Il Vecio's irresponsibility, Virginia had turned to Martelli,[4] a man they both trusted, to scold the prince for his bad behavior and ask for guarantees to protect her interests. Alarmed, Poniatowski had tried to soothe her by solemnly promising to live on his senatorial salary, to stop contracting debts, and to trust her in all things. How could she doubt, he wrote, his boundless confidence and immense gratitude? Appealing to their erotic complicity, he tried to touch her heart ("I've been through two weeks of hell. I need to see my dearest Nicchia[5]), asking her to send him a "little kiss" as a token of peace. "I looked for it everywhere in the letter but I didn't find it, I am sending 1,100 to Lisetta."[6]

Though after ten years the problem of the debt she had contracted on Poniatowski's behalf remained unresolved, the relationship between the countess and the prince had changed profoundly. Virginia had been wondering about the nature of his feelings ever since, in her solitude on a Turin hillside, she'd chosen him as her privileged confidant and asked: "What part, I would like to know, is left for me?" But even if she feared that one day Il Vecio would repay her devotion with "forgetfulness, indifference, and abandonment," she never missed a chance to tell him that, while others might turn their backs, "Nicchia alone would remain his forever, in saecula saeculorum."[7]

And in 1865—appealing to the emperor and to Count Baciocchi and Prince Napoleon as mediators—Virginia had gotten herself involved in another complicated financial venture meant to save the Poniatowski clan from financial catastrophe. Implicated in legal disputes after the death of the Duke of Morny, Giuseppe's son, Stanisław, was accused of having received illicit sums "passed from hand to hand" originating with his wife's natural father. "There is no one but Nicchia, more powerful than anyone and capable of anything," she extolled herself, and "with her pockets lined with sedatives" she fought to keep "the future from being pulled out from beneath the feet of father and son alike"—firm in her belief that "when all is said and done we will always stand together and will send all these intruders back down to hell."[8]

Still, the prince's frivolity, unreliability, and selfishness had begun to alienate Virginia, and by the late 1860s the ties that bound them had frayed. But it was not until Virginia asked him for money to repay Laffitte so as not to have to say in court that she'd acted as his frontman that Il Vecio at last took off his mask and revealed the full extent of his cynicism, rebuking her with less than "princely" language: Virginia could tell the judges whatever she liked, but even if he was the one who profited from Laffitte's loan, she was the owner of the debt. "If you turn on me I will tell the truth because I have nothing to lose, but I don't see what advantage you will gain, other than showing your ass at the window. A lovely ass it is, and certainly everyone will enjoy looking at it."[9]

Offensive and brutal as this was, the prince's behavior should have come as no surprise. It was certainly not news that Il Vecio lacked respect for her,[10] and the whole Poniatowski family had always exploited her without a word of thanks. Once, while discussing a deal that involved the Rothschild bank, Il Vecio's wife had no qualms about telling her to "keep the passion the old baron has for you burning; show him that beautiful 'little thing,' but forbid him to touch it."[11] Still, Virginia persisted in preferring the Poniatowski clan to her own, and she showed all of them boundless indulgence. We will never know whether this time, too, she would have ended up forgiving the incorrigible "Beppino," because on July 4, 1873, in London, the prince's adventurous life came to an end.

Later, Virginia would become convinced that he was the one who'd brought about her family's ruin, but just then she didn't waste time thinking about the past. Nor did she shed any tears for Napoleon III, who'd preceded Poniatowski to the grave a few months earlier. Or for the glories of the Second Empire of which she would soon become a symbol.[12] Once more she immersed herself in her great passion: politics. After creating Italy, saving the papacy, and laying the foundations of a Franco-Prussian concord, the time had come to work to free France from the republican imposture and restore it to its legitimate sovereigns.

It was not a far-fetched idea. The parliamentary majority after the elections of February 1871 was royalist and had failed to restore the monarchy only because of the rival dynasties. The legitimist pretender, the Count of Chambord—Charles X's nephew—spurned the tricolor flag stained by Louis XVI's blood and demanded a return to the white banner of the Bourbons. The Duke of Aumale, Louis Philippe's fourth-born son, was the Orléanist candidate, and though supported by the right wing and the centrists, he was disliked by the opposing camp. Furthermore, out of respect for law and the will of the people, he was squeamish at the prospect of being appointed president of the republic.

Virginia had been on friendly—and perhaps more than friendly—terms with the Duke of Aumale ever since, in her triumphant twenties, she had visited him at Twickenham, and when the Second Empire collapsed she hoped to see him become leader of France. Henri d'Orléans had all the qualities necessary for success—love of country, military valor, liberal convictions, respect for institutions—but he lacked determination. After the revocation of his exile and the restitution of his assets, being elected a deputy in the National

Assembly and reinstated in the rank of division general, he had no desire to leap into the political fray or accept the compromises that would entail. Rather than make history, the Duke of Aumale preferred to study it—conjuring up the deeds of his ancestors, collecting incunabula, manuscripts on parchment, valuable volumes, paintings, statues, miniatures, all the while transforming his Château de Chantilly into an extraordinary museum.

Virginia felt sincere admiration for him and for a long time she tried—with the support of her friend Estancelin[13]—to overcome his reluctance, urging him to take advantage of the Third Republic's atmosphere of political uncertainty to put the Orléans back in charge.

Perfectly at her ease in the role of mentor, Virginia first tried to shake the duke from his torpor. "France must be conquered," she wrote in a combative tone, "and no one is better equipped to conquer it than you."[14] And so she coaxed him out into the open. "What are you waiting for? Let them see who you are, and dictate your conditions!"[15]

Aumale was not insensitive to her interest: "Madame, I was very touched by your sympathy, I remember you fondly and am profoundly grateful to you," he gallantly replied. "I would have liked—I would still like—to thank you in person, and if I knew you were in Paris I would certainly try to come pay you a visit."[16]

But while waiting for this visit, at which she planned to display the full extent of her eloquence, Virginia confided her disappointment to Estancelin. "Brave on battlefields and brave in life, how can a prince show himself so irresolute before the offices of government?"[17] And how was she supposed to ignore the fact that, as time wore on, Aumale, surrounded by his "foolish" advisors, seemed increasingly deaf to her pleas? When will he stop seeing Estancelin as "a man devoted to women, hunting, and witticisms" and her as "a woman devoted to men and an eccentric"?[18] Written in the form of a questionnaire during the peace negotiations, a note from the countess to the general nicely illustrates how well the two old accomplices got along: "Where are you? / What are you doing? / What will you be doing? / What do you want on your side? / What do we want on mine? . . . What would you like us to do?"[19]

The worst of it was that the duke didn't ask her to come to Chantilly and took his time before paying the visit he had promised. It is true that Virginia, who was ill again, could not invite him to dinner, but—she joked to Estancelin—"you don't *have* to have dinner to see each other; you can even talk in a bedroom. Visiting the sick is the duty of kings and the right of princes who have reigned or are destined to govern." And she concluded:

> Let him come to class, then, in this sickroom, and with someone else if he wishes. Etiquette will be scrupulously observed. Tell him all this, and if he ever makes up his mind, let me know *the* day he will come, this lamb that I'm not going to make a meal of . . .[20]

Finally, the visit took place, but as Virginia reported to Estancelin soon after, it left her bitter. Upright and tall, dressed in mourning for the death of his wife, "ceremonious and prim," Aumale sat down in a chair beside the invalid's bed and placed his hat on his knees, never even removing his pearl-gray gloves. His cold detachment had given Virginia—pale, in pain, without makeup—a sense of how much time had passed since their first encounter, but she had screwed up her courage, and for two hours she tried to sound out the duke's political intentions. "He spoke of nothing except *politics*, *Gambetta*, *king*. The latter is indeed the title to which he aspires, but he would like to achieve it by being *elected*; heed my female intuition."[21] As often happened, Virginia turned out to be right: A prisoner of the lofty idea he had of himself, of his family history, and of the incompatibility between liberal principles and his secret ambitions, the duke lost his chance. The disappointment was bitter, but the stalwart conspirator already had another Orléans in her pocket (a consolation for the affront of those pearl-gray gloves, which it would take her a long time to put behind her).

Estancelin introduced her to the man in question. Young, chivalrous, and handsome, Robert d'Orléans, Duke of Chartres, had everything going for him. In the ranks of the Sardinian army, he'd taken part in the second war of independence, distinguishing himself at Palestro, and when war broke out with Prussia he'd asked Napoleon III to be allowed to fight in the French army. Virginia had personally pleaded his case, to no avail, writing a high-spirited appeal to the emperor: "Come, sire, allow a French royal to die as a soldier, and you will have one rival less."[22] But Chartres had not given up his quest. After the defeat at Sedan he'd covered himself with glory by fighting in the ranks of the French army under the pseudonym of Charles le Fort and, at the end of the war, he was still in the service of the Third Republic. Three years younger than Virginia, he was a happily married man, which did not prevent him from having a long affair with her.[23]

Chartres was uninterested in defending the Orléanist cause in the political arena, adhering entirely to the decisions of his older brother, the Count of Paris, but he was more than ready to give Virginia full satisfaction in the sexual domain. "I felt an exhilaration that almost frightened me,"[24] he wrote to her after their first night of lovemaking, and after that first night, he never stopped desiring her. "If you will allow me to come ... kiss your beautiful hands for a moment, write to me at my address in Paris ... and I will answer to the adage *Quando, Come, Dove* [When, How, Where]."[25] Over the years they would see each other many times, and despite the joking tone they both used with each other—she nicknamed him "Gianduya," and he called her "Tante" because of her connection to the Duke of Aumale—their relationship would not be free from jealousy. As we will see, it was Virginia's relationship with Costantino Nigra that made Chartres go berserk, but once this crisis had passed, Auntie and Nephew would continue commemorating their shared past every thirteenth of the month: "Goodbye balcony and moonlit night and intoxicated evenings ... Save a little love for your nephew, who is always thinking of you,"[26] he wrote to her during one of his many trips. And she replied: "To write to you I have waited until midnight, the hour of love, the hour, perhaps, of royal and military convoys, in the belief, in the hope ... that when the hour of the court arrives a son of France might appear in the Piazza dei Napoleoni, or a letter."[27] Her hopes would not be disappointed. The duke remained a steadfast friend to the last.

Her relationship with Estancelin, too, was going strong, and they remained quite affectionate. In May 1871, when her friend—who'd been appointed general commander of the auxiliary forces for the defense of Normandy—was shot in the chest and forced to return to Baromesnil for treatment, Virginia grew worried when she didn't receive replies to her letters. Knowing he was with family, she tried to ascertain whether her letters had been delivered to him, making it mischievously clear that "they were judicious *like me* and confined themselves to asking how you were." (Clearly she had, on occasion, written other less chaste letters.) But above all she wanted to know how he was doing physically, for the Prussians had obviously not touched his *esprit*: "Neither sieges nor bombs could put a scratch on that."[28]

Even in later years, Virginia would go on fondly exhorting Estancelin not to pull in the oars:

> But what are you up to in your Norman lair, among pendulous lilies and ramrod violets? Are you perhaps hoping to earn, with some specimens of the local agriculture, the color of hope on the new flag of the French republic? Come on out of that dark cave, get better, and . . . come give me a kiss.[29]

She knew she could always count on his friendship: "I have something very serious to tell you and must speak to you about an urgent matter,"[30] she wrote, arranging to meet him at the Hôtel de l'Alma. We have every reason to think that the "urgent matter" was something to do with "Georgette," whose ears, until recently, he'd affectionately pulled—and who, as we will soon see, had been giving his mother a great deal of trouble.

But there were new friends too. In early 1873, Virginia met a man who offered her one last chance to play the game of love. His name was Paul Granier de Cassagnac, a well-known journalist who wrote for the newspaper *Le Pays*, which he also edited. His columns were virulently anti-republican, arguing in favor of the restoration of the imperial regime. Five years younger than Virginia, Cassagnac was an athletic man with a handsome, virile face and a thick musketeer's mustache that suited his temperament—quick as he was to pick a fight and draw his sword. A talented polemicist and lover of provocation, he fought with equal vehemence for the throne and the altar—especially for figures he held sacred, such as Marie Antoinette, Eugénie, and Napoleon III—and attacked any and all opponents with his pen, starting with the hated Gambetta, and brooking no quarter when it came to institutions. He was the one who coined the epithet *la gueuse* (the beggar) for the Third Republic. And while his adversaries often called him to account for his insults by suing him, he preferred to take justice into his own hands by challenging them to duels and promptly cutting them to shreds. An unrepentant bachelor, he was a swaggering womanizer, and only two days after an acquaintance introduced him to the famous Countess of Castiglione he went on the attack—successfully, one would have to say, given that he was able to write to her: "Tomorrow evening, if you wish, I shall come tell you about the beautiful dream that still stirs my imagination, and my boundless desire to see it repeated . . . An irresistible bond has been formed between us, and I for one shall never break it. Yours, Paul."[31]

In reality, things didn't go exactly as his letter suggests.[32] A cocky man, he'd immediately become impatient with Virginia's erratic and capricious behavior, treating her like a splendid cocotte prone to outbursts of generosity and joy, a pleasant partner in bed. The relationship between them needed to be clear, and he didn't want to know anything about her business dealings or her links with that "old worm"[33] Charles Laffitte and his "papier-mâché principles." Only Poniatowski had treated her so brusquely—but the treatment didn't seem to displease her. She decided to take up the gauntlet, and adapting herself to Cassagnac's demands managed to overcome his resistance and become a fixture in his life. After begging her pardon for being so cruel, the journalist was forced to admit that he cared for the countess. He'd been afraid of admitting it to her, but his "stubborn devotion" had won the day. And so little by little the intimacy between them grew. Virginia called him "Le Pays," after his newspaper, and he called her his "Jolie Payse." By the summer of 1873 Cassagnac craved her company, confessing: "I am abandoning you for the countryside, but it isn't like it used to be, when I would forget about you and not give you a thought... Now, against my will, I find you're creeping into my life, and I must say I don't mind it all that much." Before setting off, he sent one last message: "I have no memory of yesterday, I don't know what will happen tomorrow, but tonight, July 23, 1873, I love you."[34] These words, which left Virginia in no doubt she had triumphed over her musketeer, could only please her, since they faithfully reflected her own idea of love: a brief epiphany, an ephemeral state of grace, not destined to last. The countess would continue to make use of men even after she was past the age of forty, but the relationship with Cassagnac, free from lies and calculations, brought with it a promise of happiness, rekindling her passion for life.

But that didn't mean she was going to give up her court of slaves.

# The Slave

He called himself "L'Esclave"—the Slave. For months he had besieged Virginia with compliments before attempting, faced with her resistance, "a decisive attack."[1] But we see in his letters to the "chère comtesse" (about twenty of them, written between 1873 and early 1874) not only the old military metaphors for courtship favored by libertine prose; we also see, as though in a mirror, the same epistolary strategy—the domination of the other through a skillful use of language—employed by Virginia to lord it over her admirers.

Various clues[2] lead us to suppose that L'Esclave was Xavier Eyma—a journalist, novelist, and playwright who enjoyed a certain notoriety. Originally from Martinique, he had written about the habits and customs of the Antilles and North America in nonfiction works such as *Les Peaux noires* and *Scènes de la vie des esclaves* before tackling the same theme in an 1866 novel, *La Chasse à l'esclave*. It was therefore with full knowledge of the facts that, subjugated by Virginia's charm and perfectly willing to place himself at the mercy of her whims, he had adopted his nom de plume.

But why did Virginia encourage the attentions of a man who was twenty years her senior and neither rich nor high-ranking? An influential journalist, aligned with conservative positions, and an expert in finance, Eyma evidently represented a valuable source of information when it came to politics and business alike. And yet, in his efforts to capture Virginia's attention, these were not the kind of subjects he raised, which perhaps explains his slow progress. By focusing on the narcissism of his "mistress" and becoming its exegete, L'Esclave applied himself to exploring her psychology, interpreting her behavior, and demonstrating her dilemmas. He hoped, as the classical moralists had taught, that by revealing her to herself he might also influence her choices.

The two of them got into the habit of seeing each other and of writing to each other every Thursday, but even in his first letter Eyma complains about Virginia's behavior. After leading him to "presume" he might "pique her curiosity," she had disappeared without a word of explanation. But he held no grudge and was confident that given time the runaway would make her feelings clear. "I see all the turmoil of your thoughts and the vacillations of your heart," he wrote, with a healthy perspicacity. "You say, 'I have conquered him, I am conquered myself; but I am still mistress of my heart, of my senses, of my reason, of my whole person, and I will cede the spoils to this conquered conqueror only on the day and at the hour that I decide.'"[3] After all it was Virginia who, during their most recent encounter, at the very moment of denying herself to him, admitted her interest, both arming him with new hope and leaving him uncertain: "Was it the moment, then, to launch my attack? . . . But no! I resisted this supreme temptation . . . I am waiting for the vanquished to say to me on her own initiative: 'Come, here is my hand, I promise it to you, do with me what you wish; soul, body, spirit—it all belongs to you' . . . It will not be merely a triumph over the senses but a triumph over the whole being."[4]

L'Esclave ran the risk, however, of waiting for a very long time. After vanishing without a trace,[5] Virginia resurfaced but refused to see him. She was seriously ill, she claimed, rebuking him for not being sensitive enough to pity her in what he called "an enchanting and wicked note."[6] Eyma took advantage of the situation to resume playing the double role of psychologist and spiritual advisor:

> My dearest countess, your crisis is more mental than physical; I am by profession a doctor of the soul and I identify my patients at a distance, without having to examine them and take their pulse. I auscultate by other means, and I am never wrong. Just try denying it, if you dare! In the case of this crisis . . . I play a small part, and so I would find myself in a difficult position even if I were to give you a piece of advice, which after all you perhaps couldn't or wouldn't wish to follow, so I'll keep it to myself. What I can tell you is that I will wait patiently for the crisis to end—we will see if it will be to my advantage or not.

He drew hope from the memory of the "auspicious day" on which she confessed to him that she was, "unfortunately," interested in him.[7]

But Eyma wondered whether these emotional oscillations—Virginia's "perfidious courtesies"—were really the result of her erratic temperament, fears, and existential discomfort. Might they not be instead part of a "calculated, clearly premeditated" plan? "In your world, there is no room for chance, which cannot satisfy your needs," he wrote. "*What you want, is*; I have already had the opportunity to observe this myself. Nothing is stronger than your will, except the superhuman forces that bend all things to their will."[8] All he could do was beg her to "resurrect" him, to write to him, and to revive their Thursday rendezvous, knowing full well that in his "capacity as a slave" he had no rights whatsoever and so remained duly obedient to his mistress, whose lovely hands and feet he kissed.[9]

Yet even as she refused to see him and hid behind excuses, she used one of her lovely hands to administer "vigorous lashes"[10]—one suspects lashes that the journalist would have liked much more if they'd been real rather than metaphorical. Had the beautiful tyrant with the fatal whip realized their relationship risked becoming a dangerous source of misunderstandings? Or did she enjoy stringing him along like a vulgar *allumeuse*? "I will not do you the dishonor, dear Countess, of accusing you of coquetries... Therefore please tell me your thoughts clearly and without hesitation. No games." As it turned out, the epistolary strategy he'd been hoping would put her under his spell did not produce the desired results:

> It would be good to liberate ourselves of all the niceties and delicacies we use in our letters. A letter is a perilous thing, I tell you again, since it is essentially deceptive; it intoxicates both writer and reader; one ends up gabbing to no purpose with whatever words come to hand or with carefully chosen words, but without the benefit of an immediate reply that permits us to explain or correct ourselves.[11]

Financial difficulties temporarily brought the Belle Dame sans Merci down from her pedestal: Virginia asked him for a loan. But it wasn't really a good time for poor Eyma. "What can I do? What should I do? I am ready to do anything, except the impossible," he despaired, explaining the sacrifices he had to make to finance his new paper. "Two hellish months organizing and raising cash to get a machine running which has so far given me more headaches than satisfaction."[12] Difficulties aside, Eyma was soon able to announce, exultantly, the publication of *Le Nouvelliste*: "The general opinion is that I will succeed. Let us pray that is right!"[13] he crowed, hoping that he the dedicated lover would soon meet with similar success. Again he attempts to ensnare her psychologically: "You resist by drawing on the energy that comes with distrust, but I . . . I have the patience of passion."[14] But Eyma had already tried preciousness, oxymoron, and subtlety, and even moralistic fables. A professional writer—in his letters he never fails to appeal to his "pen" to inspire him with the proper words—he engages her passion for the theater and shows off his talent as a voguish playwright: he composes a dialogue between Adam and Eve that illustrates the different behavior of men and women in the sentimental and moral spheres. But Virginia was tired of wasting time. Her suitor now bored her, and she studiously avoided any request for clarification—at which point Eyma sent her a very long letter retracing the stages of their relationship in scrupulous detail.

Since, right away, she had been alert to the feelings she inspired in him, the journalist argues, why not, if she found them so "unpleasant," refuse to receive him at her home? Instead she had given him a glacial welcome, avoided him for a long time, and then made up her mind to see him again—"once more opening the gates of dreams." She had told him that, if she continued to keep him at arm's length, it was out of "fear"; only to finally grant him, giving in to his insistence—and who knows whether she didn't draw inspiration from Madame Bovary?—ten minutes alone in a carriage, in the middle of the street. With hope in his heart, L'Esclave had returned to the Hôtel de l'Alma only to fall into a "trap": to his surprise, he had found her as resistant as ever. The beautiful temptress had been quick to justify that resistance with a long list of specious whys and wherefores. For too long now, she had been behaving in an ambiguous and contradictory fashion, deaf to his protests and pleas. Enough was enough. It was time for her to show her cards and let him know how her intentions. And to forestall further equivocation, he presented her with an ultimatum, demanding that she choose, if she had the courage, between two answers:

> You bore me, leave me alone and try to cure yourself of a malady that is wearing me ragged too,
>
> or:
>
> Here are my hands, do with me as you wish.[15]

For once Virginia's response must have been clear enough, considering that Eyma never wrote to her again.

# "Love Which Is Nothing and Everything at Once"[1]

THE TIME HAS COME to ask ourselves whether Virginia ever fell in love and whether she was even capable of falling in love. The only indication that love retained a special aura for her is her reticence toward anyone who felt authorized to extract a declaration of love from her. If anything, she preferred to wave it away, calling it "a stupidity," especially when speaking to those who, like Giuseppe Poniatowski, inspired her with her feelings not unlike love.

She expressed her thoughts on the subject to the banker Ignace Bauer (younger and not as tough as Laffitte), from whom she'd borrowed a great deal of money in the early 1860s, taking advantage of his devastating passion for her but never allowing him even to imagine it was reciprocated. When Bauer proposed his plan for a life together, offering her a substantial annuity, not to "buy" her but to protect her dignity and financial independence, his "lady," his "queen," his "Madonna" paid him back in kind by offering him a rare outpouring of sincerity:

> I don't believe in love, it is an illness that passes the same way it comes on, gradually, or a fitful fever like the ones I get from time to time;

> we must not count on it being anything else, nor want anything further, nor hope for anything more. I repeat what I have always said, though I have stopped reminding you of it: Take me today and don't count on having me tomorrow. I am a daughter of God who will end up in the arms of the Devil if God doesn't want her. Which is why I vehemently implore you: Stay as you are, don't change a thing about what you have been, be ready to come back to yourself, to resume your old life, if I should die.

An unusual burst of sincerity, and she regretted it when Bauer left her to marry someone else—though not even marriage protected him from the "inquests" and "indictments" of the "demon with the heart of an angel" whom he'd so desperately loved.[2]

Bauer was not the only one to have the courage to break off a relationship with her, but the imperturbable Virginia always thought of those who *had* loved her as if they still belonged to her, getting back in touch with them anytime she fancied. And if, as with La Tour d'Auvergne, the defectors happened not to heed her call, she pitied them: "I love those who have loved me, and I pity them when they no longer have the courage or the will. If some misfortune befalls them I look at them and say to myself: 'Poor things! If they still had me as a lover, or as a friend, they wouldn't be so unhappy.'"[3] This was not even to mention those who'd committed the folly of getting married:

> Oh, the wives! They are my *bête noire et mon plus grand épouvantail* [pet peeve and my greatest bugbear]. All my men have taken one, and I have lost them, and they've gained neither their affection (inevitably given to another after three months of matrimony), nor chil-

dren (for one can never *savoir au juste de qui ils sont* [know for sure whose they are]), nor money (especially since the wife often ruins him, or the money is taken back by the family), nor a true companion (only one in the eyes of the world).[4]

The idea of love as a pathology certainly corresponded to her observations "in the field." As a serial seductress, Virginia was expert in the phases of that "intermittent fever" that caused men to fall at her feet, and she also knew some tricks to prolong it—which doesn't rule out the possibility that she experienced it herself. Yet the multiple and contradictory expressions in her letters[5]— now cold, now inviting, now sad, now cheerful, now passionate—allow us to make a few inferences. The sole certainty is that, for her, sexual relations were beside the point. "I accept your promise of fidelity but only as regards friendship: I care a great deal about fidelity of the heart, but not of the body,"[6] she declared to Bauer; and she reprimanded her friend Estancelin, who was quite susceptible to erotic reminiscences, by saying: "All right, between you and me there was this and that . . . These are things of the past, when there was a reason for them. A matter of luck and chance. What's the point of poking up the ashes when the fire is no longer smoldering?"[7] The haughty countess, who made a religion of her body, employed it with the greatest nonchalance, offering or refusing it based on careful strategies of domination and trade, but also, sometimes, purely on a whim. We can assume—if it is true that she agreed to display herself in all her nakedness to a privileged few[8]—that the pleasure of showing her physical perfection was substituted for her absence of desire.

But when it was her turn to make the first move, she did not hesitate to resort to the notion of love. "I am writing to tell you something that you might have, with a bit of goodwill, realized on your own: I love you!"[9] One of her favorite expedients, beginning with her affair with La Tour d'Auvergne, was to fire up the imaginations of her suitors by using distance as a shield—"It's a shame you didn't come! You would really have enjoyed me. I got up and dressed for you"[10]—and in general by cultivating, despite all the evidence to the contrary, their illusions: "You see that I am still and in spite of everything what you wished me to be; I have not ceased to be her and I will always be her, believe me and bear this in mind, and if sometimes you find me harsh and cold, if I am abrupt and unpleasant company, it is because I have to be and there is nothing to be done!... But tonight I'm good, and I could be even better if... you were here too!"[11]

Bored by the passionate declarations of the unhappy men on whom she so easily cast her spell—men inevitably dead set on an exclusive relationship—she passed her leisure time mainly with accredited seducers like Nigra and Estancelin, who did not question her need for freedom—an irrepressible need for her, a congenital instinct, which led her to declare she was "as free as a cat."[12]

On occasion, putting aside those sexual efforts indispensable to her financial independence, she indulged herself spontaneously. She had a weakness for adventurers like Bentivoglio, or simple naval officers, and she didn't mind men with brusque manners, who treated her unceremoniously, with the bluntness set aside for courtesans. This was characteristic of the two men, Poniatowski and Cassagnac, to whom she expressed the desire to be loved just as she was. In later years, changing her mind, she spoke of "love which is nothing and everything at once," adding that "one must not hold on to anything or anyone"[13]—and Poniatowski and Cassagnac were undoubtedly the ones who to her represented the "everything" of love. Nor is it a coincidence that the handsome defender of the Bonapartist cause entered the countess's life just as Il Vecio came to the end of his many miles away.

Until the end, Poniatowski's irresponsibility and cynicism hurt her; she could never bring herself to believe that she mattered so little to him and always hoped for a conversation that might clear it all up. The countess and the prince met for the last time in Paris, probably in the summer of 1872, when he was paying a visit to the city, but their two-day "repatriation" ended badly: Poniatowski, in dire straits, scoffed yet again at her demands to repay his debt. And Virginia, once she was alone again, picked up her pen and gave vent to her indignation: "After the tears of the day and the hope of the evening came the laughter (yours . . .), the anger, the pride, the *revolt*, and so at midnight I have written this letter, which I am not going to send, because you would respond in a way that would require a reply and because, for the time being, I am in no state to read or write or speak or act."

Was Il Vecio aware of the agony he was causing her?

> I haven't been able to sleep *one minute* and *I feel ill.* After these forty-eight hours (not what you promised they would be) it is natural and unavoidable that there should be a reaction, knocking me flat. When and how will I lift myself up again? I don't know. I am not all that you think I am—I have a very great moral strength, it's true, I'm generally up to speed on *everything* and *everyone*, but certain things . . . coming from certain people, at certain moments, bring me down and keep me down—I am laid low in body and spirit . . .

> my heart is mortally wounded, and the slightest blow and the smallest thorn reopen the old wounds and set the blood flowing.

Il Vecio enjoyed being cruel to her for the pure pleasure of seeing her suffer, like those

> innocent children with an instinct for destruction who torture a poor insect by holding its legs, grabbing its wings, and dunking it in water, but not long enough for it to die, then take it out and leave it supine on the ground, knowing this will deprive it of life breath by breath if some merciful hand doesn't come along in time to spare the quadruped [*sic*] by righting it, or setting it off walking, or letting the flying ones go flying.

But she had no intention of giving up without asking him to meet and explain why he'd behaved as he had. "A quarter of an hour of proceedings and goodbye," with the promise that "for *this quarter of an hour* you won't laugh that laugh!"—that terrible laugh that was still ringing "in [her] ears."

Then, characteristically changing her mind, she regretted speaking with such open-heartedness instead of sending him "the haughty midnight letter that told him to kiss the Florentine goodbye, which is to say: merrily telling him to go get f——." She, too, wanted to make light of life, but she didn't have the strength: "I fall back into this dreadful black bed brooding on my sad fate . . . I'm tired, I'm in pain, goodbye; to hell with everything. I turn toward the wall and shut my eyes . . ."[14]

Knowing Virginia, Poniatowski avoided a face-to-face confrontation and tried to mollify her with a flattering telegram that made her as imperious as ever:

> At long last I receive *three* lines where I read that I am beautiful, that I am a genus [*sic*], and that I am (also) good. You worship! You bow and scrape! For once it isn't bad, that you say it and *think* it (or that you *think* it and *say* it)... Thank goodness that at last you have changed your mind, that you repent, and that you are just (I don't say *grateful* because I don't know what to do with the gratitude of other people, my own satisfaction and personal enjoyment are enough for me)... But *I punish* the *ungrateful* and the *unjust* harshly. You have seen how I treated you when you wanted to be *unjust* just to hurt me?

Did she need to remind him what she had done for him? "In business, however, and in extreme cases, to save you (while you go on contradicting and riding roughshod over me), *j'ai passé outre* [I got over] even my *deepest* resentment and served you without saying a word about it." And even as Virginia proclaims her generosity, she demands much more than gratitude:

> What now? Didn't you know that I am very good? I, who would give up all my *pleasure* to give *pleasure*... who would burn my own finger to be of service—who would take the bread out of my own mouth for someone else, on the condition, however, of *giving pleasure*, of *being* of service, of relieving hunger—or else no. I don't need people to tell me I am good, only that they *feel* it, *think* it, *believe* it, and don't dare say or let others say otherwise, that is, that Nicchia is wicked.[15]

Now it was his turn to give an account of his thoughts and actions, which is why she wanted to see him:

> I need to *understand*, because *I understand* right away. I understand things quickly, I understand them well. You know I'm a sight-reader (not music), but *eyes* and *facts*...!! Words matter little to me and I care nothing about *writing* even if the words keep *faith* and the writings provide *proof*, it is easy to change words, it is easy to rescind writings. But eyes don't *change* and facts aren't *overturned*, they can only be denatured. You will at least admit to the notorious *coquille* "Genus" [*sic*] telegraph. Thus *you understand that I understand*, and that *everything* is *entirely your fault*. *Passons et n'y revenons pas* [Let's move on and speak no more of it].[16]

Even if Il Vecio's behavior was unforgivable, nothing could erase the memory of the best day of her life, when she'd felt their two bodies formed one soul. And never mind if the only soul involved was her own.

Despite the bitter ending of her relationship with Poniatowski, whose sudden death had ruled out a final reckoning, Virginia remained on the lookout for a man who could understand her and love her just as she was. The man turned out to be Paul de Cassagnac, who, as we've seen, she met in the winter of 1873.[17] Soon after her affair with the newspaperman had begun, Virginia wrote him to probe his intentions and lay her heart bare. She needed to make clear to him how different she was from her public image. This was no simple task—Cassagnac was fully aware of her intimate business relationships with princes and bankers—but Virginia tried, and so bequeathed us another remarkable dramatic production. The letter is in diary form, divided into eight parts, written over the course of thirteen days. It is a full-blown theatrical monologue.

We are in Paris at ten o'clock at night on a Wednesday in the year 1873. Earlier that day, Cassagnac, about to leave on a work trip, had "very kindly" come to say goodbye with a bouquet of roses, such "a sweet delight," and to thank him Virginia picks up the pen, relishing the prospect of telling her lover all about herself. For once she doesn't ask him to return the letter but trusts in his discretion and addresses him without worrying overmuch about style. "I must warn you," she says straight off, "that I never reread myself, I write at full tilt."

A few days apart are, however, enough to make her change her tune. "As I've already told you, I feel a great foreboding about this trip of yours." And she confesses to her lover that "My hope went away when you went away, my courage has withered with the roses, and I'm still here, drowning my sorrow in my tears." Her arrival in Dieppe restores some of her courage and the new scenery presents a new opportunity to confess, every detail acquiring symbolic value. Her first task, she tells him, has been to "decorate the bedroom (the room of desires "past, present, and future") with roses, finishing the job with "objets d'art artistically placed." She has made it into a "little home" in line with her sensibility and taste, and only the essential thing is missing—"her everything": the man to whom she now declares her love. So that he is always with her, even if only in the form of a simulacrum, she has brought along a few of his gifts from Paris: a Madonna for the bedside table; a cross and a dagger to hang on the wall; a die, a horseshoe-shaped seal, a reliquary, and a handful of other cherished objects on a table nearby. And here, on stage, she scribbles (in bed as usual, under the covers) this diary-like letter in which she lays her heart bare.

The next day starts with Virginia defending herself against some accusations that her friend leveled before his departure. Her feelings, she confesses, have only "deepened and become more beautiful despite the storms that have sometimes darkened my brow but never cooled my heart, inducing me to keep myself hidden behind lock and key." Virginia wants Cassagnac to go beyond appearances and peer into the depths of her heart. "We must look beyond the ripples and concentrate on the depths, as good as they are great, as *fair* [in English in the original] as sensible, and my affrighted sadness deserves the amplest moral pardon." As for the "physical," of course he has the right to do as he sees fit, though her lover must keep in mind: "You have to take me at the right time, and above all, after a brusque separation, warm me up gradually," since any forcing risks "extinguishing" her desire. But there is to be no doubt about the authenticity of Virginia's feelings for Cassagnac, as she makes clear by returning again to the bouquet of roses, which continues to be the center of her attention: "I want to die with this bouquet, but first I will have a copy made, because, alas, reality cannot endure." She will wrest these roses from the clutches of time and carry them with her always, never to be separated from them again.

The problem of their temperamental differences, misunderstandings, the anguish of the morrow... all these remain. But out of the blue a letter from him arrives, cheering her up: "Yesterday's letter moved me tenderly; I thought I was impervious to tears, but the other night I soaked the pillows." Virginia saw "an auspicious omen" in her friend's words, but how could she still hold out hope? "My God, my God, what am I saying? The word 'happiness' sounds like blasphemy from my lips." She concludes on the suggestive image of a heartfelt plea for help: "Now I close my mouth and eyes, and I turn them in your direction... Where are you now? Far, far away, and I feel as though I'm there, it is midnight."

The next day the salvific force of love comes back into the picture. She reports a brief conversation that takes the form of a fable:

> Today an acquaintance, seeing me looking distressed, said: "You should have someone who loves you, who is always by your side!" "And if he were far away, what would you say?" "I'd say he doesn't love you." "But if it's out of necessity?" "The only necessity when you love is love. If he is not willing to sacrifice everything to live with you, if he cares about career, rank, honor, fortune, then he doesn't love you!"

Did Virginia—a woman who had never given up anything for anyone—really hope that Cassagnac would give up his political mission for her sake? That he would put his public image at risk by making such a compromising relationship official? Did she really want to persuade him that it was his love that she craved? Perhaps it's no coincidence that a few accents of *La Traviata* echo in her words:

> Dear me, all alone in this desert of misery, not to mention *miserably sick*, because in addition to the physical prostration and the moral travails I am tormented by a fever that saps me of all my strength, even the strength not to be weak. I feel so weak that I'm afraid. Afraid of what, will you say?

We know Virginia's histrionics too well to give full credence to what she writes here, but it is difficult not to believe in the sincerity of her fears, which are so profoundly human: "Fear of God, fear of the

Devil, fear of men, fear of things, fear of chance, finally fear of myself!!!...And fear of death!!!!!!!! Well yes, here she is, this woman who has become afraid for you, for herself, for us..."

Bringing the tragedy to its climax, Virginia changes the mood and opens the door to hope again. She feels better, but she can't shake her desire to have Cassagnac there with her. Why, then, does she find herself "on this terrace alone, free, undisturbed?...What nonsense, when we could be so happy here together!" Of course she treasures the tranquillity, the solitude, and the melancholy of Dieppe, but, she repeats, she is missing something essential—that "everything" which she now proposes to her correspondent in the form of a "love between friends." Not an *amitié amoureuse* toying with romantic ambiguities but a tacit pact between two free people who are capable of accepting and loving one another as they are.

As she'd done many years earlier in her letters to Poniatowski, Virginia attempted to lay herself bare to him in all her contradictory truth: her habits, rituals, moods, fears, hopes, and her will to live. But where there was no need to give a name to an obvious feeling with Il Vecio, with Cassagnac she grasped that she must respect convention. She had resigned herself to using the word "love" so that he might love her without judgment. She put herself in his hands and waited anxiously for a response: "Write to me. Do it quickly, quickly." Cassagnac did agree to try the experiment, but their "friendly love" was not destined to last.

# The Rebellious Child
## 1866–1879

Virginia's well-intended resolutions did not change her behavior, and Cassagnac, weary of her foul moods and "funereal airs,"[1] went his way. The outcome strengthened her belief that even her most fervent suitors could not stand up to her and, in the end, were sure to beat a cowardly retreat. But the last thing she expected was for her son to rebel. This was not to be tolerated. But let us backtrack a little.

As we have seen, the thankless task of informing her grandson of his father's tragic death had fallen to Marquise Oldoini. "The poor child was inconsolable," she reported to her husband, worried as always about Virginia's possible reaction, "but his pain is twice as terrible because of the way he fears his mother. You must not mention this, or she'll make mincemeat of him."[2] A short while later, her worry would be replaced by dismay: Isabella saw her daughter and grandson arrive in Florence "without even a maid or a servant, dirty and dressed in disgusting rags." In another letter to Marquis Oldoini, she vents her spleen at the "truly unfair way poor Giorgio is treated even as he tries his hardest to make up for the absence of servants by acting as her servant. All he gets in return are shouts and blows, and I assure you the child is fed up."[3]

Having dismissed Mademoiselle Rauch—who had grown to hate her during Giorgio's time in Italy[4]—Virginia made up her mind to look after her son on her own. This was what the child had always dreamed of, but unfortunately the mother he had longed for turned out to be a wicked stepmother. Not only did she use him like a slave but she "treated him with her own methods when he was ill," and "it was a miracle she didn't kill him."[5] In his memoirs, Dr. Blanche's youngest son, Jacques, speaks of the "curious health regimen" to which the Countess of Castiglione subjected her son on a holiday in Dieppe. Standing at the window, in her "hoarse, harsh, and imperious" voice, she ordered the "frail child to run all around the meadow in the blazing sun, shouting all the while, 'I want you to breathe!'"[6] One day Isabella noticed Giorgio was "missing two teeth in the front of his mouth," and her grandson told her in strictest confidence that his mother had sent him to Paris to deliver a letter to a dentist who, without warning, "pulled out both of these teeth, which had been there for five years and were strong." But that wasn't the end of the story. "He told me," the marquise wrote to her husband,

> that he thought he was going to die, and all alone on the street, wanting to get home, he felt faint and climbed into a cab. When he got back to the house, she saw him crying and covered with blood, and asked him: "*Qu'avez-vous, êtes-vous tombé?*" [What's the matter, did you fall?] I didn't answer, Giorgio said, I threw my teeth on her bed and left.

A horror story, for which Isabella herself was unprepared: "Such atrocities make me shudder, and I cannot forgive myself for having given birth to such a hard-hearted daughter."[7]

But even when—distracted by other concerns—Virginia wasn't actively cruel to her son, the situation remained a dramatic one. At the age of thirteen, Giorgio was forced to live in a house with "no fire, no cook, and no servant,"[8] where he spent his days wandering around, eating wherever and whenever he could. Though he was forced to deny it, he no longer had tutors; he'd gone a year without cracking a book; and his mother intended to put him in a pension instead of a boarding school, which did not bode well. "It is inconceivable for a mother to do to an innocent child the horrible things she does to Giorgio," Isabella writes in another letter. "It wouldn't surprise me if, out of desperation, he did something crazy. If he does, many people will have a stain on their conscience."[9]

In the years after his father's death, the boy accompanied his mother to Paris, Turin, and Florence, and then again to Paris, when after the Commune the city returned to normality. But there was no room for him in the furnished apartment Virginia rented in the Hôtel de l'Alma, and so, after a long period as a guest of the Rothschilds', he moved to a small furnished room on rue Saint-Arnaud, where his mother as good as abandoned him until Betty de Rothschild intervened. The baroness had known Giorgio since childhood[10] and was fond of him. She ventured to urge Virginia to take better care of her son, now eighteen years old, but whom she still treated like a child—left "without education or moral guidance at precisely the most important and decisive age."[11]

Virginia cared too much about the baroness's friendship to incur her disapproval, and she sprang into action. At the suggestion of Abbé Maurette[12]—Giorgio's spiritual director since his first communion[13]—she hired a tutor who seemed to have stepped straight out of the *Scènes de la vie de bohème* rather than an educational institution. Genulphe Sol, the son of a tax collector, was born in 1841 in Beauregard, a small village in Occitania; he had unsuccessfully tried his hand at various professions, including journalism, and was living in Paris with a widow, Joséphine Bellande, who made ends meet by renting rooms to girls of dubious repute. He was a handsome young man with dark eyes and symmetrical features, his hair artfully disheveled to conceal his incipient baldness; he had a thick black mustache and a brash demeanor that was anything but reassuring.

After the count's death, Virginia had become the arbiter of Giorgio's fate. She treated him like a servant. She had him, among other things, copy out letters for her in his beautiful calligraphy.[14] But Giorgio, while living with his father in Turin and Florence, had acquired an awareness of his social position as a Piedmontese gentleman, and having passed the age of innocence, he viewed his mother's eccentricities, money problems, and revolving-door lovers as so many embarrassments and humiliations. Every now and then, confronted with certain maternal demands—ordered, for example, to serve as copyist for Prince Poniatowski—he lost his temper:

> If it goes on like this, Countess, I'll end up in the cemetery. The other night and all day yesterday I had a bad attack of the very grave illness I had before, which rears its head whenever I'm annoyed or work too much. And the prince says I'm having a good old time. I'm finally out of danger, says the doctor, I need rest, *dolce far niente*, peace and pleasure . . . In the meantime, however, I have to copy this

> letter immediately on behalf of the prince in the room down the hall no time to waste time chatting.[15]

Futile protests—as futile as his requests for the freedom and the money to finish his studies. Giorgio asked his father's brothers and his mother's father for help, but (as he would later remind the marquis, not without bitterness) none of them "deigned" to exercise their authority on his behalf to allow him "to embark on the social and intellectual life" that was his birthright.[16] Abandoned by his relations, afraid of clashing with Virginia, and without his beloved grandmother as confidante, Giorgio turned to his tutor. Indeed, Sol was the first person not to treat Giorgio like a child and to treat him like man. He kept his mother in the dark about his shortcomings, introduced him to friends, and, through Madame Bellande, may have arranged rendezvous with acquiescent girls, providing a sexual initiation. Sol, like Mademoiselle Rauch and Abbé Maurette, disapproved of the countess's treatment of her son, and unencumbered by the professional ethics of the former or the Christian resignation of the latter, he incited his pupil to revolt. He did so with extra gusto knowing that, should Giorgio and Virginia fall out over money, he might find himself transformed into the mentor of a young gentleman with a brilliant future. In any case it's clear that, without Sol's psychological support and advice, Giorgio could never have stood up to his terrifying mother.

At eighteen, he laid claim to his share of his father's inheritance: the principal of a 4,000-franc annuity that Castiglione had earmarked for his education, as well as the 100,000 francs of the matrimonial "dower"[17] he'd committed to providing, in the event of his death, to his wife and descendants. Virginia, however, had already disposed of the dower.[18] How was she to be induced to give him what he was owed?

Did the idea originate with the boy or the tutor? Hard to say. In any case, on November 25, 1873, young Verasis di Castiglione secretly left Paris after taking a great many sensitive documents from his mother's house, including "business correspondence, private letters, as well as two ciphers from the king," and handing them over to Sol.[19]

Virginia, who didn't realize until a few days later that the documents had disappeared, was distraught at her son's shameful larceny. She would henceforth call him "le Tigre." The stolen papers were too compromising not to throw her into a panic, since they constituted proof that she had once been a spy for the Savoyard government and gave clear evidence of her intimate relationship with Victor Emmanuel II. There may also have been some extremely compromising letters from her current lover, Cassagnac, whom Virginia told about the incident straightaway. "My dear Nicchia, your letter brought me to tears, I am sorry to see you in this impasse and not be able to help you," he replied.[20]

Giorgio's missives to the tutor as he made his getaway—letters the police seized two years later from the widow Bellande[21]—allow us to reconstruct how it all transpired. The first thing Virginia did was mobilize Abbé Maurette[22] and appoint Sol to go to Italy, flush out the fugitive, and escort him back to France.[23] Pretending not to have a clue—and lavishly subsidized by the countess—Sol traveled to Turin and Florence, writing to let her know he'd been unable to locate his pupil, then telling her that he'd received a letter from him posted from Paris. Meanwhile, Giorgio, who'd left La Spezia for Genoa, wrote to his mother to lay out his terms: He would return the stolen documents only in exchange for emancipation and the inheritance from his father.

Virginia, enraged, decided to do battle to the bitter end: Was Giorgio not a minor? Until he turned twenty-one, was he not her dependent? This gave her the right to dispose of the annuity earmarked for him as she saw fit. And it was "[her] duty as a mother" to "preserve that annuity for him, which secures a man's independence and guarantees him, regardless of his career, an honorable existence."[24] But Cléry, the lawyer friend to whom she'd immediately turned for counsel, strongly advised her against resorting to legal action. The scandal would be immense, and there was also a risk that the court would grant the request for emancipation. In turn, Giorgio warned her he was prepared "to bring a suit against her for forfeiture of the guardianship, with a view to legal emancipation,"[25] citing the "thousand physical and moral sufferings"[26] he had endured. At this point, Virginia yielded and wrote to Sol, ordering him to conclude the negotiations and "take Mr. Georges to Turin, to the lawyer Mongini, thanks to whose intervention the guardianship will be extended, and the emancipation will be granted in due time." In return, the countess recommended that the preceptor have all the stolen documents handed over to him and brought back to her in Paris.[27]

The letter—four pages in length—is verbose, overflowing with allegations against her son, but it also shows us a strong-willed and clear-thinking Virginia, who, following Cléry's instructions, in legal language, aptly and accurately describes the course to be followed. Then again, in a rough draft of another letter to the tutor we glimpse a deluded mythomaniac taking refuge from her difficulties in an imaginary world. Apropos of nothing, Virginia confides to Sol that she used to be a consummate artist who refused, however, to take credit for her work: "In my day I was a musician and a writer, an author of plays, songs, and stories which, perhaps wrongly, I never chose to sign, all the while giving, out of my own soul, the most important thing of all: an *idea* for the benefit of others. I have been the mind and soul of Italian, Prussian, and French *History*, letting Thiers take all the glory, and never breathing a word about it to anyone." Her image of her son splits in two: There was a "great" Giorgio "full of goodwill," and to him she made her appeals; then there was a "little" Giorgio "stubbornly intent on doing wrong, delaying, starting over, confusing things," who would soon discover, to his loss, what it meant to incur her wrath. This eighteen-year-old who dared to defy her would remain for her the child he had once been—the child she bullied into staying locked in his room, telling the truth, obeying her without any argument. "My nature does not permit a show of will from others," she announces in a flash of lucidity, "nor can it tolerate reasons; it demands and imposes passive obedience." Finally, abruptly returning to the present, she is sorry to say that her degenerate son entirely lacks his mother's heart, courage, and intelligence.[28]

So the thirty-five-year-old Virginia—unable to handle a reality that failed to align with her desires—contrived for herself a fictitious past. Meanwhile, her son was making every effort to free himself from her tyranny and to lay the foundations for his own future. From Genoa, where he was a guest of the barons di Morand (to whom Virginia had provisionally delegated his guardianship), Giorgio wrote to Sol almost daily, updating him on what he was doing and the state of negotiations, asking him for advice and guidance.

On December 9, 1873, he reported: "The countess wrote yesterday to Baroness Morand that she was ready to agree to the conditions requested."[29] But how could she be trusted? Clearly she hadn't thrown in the towel, since shortly afterward she asked Baron Morand to persuade her son to meet her and Marquis Oldoini in Bordeaux. Perhaps aware that he couldn't withstand a direct confrontation with his mother—but also fearful of setting foot in France, where he ran the risk of being arrested for theft—Giorgio replied that he wouldn't leave Italy "without certain guarantees."[30] Meanwhile, the marquis told his daughter he would brook no further discussion of the decisions he had already made:[31] As Giorgio himself wrote exultantly to Sol, his grandfather had abandoned his usual policy of neutrality and, on his way through Genoa en route to Portugal, had taken Giorgio's side, even assuring him of the protection of the old Marquise Doria, the mother of the first lover whose heart Virginia had broken.[32] Hoping to win the support of influential figures, the young count also intended to pay his respects to the Duke d'Aosta (back in Italy after his brief and ill-fated Spanish adventure), who would certainly look out for the son of an official who'd met his end while escorting his carriage. Though everything pointed to a happy ending, Giorgio knew his mother too well not to worry there might be a plot twist, and as week followed week, the drawn-out negotiations and nerve-racking wait in an unfamiliar city tested his limits. On Christmas night, he sought to exorcise his loneliness and bewilderment by writing Sol an eleven-page letter that he began at half past three in the morning and finished twelve hours later. This time it was not advice he needed, but comfort, and he knew that his tutor was the only one who could provide it. So he told him the "sad story" of his lonely Christmas "in a big city where he had no friends." After Midnight Mass, he had lingered in the church for another quarter of an hour, then, "going out into the street crowded with people singing, laughing, celebrating the holiday," he had been overcome with sadness and burst into tears. "Oh, when will the *life* begin for me that until now I have only glimpsed, unable to get the least bit close to it?" he asked, in a cry from the soul that called his whole existence into question. At half past two, after dining in a cheerful crowded restaurant where he'd felt even more alone and bewildered, he'd returned to the Morands' palace, and then, finding the door shut, he'd wandered off to the harbor, boarded a boat for rent, and asked the boatman to sail around the gulf. He wanted to get to the bottom of his perplexity, to find himself again:

> The sky full of stars, the sea calm as a lake. In the distance I could see a few gas lamps, reminding me there was a city over there where thousands of people were celebrating while I had nothing but the sea. No, that's too sad, I don't want to go back over it, you can't imagine all the things I thought and understood in that lonely hour in the sea's immensity.[33]

A few hours later, returning to the palace to find a telegram from his mother, Giorgio realized that "real life" was finally about to begin. Virginia had discovered that not only had the vile tutor made a fool of her but that Abbé Maurette and her friend Rothschild had taken part in the plot. It was now clear to her that she had lost.

She would not, however, fail to take vengeance on Sol. First she threatened to sue him and everyone she considered his accomplices for child abuse, then, recalled to her senses by her lawyers, she backed down, zeroing in on the tutor. The charges—concubinage, aiding and abetting, receiving stolen goods, immoral acquaintances—were not groundless, and Giorgio was forced to abandon Sol, who found himself with nothing to show for months of frenzied activity, travel, and inconvenience, his future uncertain, and a charge of immorality hanging over his head. But that wasn't the end of it. Forsaken by her lover and left without a sou, the widow Bellande attempted to sell the Countess of Castiglione some of the documents still in her possession; Virginia, however, did not bite. She reported Bellande to the police, who confiscated the papers in question.

Finally, on January 27, 1874, Giorgio was given the deed of emancipation, signed by his mother's proxy. In exchange he returned all the documents in his possession. To save face, it had been agreed that Virginia would declare that, as a resident of France, she was renouncing the guardianship *sua sponte* [of her own accord] since her son had gone to study abroad. For the fugitive, it was the end of a nightmare. "I am emancipated, I have the right to speak, to express my will, to work . . . I enjoy the same advantages as an adult, I can do what I like with my annuities, do whatever I see fit,"[34] he gushed to his grandfather. And he wasted no time demonstrating that he knew how to make good use of his freedom. He settled in Turin, where he was born and where his father's family lived, doing his best to make up for lost time. "I am getting right to work," he announced to his grandfather, "I am studying as much as I can and also doing a great deal of exercise. Riding, Gymnastics, Fencing, etc. I am learning History, Geography, Mathematics, Political Economy, and Law, and plan to undertake still other subjects. My health is excellent."[35] Demonstrating remarkable willpower and self-discipline, as well as an extraordinary capacity for scholarship,[36] he studied "without stint, nine or ten hours a day"[37] to become a diplomat and serve his country.[38] In early 1875 he passed his exams with distinction, but not having a law degree he could only enter the foreign ministry through the back door. Thanks to the personal intervention of Victor Emmanuel he was taken on as an "honorary attaché," and while he looked forward to the day when he might become a "real attaché," he resigned himself to the fact that his first destination would be distant and destitute Buenos Aires.[39] When he broke the news to his grandfather, he struggled to explain that the choice of Argentina was not his, and the marquis, who'd been hoping he would come live in Lisbon, took it as a betrayal. And since Virginia had cut all ties with him, guilty as he was of siding with his grandson, the old diplomat felt abandoned by his whole family. From now on, he wrote to the innocent Giorgio, it would be "every man for himself, and God for us all."[40] He was placated, however, by the young man's explanations, and it wasn't long before he resumed his role as the noble father, appealing to Virginia's goodness and intelligence to put an end to these family quarrels.[41] His daughter answered him with a letter so long that it "wrecked the wrist" of loyal Passera, who'd become her amanuensis. Amidst a thousand galloping recriminations she told her father she'd received a visit from "Mr. Georges," with whom she'd reached an agreement regarding the dower, which had remained unresolved even after his emancipation. Not that this meant she was willing to forgive the affront she'd suffered: "Know that in future those who wish to be my friends will have to choose between him and me." And she concluded with a riddle: "As for him, I am still his mother, but he is no longer my son."[42]

Their two accounts of the visit, which took place on February 18, 1875, and ended with an agreement written on stationery from the Italian consulate,[43] depict the same drama from opposite points of view. Giorgio's letter to his grandfather concentrates on his desire to resolve the monetary dispute and be reconciled with his mother before leaving Europe. Having traveled to Paris and managed, with great difficulty, to visit Virginia, he had, in order to avoid a trial,[44] accepted the proposal that he receive only half the dower, which would otherwise have been his in full. Convinced that by doing this he had secured his mother's indulgence, he fell into the trap of impossible expectations: "Well then, after we'd discussed the matter (in front of the lawyers) my mother let me go without saying a single affectionate word of the sort that a mother can always find for a child. And that by itself hurt me more than you can imagine."[45] Virginia, meanwhile, sent Cléry a victory bulletin: Le Tigre had lost on every front.

> He's not that strong, you tell me! Eh, by Jove, those Piedmontese have made him soft in the head. No wonder he isn't so strong anymore. Indeed, I found him very *weak* and foolish, and ugly and wretched, poor fellow... He had brought three handkerchiefs with him, all set to weep. But I made him *laugh* the whole time. We talked like two lawyers bickering over somebody else's affairs, and for the moment I've won. *He accepts everything.*[46]

But Virginia was too intelligent not to realize this was a Pyrrhic victory: her son had permanently cast off her yoke. She would never recover.

In another interminable letter to Marquis Oldoini written not long after these events, Virginia took stock. The picture she painted could not have been bleaker. For six months she'd been laid up in bed with a broken leg. The accident happened in her sleep, and was caused, according to the well-respected surgeon who'd been treating her, by "constant ebullitions and bad blood" that had "crystallized" her bones. The diagnosis did not surprise her. After paying "more than a million to cover her husband's debts" and shelling out everything she had and everything she didn't have, now reduced to poverty and living in "two miserable little rooms in a hotel," she had even been betrayed by her own son! She was bitterly shocked to learn that her father had sided with his grandson, but she preferred to let it go: "I will neither hurl accusations nor recriminate, I have always given everything without ever thinking of myself, and I ask nothing of anyone. I will live as best I can, come what may." Still, it pained her to think that she could not end her days peacefully on her childhood hill in La Spezia, the place she loved most in the world. In fact, expropriations, mortgages, a thousand problems, lack of money, and her disastrous health were forcing her to put her share of the properties up for sale, and, incidentally, she suggested to him that perhaps he might purchase it. One had to resign oneself: "There are some fates against which it is pointless to rebel. Mine is to own nothing, to hold on to nothing, to live alone and far from my country."

Then, contradicting what she'd said a few lines above, she returns to the filial affront she'd suffered, changing her tune. All she wanted was for the whole thing to be behind her: "But since in Italy *all these ingrates* and miscreants talk to you and gossip about me, at least you'll know what to answer. As for me, I don't say anything to anyone. Let them all go hang themselves—kings, princes, ministers, friends and enemies—but let them leave me alone. If not, I bite." Well, anyway, her health was so poor that she was not long for this world. She had faith that a just God would welcome her into heaven.

Having deftly blended aggression with detachment and victimhood with self-aggrandizement, the countess could have ended the letter on this note, pathetic and dignified. Unable, however, to control her overwhelming resentment and despair, she launches into a long litany of woes. Disaster has befallen every "good and beautiful" thing she ever possessed, and the Virginia of old is gone forever: "I am nothing now but a hideous, exhausted woman, indifferent to all. This is what comes of misfortune and misery." And again she circled back to the "horrible infamies concocted" against her by her son, whom the marquis had refused to shun, and went on to expiate on the properties at La Spezia again, not ruling out, this time around, that she might in fact hold on to them. Since in the absence of a suitable secretary she would no longer be able to write to him, she bade her father farewell, wishing him all good things—"balls, parties, dinners"—down there in Portugal. With the death of their "dear marquise, *qui était notre rassemblement à tous* [who held us together]," it would be difficult to find occasions to see one another. Besides, she concludes sardonically, at this point her "perpetual solitude and categorical rejection of the stagecraft and spectacle of society" deprived her of the pleasure of being "of any help to his career."[47]

If Virginia hoped for her father's sympathy and compassion, she was sorely disappointed. Marquis Oldoini's reply sounded like a *de profundis*:

> You must be truly desolate, dear Niny, to write such distressing things as the twenty-four dense pages I've just finished reading... All my life I've done nothing but warn you against your intransigence, even

> during your marriage, at the risk of seeming almost a tyrant. Like the Titans who wished to scale the heavens and ended up flat on their backs, you presumed to change the world instead of taking it as it is, and you have destroyed yourself.

In short, having refused to listen to him, she had dug her own grave.

> You used to be as beautiful as a dream, intelligent, with all the virtues of a character of the first order... prepared to sacrifice yourself...; now here you are at war with the whole world, isolated, a recluse, not tied to anyone anymore, perpetually suffering, full of pain and remorse, in short condemned to unhappiness.

Could she—his "good Virginia"—ever change her attitude? Her father despaired of it, because unfortunately her ideas had now become "second nature."[48]

Marquis Oldoini's diagnosis was incontrovertible. Worse was still to come.

In July, the young Count of Castiglione received orders to set sail for Buenos Aires on the first of August, but Oldoini begged Artom—then secretary general at the foreign ministry—to postpone the date until September 1 to give him "the consolation" of going to Italy, embracing "his Giorgio," and "talking with him about Family."[49]

Strange as it may seem, during Giorgio's time in Buenos Aires, his relations with his mother became affectionate again, and the two resumed their correspondence. Giorgio even conjured up their old symbiosis, though, after so many years, he could not escape the perverse mechanics of his eternally disappointed expectations:

> Oh, has Mina already forgotten Le Demoiseau? Has the ocean that separates us already swallowed even the memory of Il Piccino? I would have expected it from everyone else, but not from Mina. If you knew how much joy it gives me to receive your letters, you would not make me pine in vain.[50]

For all that, Giorgio's thoughts had turned to the future. After two years of apprenticeship in Argentina he returned to Turin, where he now felt at home. Proud of the name he bore, he was on excellent terms with his uncle Clemente and his aunt Maria, and, having no children, they looked to him as a possible heir, and though Victor Emmanuel had broken his promise to buy back the Castello di Costigliole,[51] Giorgio further enjoyed the protection of the House of Savoy. After so much loneliness, he longed to find the family happiness he'd been denied, and on November 18, 1878, he married his cousin Amalia Asinari di San Marzano e Caraglio.[52] Her upbringing and temperament made the young bride the polar opposite of his mother, yet the classical perfection of her features inevitably make one think of no one so much as Virginia. A year after their wedding the couple set out for Portugal, where Giorgio was to take up the post of attaché to the Lisbon legation run by Marquis Oldoini. Everything suggested the time had come for him to savor the fullness of life, for which he'd fought so tenaciously. But fate had other plans. On November 14, 1879, in Madrid, at the age of twenty-four, Giorgio Verasis di Castiglione was abruptly mowed down by smallpox.

"An irreparable loss for the Oldoini and Castiglione families,"[53] his grandfather noted on the back of his grandson's last letter.

Virginia, in a last attempt to claim possession, tried to recover his body, to have it next to her forever in the tomb. But the *picchinicchi*'s remains stayed in Spain. Virginia would have to face the descent to the underworld alone.

# Odi et Amo

THE BREAK WITH HER SON also marked the end of the countess's twenty-year friendship with Costantino Nigra, who was guilty of sticking up for the boy. In the grip of her resentments, Virginia did not scruple to sever ties with her longtime companion. It was, after all, a settling of accounts with a man whose subservience she'd never quite secured.

In the winter of 1856—young, beautiful, elegant—they had both left Piedmont for Paris, and through Cavour they'd become friends. In Turin, this would have been unthinkable: In the Savoyard capital, where the nobility, entrenched in its privileges, still formed a world apart, an official of humble origins like Nigra would never have had the chance to associate with a high-born lady like the Countess of Castiglione. One could appreciate the professional merits, the culture, and the courtesy of a person like Nigra, but inviting him to dinner was out of the question.[1] In the Paris of the Second Empire, however—at least outside the Faubourg Saint-Germain—the only credential the beau monde and the court demanded was success, regardless of origin. Certainly in the first two years they spent in the French capital, the social distance between Castiglione and Nigra remained considerable, and it was she, not he, who shone in high society. "We have read in the newspapers all about your balls and parties where, as everywhere else, you reign supreme,"[2] Nigra wrote to her, deferentially, when she was working behind the scenes in a constant to and fro between Turin and Paris. But a sturdy bond was soon established, as Nigra relayed the coded instructions from Cavour.

A few years later, Virginia learned that Nigra was back in Paris, where he'd been promoted to the rank of envoy extraordinary and minister plenipotentiary before becoming, in August 1861, at only thirty-three, the King of Italy's first representative in France, entrusted with the arduous task of bridling disappointments and resentments, restoring trust, and convincing Napoleon III that it was advisable to persist in his support of the unification of the Bel Paese. Having stepped out from Cavour's shadow, the young Piedmontese remained in the capital for a full fifteen years, demonstrating an ability and professional resilience destined to make him a source of pride for Italian diplomacy. He combined, in the words of Federico Chabod, "the highest sense of national dignity with a deep sense of personal dignity, and he refused to compromise either one."[3]

We know rather little about the private life of this celebrated diplomat so used to living his life in public, partly because the man himself arranged to erase his traces. He was born in Villa Castelnuovo, a small village in Canavese, into a close-knit petty bourgeois family that was far from rich. He volunteered for the first war of independence and was wounded in the Battle of Rivoli. After returning from the front, he earned his law degree, never ceasing to write poetry, which testified to his patriotic passion and his profound attachment to the peasant world of his childhood. "La rassegna di Novara," a poem about the fecund heroism of the vanquished (whose lines "Obey in silence, / and in silence die" would become the motto of the Carabinieri), was a touching expression of his faith. As the historian Adriano Viarengo writes:

> A child of Romanticism, Nigra had been formed by the liberal ideals of 1848, in a vibrant Turin that saw in the [Albertine] Statute granted by Charles Albert the first stirrings of that "Italian revolution with a king," which Mazzini bitterly mocked in 1840 and which came to fruition between 1859 and 1860.[4]

In the summer of 1852, he won a competition that allowed him to enter the foreign ministry, where he was appointed secretary to Massimo d'Azeglio (then the prime minister), and he, at the end of his term, turned him over to Cavour. It was therefore under the auspices of a statesman, a novelist, and a painter that Nigra took his first steps behind the scenes of Italian politics, after which he entered European diplomacy at large, sealing his fate.

The first price he paid for this career was the collapse of his marriage. In 1855 he had pledged his troth to the daughter of Giovenale Vegezzi Ruscalla, an expert in philological and ethnological studies. Cavour himself seems to have been the instigator of the match, working closely with the bride's family.[5] The worthy daughter of an idealistic and patriotic father, Emma was beautiful, cultured, sensitive, passionate about poetry, and averse to compromise; she hoped her husband would follow his vocation as a poet and philologist, and saw his choice of politics as a betrayal. The birth of a child failed to lift her spirits, and Nigra tried in vain to convince her to come with him to Paris. Staying behind in Turin, in her parents' house, Emma gradually detached herself from the outside world, shutting herself away in a dreamy silence, slipping, by degrees, into insanity.[6]

Despite the distance between them, Nigra would never cut ties with the vast Vegezzi Ruscalla family; he made sure that his wife was taken care of and supervised his son's education; but the end of the marriage initiated a long series of futureless affairs.

From the moment he landed in Paris, the diplomat dedicated himself to a comprehensive seduction of the Second Empire's high society. "With his calm but amiable demeanor, his simple and elegant manners," recalled a politician who had seen him in action,

> he was an exceptional and tenacious negotiator, but never intrusive—capable of saying anything without causing offense and listening to everything without letting himself be offended, skilled at suggestions, intuitive, ingenious when it came to debunking differences and burying the hatchet, never discouraged by failure or intoxicated by success, level-headed when faced with the unexpected, not inclined to delusion though in no way pessimistic. Fortified by his perfect French, he did not limit himself to the artificial conversations of official diplomacy but was able to enter the salons of high society, had established connections with various prominent figures, and, between a reception and an invitation to dinner, dedicated himself to a sustained but discreet appeal to public sympathy.[7]

Not that there was any shortage of people who treated him with disdain. Maxime Du Camp—snobbish, and perhaps also envious, not to mention hostile to the politics of the Risorgimento—wrote of him:

> The good looks... the cunning in place of wit, and the air of self-importance he displayed in certain circumstances were not enough

> to deceive me about his worth; to me he seemed like one of those men who make you say "I wouldn't give him a penny"; and, truth be told, I never gave him one.[8]

But Nigri's personality made even his defects attractive: "An elegant young bachelor, a man of letters, a gentleman, a handsome, self-assured knight—though he had the air of an artist rather than a statesman—he enjoyed considerable success with women, despite a marked Piedmontese accent and a lisp which, in the final analysis, contributed to his charm." Even as he pursued success in society—essential for a diplomat—Nigra had not given up his original vocation and still diligently cultivated "relationships with the greatest exponents of art, literature, and theater, and was always well aware of what was going on behind the scenes of Parisian life."[9] A careful curator of his public image, Nigra took a line in politics and diplomacy, as well as in his private life, characterized by reserve, prudence, and moderation. And since he was as discreet with the fairer sex as he was in his profession—almost nothing has survived of his romantic correspondence—we must content ourselves with the generic testimonies of his contemporaries. However, a note from Princess Emanuela Potocka, who had no reputation to defend, speaks volumes: "I authorize His Excellency Nigra to declare, if he so wishes, that the present photograph portrays one of His Excellency's numerous victims."[10] According to Count Ressmann, the enchanter was capable of sending fifteen Parisian grandes dames as many bouquets of flowers, which he had shipped in from Florence at his own expense.[11] A colossal bouquet, for the empress's birthday, without an accompanying note, had as its sole signature a "profusion of rosettes in the colors of Italy."[12]

When Virginia returned to Paris in the early 1860s, the relationship between the two accomplices was bound to change. Now it was Nigra who enjoyed the good graces of Napoleon III and the favor of the empress; who was a guest of honor at the Tuileries and Compiègne;[13] and who was squabbled over by the members of Parisian high society. It was up to him to extend his hand to his fascinating companion in adventure, who'd fallen into disgrace. He also took the opportunity to court her. Their complicity, extended into the erotic sphere, grew stronger, especially since both liked to play the game of love and made no secret of it. But libertinism answered different needs. While for Nigra it brought pleasures that allowed him to forget his unhappy family situation, for Virginia—who as a rule gave herself to men only if they could be useful to her and was always prepared to punish them for forcing her to give herself—the game of pleasure was a diversion from all her exhausting schemes, which engaged her on many fronts and all at once. It wasn't easy finding men who were up to such games—Estancelin was one—but nobody's hand was more competitive than the handsome Costantino's. Few took her measure with such a dispassionate eye. With his writerly acumen and diplomatic talent, he intuited her intellectual audacity, her political insight, her pride in serving a noble cause—not to mention her capriciousness, her arrogance, and her boundless confidence in her own beauty. And he'd guessed the nature of the worm eating away at her straight off. From the very start of their partnership, in the spring of 1857, after congratulating her on her success, Nigra perfectly captured the restlessness that never left Virginia, even in the midst of her triumphal advance. "Beautiful Lady," he writes to her, "in the name of God don't let yourself be laid low by the black melancholy that oozes from one of the phrases in your darling letter." And with equal perspicacity, taking notice of her epistolary verve, he apologetically delivers a little "sermon":

> I will suggest one way—an excellent way, I think—to get rid of [this melancholy]. You are a witty and cultured woman. You write well, and with a bit more attention, you could write *very* well. Everyone around you finds you sincerely charming, which is partly the effect of your beauty, but more so of your character, which, though capricious at times, is ultimately gentle and good. You are in touch with people who have a certain role in things. Your perceptions are accurate, insightful, and precise, as far as I can judge. Well, given all this, you are in an excellent position to write your memoirs. That will have the advantage of sternly banishing sad thoughts and melancholy for a few hours a day, and it will be a great consolation in the future. Forgive me for sermonizing.[14]

Always consumed by an exaggerated sense of emergency, and caught perilously between her two tongues, Virginia would never have the "attention" necessary to make better use of the vivacious, original style evident in her letters, and only when her lucidity had abandoned her would she entertain the prospect of writing her memoirs. Nigra, however, received unambiguous confirmation of her artistic sensibility in the form of a "magnificent" photo album containing twenty-five images dating back to the years 1857–1859.[15] Pasted on both sides of eleven sheets of ivory-colored cardboard, these portraits—in different shapes and sizes—are framed by imitation wood lacework probably applied by Virginia herself. The decorations on the cardboard binding match these frames, and on the inside cover there is an empty secret pocket, perhaps meant to hold a more intimate image.[16] Chosen specifically for Nigra, the photographs—the only complete album of Castiglione's that, to our knowledge, has come down to us intact—are a visual chronicle of Virginia's first sojourn in Paris and a document of her chameleon-like talent. In shot after shot, we see her embodying very different aspects of femininity: maternity, spirituality, contemplation, seduction, playfulness. All of the poses reflect the pictorial canon then in vogue, calling to mind the painter Claude-Marie Dubufe's *têtes d'expression*.

When Nigra received it, he was over the moon: "Thank you for the *album*, which is truly magnificent. The portraits are far from representing all your divine beauty, but they demonstrate that whoever dreamed up the poses is an artist at heart. And then, how much expression in that gaze! God! God!"[17] And he was not the only one to be impressed by the gaze of the model in the most notable of these portraits, which Baron Robert de Montesquiou christened *Le Regard*, and which is rightly considered one of the most beautiful portraits in the history of photography:

> Emerging seminude from a tulle corolla, seductive yet simultaneously aloof, the countess confronts the viewer. She exudes that glacial eroticism, that "cold fire"—that "tropical winter"—that so impressed her contemporaries. Offered up for admiration, her arm looks like an ancient marble fragment. The countess's incredible ability to "hold" the lens is largely thanks to the expressive power of her gaze, which she is able to modulate as she pleases and which Pierson manages to convey. Model and photographer demonstrate perfect col-

> lusion in their effort to achieve the effect desired. *Le Regard* is their first masterpiece.[18]

With that gift, the new ambassador received a token of goodwill that Virginia reserved only for a select few. And she threw in something even more intimate:

> I am sending you the brunette and the blond with two hairs of the same colors, much discussed by people who, never having seen me one way or the other, don't believe in such a freak of nature. But nature itself has granted me the privilege of being able to appear imposing or petite by turns, but always as myself. That is my crime! The portrait in white is *art*, but the third hair plucked from my twenty-year-old head is no more artificial than the others. Everything about me is true, including my friendship.[19]

Even if otherwise engaged—she in simultaneous relationships with Poniatowski, La Tour d'Auvergne, and Laffitte; he in a very intricate and constantly evolving political situation—the old accomplices seem to have found ways to see each other often. And Virginia sent him the most disparate requests, once even asking his advice on which outfit to wear to a ball.[20] "Dear and beautiful countess," Nigra protested, "what the hell are you doing asking me to decide on the color of your clothes?" And quoting from a book of Tuscan, Corsican, Illyrian, and Greek folk songs collected by Niccolò Tommaseo, he teased her: "You are the loveliest girl / who can be found in heaven or on earth / and more colorful than a fresh-blown rose / and whoever sees you falls in love." To which he added: "If you come by at 4 we'll talk. I kiss your beautiful hand."[21]

Knowing her volatility, the diplomat courted her with caution, sending her the customary floral tributes. The bouquet she received on her name day allowed her to invite him, quite provocatively, to come clean: "Thank you for the roses gladly received for Sainte Virginie *May 21.* I repeat: Please do me the favor of not making use of *uselessness* and inventing a *utilitarian reason* for the pleasure of seeing me." And when her friend requested her presence at the embassy without explaining why, she put her foot down. Her tone was provocative, her language a fantastical Franco-Italian:

> With your note, you failed to *vous faire croire* [make me believe] and gave me a pain in the chest, getting out of bed cold and shivering *parceque* [*sic*] *Nigra a dit "il le faut"* [because Nigra said "you must"] . . . *je n'accepte pas les surprises, si vous voulez de moi il faut me dire pourquoi* [I don't accept surprises, if you want me you must tell me why]. I've gotten to be worse than Saint Thomas, if I don't touch I don't believe, if I don't see I don't go. *Tant pis pour ceux qui attendent* [So much the worse for those who wait]. If you have something to tell me, write or come and tell me this evening. *Ce que je vois de très clair c'est que vous n'acceptez ce que l'on vous offre, M. le Ministre!* [What I see very clearly is that you aren't accepting what you are being offered, Mr. Minister!]"[22]

Nigra tries to appease her by resorting to a more gallant style:

> You are as adorable as always, beautiful Countess, close up or from afar, present or absent, in Passy or in Paris. This evening I will go to the Tuileries; but the moment I'm free I shall come knocking at your

> door and tell you out loud what this note, however fragrant, cannot express . . .[23]

Released from her foul mood, Virginia immediately turns flirtatious again, even paying some "attention" to her Italian:

> Would you be *in love*! And could you have by chance made a blunder with your letter? If so, write another; this one is too darling for me to send it back and I'm keeping it close to my heart as an example of what *you could be*. If everyone loves me, come and tell me today when you want to reschedule yesterday's match. Monday evening instead of Tuesday evening if you can.[24]

Nigra responded in kind regarding his invitation to the embassy, which had angered her so much, and made clear how he felt about her:

> I don't see any real point in your coming here. However, it does seem right for you to show yourself at least once. When you make up your mind, let me know and I will be there to welcome you with open arms. Do you think I'm in love? By God, you must know me pretty well. I kiss your beautiful hand, let me know when you will have me, or come and see me![25]

Meanwhile, their time together was becoming more intimate. "I waited for you the other evening until midnight; but in vain! Patience. Another time. I was told you looked very beautiful and I believed it."[26] Soon Nigra would no longer need permission to visit her: "I will come to you this evening at eleven. Don't make me do too much time in the antechamber. Without *useless* phrases, I call myself your N."[27] Or, even more bluntly: "I will come see you tomorrow evening, *on condition however that you don't wear anything*."[28] Or even: "See you this evening, at nine, Without."[29] And if she played hard to get, he didn't make a fuss: "I will come see you when you can devote a whole evening to me alone and when you aren't tired, or dressed, or in a foul mood. If not until Sunday, fine."[30]

Until such time as the "passionate letters" Virginia sent Nigra resurface in some archive or private collection,[31] we have more than enough evidence to surmise that, starting in the summer of 1862,[32] the two compatriots freely and gleefully played an erotic game whose sole objective was pleasure. But the understanding between them went on even after the game was over, and Nigra always had a fond affection for—and the utmost patience with—Virginia. He was quick to offer her his arm for her much talked-about return to the Tuileries in the costume of the Etruscan queen,[33] advising her to arm herself with a female chaperone as well;[34] to accompany her on an "incognita" visit to the prince [Napoleon] "without running into women or children";[35] to invite her to dinner with Plon-Plon;[36] to inform her that Prince Umberto of Savoy was passing through Paris;[37] and to put the services of the Italian legation at her disposal. It was he who broke the news of the imminent death of her grandfather Lamporecchi[38] and the sudden death of her husband, and it was he who went to visit, when she was not in Paris, little Giorgio—who was only a year older than his "baby,"[39] who lived, to his great sadness, so far away.

No less important to their continuing bond were the dinners *à trois* with the highly intelligent and trustworthy Artom, Cavour's former secretary, since transferred to the Parisian legation, and the simple, lighthearted moments they shared together: "Spring has come, the air is warm, the sky is clear, why don't you come take a walk with me at 7?";[40] "Do you want to come for a walk in the woods today at 2? I will pick you up, if you wish, in a closed carriage. R.S.V.P.";[41] "When are you going to the theater? Artom and I are at your disposal any evening you choose."[42] And one Sunday in April 1865—a disastrous year for Virginia in terms of finances and family—knowing his friend's passion for the opera, he wrote to her: "Following your advice I bought a ticket for the Opéra comique, *faute de mieux* [for want of anything better]. We will therefore expect you for dinner tomorrow, *Monday*, 6 sharp. I have a message to give you. Please come. All yours, N.!"[43] But soon it would be Virginia who had to find words to comfort her friend, who'd gone back to Italy to bury his father. "Dear Contessa," he wrote in reply,

> I have arrived, following a trip I found rather sad, as you might imagine. In Florence, before I left, I received a truly lovely letter from you, for which I am most grateful. Please believe that this proof of sympathy moved me deeply, and my gratitude is entirely sincere. If you have a little time, let me come see you. I can tell you how your son is doing, I saw him in Florence. Your affectionate Nigra.[44]

His affection was real, as he demonstrated by worrying about her and tolerating her mood swings, her diffidence, and her ambiguity: "I'm sorry to hear you're unwell," he wrote, "but I will come tomorrow, either during the day or in the evening, to keep you company with Artom and *vous soigner* [take care of you]."[45] Depression and melancholy were pathologies that he, sadly, understood all too well, and he urged his friend not to yield to inertia and to force herself to get out of the house.[46] Knowing that she was laid up in bed, he attempted to take her mind off her woes by telling her what had happened the previous evening:

> Yesterday I nearly broke my neck. I'm not kidding you: servant falls and breaks his leg; coachman falls and is covered with bruises; the horse, sans coachman, takes off into the Rondpoint des Ch. Élysées and barrels to a stop, running one wheel smack into the belly of a *cab* horse that was clopping by. All the while, I was inside—not pleased as Punch, as you might imagine, but blasé. As soon as I saw that our run-in with the *cab* had curbed the progress of the carriage, out I jumped, lean and light.[47]

And Nigra never forgot that it didn't take much for Virginia to feel neglected, betrayed, abandoned. And how could she not be jealous of the sympathetic bond forming between her friend and the imperial couple? Was it only out of duty, and only thanks to a silver tongue, that the diplomat managed to blunt Eugénie's hostility toward Italy (the empress, an Austrian and fervent Catholic, did not want to hear a word about either the Roman question or the annexation of Venice) and win her friendship and trust? The countess was too perspicacious not to notice that the diplomat felt a chivalrous admiration for the sovereign that went beyond mere professional duty. And then some news reached her that irritated her profoundly. The two crucial problems the Italian representative found himself facing in Paris were the Roman question and the non-annexation of Veneto, which—in contravention of the agreement made in Plombières—the Armistice of Villafranca had left under Austrian dominion. The empress was inflexible on both points. Nigra, however, had not lost heart. One evening in June 1863, while the court was in Fontainebleau, Eugénie invited her guests to take a gondola ride on the wide pond by the castle, but it was discovered, to her disappointment, that the gondolier had lost his voice and couldn't sing Venetian songs as usual. Nigra seized the opportunity and, overnight, like a troubadour of old, had composed a barcarolle[48] for the sovereign in which the city of Venice begged the "blond empress" to liberate her from Austrian chains.[49]

Published a few months later,[50] the barcarolle made a splash, but we have no idea what effect it had on its addressee. Initially sensitive enough to Italy's fate that she admired Felice Orsini's patriotism and deplored his death sentence, Eugénie now saw the changes taking place on the peninsula as a threat to European equilibrium and the security of the papal state. But that wasn't the whole story. What made her truly bitter was the ingratitude "of an entire people toward a country and a sovereign who risked everything to make the Italian nation a reality instead of a utopia"—the conduct of a country where "it seems as if justice has been banished from every heart"—making her feel obliged to "repay hatred with hatred."[51] The events of the following years would make clear that, even if Nigra didn't change Eugénie's political convictions, he did manage to temper her hatred. The question remains what sorts of arguments he might have mustered. A rumor went around that "Cavour had entrusted him with the Italian embassy in Paris more for his physical prowess than for his qualities as a politician, in the hope that, with a little luck, he would have an effect on the empress equal, or nearly equal, to the effect the Countess of Castiglione had had on the emperor."[52]

Should we believe Prince Bernhard von Bülow, a great admirer of Nigra's, when he claims that the handsome Costantino "had been able to win Eugénie over with his exquisite manners and tactful poems"?[53] If so, it was probably an amorous friendship that did not impugn the proud empress's virtue or reputation. Moreover, as we have seen, what saved Eugénie from romantic slings and snares was not only her sincere religious faith and unremitting awareness of her duties as a sovereign but her absolute frigidity. On the other hand, a story relayed by Carlo Richelmy, a cousin of Nigra's wife's, allows us to wonder, assuming we are willing to rely on the memories of a four-year-old child. "Costantino's son, Lionello," Richelmy says,

> remembered having seen the empress arrive alone, attempting to hide herself under enormous veils, at his father's small private apartment. A very serious concern must have led Costantino not to send his son away in such an intimate circumstance. He expressed his hesitations in a letter, which he sewed into the lapel of one of Lionello's jackets, and then sent the boy to Turin with his tutor. It was Cavour himself who, welcoming the child into his study and patting him on the shoulder, discovered the document.[54]

The great statesman would respond to Nigra's "hesitations" in a letter that ended: "For the good of Italy, do not act like a chaste Giuseppe."[55] Alas, we don't know what happened next, though we do know that Nigra would always keep a marble cast of Eugénie's hand—a gift from the empress herself—in plain sight on his desk. Nor can we doubt the tender friendship she offered in exchange for his devotion when we consider that, in the spring of 1907, at the age of eighty, having learned that Nigra was dying in his villa in Rapallo, she rushed to bid him a final farewell.

Victor Emmanuel's envoy would make use of other arguments to convince the "mute imperator" to work toward the liberation of Venice and the Bel Paese by maintaining a benevolent neutrality despite the Italo-Prussian alliance against Austria, and by drawing up an agreement[56] that provided for the withdrawal of French troops—stationed in Rome for the protection of the pope—in exchange for the king's commitment to not invade the papal state and to the relocation of the capital from Turin to Florence.

Cautious and discreet as he was, Nigra could not, of course, risk informing Virginia of the secret agreements being laboriously thrashed out between Italy and France, and it is probable his old friend—now out of the game of politics, but always avid for news—begrudged him his knowledge. Furthermore, there is no clear indication that the diplomat, who was in contact with important Parisian bankers and didn't disdain playing the stock market himself,[57] was ever inclined to share any of his lucrative information with her. Virginia—unable to keep him in her pocket—did not spare him her sourness and sarcasm. Sometimes, even as she begged him to pay her a visit, she made no secret of the welcome that awaited him:

> Yes tonight . . . though for me it's a *bad* night, *désagréable*, *fatiguante*, and there are no distractions of the kind that a minister like yourself craves after the aggravations of the day. I ask you to come only if it's really indispensable, because with this great heat and my malaise, running around the streets in the sun makes me sick, angry, and doubly unbearable.[58]

She also accused him of shamefully neglecting her:

> If I'd died I would have called you afterward to bury me, this being *de toute nécessité* [necessarily] something I can only have others do. I don't want to see you and if you wanted to see me I would tell you that it is damaging and useless to you . . . but I must tell you *for your own sake* it is ridiculous to pretend you didn't know anything about my illness and I beg you *for my sake* not to claim not to have known (even if true) because no one believes it and so you're only trying to put people on for no reason.

And she concluded with a lapidary sentence: "Tell me: Is there is another woman like me? You will never find one."[59]

There certainly wasn't another woman so insufferable, and even her friend's patience had its limits. While she was waging war with her husband over custody of her son, the countess learned that Nigra was corresponding with Castiglione and accused him of plotting against her.[60] This was more than the diplomat was willing to tolerate. After explaining that the count had written to him "regarding a private matter concerning the king," he gave her a thorough dressing-down:

> If I didn't know you—if I didn't know that you were good, and if I didn't love you—I would tell you to go straight to hell. You should know from experience that I do not meddle in your affairs. I never talk about you, except to the Rothschilds when they ask about you, and even then I reply that I know neither what you are doing nor where you are. I have never spoken about you or written about you

to your husband . . . So get hold of yourself, and don't write me rubbish like that lovely little note today. Now that I've vented my spleen too, I send you a thousand affectionate greetings and *sans rancune* [no hard feelings].[61]

But at the beginning of the third war of independence, telling Virginia about the disastrous defeat at Custoza, Nigra could be sure he was speaking to a loyal friend who would share his dismay:

Today I'll be gone all day, don't come. *Je suis d'une humeur de chien* [I'm in a foul mood]. There is no other news except what everyone will read in the newspapers. We were defeated at Custoza and forced to go back across the Mincio. The Austrians took 2,000 prisoners from us, we took 600 from them. A fierce fight. Prince Amedeo wounded, 30 days to heal. General Villarey is dead . . .[62]

With the war over and unification almost complete, the handsome seducer recovered his lightheartedness and gallantry. Disappointed at not having been able to celebrate the end of 1866 with Virginia, on January 1 he sent an enchanting gift designed especially for her, with an exquisite note:

Dear Countess, We waited for you until after 10. I wanted to give you a small *Etruscan* fan. I am sending it to you, asking you to accept it as a memento from a friend. I would have liked it if the portrait of the *Etruscan queen* had come out as well as this. But when one has a face as beautiful as yours, there's not a brush up to the task . . . I kiss your beautiful hands. Nigra.[63]

When the empire collapsed, Nigra was quick to demonstrate his devotion to Eugénie by rushing to the Tuileries and offering to escort her, like an ancient knight, out of a back door of the palace before the angry mob swarmed in.[64] The next day Clotilde of Savoy cleared out of Paris, but her departure was very different from her cousin's. The princess left the Palais-Royal in a carriage with her insignia, escorted by a guard of honor and valets in imperial livery, reaching the Gare de Lyon "without receiving anything other than shows of sympathy and respect."[65] As she'd written to her father and her husband, who was already in Italy, she felt obliged to stay in her new homeland despite the disastrous progress of the war, because she was "not a Princess of Savoy for nothing."[66] But it was less her dynastic titles than her tireless charitable work for the poor and derelict that had won her the respect of the people, allowing her to leave with her head held high.

In the Paris of the Third Republic, Virginia found Nigra playing the same role he had before, but in a profoundly different frame of mind. He was now in the tricky position of representing a country that hadn't come to the aid of its former ally, and if in France the diplomat was now despised by Prince Napoleon and the Bonapartists, who considered him a traitor who'd gone over to the republicans, in Italy he was regarded with suspicion by the leftists, who saw him as "Italian Bonapartism incarnate," and also disliked by the king himself. As Federico Chabod explains in a masterful biographical sketch,[67] Nigra had lost his self-confidence, and in June 1871 he told his friend Visconti Venosta that he intended to abandon not only Paris but his diplomatic career:

> I no longer have the happy confidence of youth. If the slightest disagreement occurs [between Italy and France] I fear it would be

> attributed to the good relations I had with the empire. I also feel very tired. The mistrust, and the thought of no longer being up to the task, often keep me up at night.[68]

Abandoning the idea, he remained in Paris for another half-decade, and he went on to serve his country in Saint Petersburg, London, and Vienna, but by then he was a different man:

> Not that he lacked the energy to do what he needed to do, or to take a clear position when necessary... or that he had entirely lost the ability to assert himself, even in the difficult environment of Vienna, with a great personal prestige that, within limits, made up for the less-than-great prestige of the country he represented. But increasingly he seemed less a politician than a man of learning and a man of the world.[69]

The same could not be said of Virginia, who, as we have seen, had not given up hopes of exerting political influence and someday seeing the Orléans back on the throne. It is not known whether her maneuvers had incurred Nigra's censure, but it was certainly incumbent upon her to allay the suspicions of the Duke of Chartres, who made no secret of his jealousy of Nigra. The very long letter Virginia wrote to him constitutes an impassioned vindication of freedom, an authentic feminist proclamation avant la lettre, and, at the same time, amid the repetitions, inconsistencies, mystifications, and intimidations of Virginia's mounting rage, it shows how conflicted her relationship with Nigra was, but also the inalienable place that, in spite of everything, he'd occupied in her life for so many years. "You ask me if I am N[igra] C[ostantino]'s lover? Does it matter?

There's no need to go over this again, it's something that infuriates and disgusts me and I can't take it anymore!" she writes, and her anger—though always somewhat "dramatized"—rings true.

> I find it offensive and hurtful, because frankly I could do better, and even if I at least had a good opinion of him and did not find him *evil, false, spiteful, deceitful albeit very intelligent and adroit*, I would have had him and said so plainly and clearly—what have I got to hide? and from whom? But then there's nothing to hide, it is no mystery that his behavior changes daily depending on whether we're bickering or making up *because of all those falsehoods* and ruses I find so revolting. He comes here often, *every day and night* to work... People are free to believe (and it is natural enough) that we are working *on multiplying* [the human race]...
>
> And so what? None of that proves anything. Besides, it's *idiocy* on your part, you, a johnny-come-lately, to ask me, a widow, free, at my age, who has had me and how many men I've been with...The truth is that I'm free and I intend to stay free, otherwise I'd get married...Let's drop the whole subject and not go anywhere near it again. Agreed? Enough, enough, or we'll quarrel and not be able to come back...Woe unto you (forewarned is forearmed).

However, Chartres's accusation touched a point too sensitive for her *not* to feel the need to go back over it:

> But when you bring up N.C. for the umpteenth time, and something that is and is not love between him and me...then I will, for the umpteenth time, answer as follows:

1. *I was not, and am not,* his lover.
2. I have never loved him, and I do not love him.
3. I am not at all sorry that I am not seeing him at this time (on the contrary!).
4. Therefore I don't see why I should be angry with him, and in fact I am not... It is I who prefer to keep him at a distance, because he is constantly irritating and repulsing me with his mysteries, his *tricks, his lies*.

On this last point Virginia was telling the truth, since she was indeed very "vexed" by Nigra's professional diplomatic reserve; this, however, did not affect a relationship cemented over the course of years under extraordinary circumstances. Had it not been Nigra himself who rushed to her side after the nocturnal attempt on the emperor's life, to keep her "from taking the Spaniard's head off and exposing and revealing her accomplices in the ill-fated *blackmail* attempt"? The Duke of Chartres had to understand that this was reason enough for her to find it "necessary and advantageous to remain on good terms with him, though I have no other relations with him... And besides, what, I should show this man to the door merely at the whim of another? Even of the man I love best? Even my lover? *Certainly not... Ask me no more questions and be done with it.*"[70]

After he left for Saint Petersburg in the spring of 1876, Nigra would never have a chance to see Virginia again, but the "dear and beautiful countess" would never forget him, and many years later she would have a photograph of herself delivered to his door. To Nigra's subsequent letter of thanks, which she carefully transcribed in her diary, she added a few lines of commentary in her own hand which confirm how vividly she recalled the bond they had shared:

> The letter from [Nigra] (who has neither written nor seen me for twenty years because of our *brouille dans* l'Enlèvement [quarrel after the *Theft*] and slanderous attack committed by my son) is a *bijou* of lofty, sad, and youthful remembrances that touched me to the core.
>
> "Dear Countess, the Count of... has given me your letter and photograph. I thank you from the bottom of my heart for remembering me so kindly. I see from the photograph that you are still beautiful and young and I congratulate you, there is no woman like you and never will be...Do not forget your old admirer and worshipper."

A handful of courteous and matter-of-fact phrases, but among them one that she alone would understand, since she was the one who'd asked him: "Tell me, is there is another woman like me? You will never find one." After so long a silence, Nigra's reply was a ray of sunshine in the darkness of her existence: "Lovely! for a man with no heart, but full of Poetry! Receiving this gift, I feel as if I were out of jail here just for today."[71]

By that point both of these exceptional personalities were declining in very different, though equally melancholy, ways. Virginia confronted these years as a final challenge, fleeing the malevolent curiosity of a world that had failed to do her justice, while the diplomat, much as he felt like a relic, continued to maintain, with elegance and dignity, the position he'd secured in society on his own merits. In 1882, Umberto I granted him the title of count with the corresponding coat of arms, for which Nigra chose a Piedmontese motto, AUT ET DRIT (tall and straight), which fitted him perfectly. On December 4, 1890, he was appointed senator of the kingdom of Italy and, two years later, awarded the Supreme Order of the Most Holy Annunciation. As the years passed, he also resumed his research in comparative philology, linguistics, and ethnology, for which he had earned the praise of Mérimée in Paris.[72]

He returned to poetry, too, with his parallel translation of Catullus and Callimachus;[73] a collection of his own verses, *Idilli* (1893); and a collection of the popular songs of Piedmont, which was perhaps his most original contribution, since it inaugurated a new method of study in the field of popular poetry that "marked the passage from empirical or abstract or purist grammar to comparative and historical linguistics."[74] Yet in old age he never went back to live in Villa Castelnuovo—the hometown to which he was so deeply attached. As had happened to Virginia with La Spezia, albeit for different reasons, the places of his childhood became paradises irremediably lost. His falling-out with a son on whom, after his marriage had failed, he'd pinned all his emotional hopes—and who had deeply disappointed him—only deepened his loneliness. Professional and worldly success did not keep him from feeling estranged, like many of his peers, from the course taken by Italian and European history after 1870, and he began to feel himself among the ranks "of the dead embalmed in their vestments."[75]

Precious few remembered the Italy for which the men of his generation had fought, and faith in Cavour's liberal and reforming ideals had waned. Now that many of the protagonists—Victor Emmanuel II, above all—of the age that ended with Cavour's death were themselves dead and buried, Nigra felt the time had come to sketch out the backstory of the crucial events he'd witnessed firsthand. For years he worked on his *Ricordi diplomatici*, drawing on the many valuable documents in his possession, and in 1903 he finally completed them.[76] Yet despite the many memoirs being published in Europe in those years, Nigra let only a few pages of his appear in a journal,[77] perpetually postponing their publication. There is no reason for us to pore over the vexed question of why he was so reticent, or the mysterious disappearance of the manuscript he carried with him everywhere in a briefcase. Was it Nigra himself, overcome by scruples, who fed it to the flames, along with all his private papers, in his home in Venice on the Grand Canal? Or did the memoirs fall into the hands of those who feared they might interfere with the official narrative of the Risorgimento?

When he learned that some unidentified men had broken into the villa in La Spezia, where Virginia kept part of her archives, and burned many letters from distinguished correspondents right then and there, Nigra very likely became distraught. In any case, when submitting his own private papers to an auto-da-fé, the diplomat spared only one item: the photograph album that Virginia had given him more than forty years earlier. This gesture was a final tribute to the friend who had preceded him to the grave, and was, in its way, an act of repair. The great *commis d'état* failed to acknowledge Virginia's full contribution to the Italian cause, but the gift he saved from the flames has given posterity tangible proof of her "divine beauty." And by donating it to the Museo del Risorgimento in Turin, Nigra's heirs have, in turn, allowed the countess finally to find a place in the temple of memory consecrated to those who "made Italy."

# The Supreme Shame of Decline

> . . . like the beautiful Countess Castiglione,
> who, they say, when her season waned,
> vanished from the world, sealed the doors
> of her house, and remained its prisoner.
>
> Alone with Time, among the colorless fabrics,
> she waited out the years without friends or mirrors,
> concealing from the People and the Court alike
> the supreme shame of decline.
>
> —GUIDO GOZZANO, *The Colloquies*

"IT TAKES COURAGE AND PRIDE to be a victim or a martyr. And the executioners, whatever their nature, can all go to hell,"[1] Virginia wrote to her lawyer, who was trying to get it through her head that she might well lose her battle with her son. The role of victim and martyr would be the last and most memorable performance of Virginia's ever theatrical career. She'd always favored tragic parts. When the actress Mademoiselle Rachel's effects were auctioned off, the countess acquired Adrienne Lecouvreur's dagger.[2] And the final scene of the countess's play *Le mariage et la mort*[3]—in fact the *only* scene she drafted—confirms her penchant for the tragic: It depicts a heroine about to climb the scaffold to spare the life of her beloved, who stands helplessly by and watches her make this sacrifice. But Virginia was still a long way from death. She would dedicate the time she had left to gathering the evidence needed to confute the slanders slung at her, and to ensure that the truth would prevail. Her carefully considered exit from the stage was to make her a legend, but in the meantime her life would become an "ordeal."[4] Overwhelmed by her physical and mental suffering, she lost her mind. She was not yet forty years old.

Beyond the waning of her beauty, Virginia was now forced to endure a long series of bereavements. The most painful were the betrayal of her son, her final break with Cassagnac, and her estrangement from her father—about to tie the knot with a Portuguese noblewoman, who was, to crown it all, younger than Virginia herself. In the space of a few years, most of the people who, for better or worse, had mattered to her died one by one. After her husband and mother, La Tour d'Auvergne, Napoleon III, Poniatowski, and Laffitte died in rapid succession between 1871 and 1875, and in 1878 it would be Victor Emmanuel's turn. "The 48 died, sometime between yesterday and today," Virginia wrote to Léon Cléry after Laffitte passed away.

> Another friend I will go and see before long. What am I doing here, still? I have *nothing* left, and *no one*—no one and none of what I had from when I was a child.
>
> And yesterday another of my beloveds gone, a man who loved my heart and admired my brain.—All of them are dead now!...
>
> You cannot be close with someone for twenty years in your youth

> and *not* mourn them bitterly. It is the whole past going away, and it never comes back; even if you are lucky enough to make new friendships, there is one thing you will never find again: that dialogue between the memories of two lives; of course, it is almost impossible for two people of different sexes to experience a mutual interest without some psychological or material love playing a part.
>
> Yet even the sublimest loves, with their quarrels, jealousies, and storms, last but a little while, whereas simple affections, such as the one between 48 and me, last forever, cloudlessly: they pass through a life and yet remain outside of it.[5]

The last lines of the letter indicate her tendency to revisit the past in the light most flattering to her—in this case the light of a pure, disinterested friendship—hoping to bring it into line with the self-image she intended to bequeath to the world. To cope with a present beset by practical and financial worries, she could fortunately rely on the unfailing support of the two great friends she had left: General Estancelin and the lawyer Léon Cléry, who had been introduced to her by Thiers in Florence in October 1870, when Cléry was representing the government of national defense to Victor Emmanuel II. In those difficult days, Cléry had become close with the beautiful Italian so eager to help France,[6] and he would not fail to do right by her after her death:

> She was by no means an adventuress. On the contrary, she was a great lady... A very intelligent woman, highly competent in all things pertaining to diplomacy and politics, she juggled with both the ease and the talent of a true Florentine with some drops of the Medici blood in her veins.[7]

They had a "steadfast" friendship. In his affectionate efforts to chase away Virginia's anxieties—dispelling her suspicions and fears—the acclaimed lawyer would patiently take the time to decipher her "infernal chickenscratch."[8] Most importantly, he would never fail to provide her with professional assistance in her many disputes—from the one with her son to the tangle of trials related to the La Spezia properties, to the tug-of-war with the owners of her last residence.

That Virginia's correspondence reflects the inexorable worsening of her nervous illness there can be no doubt, but it also reveals her discernment, her powers of observation, her irony, grace, worldly knowledge, and, not least, the undoubted writerly talent noted by Nigra. Her correspondence with the Clérys especially—of which Montesquiou published a small anthology[9]—reveals a mastery of classic French epistolary art, eschewing "five-penny"[10] literary formulae in the name of originality and surprise.

The birth of a baby girl in the Cléry household, for example, allows her to express her gratitude with an expensive gift accompanied by a message that politely minimizes the gift's costliness, instead emphasizing its auspicious significance. But in voicing her hopes for the child's beauty, Virginia yet again celebrates the cult of her own:

> You have authorized me to peel off a *pearl* for your daughter... but no, I will not give it to her, for it is a symbol of *tears*. She must let her eyes sparkle, following in my footsteps, and dazzle the last decades of our century. I hope she will be beautiful; one must be, in order to face the world. And that is why I wouldn't wish to bedizen her cradle with a pearl. For her, I prefer an emerald, signifying *gratitude*, for green is the color of hope.[11]

New Year's Eve greetings were a more challenging rhetorical exercise, but Virginia handled them expertly by reaffirming her relationship with the Clérys. Written in late 1874—the ill-starred year of her son's emancipation—her note takes it cue from the gift the Clérys had sent her:

> And do you think I need *ivy* to feel attached to you, whom I love with such a powerful love, because you love me so deeply!
>
> No, I have no need of fruit and flowers to find you in my thoughts. But what fruit, and what flowers, arranged with such grace—what a magnificent basket has just come to brighten my sad and lonely little corner with its thousand shades, surprising me in my meditations on the sad year just passed!
>
> But during the twelve chimes of midnight I shall eat twelve good-luck seeds, thinking of you and yours and all our *wishes granted*, for I want us to be *brothers in happiness*, assuming some happiness is possible in this life![12]

Three years later the future had grown still bleaker, and Virginia, aware of the headaches she was causing her lawyer friend, used well-wishes as an excuse to apologize:

> On the last day of 1877 I was too distressed, confused, and melancholy to ask you to pardon me the three hundred and sixty-five annoyances my miserable legal disputes have, against my wishes, caused you, both this past year and in years previous... As for me, I can only rejoice in these eight years of pleasant and unbroken association, which has become a "steadfast" friendship that is by now indestructible; a reciprocal friendship that is my *bulwark*, my *right*,

> and my *pleasure*, and that offers me, in addition, a firm footing, allowing me to pester you even from my grave (and I will be in it before long, at this rate . . .).[13]

In June 1878 Virginia left the Hôtel de l'Alma and moved into an entresol apartment on the Place Vendôme. There at number 26 on what, a century earlier, Marquis Domenico Caracciolo had called "*la plus belle place au monde*" [the most beautiful square in the world], the most beautiful woman of the century set the scene for her exit. Ever since her husband's death, she had taken to wearing mostly black, which, besides foregrounding her widowhood, had the merit of suiting her complexion. Black reigned, too, in the apartment that now served as her refuge from pitiless daylight and prying eyes.

After the classic red and gold of her bridal chamber and the excessive candy pink of her room on the rue Castiglione, Virginia brilliantly anticipated modern architects and decorators by creating an effect that had until then been reserved for funerals. Was she perhaps remembering the legend of the Countess of Châteaubriant—a great passion of Francis I's and the first maîtresse-en-titre of a French king? It was said that, after she'd been deserted by the sovereign, her husband paid her back for her betrayal by locking the adulteress in a room bereft of light and wallpapered in black like a coffin. Instead of the unhappy chatelaine, it was now the mistress of France's last emperor celebrating her own living funeral by choosing to seal herself away in the heart of Paris, in sight of the column commemorating the feats of Napoleon the Great.

Montesquiou would visit the apartment after Virginia's eviction, noting the consistency of the decor:

> I found a ruined salon with walls painted black like the background of Pompeian frescoes, with a small white meander as on a funeral frieze, recalling the costume jewelry of the Queen of Etruria which she wore at the famous ball.[14]

The floor, too, was covered with black carpets, and the fabrics upholstering the sofas and armchairs were likewise black. We do not know for certain whether, as legend has it, the mistress of the house had veiled the mirrors to shield her eyes from the sight of her own decadence, but there was surely no need; from the permanently closed shutters, very little light filtered into an apartment immersed in murk. (Yet Virginia could not have done completely without a mirror when she faced the camera in the last years of her physical decline.)

Closed in on itself, with all the doors and windows barred against the world, her residence on the Place Vendôme was not only a refuge from a present in which she no longer had any place; it was a treasure chest in which to guard her past and a temple constructed for her future glory. The walls were hung from floor to ceiling with photographs that immortalized the countess's beauty and triumphs, and scattered over the tables or arranged in display cases were fans, trinkets, and precious objects that reflected her refined taste. Letters, telegrams, dispatches, secret codes, and ciphered messages were carefully locked away in a trunk—another was stored in La Spezia—as evidence of the role Virginia had played in the making of history.

The evocation of the past, however, was inseparable from the memory of the dead, which, as she wrote to Cléry, became increasingly persistent: "The prince is dead, my mother is dead, my grandfather is dead, my husband is dead... Must I, then, also die—despairingly?"[15]

After the death of her son, thoughts of mortality never left her alone. Yet she still had twenty more years to live.

In reality—as with her periods of isolation at Villa Gloria and Passy—her confinement on the Place Vendôme was less rigorous than Virginia made it out to be. In addition to visits from Cléry and Estancelin, who announced his presence by whistling under her windows whenever he happened to be in Paris, she still regularly received guests important enough to attract police attention. An 1881 report names Prince Napoleon, the Duke of Aumale, and the Orléans princes. But what most disconcerted the diligent officials were the apartment's security features: With two entrances—one on the square and one on a side street—the countess's visitors could come and go without running into one another. And access to the mezzanine required passing through three doors on three different levels, each equipped with a complex system of locks. The policemen would have been even more perplexed if they'd known that the keys to the front doors were hidden in a secret compartment of a finely chiseled cross on display in the apartment—the one engraved with the double V for Virginia Verasis[16]—and that those doors were opened only after the visitor had given the landlady a password that changed regularly. "These eccentricities of hers," the report concludes, "are well known in the neighborhood. Some say she is a madwoman. According to others, strange things must go on in that house."[17]

But no lock or bolt was strong enough to protect Virginia from her own obsessions. Her persecution mania, whose early symptoms her mother had recognized decades earlier, was by now chronic. Her fears and suspicions never left her alone. She was afraid of being spied on, robbed, and murdered, and life in general seemed laden with threats—chief among them the threat of ending up impoverished. Yet she wasn't afraid to go out alone at night, veiled and mantled in a big cape, and wander with her little dogs through the empty streets, sometimes walking down rue Castiglione to contemplate the ruins of the Tuileries, whose marble fragments she was collecting;[18] sometimes walking as far as rue Saint-Florentin, where she would stop and stare for a long time at the window of Gustave de Rothschild, the friend who'd never failed to offer a helping hand . . .[19]

All through her days and long sleepless nights, lying in bed or on a chaise longue, Virginia exorcised her loneliness by jotting down her thoughts on loose-leaf paper, filling pages in her diary, or letting it go in interminable letters. She'd always loved to write, but as she confessed to Estancelin, letter-writing—that "dialogue between the memories of two lives"[20] which was the exclusive privilege of friendship—was now her sole consolation.[21] It allowed her to escape her confinement, to give and get news, to comment on current events, make judgments, and tell her story according to her moods and fancies of the moment. Sometimes incisive and lapidary, at other times erratic, her prose combines a taste for portraiture with the pleasures of amplification—with a barrage of adjectives, epithets, and synonyms meant to reinforce her claims (not to mention her tendency to underline with abandon).

What stopped her from pursuing her dream of wielding her pen and revealing her truth once and for all? On one of many scattered loose-leaf sheets she confesses: "This is one of my dreams, one of the few great ambitions I have left. I would like it to remain as a legend to posterity written by me as a National reward (to memorialize a time and place) for the one great thing I have made *by myself* . . . Italy!"[22]

The emperor's decision to go to the aid of the Savoyard kingdom was made in her arms—why should she deny it? She'd even gone so far as to threaten:

> *Now I am alone, old,* and *free*, and I will not keep silent; I will fiercely *avenge* myself on everyone, I will tear apart anyone who has ever tried to destroy me, rob me, annihilate me, bury me alive—my youth, my beauty, my intelligence—to kill my power and my knowledge, even should it be my ruin.[23]

But in the end she held her silence. Why?

Perhaps, simply, out of fear. Virginia's financial situation was always chaotic and unpredictable, but she could rely on two fixed incomes: the pension awarded to her by Victor Emmanuel II and the pension paid out by the Rothschilds, in the name of friendship and information received in the past. But by now the income from Italy depended on the blessing of Umberto I, who certainly wouldn't have appreciated revelations about the private and political underside of the Risorgimento at odds with his father's image as a "gentleman king" or with the official narrative of the national epic. And with the Rothschilds, too, caution was called for. In republican France, the fact that she'd once been Napoleon III's mistress had become her chief liability. When in February 1873 the newspapers reported a theft at the Italian legation—a theft in which "confidential documents" she received from the emperor had been taken[24]—Virginia hastened to issue a denial in *Le Pays*. No sooner was the French army defeated at Sedan than she decided to protect her position in France by repudiating her relationship with Napoleon III, even shamelessly asking Thiers to have the new government safeguard the effects she had stowed in Paris.[25] And afterward, whenever she was confronted with accusations leveled by the gutter press, she always denied what had been. But after all, weren't even the Rothschilds trying to make people forget their hegemonic role in the financial life of the Second Empire? The rise of anti-Semitism and the political volatility in republican France did not bode well for them.

Having convinced herself once and for all that it would always be inadvisable for her to claim her rightful place in the history of the Risorgimento—but still determined to refute the malicious judgments and calumnies meted out by memoirists of the Second Empire[26]—she considered entrusting the task to Estancelin. The Norman, who also entertained writing his memoirs, was immensely knowledgeable about history, had closely followed the political vicissitudes of France from the July Monarchy to the Third Republic, knew Virginia well, and was sincerely fond of her. He therefore accepted the proposal, on the condition that she provide him with reliable facts, names, and dates, and that he be allowed to inspect the documents in his friend's possession. But Virginia was not about to produce any evidence, believing that beauty, intelligence, and a flair for diplomacy were more than enough to explain the extraordinary prestige she'd enjoyed among all the crowned heads of Europe, not excluding the pope. And when Estancelin persisted in trying to obtain more precise information, they immediately locked horns.

"But you're demanding too much," she protested in the face of her friend's tenacity. "I'm throwing in the towel. You've made me want to forget the whole thing with all your doubts and refutations."[27] When he asked her for clarification about Orsini's assassination attempt, she replied: "Don't breathe a word of it! Do you want to make me out to be an accomplice of that murderer of emperors and people?"[28] When he retreated to friendlier territory and asked about the famous costumes she'd worn in the days of the *fête impériale*, she grew indignant at "those details manufactured by hateful slanderers, those costumes of undress flaunted before all and sundry." How dare he imply she'd led a worldly life? She had spent almost all her time in "the remote solitude of her Passy"![29] When finally he dared to question her regarding the rumors about her private life, she started calling him names: "It is incredible that an intelligence like yours should dwell on such vile matters. Stop, you wretch! It would be worse than a storm, it would be the end of everything. To load such fantasies on my poor infirm shoulders, when I am too old to retaliate..."[30] Because Estancelin kept repeating "I don't know everything, therefore I don't know anything,"[31] the project fell through, and no trace remains of the book, which was to be called *La plus belle femme du siècle* [The most beautiful woman of the century], except the title. But another trial awaited her.

"The hermit of Passy, the solitary of Dieppe, the recluse of Paris"[32] had been living on the Place Vendôme for a decade and a half when her landlord notified her that he intended to take back possession of her apartment. At the prospect of leaving this sanctuary where she had planned to end her days, Virginia lost control. Although the landlord said he was willing to throw her a golden bridge, an all-out war soon broke out, complete with legal action, insults, threats, and reprisals. Even the mice joined the fray. In the list of grievances Virginia gave Cléry, there were plenty of comic moments:

> No sooner was the chicken on the table than the famous mice tore it to shreds, and the same fate befell the precious documents you saw on my desk, and even a bouquet of cornflowers; not one was

> spared. And my bed . . . at night the mice do the contradance there under my pillows, devouring lace, plush, batiste, handkerchiefs; they don't miss a thing, linens, furs, and fichus; when they gnaw at the floorboards, the noise of it doesn't let you close your eyes . . . But it's not like I can hypnotize these rodents the way I used to hypnotize the men of the empire![33]

After three years of grueling disputes the landlord prevailed, and Virginia was forced to leave the entresol, which would later—ironically—be home to the famous jeweler Boucheron, whose shop still stands on the ground floor of the building.

"The death sentence shocked me . . . All's bad that ends badly!"[34] she wrote to Cléry, who urged her to make a virtue of necessity, to change her life, to choose a brighter and healthier place to live. But she had given up—"It is too late to start a new life when one has already begun to die"[35]—and on January 15, 1894, Virginia moved with her two little dogs to 14 rue Cambon. Determined not to move too far from "her column," she retreated to a grim, dark, airless little apartment above Le Voisin—the restaurant where she regularly dined. Fate had dictated she would "come to an *ugly*, *miserable*, *squalid* end,"[36] and yet all she asked for was "*a bed* and some peace and quiet, by the grace of God; because it isn't my place of residence that's changing but *my life*."[37]

During the years she was desperately struggling to stay in her funereal entresol, Virginia often thought of Italy and what her life might have been there. "I was born in greatness and for greatness," she wrote to Estancelin. "Ah, if you had seen it with your own eyes—that palace you might well imagine nestled in the clouds, and all my villas and lands, with the vassals kneeling to kiss my hand!"[38] Yet since she'd gone back to living in Paris she had confined herself to brief sojourns in La Spezia, which turned out to be anything but idyllic.[39] She found herself constantly grappling with new expropriations, legal battles, unpaid mortgages, and claims from peasants, and after appealing to the government, quarreling with the mayor, and letting administrators and lawyers take over with the creditors, the only thing left for her to do was flee. Her father's death[40] forced her to take matters into her own hands again. After he remarried, the marquis stopped communicating with his daughter, but he nevertheless bequeathed her what remained of his properties, along with their numerous mortgages, whose interest he'd always paid, though he could never pay them off in full. Virginia did not follow suit. But when in November 1891 her properties went to auction, she refused to resign herself, and the next year she returned to La Spezia to buy back the houses and land from the new owner.[41] Her feelings may have fluctuated, but her sense of ownership remained unchanged. She stayed in La Spezia from September 1892 to February 1893, intending to put her affairs in order. To recover her property, she'd been forced to take out a loan and a new mortgage,[42] but instead of paying her creditors, old and new, she dreamed up grandiose projects, such as modernizing the Castello di San Giorgio and turning it into a refuge for noblewomen who had fallen on hard times.

After returning to Paris—wholly absorbed as she was in the War of the Entresol—she paid no heed to warnings about her unpaid mortgage interest or subpoenas from administrators, lawyers, and engineers who had handled her problems without ever seeing a cent in compensation. Justice took its course, and the Oldoini properties were auctioned off again.[43]

In this tumultuous atmosphere, which culminated in her move to rue Cambon, Virginia tried to collect her thoughts by writing fifty-some pages to an unknown correspondent which make it clear that her mental condition was worsening.[44] Too many defeats had upset the fragile balance between vital élan and nervous pathology, between lucidity and hallucination, and Virginia, who by now was unable to keep her demons at bay, wrote in, and out of, her insanity.

The letters, which date from May 1894,[45] were addressed to a devoted friend[46] to whom the countess entrusted the complex management of the La Spezia estate. Urged to make decisions and send money immediately to cover her most recent legal troubles, she could do no more than voice her despondency.

A full fourteen pages long, the first letter is dated May 12, 1894, Pentecost Saturday:

> After last night's bomb,[47] about which I'm enclosing a clipping, whose blast I was near and fatefully eluded, as I eluded the promise of strangulation contained in a note slipped under my door, death clearly doesn't want me, yet I want death, slow, beautiful, and serene, but certain, and soon, life loathes and rejects me from every side, in every shape and form.

Some time before, a mysterious friend, who "had hung his helmet on the door on the Cappuccini hill," had sworn that he would "take Mina out of this ugly world with his own hand if she could no longer be at peace in it, give her love and beautiful sweetness, rescuing her from the discontent, the pain, the terror of people, the filth, the baseness, the loathing, the fear, the sickness, lifting her up out of danger and keeping her safe from threats so that she would no longer be a *cible* [target].” But alas, the man with the helmet had died, and she could no longer find anyone “capable of such sacrifice and virtue.”

Why, instead of tormenting her with unsolvable problems, didn’t her correspondent help her die?

> Do you want to come? In any case I can’t stand any more of this deplorable life, I’ve had all I can take, and I’m at the end of my strength, my courage, my endurance, my physical, moral, and physical will, wherever I am. So stop fanning the flames with these withering, *perplexing*, *confusing*, tormenting, punctilious, plaintive, suspicious, curious, accusatory, quibbling, bargaining, imperious, hazardous-to-things-and-facts, saddening, chilling, alienating letters—*entraînantes au silence ou à la révolte* [inviting silence or revolt].

All this aggravated her “terrible psychological state . . . to the utmost” and kept her “from sleeping, dreaming, resting, calming down, or thinking good thoughts, to the point that one feels an urge to do harm or wreak havoc on everything around.” “Wanting me to do as you wish is not the same as wanting me to do what ought to be done,” she wrote, and it was not “caprice or malice” but her nature that made it impossible to “suppress [her] feelings.” She concluded: “A madman knows more in his own home than a sane person knows in the homes of others.”

Virginia’s thoughts wandered dangerously, without order or logic:

> The wind drives me here and there and I cannot stop the wheel of misfortune and tribulation. I go wherever destiny takes me and the current takes me away. I don't know where, or how, or when I could find someplace that could tell me what or how tomorrow will be. Nor would I believe my eyes if I saw such a place. I am like a ship on the high seas *en détresse* which no one can or will ever know anything about . . . So stop tormenting me to no purpose . . . Let me follow my destiny, let me do as I will do however good or bad it seems . . . Neither calculations, nor plans, nor schemes, nor negotiations matter to me. *Le hasard seul me guide, la fatalité me conduit* [Chance alone guides me, fate leads me]."

The memory of the pain she felt on arriving in La Spezia after her properties were auctioned off became inseparable from the agonizing financial worries that gave her no rest in Paris:

> I have seen all my poor movable property sold. My beautiful jewels at the pawnshop (to pay the Oldoini debts last year, when I came to La Spezia). I don't have two centimes to rub together in either Paris or London. How will I get by? God help me if I don't die of sorrow . . . I have seen all my precious mementos, portraits, books, clothes, objets d'art, crystal, porcelain, and bronzes broken, dirty, ruined, wrecked from being cleared out by third and fourth parties . . . Where to put all this?

She no longer had "the loins or the lungs to climb up and down the Cappuccini hill"[48] and look in on her villas and farmhouses, and besides, everywhere she went there were threatening, vindictive peasants who forced her, when she was in La Spezia, never to leave the house unless she was escorted by servants.

The second letter was written on Pentecost and begins with her disappointment at not having experienced "anything good, anything profound" on that special day:

> It is precisely because I wanted something that I didn't experience it! And this holiday, which is generally jolly and lush for all and sundry, when even children have fun, play games, dress up for the big festivities. Poor me, in bed, not even naked, with nothing good enough to put on or take off, nothing to distract myself, nothing to occupy my time, neither books nor writings nor mementos nor portraits. Nothing.

In the squalor of rue Cambon—where the furniture was piled high for lack of space—her thoughts turned back to the house of her youth in La Spezia, where everything was "clean, tidy, pristine, and beautiful." She had always been fiercely protective of "things I cherish whose provenance, memories, and history I alone know."[49] And she had religiously preserved a handful of childhood heirlooms with the power to precipitate the process of memory, freeing her from the anxieties of the present:

> I want to speak here of my little armchair, the little armchair I had as a little girl, which Marietta always carried to wherever I was and from which Paolinella, with her overlarge head, was always falling and hurting herself. I would put her back, give her two slaps, then two kisses, then I would sit her in the little chair, and I would tie her

up with my jump rope so that she would never fall again, and then she would struggle so much that she'd tip over together with the chair and bump her head and cry and beam and throw punches and say, "Niny tied me up and made me fall," and Guglielmina the madwoman would laugh.

The memory was so vivid that Virginia felt she was back in La Spezia, and, like a queen, gave orders to clear a space for the little chair in her bedroom:

> I want to put it under the window in my room between the horn armoire and the Venetian bed... but if the bed doesn't fit... let it be taken back to the chapel. Write, see to it. Take care not to break the Murano vase on the terrace and bring it back inside.

Then, coming back to herself, she asked:

> But where I have let my thoughts wander? I have other things to think about. Recollections of *innocent youth* on the immolated Golgotha. It is quite clear I am at death's *door*, and ending my life amid so many worries, I keep remembering my happy childhood! What human foolishness in this world—nothing but movement, loss, and love which is nothing and everything at once; and so one mustn't care for anything, nor for anyone; that is what religion commands, and *the real monks and nuns* have always been my vocation and passion... It is quite clear there is truly a thread that pulls and draws us toward our cradle when we are about to climb into our coffins. It is death, death, day in and day out, and it drives one to tears, to keen and *curse. Alas, alas.*

Accustomed though she was to self-observation and self-analysis, Virginia also noted the progressive estrangement of all the landed gentry from their roots:

> Everything that was never mine nor will ever be mine, now that I have to lose it after having just recovered it, seeing and savoring it all again . . . is like a return to earthly paradise after emerging from hell but in fact it would be as it always was a prison and perpetual hard labor with a whole string of humiliations, and the *red cap*,[50] chains, and the anchor, and death. I am well aware—and the fateful "I" has foretold it—that I will end my days and die where and how the old masters have ended up dying, for two or three generations now, all of them living abroad and being robbed blind, ill-treated, mocked; my death sentence is written, the same as theirs was, and more so, inexorable fate has made it doubly clear. So be it, then, but so be it *quickly*, you understand? I am not doing anything in this world anyway.[51]

In the third letter Virginia seems to have regained her composure. She finds elegant phrases to express her melancholy, conjuring up an ancient legend:

> For I've set my sights on a ray of sunshine that floods my heart with an emotion sad and *deep*, which my desperate Elkovan,[52] mortally wounded by chains, carries all the way here and so no longer has the physical, moral, or material strength to go soaring over our Cappuccini peaks! It must be beautiful and sweet . . . the *saisissement* [the sudden shock] of the celestial land.

To recover her physical and mental health, Virginia had always needed light, fresh air, and the sea. La Spezia and Dieppe were places where she could find her footing. She'd been forced to give up Dieppe, and now even the *joli golfe* was off-limits to her. Finally, the city she'd loved so much, the ultra-modern Paris, was turning out to be a "hell" on earth—a place of collective alienation:

> At least here everything and everyone has an indifferent and banal realism. No one either lives or dies! They all vegetate day after day and grow hardened, foolishly ignoring, criminalizing the nature that none of them ever sees either day or night until they no longer feel its emotional or sensory effects; like the plant with the feeling leaves that shrink back when touched. When I was a child that little plant frightened me and I didn't understand it. I used to look for those Mors et Vita plants, but I never found them again. A rare and misunderstood plant. I have always resembled and abided by it.

For someone who considered herself without equal, only the plant world provided examples of things rare enough to bear comparison:

> A unique flower spontaneously born in the barren wastes on the desolate peaks of the Alps. The edelweiss is the flower of the wilderness and whitest sadness. The flower of pale melancholy, the leaves of hopelessness, for edelweiss represents desolation and despair... and that is why an idealistic and compassionate poet[53] wrote some verses about that flower for me, mentioning my name!!! on black

> paper which stands for tears and cold! Edelweiss is a flower that weeps and smiles (like me)!!! Edelweiss *fleur de bonheur fleur de malheur* [flower of happiness flower of unhappiness].

At this point Virginia is torn from her "vague *dreams*, past and future . . . only to fall back suddenly and deeply into the vile, ugly reality of all her hideous, dreadful, disgusting, irritating affairs . . ."[54] But even more intolerable than reality were the impostures of hypocritical morality, which even now raged against her:

> Enough, enough, I don't want anything more of the kind. No more simulations of *love, honor, affection, esteem, respect, deference, friendship, trust, confidence, sentiments* . . . It would make me weep with anger and lash out like a dog if I had their low character, but I am by nature lofty and proud, frank, clean, and clear, I don't care for half-measures, half-words, half-trusts, half-suspicions, half-accusations, half-ignorances, half-loves. For me it's all or nothing.[55]

The death of Valentine Delessert—also in May 1894—roused Virginia from her delusions and induced her to leave her sickbed, though "barely able to stand," and attend her old friend's funeral in Passy. "Never have I seen or described a gloomier burial, which, on the *orders* of the dead, was *sans fleurs et sans femmes* [without flowers or women]," she recounts in her fifth letter. The sole surviving member of the large Delessert family, which twenty years earlier had offered her their friendship, was Édouard. The sadness of this ceremony did not, however, prevent Virginia from noting with satisfaction that she could still be the center of attention:

> Everyone was looking at me, the *fossoyeurs* [gravediggers] and the nuns who *seemed* to want to make me one of *theirs*... serious and *sévère* under my "negro" veil. "Madame la Reine"—they took me for the empress, as usual, in mourning and out of doors, where there were people... and they sang praises "oh *la jolie femme*."

And she pictured herself back in the radiance of her youth:

> Out there in the sun among the roses and greenery, I smiled sadly at that crowd and imagined myself back in that same cemetery that *has been* and *will be* mine, in that country where with the dead woman and her children I spent my best (and worst) years with the boy... Yesterday I saw the author photographer painter [Édouard Delessert] still in love and perplexed to find me *unchanged*! (he wept, poor Old Man, with pity).[56]

Valentine Delessert's funeral was not the first to lead Virginia back to the "greenery" of the 16th arrondissement. Ten months earlier, the news that Dr. Blanche was on his deathbed made her linger at the gate of the house in Auteuil, though she never summoned the courage to ask how he was, only, on the day of the funeral, laying a bouquet of flowers on the coffin of her "oldest and dearest friend." In the long letter of condolence she wrote to Jacques Blanche a month after his father's death, the pain she felt over the loss of the illustrious clinician who'd taken such fatherly care of her is inseparable from self-pity. She wonders why she continues to be the victim of other people's ill will: "Why is there so much curiosity about my person and my images, about this strange Lady of other times and other customs... I have undergone, borne, endured enough." With a twinkle of irony, Virginia concludes by asking him not to show her letter to anyone so she doesn't come across as "a patient recently escaped from Dr. Blanche's madhouse."[57]

But the persecutions she complained of were not exclusively the fruit of her imagination. Using her move from the Place Vendôme as a pretext, the newspaper *Le Gaulois* had published outrageous articles with headlines such as "One of the Many Ladies of the Imperial Decameron," "The Empire of Beauty," "Salammbô at the Tuileries," "The Shame of Old Age," "Buried Alive?" Deeply vexed, Virginia broke her silence, sending a journalist from *L'Événement* a reply of great dignity, without a shred of madness:

> Tell me, Monsieur le François, where does this need to concern yourself with a woman who doesn't concern anyone come from?... Why devote yourself to denigrating a woman who has never done anything other than serve her country... and yours too? And tell me how it is possible, in this land famous for courtesy and good taste, that a man like Mr. Arthur Meyer would allow a piece to be published which, using my change of address as a flimsy excuse, cruelly mocks my old age and ugliness? If I am old and ugly it is no fault of mine and until today I believed that old age, if not ugliness, at least merited the respect of respectable people.[58]

Without Dr. Blanche's support, Virginia resorted for the last time to a therapy that in the past had proved infallible. On September 1, 1893, after twenty-six years' absence, she returned to Pierson for a long series of photo sessions that would go on for another two years, representing a clinical record of her descent into madness.

Titled *Rachel*, in homage to the famous interpreter of Phèdre who died in 1858, the first portrait of the *Saint Cécile et Rachel* series is quite impressive. Like "a great actress who graciously allows the lens to capture her in a few poses representing the roles that have made her famous,"[59] Virginia is portrayed full-length against a neutral backdrop, wrapped in a black burnoose[60] embroidered with shining sequins and jets. Her headwear is black—an embossed scarf with horizontal bands that falls over her chest, where the famous pearl necklace can just be glimpsed—and the gauzy dotted veil that sets off the paleness of her still-beautiful face is black, too. Her large, made-up eyes stare at us sternly, evoking the legend of the Hermit of Passy. Virginia, it seems, hasn't forgotten the tricks of the trade. She makes her figure slim by choosing a cylindrical hairstyle and climbing onto a bench hidden by her long dress, which skims the floor, while Pierson, for his part, lights her face without revealing any of the marks of age. It is an image in sharp contrast with the anecdote relayed by Jacques Blanche around the same time, when, shortly after the death of his father, Virginia asked him to paint her portrait. Summoned to a room covered in dark fabric with all the shutters closed, he found himself face-to-face with the irreparable:

> My model entered without a sound, gliding over the carpet, like an "apparition." She posed in profile, her back straight as a board. Despite her tall, tiara-like hairstyle, she was a poor thing. One by one, her veils fell to the ground . . . and I recognized the Etruscan queen, the Hermit of Passy—idol of the court of Napoleon III—a famous but painted, ruined, shopkeeper's face; a piece of half-sucked barley sugar in the hand of a child.[61]

Blanche fled the scene, yet that tragic image must have left its mark if ten years later he evoked Virginia in a ghostly portrait[62] titled *Revenante, ou La comtesse de Castiglione: Souvenir de 1893*, based on the *Rachel* he received as a gift from the countess.

Pierson's artistry, and the deep affection he felt for his client, cannot prevent the next series of photographs (the *Série des roses*) from being increasingly disturbing, and it is hard to fathom what prompted Virginia—almost bald, toothless, her face swollen, her body withered—to exhume her old costumes and pose in front of the same mirror that, thirty years earlier, had replicated the perfection of her features, or to be photographed half-length in the famous cape of now-mangy ermine with epaulettes askew and sporting a helmet-shaped cap. Did she still *feel* beautiful, and was she still counting on Pierson's mastery and his skillful alterations after the fact?[63] Locked in her isolation, unconcerned about the passage of time, had her self-image become frozen in that remote era? Yet she'd been cruelly humiliated when her faithful admirer, George of Prussia, on a visit to Paris in 1892, had invited her for a stroll in the Bois de Boulogne. To please him, she dressed as she had for their first meeting, when the prince offered to escort her to the Exposition of 1867. Wrapped in the same cashmere shawl she'd worn in that long-ago spring, with a bullfighter hat haloed by a vaporous white veil, she walked beside her old cicisbeo down avenue des Acacias (where, not long after, Boldini, Sem, and Helleu would take up their posts and study the modern-style clothing of the fashionable crowd). The couple had "gone just a few steps when they heard laughter and exclamations behind them and realized someone was following them. Not understanding the reason for this hilarity, they sought refuge in their carriage, which was just then passing by."[64] Years before, it had been the laughter and mockeries of the urchins of La Spezia, who waited for her at the gate when she ventured out into the street, that led Virginia never to set foot in her lost paradise again.[65]

Pierson's final photographs document her surrender to the devastation of old age and the masochistic fury it unleashed in her. It was no longer a question of concealing her physical decline but of pillorying it, in one last act of defiance. At the height of her beauty the countess had dared, with outrageous immodesty, to lift her dress above her knees and immortalize the statuesque perfection of her legs and bare feet in a series of photographs destined to become famous. She now exposed them to the camera again, resting them on a dark pillow, like the feet of a dead woman in a coffin. "A cruel echo of the libertine and careless images of thirty years before," those swollen feet—of which she was once so proud—suggested to her the title *Le Pé. L'amputation du Gruyère*. As Pierre Apraxine rightly observes, "it is less an image of a mythical past than a morbid prognostication."[66]

Virginia seemed just as delighted by her social decline. She had gotten into the habit of spending many hours in a private room at Le Voisin, the restaurant on the ground floor of her building on rue Cambon, chatting with the waiters and drinking too much champagne. And in the photograph *Nostalgie* she had herself portrayed at the table, framed between two bottles like a Toulouse-Lautrec prostitute. But the most appalling portrait of her is the one from 1895, entitled *Ti-fille brune*: Dressed as a commoner, with a crooked mouth and a crazy expression, Virginia clasps her hands at waist height, pointing her index fingers in the direction of her pubis.

Before the camera came to substantiate the scandal of her decline,

Virginia entertained one last dream: Instead of telling her life in words, she would do so through images, putting on a major exhibition of photographs for the Exposition Universelle that was to be held in Paris in 1900. It would be called *The Most Beautiful Woman of the Century* and would consecrate her artistic talent. Virginia had always known she was an artist. She was a born actress—unexcelled at commanding a stage, capturing the audience's attention, inventing extraordinary costumes, embodying every state of mind—and in a moment of elation she even went so far as to declare that she was also a musician and writer;[67] but it was photography that allowed her to bypass the prohibitions of her social status. In the rooms of the Mayer & Pierson atelier, safe from prying eyes, she was able to put her talents at the service of an art that had been born only about ten years before her. In those rooms it was Virginia who imposed her choices, orchestrating her appearance, dictating the poses, the expressions, the clothes, and the characters. And she found an ideal partner in Pierre-Louis Pierson, who had personally looked after her since they'd first met in July 1856. Their pact lasted for four decades—the longest collaboration of its kind in the history of portraiture—and produced more than four hundred photographs.

> From her first happy experiments in front of the lens, the countess knows that the photographic negative faithfully records every nuance of her gaze. The exposure time—a few seconds—condemns physiognomies to permanent immobility, but her eyes bring the image to life. She manages to modulate her expression with astonishing mastery... But in a justly famous portrait, entitled *Scherzo di follia*—an homage to Verdi's opera *Un ballo in maschera*—she goes so far as to make her gaze the true protagonist. By holding an empty

frame very close to her face, the countess hides it and isolates her right eye. It is a striking image. The eye *framed* in this way seems to take on a life of its own, and the resulting gaze eludes description. The countess's identity is erased. She becomes immune to time. And the image becomes symbolic: the primacy of the visual heralds the prominent role that the century will reserve for photography.[68]

Though they began as a lark, the sessions with "Papa Pierson" turned out to be crucial experiences for Virginia. Photography not only immortalized her beauty and memorialized her triumphs but opened the doors to a universe that abided solely by her imagination—a marvelous creative process that did not end in front of the lens, since it could be continued in the process of altering the photographs, retouching them, perfecting them, and transforming them into gouaches.[69]

Strange as it may seem, Virginia always maintained the utmost secrecy about her artistic enterprise,[70] giving portraits and albums only to a small circle of close friends and a handful of notable personages by whom she wished to be remembered[71]—only to regret it later, and ask for their return.

At the Paris Exposition of 1867, however, in addition to authorizing Pierson to exhibit her portrait as the Queen of Hearts—in the gouache version by Aquilin Schad—she asked in vain to be listed as an exhibitor, thereby claiming "her status as an artist."[72] Thus, as the Exposition of 1900 approached, she was planning to return to the scene with a photographic retrospective in which she would be author, director, costume and set designer, as well as the sole performer. But fate had other plans. For many years, death had been Virginia's uppermost thought—an entrancement that prescinded the bonds of friendship, eliminated the element of time, and drove her to leave her refuge and come face-to-face with other people. When in 1889, after the funeral of Madame de Canrobert—one of Empress Eugénie's former ladies-in-waiting—the Tuileries faithful saw her unexpectedly reappear after more than thirty years and write her name in the register of visitors, they all felt a "thrill": "That woman was a piece of living history. Her mere presence was enough to evoke a distant past." But it was chance that granted this distant past an epilogue. As Virginia was leaving, she passed another woman dressed in black just about to go in. Recognizing the empress—who, being in Paris, had decided to bid a final farewell to her loyal lady-in-waiting—Virginia respectfully stepped aside to let her pass. The two old rivals did not exchange a single word, although, when she spoke of the meeting later, Eugénie gently wondered: "But why didn't she greet me? I would have returned her greeting with pleasure. I haven't been angry with her for a long time now."[73]

The memory of her dead family members had begun to haunt her too. Once they were gone from the earth, she could no longer avoid dealing with all the unfinished business. Was there a single one of them—above all her mother, her husband, her son—she felt no bitterness toward? She couldn't erase them from her memory; she needed them in order to remember how much she'd been loved. And so she adopted the solution most congenial to her: she appropriated them and turned them into tutelary deities. Pierson's last photograph is, in this regard, emblematic. It shows her sitting before an easel, retouching two portraits of her parents. The need to reinvent her dead, as she'd reinvented her own life time after time, convinced her of her own sincerity. How else could she have the impudence to proclaim, to Poniatowski no less, her love for her husband and her mother: "Do you believe that one of them had or would ever have tormented or bothered or grieved or abandoned me? No, they loved me, their affection and their devotion, their self-denial, their idolatry was proof enough, and that is why I love them so much."[74] She loved them because they had put no limits on their love:

> That's how my dead were, and is that why I love them *so dearly*? And now where am I? In old age without anyone who knew me when I was young, *beautiful*, rich, powerful, useful, and helpful to them, as to all the truly needy. By nature good and generous I find myself alone, sick, miserable, ill-treated, powerless in every sense and no longer able to move *forward an inch*. Changing my life, changing my death, losing my country, which I made, of Italy!, parting with it, remaking myself as a *French* woman of *Russian* religion, and bidding farewell to everyone and everything.[75]

Meanwhile, she had been denied even the consolation of being able to lie beside them in her tomb. She'd tried and failed to have her son's remains repatriated from Spain. She longed to reunite them with her husband's and be buried alongside them. But instead she was forced to "abandon the bones of my 'Demoiseau' to the rats, though on his deathbed he asked that Mina reunite them. No these are *cruel* things and *unparalleled* things from the centuries before Christ. And who knows where the man who was my husband lies? And the illustrious ancestors and uncles—who can say? As for me, 'I *lived alone* and I died alone!' Amen! Amen!"[76]

The only thing left for her to do was stage the spectacle of her own death. Her preparations were painstaking. She entrusted her last wishes to, among others, the Clérys, her friend René Brizard, and Estancelin. "No heirs . . . and no family members, neither in France nor in Italy." The newspapers were to be paid off to refrain from reporting her death. The only people who needed to know were the King of Italy and the Rothschilds. The clothing for her coffin was described in detail: "*Compiègne nightgown*, 1857, batiste, lace, and long striped peignoir, black velour, white plush (located at 14 rue Cambon); on my neck the *petite fille* pearl necklace with nine rows, six white and three black, and the usual necklace, the one I have always worn, with the perforated coin and the crystal clasp, the initials and crown, which all my dressers know well; on my arms, bare and laid out, my two bracelets, one onyx with a pearl in the middle, and one black enamel, star-shaped and lustrous, which are elsewhere." At her feet, as cushions, she wanted Sandouga and Kasino, her two stuffed Maltese, "beautiful, all dressed up in blue and purple coats with [their] initials and collars with a pink flower and cypress pattern." And finally she summarized her last wishes:

> (1) No Cross. (2) No Priest. (3) No Church. (4) No Ceremony. (5) No Flowers. (6) No Viewing. 7) No Vigil. 8) No Doctor. 9) No Judge. 10) No Commissioner. 11) No Consul. 12) No Ambassador. 13) No Special Representative. 14) No Seals. 15) No Heirs. 16) No Cortege. 17) No Mortuary. 18) No Invitations. 19) No Announcements. 20) No Newspapers.[77]

Death, prayed for and feared, came to her on November 29, 1899, in the early hours of the morning. Virginia suffered a stroke and passed away quietly, watched over by her elderly maid, Luisa Corsi, and some waiters from Le Voisin. She was sixty-two years old.

# Postmortem

None of Virginia's provisions would be respected. She would not go "set Paradise ablaze,"[1] wearing her Compiègne nightgown and all her jewelry, nor would she even escape a religious ceremony at the nearby Church of Sainte Marie-Madeleine. They would bury her not in La Spezia, where she had so often longed to go to ground, but in Père-Lachaise Cemetery in Paris. Furthermore, upon hearing the news of her death, the Italian ambassador immediately sent a young diplomat with a great future, Count Carlo Sforza, to rue Cambon with an order to affix the seals and destroy all papers found in the apartment. Even her statement about the absence of heirs was promptly discredited. Some cousins from Genoa, the Trigones, whose existence the countess had forgotten, would justly claim the right to her assets. In addition to the properties in La Spezia, Virginia had left, piled up in four rented apartments—two on rue de Castiglione and two in the Batignolles district—furniture, mirrors, porcelain, crystal, silver, cosmetic items, and ornaments of all kinds, not to mention trunks upon trunks overflowing with fabrics, lace, clothes, furs, precious Indian cashmere shawls, and various other accessories. One trunk contained a quantity of umbrellas with jeweled handles; another, "hundreds of mother-of-pearl, chased silver and gold fans, all painted with splendid watercolors, and each corresponding to a dress worn to a particular reception or ball."[2] The great auction at Drouot in June 1901[3] would disperse this extraordinary collection of relics from her glorious past, from which Virginia never wished to part. The centerpiece was obviously her jewels, and first and foremost the famous necklace from the emperor, "weighing 3,838 grains [almost 300 grams] and with 279 pearls," which would be purchased for about half a million francs—roughly equivalent to three million euros today.

But Virginia needed no grave goods to ensure she would live on in the collective imagination. She had already become a legend in her own time. Even in the early 1870s, the great memoirist of the Second Empire, Arsène Houssaye, crossing the Place Vendôme late one night, felt his heart skip a beat when he saw "a passerby taking shape in the nocturnal dark . . . preceded by two little dogs [like] two balls of fat . . . covered, more than dressed, in a light cloak with a frilled hood . . . 'Behold, take heed, *there is Castiglione*,'"[4] he'd whispered to Ferdinand Bac, who had recently arrived in Paris, and he explained why that name alone was enough to conjure an era.

A decade later, it would be Robert de Montesquiou who was overcome with emotion when he discovered "that in a certain building on the Place Vendôme, behind shutters eternally closed, there lived a woman, and that this was the woman whose name has become, for a particular historical period, but perhaps also for all time, synonymous with *beauty*."[5] The writer would subsequently wander more than once under the windows of the entresol, hoping to catch a glimpse or the merest movement of his idol through the cracks in the shutters. When she learned of the interest of this refined poet twenty years her junior, Virginia read and annotated his *Les Perles rouges*,[6] making it her own and retitling it "Hortensia bleu" after the title of his latest collection of verses; but she never wished to meet him. It was only after the countess died that, thanks to one of the doctors[7] who pronounced her dead, Montesquiou was permitted to set eyes on her:

> Having been summoned to come the following morning, when the body would be placed in the coffin, I went up a small staircase above Le Voisin that led me into the humble rooms that had served as the exile's refuge for many years. For we really must call it exile—the way she was obliged to leave, as she said, her Column.
>
> A narrow door opened before me, and the doctor came to welcome me. A dozen or so persons were huddled together in the room—among them a representative from the Italian embassy and Maître Desouches, the countess's lawyer... as well as a few suppliers and servants.
>
> On the floor, at the center of the room, lay the coffin, ready to be closed again.
>
> I have an impression of what I saw more than I have an image. A sculptural mask, with imposing features, strong lines, and rigid cheekbones; the brow bone, wide and magnificent, attracted and captivated one's gaze, as though it were a span of light. The banal expression "it was a bolt from the blue" takes on its full force, grandeur, and precision in this case. It was truly, for me, a bolt from the blue—the pale and abrupt appearance of this beautiful, this grave, this noble face, which was about to disappear forever.
>
> But these adjectives are insufficient; there was also something august and heroic about those features. Yes, what struck me most forcefully, during that fleeting minute and the memory it bequeathed

> me, is that her face seemed less supernatural than superhuman, and almost asexual; one could easily have mistaken it for that of a great man, an illustrious captain, a famous poet.
>
> Isn't that as it should be, though? Wasn't she a woman with a virile spirit—a spirit of *domination* and, at the same time, *poetry*?
>
> ... The lid was set back in place.[8]

Obsessed by this vision, Montesquiou would go to great lengths to bring the femme fatale he'd never had a chance to know back to life. To reconstruct her personality, feelings, tastes, and life choices, the writer threw himself into wide-ranging investigations, questioning every living soul who'd known her, acquiring her letters, stockpiling her photographs, and buying up any object that had belonged to her until he created a shrine at the Palais Rose in Vésinet, where worshippers could pay their respects. Twelve years later his quest culminated in the publication of *La divine comtesse*, the book that would establish her myth—a myth that mirrored the image the writer had conceived of himself. For he and Virginia in fact share many traits. With a prestigious family tree and a fortune sufficient to satisfy his costly whims, Robert de Montesquiou had made aesthetic supremacy his raison d'être, not unlike the *divine comtesse*. "His cold temperament, combined with his perfectionism," writes Philippe Jullian, "makes him one of France's rare dandies."[9] Tall, thin, with aristocratic features, the count presumed himself inimitable. Everything about him—his gestures, his tone of voice, his mode of dress—was studied down to the smallest detail. And he became a literary character even before he disclosed his own writerly ambitions. In 1884, Joris-Karl Huysmans had taken him as a model for Des Esseintes, the decadent aesthete of *À rebours*, thus inaugurating a series of portraits *à clé*,[10] the last and most famous of which would be that of the Baron de Charlus in Proust's *Recherche*.

A tireless promoter of his own image, and an unrivaled narcissist, this "sovereign of transitory things," as he proclaimed himself in a dedication to Proust,[11] "had himself photographed no less than 189 times in the course of his life. Each of these photographs was labeled and pasted in large albums with a fastidiousness no diva ever demonstrated. Only Mme de Castiglione posed so frequently before the camera."[12] And there is no lack of similarities when we examine their ways of presenting themselves. Like Virginia, Montesquiou in his photo sessions flaunted his very elegant wardrobe; had himself portrayed in a mask; dressed up as characters from the Arabian Nights, or as Zanetto or Saint John the Baptist. Also like Virginia, he presented a wide range of poses and moods and, for example in *Robert de Montesquiou's Hands*, took pleasure in isolating an anatomical detail of which he was particularly proud.[13]

Not content with pursuing his own aesthetic perfection, Montesquiou acted as Pygmalion to his young cousin, the beautiful Élisabeth Greffulhe (whom Proust would soon take as a model for the character of Oriane de Guermantes), expediting her debut in society. In the 1880s, when Virginia was still alive, it was Countess Greffulhe, twenty years her junior, who became the beauty of beauties of the new generation; who arrived late at balls only to make swift and dazzling appearances; who went on holidays in Dieppe; and who laid down the laws of "modern style" with clothes of her own devising, expertly tailored by the eternal Charles Frederick Worth. Sometimes, however, to avoid criticism, Élisabeth permitted herself *not* to follow the advice of her cousin, who found in the Countess of Castiglione the freedom, the irreverence, the originality, and the erotic provocation deficient in the overly perfect, overly conventional Élisabeth. And so he made the countess the symbol of his personal idea of the eternal feminine. By conjuring her up, putting words in her mouth, and interpreting the feelings and desires and metamorphoses of the modern Magdalene, he infiltrated her private life and experienced, through her, emotions that were otherwise off-limits to him. And he could do so without any qualms, because his idol was no longer able to contradict him. Clothes, jewelry, and photographs became excuses for exercises in style in which linguistic preciosity went hand in hand with the exegetical acrobatics of an erudite imagination. Like a princess from the Arabian Nights, the *divine comtesse* rode beside him on a flying carpet through civilizations and centuries only to become, once and for all, the quintessential heroine of fin-de-siècle decadence. Her portrait in *L'Ermite de Passy* becomes, in retrospect, the symbol of unattainable beauty: "The Countess of Castiglione, a voluntary recluse for more than twenty years in the lay cloister of silence and in the secular convent of solitude, was a Carmelite nun devoted to her own beauty; she withdrew, not into God, but into herself."[14] Asked to write the preface to his French friend's book, a perplexed Gabriele D'Annunzio preferred to take cover behind the generic statement that "with each step, each gesture, each glance," Montesquiou's heroine "seems to be imprinting her own figure in the very substance of the poetry." But after he himself imbues the countess with the solemn aura of Tuscan humanism, he cannot help but wonder: "Is this man who loves and celebrates her in the perfection of death perhaps forgetting that she, too, had a Dawn?" And he reminds us of the days when she "bore her youth like an immortality."[15]

For the first time the seasoned seductress, the beautiful one accustomed to chaining men to her chariot, found herself prisoner, possessed by a suitor and at the mercy of his fantasies. Yet by appropriating her Montesquiou consecrated the legend whose foundations Virginia had laid, transforming her defeat into a triumph.

# Acknowledgments

I AM, FIRST OF ALL, touched and grateful to Roberto Calasso for having welcomed me once more into the catalog of his Adelphi Edizioni. Heartfelt thanks also to Teresa Cremisi, who encouraged me to hazard a new biography of the countess, followed its progress, and supervised the French edition, and to Ena Marchi, who, with the help of Daniela Salomoni, edited the Italian text.

Among scholars and friends, I would above all like to express my gratitude to Adriano Viarengo, who, with great generosity and inexhaustible patience, helped me orient myself in the complex landscape of preunification Italy, and to Rosanna Roccia, my guide through Cavour's correspondence. Benedetta Cibrario provided me with information about her ancestors and Duilio Cortassa with clarifications regarding Piedmontese toponymy.

I am grateful to friends from La Spezia for infecting me with their enthusiasm, which keeps the memory of Virginia Oldoini poignantly alive in her *joli golfe*: to Giuliana Zecchini, who knows everything about her; to Marzia Ratti, for the impeccable edition of the documents preserved in the municipal archive; and to Annalisa Tacoli. Lucia Lazzerini offered me her linguistic expertise when I came to Virginia's picturesque Tuscanisms. Francesco Margiotta Broglio, who generously advised me on which archives to explore, entrusted me to Claudio Lamioni when I turned to the archives of Florence. Also in Florence, Cosimo Ceccuti suggested some essential readings on nineteenth-century Tuscany. I feel a great debt of gratitude to all.

I owe the diagnosis of my heroine's pathology to Francesco Montanari, the description of the clothes and hairstyles to Nanà Cecchi, and the facts about her jewelry to the historian Lia Lenti. Mariolina Bertini briefed me on Proust's relationship with Montesquiou; Daria Galateria and Giuseppe Scaraffia on fashions, courtesans, and eroticism in nineteenth-century France; and Alberto Chiesa and Massimo Fino on the vicissitudes of the countess's manuscripts. In Naples I could count on the unfailing kindness of Teresa Leo and Rosario Scuotto. And, not for the first time, I express my gratitude to Pietro Corsi, who holds the passkey to all bibliographical references.

I can never thank Pierre Apraxine enough for his enlightening suggestions. Thanks, too, to Georges-Henri Soutou for alerting me to the existence of the Fonds Poniatowski; to Charlène Fanchon of the Département des archives privées, Archives nationales de France, for her indispensable assistance; to Philippe Levillain, who helped me identify the author of the letters to Virginia preserved in the Bibliothèque historique de la Ville de Paris; to Laure Murat for information on Dr. Blanche's archive; to Éléonore Reverzy for particulars relating to the "*notes préparatoires*" for Émile Zola's *Son Excellence Eugène Rougon*; to Jean-Claude Casanova and Georges Liébert for their many generous suggestions; to Brigitta Loconte for her research at the Bibliothèque nationale. An immense thank you to Antonio Manfredi and Luca Carboni for rummaging through the Vatican Apostolic Library and the Vatican Secret Archive; to Rosanna Rummo and Anna Maria Buzzi for their eminent attentiveness; to Carla Ceresa of the Fondazione Camillo Cavour Santena; to Isabel Costa and to the heaven-sent Marco Testa of the Turin State Archives; to Edi Perino of the Museum of the Risorgimento in Turin; to Piero Marchi and Manuela Bardi of the Florentine State Archives; to Paola Businaro of the Historical Diplomatic Archives of the Ministry of Foreign Affairs; to Maurizio Serra for elucidating the diplomatic career of Costantino Ressmann; and finally to Peter Glidewell and Beppe Manzitti.

Few members of my family have managed to elude my inquiries. I am grateful to my brother Piero for his many suggestions; to Cinzia, who helped me with bibliographic research; to Masolino and my daughters Margherita and Isabella, who were the first to read *The Contessa*; to Caterina, who confirmed, with photographs in hand, the hypothesis that Alida Valli's black burnoose in *Senso* was modeled on Virginia's burnoose in the portrait by Blanche. A conjugal thank you to Benoît, who has demonstrated uncommon patience. And it is impossible for me to conclude without expressing my gratitude to Davide Tortorella, who, even before he contributed his beautiful translations to the Italian edition of *The Contessa* enjoyed himself, as a puzzle enthusiast, helping me decipher Virginia's "*crayonnages infernaux*," and in the end, falling victim to his curiosity, let himself be yoked to Virginia's chariot.

George Frederic Watts, *Countess Castiglione*, 1857; private collection

Pierre-Louis Pierson, *Béatrix*, 1856–1857; the Metropolitan Museum of Art

Pierre-Louis Pierson, *Le Regard*, 1856–1857;
the Metropolitan Museum of Art

Pierre-Louis Pierson, Aquilin Schad, *The Queen of Hearts*, 1861–1863

Pierre-Louis Pierson, Aquilin Schad, *The Etruscan Queen*, 1864;
PVDE/Bridgeman Images

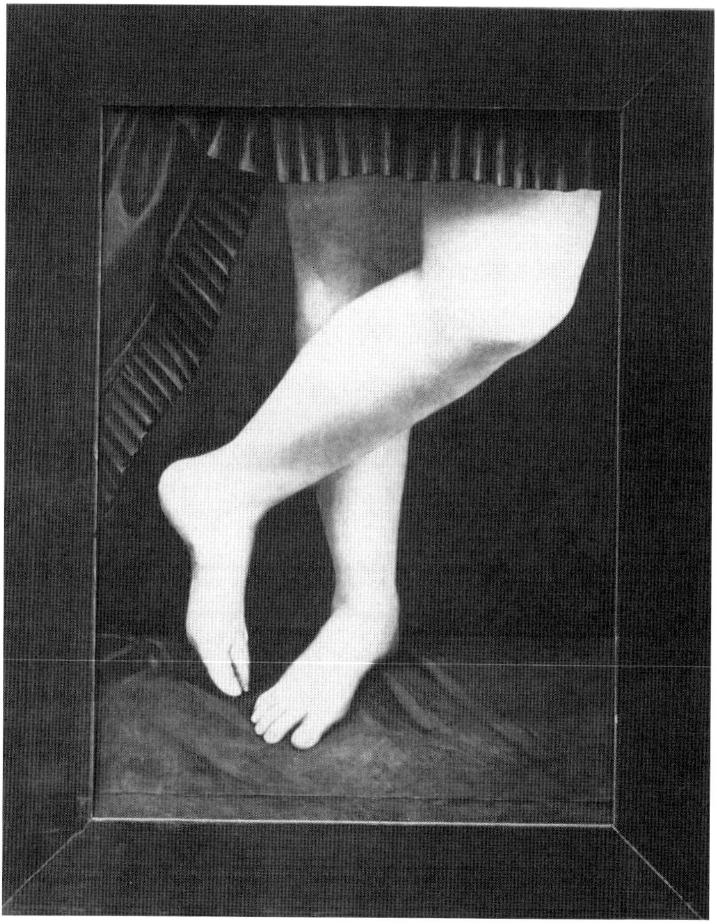

Pierre-Louis Pierson, *The Countess of Castiglione's Legs*, 1861–1867; akg-images

Pierre-Louis Pierson, *The Murder*, 1861–1867;
Musée Unterlinden, Colmar / Christian Kempf

Jacques-Émile Blanche, *The Countess of Castiglione*, 1893;
the Metropolitan Museum of Art

Pierre-Louis Pierson, *Scherzo di follia*, 1861–1867;
the Metropolitan Museum of Art

Pierre-Louis Pierson (?), retouched by an unknown artist,
*The Hermit of Passy*, 1863; the Metropolitan Museum of Art

Pierre-Louis Pierson, *Giorgio di Castiglione*, 1863–1864;
Musée Unterlinden, Colmar / Christian Kempf

Pierre-Louis Pierson, *The Countess of Castiglione*, 1861–1867;
Musée Unterlinden, Colmar / Christian Kempf

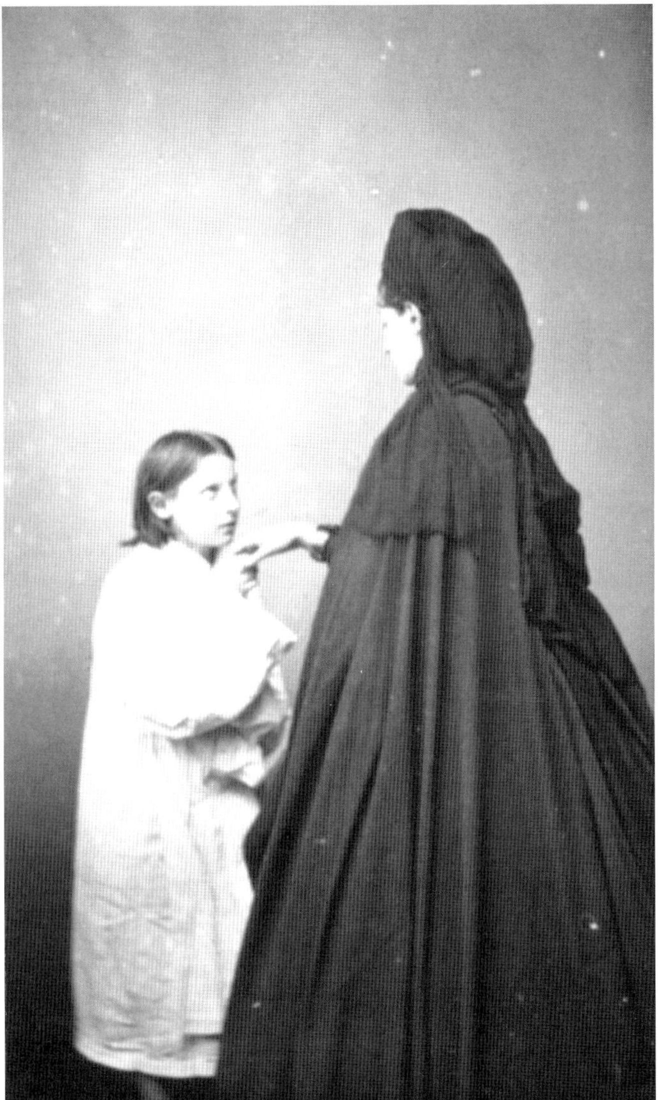

Pierre-Louis Pierson, *La Baise-main*, 1867–1868; akg-images

Hippolyte-Jean Flandrin, *Napoleon III*, 1862;
Museo Napoleonico

Gustave Le Gray, *The Empress Eugenia kneeling on a prie-dieu in the salon of the palace of Saint-Cloud*, 1856;
Musée d'Orsay, dist. RMN-Grand Palais / Patrice Schmidt

Luigi Built-in Cretté, *Costantino Nigra*, date unknown

Mayer & Pierson, *Camillo Paolo Filippo Giulio Benso, Count of Cavour*, ca. 1855

Anonymous, *Count Francesco Verasis di Castiglione*, ca. 1856

Cesare Bernieri, *Victor Emmanuel II*, 1863–1867; the Metropolitan Museum of Art

# Bibliographic Note

THE FIRE PERPETRATED on rue Cambon by order of the Italian government the day after the Countess of Castiglione's death—a true auto-da-fé, as Carlo Sforza would say years later—was preceded and followed by violations and thefts of the documents that she kept in La Spezia. This quite successful censorship operation aimed to eliminate every trace of her role in the history of the Risorgimento; in France, on the contrary, the divine countess became a symbol of Second Empire Paris. To reconstruct her personality, habits, and tastes, Robert de Montesquiou not only collected the testimonies of those who had known her; he was also able to consult her illuminating correspondence with Léon Cléry, amass photographs, and take part in auctions of jewelry and objects that had once belonged to her. *La divine comtesse. Étude d'après Madame de Castiglione* (preface by Gabriele D'Annunzio, Paris, Goupil & Cie, 1913) and the folder of preparatory material preserved in the Bibliothèque nationale de France are fundamental for anyone interested in her. Published the previous year and also very useful is Frédéric Loliée's *Le Roman d'une favorite. La comtesse de Castiglione, 1840–1900 d'après sa correspondance intime inédite et les Lettres des Princes* (Paris, Émile-Paul, 1912). A specialist in the society of the Second Empire, Loliée was able to read—before they were destroyed—the letters that Virginia wrote to her friend Estancelin over a forty-year period, and he quotes numerous and significant excerpts, helping us reconstruct the countess's relationships with the Duke of Aumale and the Duke of Chartres. For their part, Elena Henrisch and Costantino Nigro, authors of *La contessa della leggenda, attraverso la sua corrispondenza intima, diari e documenti inediti, 1837–1899* (Florence, Marzocco, 1912), were able to view a number of Virginia's papers still in the possession of the Trigone heirs and various other correspondents, which are now untraceable. In 1951, the sale, initiated by Carlo Alberto Chiesa, of the documents found in La Spezia after Castiglione's death—and preserved by the Trigones in Genoa—revealed the existence of thousands of letters (see Carlo Alberto Chiesa, *"Un mestiere semplice": Ricordi di un librario antiquario. Per i novant'anni di Gianni Antonini*, Milan, Officina Libraria, 2016, 18–19). Divided into ninety-four lots, the catalog of Drouot's Parisian auction contains the *Correspondances inédites et archives privées de Virginia Vérasis, comtesse de Castiglione*, with a preface by André Maurois (Paris, G. Blaizot, 1951) and a quick glance at the contents is enough to grasp their importance: *Lettres de personnages politiques, et de diplomates français et italiens, du XIXe siècle: Thiers—Cavour—Nigra—Walewski—Fould—Baciocchi—Cassagnac—F. de Lesseps—d'Ideville—Imbert de Saint-Amand—La Tour d'Auvergne—J. Poniatowski—Nieuwerkerke—Charles Laffitte—Louis Estancelin—etc.—Lettres de Napoléon III et de sa famille, des Princes d'Orléans (Duke of Aumale, Duke of Chartres, etc.).—Important Dossier de la famille Rothschild.—La famille et les amis de la "Divine Comtesse," son Journal intime (autographe inédit).—Nombreuses LETTRES D'AMOUR reçues par elle ou adressées à divers correspondants.—Correspondance des hommes d'affaires (Léon Cléry, de Morand, etc.).—Souvenirs et reliques diverses.—Collection de photographies de la Comtesse de Castiglione et des personnages célèbres. Peintures et Aquarelles: "Le peignoir rose," etc. Coffret contenant les bas de dentelles portées par la célèbre favorite.*

Before this treasure trove of manuscripts, which resurfaced unexpectedly after half a century, was dismembered and dispersed, a young historian who was not yet thirty years old managed to view them and make contact with some of the buyers—which served as the basis for the first solidly documented and reliable biography: *La Castiglione, dame de coeur de l'Europe, d'après sa Correspondance et son Journal intime di lei inédits* (Paris, Amiot-Dumont, 1953). To this day, Alain Decaux's book remains an indispensable source of information—particularly the extensive excerpts from the diary kept between 1854 and 1856, which was purchased by Gérard Magistry before being stolen and lost.

The centenary of the countess's death led to the rediscovery of her photographs, as attested by the exhibitions in Paris (*La comtesse de Castiglione par elle même*, Musée d'Orsay, October 12, 1999–January 23, 2000); New York (*"La Divine Comtesse": Photographs of the Countess de Castiglione*, Metropolitan Museum of Art, September 19–December 31, 2000); Turin (*La Contessa di Castiglione e il suo tempo*, Palazzo Cavour, March 31–July 2, 2000): an extraordinary autobiography in images, which has opened up new prospects for research and inspired artists and writers. Both Nathalie Léger's penetrating essay *L'Exposition* (Paris, P.O.L., 2008) and the valuable *La Castiglione: Vies et métamorphoses*, by Nicole G. Albert (Paris, Perrin, 2011) illustrate the variety of interpretations licensed by Virginia's photographic enterprise. But the renewal of interest in her—and in the history of the customs and fashions of the Second Empire—did not lead to deeper study of her complex biography. Given the irreparable loss of so many documents, I cleaved most closely to Decaux's book and to passages from the letters that appeared in the 1951 auction catalog.

As I was able to observe in the course of my research, though many of Virginia's most important letters are unobtainable, thousands of documents concerning her have fortunately been preserved in Italian and French archives. In the abundant Castiglione collection at the Turin State Archives, we can view the many precious lots purchased by the Italian state at the Drouot auction and in subsequent auctions. In this book, I confine myself to quoting letters written to her by her father, her mother, her husband, her son, her lover La Tour d'Auvergne, and what remains of her correspondence with Nigra and Victor Emmanuel II, in addition to countless drafts of letters, notes, and fragments of diaries in Virginia's hand. Preserved in Rome, in the Historical Diplomatic Archives of the Ministry of Foreign Affairs, the Marquis Filippo Oldoini collection, too, gathers many hundreds of letters that his daughter wrote to him from her childhood on, as well as copies of some of his replies. His correspondence with his wife, son-in-law, and grandson is particularly interesting, and sheds new light on Virginia's character and behavior. Unfortunately, with the exception of the few preserved in the Turin State Archives, I have not been able to locate Giuseppe Poniatowski's letters to Virginia, whose importance is made clear by both Decaux's biography and the Drouot auction catalog. The letters she wrote to the prince, held by the Archives nationales in Paris—letters whose existence Decaux does not appear to have been aware of—are startling to say the least. The situation is similar with the correspondence—which has been quoted, though largely neglected—with Estancelin, Thiers, and Laffitte preserved in the manuscript department of the Bibliothèque nationale de France, as well as that of her son Giorgio with his tutor Genulphe Sol in the Archives de la préfecture de Police in Paris. And the still unpublished letters of "L'Esclave" preserved in the Bibliothèque historique de la Ville de Paris reveal new and surprising facets of Virginia's character. While groups of letters from the Drouot auction gradually reappear on the antiquarian market, and while we wait to see further important pieces of the indefatigable epistolographer's oeuvre reemerge into the light of day, it should be noted that the collections of the archives of Turin, Rome and Paris still have many new discoveries in store. I therefore hope that, difficult though the task of deciphering Virginia's "infernal scribbles" may be, this book will encourage further research.

# Notes

## ABBREVIATIONS

| | |
|---|---|
| ADPP | Archives of the Police Prefecture of Paris |
| AFC | Archive of the Camillo Cavour Foundation of Santena, Camillo Cavour Fund, Olivetti donation |
| AIA | Isaac Artom Archive, Union of Jewish Communities Italian |
| ASD | Diplomatic Historical Archive, Ministry of Foreign Affairs, Filippo Oldoini Fund 1848–1888 |
| ASF | State Archives of Florence |
| AST | State Archives of Turin, Court Section, Castiglione Papers |
| BHVP | Bibliothèque historique de la Ville de Paris |
| BNF | Archives de la Bibliothèque nationale de France, Département des manuscrits, Archives of the Countess of Castiglione |
| FP | Archives nationales, Fonds Poniatowski |
| NAF | Nouvelles Acquisitions Françaises |

## FLORENCE (1837–1853)

1. Marco Tabarrini, *Ricordi biografici sul cavaliere avvocato Ranieri Lamporecchi*, Florence, Le Monnier, 1863, 10–11.
2. See Andrea Corsini, *I Bonaparte a Firenze*, Florence, Olschki, 1961.
3. Mathilde Bonaparte, *Mémoires inédits*, edited by Carole Blumenfeld, preface by Philippe Costamagna, Paris, Grasset, 2019, 45.
4. When Piedmont fell under Napoleonic rule, Massimo's father, the Marquis Cesare Taparelli d'Azeglio, was exiled to Florence with his family.

5. Massimo d'Azeglio, *I miei ricordi*, edited by Massimo Legnani, Milan, Feltrinelli, 1963, 76.
6. Ibid., 548–49.
7. In 1806, Filippo's father, Marquis Grimaldo Oldoini, married Elisabetta Antonia Isabella Lamporecchi, Isabella's father's sister.
8. As stated in the marriage certificate: "Oldoini Filippo, landowner, aged nineteen, bachelor, son of Grimaldo and Lamporecchi Elisabetta, was wed in Florence, Church of Saint Simone, January 31, 1836, to Lamporecchi Isabella, landowner, aged nineteen, maiden, daughter of Ranieri Lamporecchi and Chiari Luisa," ASF, Fondo Stato civile di Toscana 1808–1865, vol. 10683, internal no. 24, year 1836.
9. As stated in the birth certificate, ASF, Fondo Stato civile di Toscana 1808–1865, vol. 10549, internal no. 876, 1837.
10. See Alfredo Poggiolini, "La contessa Verasis di Castiglione nel romanzo e nella realtà, con documenti e particolari nuovi," in *Rassegna Nazionale*, 188, 34, November 16, 1912, 194–222, and December 1, 1912, 343–69. Reprint edited by Gabriella Chioma, with an introduction by Marzia Ratti and a bio-bibliographic note by Rossana Piccioli (La Spezia: Edizioni del Tridente), 20.
11. April 27, 1848 and January 28, 1849.
12. See the letter from Massimo d'Azeglio to Filippo Oldoini, Turin, May 12, 1849: "I have not forgotten your plans to serve the state. If I can be of use to you in my new position, let me know your thoughts . . . and within the limits of my powers, I shall place myself under your command," in Massimo d'Azeglio, *Epistolario, 1819–1866*, edited by Georges Virlogeux, 12 vols., Turin, Centro Studi Piemontesi, 1987–2021, vol. 5, 3.
13. The same Emanuele d'Azeglio had offered, in a confidential note to the ministry, "certification that he was among the poor in spirit" (Emanuele d'Azeglio's letter to Camillo Cavour, Park Lane, January 16, 1858, in Camillo Cavour, *Epistolario*, edited by the Commissione Nazionale per la pubblicazione dei carteggi del conte di Cavour, 21 vols. (Florence: Olschki, 1862–2012), vol. 15, 43 [fragment]). See also Francesco Bacino, "L'archivio di Filippo Oldoini," in "Rassegna storica del Risorgimento," 38 (1950), 40–45; Francesco Bacino, *La legazione e i consolati del Regno di Sardinia in Russia, 1783–1861*, Rome, Indices of the Historical Archive at the Ministry of Foreign Affairs, 1952, vol. 5, 47ff.

14. Letter from Camillo Cavour to Alfonso La Marmora, July 12, 1852, in C. Cavour, *Epistolario*, vol. 9, 163.
15. On July 15, 1856, Cavour wrote to his nephew Ainardo, who was about to leave for La Spezia: "I hope that you enjoy your stay in La Spezia, but there's no need to fall in love with Ninì's mother; only gray-bearded men such as myself are permitted to prefer her to her daughter." See C. Cavour, *Epistolario*, vol. 13, 597 [fragment].
16. Cavour held the office of president of the council of ministers from November 4, 1852 to July 19, 1851, and from January 21, 1860 to June 6, 1861.
17. Letter from Camillo Cavour to Ruggero Gabaleone di Salmour, Leri, [September 26, 1856], C. Cavour, *Epistolario*, vol. 13, 757. In Piedmontese dialect "ciola" (pronounced "chula") means "fool," "simpleton."
18. Letter from Isabella Oldoini to her daughter, December 18, 1855, AST, bundle 1, folder 4, letter 34.
19. Isabella was born in Florence on March 26, 1816. Cf. ASF, Fondo Stato civile di Toscana 1808–1865, folder 1463, internal no. 2415.
20. Ranieri Lamporecchi (b. Pietrasanta, December 1, 1776, d. Florence, March 25, 1866) was the son of Vincenzo, made a nobleman of Pisa by decree on June 18, 1794. Cf. ASF, Fondo Nobili, volume 2, n. 54.
21. The work of a whole lifetime, entitled *Il Bonaparte*, the poem is divided into twelve cantos and 948 octaves. In May 1861, Lamporecchi submitted it to Chevalier Marco Tabarrini. Cf. ASF, Carte Tabarrini, Inv. 221, CP 5826, volume 2.
22. Five children were born to Ranieri Lamporecchi and the actress Luigia Teresa Chiari (married in 1813): Vincenzo Carlo Giuseppe, born October 13, 1814; Isabella Teresa Maria Antonia, born March 28, 1816; Antonia Giuseppina Aurelia, born May 28, 1818, married to Baldino Baldini; Giovanni Grimaldo, born July 11, 1820; Alessandro Giulio, born May 30, 1824, died in 1866. Cf. ASF, Ceramelli Papiani Collection, file 5826.
23. Letter from the family lawyer to Isabella Lamporecchi, no place specified, August 28, 1852, ASD, "Lettere della famiglia Oldoini e affini e ricevute, a Londra, Parigi, Turin, Monaco e Dresda, 1851–53," binder 3.
24. "Oldoini has a smaller fortune than you suppose, and he cannot dispose of it, for it is his wife who holds the purse strings," Alessandro Jocteau writes to Emanuele d'Azeglio, in Federico Curato, *Le relazioni diplomatiche fra il Regno di Sardinia e la Gran Bretagna*, 8 vol., 3rd series: 1848–1860,

Istituto storico italiano per l'età moderna e contemporanea, Rome 1961–1969, 39, quoted in Massimo d'Azeglio, *Epistolario*, vol. 51, 256, note 1 [French].

25. An impenitent Don Juan, Filippo did not disdain extramarital love affairs and one of his natural children, Luisa Comparetti, looked after his properties in La Spezia. Cf. AFC, 11.

26. In a letter to Massimo d'Azeglio written on August 9, 1849 (in M. d'Azeglio, *Epistolario*, register no. 204, vol. 5, 423–24) Vincenzo Ricasoli writes that he had defended him "against accusations of luxury"—which Isabella Oldoini also challenged—formulated against him by his wife, though he had not been able to convince her of his innocence.

    Cf. M. d'Azeglio, *Epistolario*, vol. 5, 201, note 1, in the margins of a letter from Massimo d'Azeglio to Giovan Battista Giorgini written on August 12, 1849. See also Georges Virlogeux, "Costantino Nigra 'inventé' par Massimo D'Azeglio," in *L'alliance entre le Royaume de Sardaigne et l'Empire français dans le processus d'unification de l'Italie*. Proceedings of a conference held at the Italian embassy in Paris, Saturday, April 14, 2018, under the patronage of the Italian Embassy in France, the Sorbonne University, and the Institute of Italian Culture in Paris.

27. Letter from Massimo d'Azeglio to Teresa Targioni Tozzetti, La Spezia, March 24, 1849, in M. d'Azeglio, *Epistolario*, vol. 4, 326.

28. Gabardo Gabardi, *Firenze elegante*, Florence, Ricci, 1886, 146.

29. Born in Rome in 1816, Giuseppe Poniatowski married Countess Matilda Perotti (1814–1875) in Florence in 1834. They had one son, Stanislao Augusto Federico Giuseppe Telemaco (1835–1907).

30. Following the Congress of Vienna only the major powers had the right to embassies led by an ambassador, while the minor states (designated by the phrase "powers with limited interests") were represented by legations, led by a minister plenipotentiary.

31. Alain Decaux, *La Castiglione, dame de coeur de l'Europe, d'après sa Correspondance et son Journal intime inédits*, Paris, Amiot-Dumont, 1953, 21.

32. ASD, binder 3.

33. This information comes from Alfredo Poggiolini, who, after Castiglione's death, was in time to take down the oral testimonies of the inhabitants of La Spezia. A. Poggiolini, *La contessa Verasis di Castiglione*, 27.

34. "Variety" column, signed by Aristide Cola, in *L'Arte* (which called itself "a literary, artistic, theatrical newspaper"), Saturday, September 11, 1852, 290.
35. Letter from Isabella Oldoini to her husband, [Florence, September 1852], ASD, binder 3.
36. Ibid.
37. A. Decaux, *La Castiglione*, 22. Consisting of approximately two hundred pages bound in red, the *Journal intime* kept by Virginia in French between 1854 and 1856, and auctioned by Drouot in June 1951, was purchased by Gérard Magistry, from whom it was later stolen. Fortunately Alain Decaux, who had had a chance to consult it before it was stolen, described its characteristics and transcribed many significant passages in his invaluable biography *La Castiglione, dame de coeur de l'Europe.* The three handwritten pages (running from January 26 to March 4, 1856)—part of the Olivetti donation and preserved today at the Fondazione Camillo Cavour Santena—suggest that the diary was dismembered and the pages sold separately. A similar fate must have befallen the *Journal intime* kept by Virginia from February to March 1863, which was likewise auctioned by Drouot, seeing that a page about the masquerade ball at the Tuileries on February 6, 1863, is also preserved in the archives of the Cavour Foundation. On the other hand, the journal written in pencil, in Italian, and difficult to decipher, which can be found in the State Archives of Turin, dates to the years of her old age. Castiglione Papers, bundle 16, one fascicle, sub-fascicle with annotation in pencil, "Giornale pag. 78."
38. Letter from Isabella Oldoini to her husband, [1852?], ASD, binder 3.
39. Ibid.
40. Ibid.
41. After he was engaged to Virginia, Count Verasis expressed his gratitude to Isabella Oldoini for her support: "You have kept your word, and I cannot but offer you a thousand blessings for all that you have deigned to do on behalf of my happiness." La Spezia, September 3, 1853, ibid. [French].
42. Cf. Enrico Della Rocca, *Autobiografia di un veterano. Ricordi storici e aneddotici*, Bologna, Zanichelli, 1897, 347–49.
43. Francesca Trotti (1829–1851).
44. Letter from Francesco Verasis to Virginia, La Spezia, night, [July 1853], AST, bundle 14, fascicle B, unnumbered letter [French].

45. Letter from Francesco Verasis to Virginia, [La Spezia], after dinner, ibid. [French].
46. Letter from Francesco Verasis to Virginia, La Spezia, July 23, [1853], ibid.
47. Letter from Francesco Verasis to Virginia, [La Spezia], evening of the 8th, *ibid.* [French].
48. Letter from Clemente di Castiglione to Filippo Oldoini, August 31, 1853, ASD, binder 3.
49. Letter from Filippo Oldoini to Clemente di Castiglione, La Spezia, 3 [September 1853], ibid. [French].
50. The marquis would reiterate this to Virginia when she requested a separation from her husband.
51. The count made allusion to it in a letter to his father-in-law (Turin, January 6, 1855, ASD, folder 4), hoping to earn his trust. For his part, considering the terrible upshot of the marriage, the marquis would not fail to remind both spouses of the reservations he had expressed at the time.
52. His father, Vittorio Luigi, who died in 1839, had been Charles Albert's grand master of ceremonies.
53. See their marriage certificate, ASF, Fondo Stato Civile di Toscana 1808–1865, vol. (4969), internal number (5). "The wedding was celebrated in the Parish of SS. Annunziata on January 9, 1854. Verasis di Castiglione, Francesco, son of the late Luigi and Sigala [*sic*] Vittoria, count, aged twenty-eight, widower of Francesca Tretti [*sic*], at the Cathedral of Turin, married on January 9, Olduini [*sic*], Virginia, aged seventeen, daughter of Marquis Filippo and Isabella Lamporecchi. Witnesses Ponjatoschi [*sic*] Carlo, Lamporecchi Ranieri, Martini Giuseppe, Verasis Clemente."
54. Purchased by Francesco's father, the building at via Lagrange 29, where the mathematician and astronomer Joseph-Louis Lagrange had been born in 1736, was in the Conciatori district (Des Courroyeurs during the French period), and its garden, complete with two large greenhouses, bordered via Carlo Alberto, then the Madonna degli Angeli or des Anges district. The Castiglione palace adjoined that of the Cavours, designed in 1729 by the architect Gian Giacomo Planter on the orders of Marquis Michele Antonio Benso, constructed around two courtyards. The court of honor opened onto the Arcivescovado district, renamed, around the time Camillo was born, rue d'Austerlitz, at number 8 on present-day via Cavour, while the rustic court, at number 27 on present-day via Lagrange,

still opens, through a large wooden door, onto the courtyard of Palazzo Castiglione.

55. Letter of Francesco Verasis to Filippo Oldoini, Turin, March 20, 1854, ASD, binder 4 [French].
56. Letter of Francesco Verasis to Filippo Oldoini, Turin, April 8, 1854, ibid.
57. Letter of Francesco Verasis to Filippo Oldoini, Costigliole, August 24, 1854, ibid. [French].
58. Letter of Francesco Verasis to Filippo Oldoini, Costigliole, November 20, 1854, ibid.
59. Letter of Isabella Oldoini to her husband, no place specified, undated [Winter 1854], ibid.
60. Letter of Isabella Oldoini to her husband, no place specified, undated [Winter 1854], ibid.
61. Letter of Isabella Oldoini to her husband, no place specified, undated [Winter 1854], ibid.
62. Quoted in A. Decaux, *La Castiglione*, 34.
63. Francesco mentions his wife's refusal to address him informally in a letter to Virginia, Milan, July 13, 1854, AST, bundle 2, item 5, letter 8, and complains about it to his father-in-law in a letter dated October 25, 1854, ASD, binder 3.
64. Letter from Francesco Verasis to Filippo Oldoini, no place specified, June 29, 1854, *ibid.* [French].
65. Letter from Francesco Verasis to Filippo Oldoini, no place specified, October 25, 1854, *ibid.* [French].
66. Letter from Isabella Oldoini to Virginia, AST, bundle 1, item 4, letter 5 [French].
67. See letter from Francesco Verasis to Filippo Oldoini, Turin, June 29, 1854, ASD, binder 3.
68. Letter from Isabella Oldoini to her husband, no place specified, undated, ibid. [French].
69. Letter from Isabella Oldoini to Virginia, AST, bundle 1, item 4, letter 12 [French].
70. Letter from Isabella Oldoini to Virginia, *ibid.*, letter 5.
71. Letter from Isabella Oldoini to Virginia, *ibid.*, letter 2.
72. Letter from Isabella Oldoini to Virginia, *ibid.*, letter 23.
73. Letter from Isabella Oldoini to Virginia, *ibid.*, letter 16.

74. Cf. letter from Isabella Oldoini to Francesco Verasis, ibid., letter 18.
75. Letter from Costanza d'Azeglio to her son Emanuele, Florence, March 19, [1851], in Costanza d'Azeglio, *Lettere al figlio* (1829–1862), edited by Daniela Maldini Chiarito, 2 vols., Istituto per la Storia del Risorgimento Italiano, Rome 1996, vol. 2, 1156.
76. Letter from Filippo Oldoini to his daughter, Karlsruhe, February 3, [1864], AST, bundle 1, item 2, letter 76.
77. Isabella's concern for the fragility of the marquis's nerves is a leitmotif of their correspondence. "In any case I don't want you to suffer from the spleen as usual," she wrote to her husband in 1853, ASD, folder 4; and, on January 3, 1860: "I was sorry to hear that you have had another nervous attack," *ibid.*, folder 3. See also Isabella Oldoini's letter to her daughter, AST, bundle 1, file 4, letter 10.
78. Letter from Virginia to her father, no place specified, undated, ASD, binder 4 [French].
79. Letter from Virginia to her father, Costigliole, 2 A[ugust, 1854], *ibid.* [French].
80. Quoted in A. Decaux, *La Castiglione*, 53, note 1.
81. Ibid., 54.
82. Ibid., 54.
83. Ibid., 56.
84. Letter from her husband to Virginia, Costigliole, September 5, 1855, AST, bundle 2, item 5, letter 14 [French].
85. Quoted in A. Decaux, *La Castiglione*, 62.

## TURIN (1854–1856)

1. Marquis Lorenzo Litta Modignani (1797–1874) was the brother-in-law of Margherita Provana di Collegno, having married her sister, Carolina Trotti Bentivoglio. He was a scholar of philosophy and a close friend of Manzoni's.
2. *Diario politico di Margherita Provana di Collegno, 1852–1856*, edited by Aldobrandino Malvezzi, Milan, Hoepli, 1926, 158–59, note to entry for January 12, 1854.
3. C. d'Azeglio, *Lettere al figlio*, vol. 2, 354 [French].

4. Cf. Mario Mazzucchelli, *L'imperatrice senza impero (la contessa di Castiglione)*, Milan, Corbaccio, 1927, 30, note 2.
5. Letter from Massimo d'Azeglio to Teresa Targioni Tozzetti, Turin, January 18, 1854, in M. d'Azeglio, *Epistolario,* vol. 5, III, 151.
6. Henry d'Ideville, *Journal d'un diplomate en Italie. Notes intimes pour servir à l'histoire du Second Empire. Turin, 1859–1862*, Paris, Librairie Hachette et Cie, 1872, 50.
7. C. d'Azeglio, *Lettere al figlio*, vol. 1, 258, quoted in Adriano Viarengo, *Vittorio Emanuele II*, Rome, Salerno Editrice, 2017, 47.
8. Cf. Comte de Reiset, *Mes souvenirs. Les débuts de l'indépendance italienne*, 3 vols., Paris, Plon, Nourrit et Cie, 1901–1903, vol. 1, 441–42.
9. H. d'Ideville, *Journal d'un diplomate en Italie*, 56–57.
10. Comte de Reiset, *Mes souvenirs*, vol. 1, 441–42.
11. Rosario Romeo, *Cavour e il suo tempo*, 3 vols., Bari, Laterza, 1969–1984, vol. 3: 1854–1861, 109–112.
12. Once he had become king, Victor Emmanuel II delegated the task of forming a government to the conservative general Claudio Gabriele de Launay, but less than two months later, in May 1849, he replaced him with Massimo d'Azeglio.
13. On December 2, 1851, Louis Napoleon's coup d'état had sowed fear, among Italian liberals, of a reactionary surge, and despite the contrary opinions of Victor Emmanuel II and d'Azeglio, Cavour—who became a minister in October 1850—opened himself to Rattazzi's center-left, in order to strengthen his and the government's parliamentary base with a view to maintaining the statute and supporting the Italian national movement. In this way, now the leader of a majority in the chamber, on November 4, 1852, he secured the presidency of the council.
14. In 1713, based on the agreements following the Treaty of Utrecht, Duke Victor Amadeus II of Savoy obtained the cession of Sicily on the part of Spain and the royal title. Five years later, though he retained the title of king, he was forced to exchange Sicily for Sardinia.
15. A. Viarengo, *Vittorio Emanuele II*, 9.
16. Quoted in Nassau William Senior, *L'Italia dopo il 1848. Colloqui con uomini politici ed eminenti perseguitati italiani,* edited by Adolfo Omodeo, Bari, Laterza, 1937, 284.

17. A famous phrase attributed to Victor Amadeus II, meaning that Piedmont ought to expand its territories the way one eats an artichoke, leaf by leaf.
18. Comte de Reiset, *Mes souvenirs*, vol. 2, 165—from a report written by the count for Napoleon III.
19. At the beginning of the conflict, it was hoped that Austria might side with Russia, creating the conditions for a European war against the two pillars of the Holy Alliance and giving the Sardinian kingdom an opportunity to take revenge against Austria. But Vienna did not come to Russia's rescue, and in April 1854 Austria signed an agreement with France and England, obtaining, in exchange, London and Paris's willingness to support the status quo in Italy. When England, finding itself in difficulty in the Crimea, asked the kingdom of Sardinia to send a military contingent, the latter thus ran the risk of fighting alongside Austria, estranging Italian patriots. Victor Emmanuel had intended to fight whatever the cost, but Cavour had not counted on the resistance of the minister of war, Dabormida—who asked for compensation in exchange for assistance—and assumed responsibility for accepting England's request. Fortunately, Austria did not intervene and, after the fall of Sevastopol, forced Russia to make peace.
20. On January 12, Russia broke off diplomatic relations with London and Paris.
21. Quoted in A. Decaux, *La Castiglione*, 32.
22. Letter from Massimo d'Azeglio to Giuseppe Magnetto, [Turin], 27 [January 1854], in M. d'Azeglio, *Epistolario*, vol. 5, III, 155. [Perhaps not insignificantly, "Massimo" is the word for "maximum" in Italian.—Translator's note.]
23. Letter from Massimo d'Azeglio to Filippo Antonio Gualterio, [Turin], February 9, 1854, ibid., 159.
24. From the diary of Virginia, June 5, 1854, quoted in A. Decaux, *La Castiglione*, 37, note 1.
25. Letter from Francesco Verasis to Filippo Oldoini, July 20, 1855, ASD, binder 4.
26. See the beautiful letter of June 27 in which the Count of Castiglione informed his father-in-law of the death of the queen, of whom he was extremely fond, ibid.
27. Quoted in A. Decaux, *La Castiglione*, 47.

28. The kinship, reasserted several times by Cavour and Virginia, is never explained. Franco Della Peruta speaks of a "common kinship" between the Cavours and the Oldoinis—see "Un profilo della contessa Virginia di Castiglione," in *La contessa di Castiglione e il suo tempo*, catalog of the exhibition at Palazzo Cavour, Turin, March 31–July 2, 2000, edited by Martina Corgnati and Cecilia Ghibaudi, Silvana Editoriale, Cinisello Balsamo, 2000, 43—though the Lombard origins of the Oldoini and their settlement in Liguria make the hypothesis seem problematic. But, as Dr. Rosanna Roccia, the erudite editor of Cavour's *Epistolario*, has kindly pointed out, there is no evidence of a relationship between the Cavours and the Castigliones apart from two marriages, in 1747, of Bona Gabriella Birago to Aurelio Michele Verasis di Castiglione, and of a Francesco Lodovico Ignazio Birago (1719–1790) to Maria Felicita Benso di Cavour, who died in 1767.
29. The death of Queen Maria Adelaide on January 20 had been preceded by the death of the queen mother, Maria Teresa of Habsburg-Lorraine, on January 12. On February 9 Victor Emmanuel's younger brother, the thirty-three-year-old Ferdinand, Duke of Genoa, passed away, followed, on March 17, by the king's last son.
30. *Souvenirs du Général Cte Fleury*, 2 vols., Paris, Plon, Nourrit et Cie, 1897, 3rd edition., vol. 1, 350.
31. At the Battle of Traktir, during the Crimean War, Victor Emmanuel II's troops had supported the French and British in their victory over the Russians.—Translator's note.
32. *Souvenirs du Général Cte Fleury*, 351.
33. Ibid.
34. An intervention that, according to the clause of April 10, 1854, was "disinterested."
35. Letter from Camillo Cavour to Massimo d'Azeglio, Paris, December 9, 1855, in C. Cavour, *Epistolario*, vol. 12, book 2, 614.
36. R. Romeo, *Cavour e il suo tempo*, vol. 21, 199.
37. Letter from Francesco Verasis to Filippo Oldoini, Turin, March 30, 1855, ASD, binder 3.
38. Letter from Francesco Verasis to Filippo Oldoini, [October], ibid.
39. Cf. A. Decaux, *La Castiglione*, 71–72.
40. Plenipotentiary minister of the kingdom of Sardinia to Florence from 1848 to 1852, Villamarina had been sent to Paris in 1852.

41. Marquis Lorenzo Centurioni, legation official.
42. Virginia's misspelling of *fleuron*, a French term that, in heraldic language, indicates the gold "opium flower" (poppy) placed on the marquis crown (Piero Guelfi Camajani, *Dizionario araldico*, Bologna, Arnaldo Forni, 1940, 266). A *fleuron*, in the shape of a clover, can also indicate the comital crown, and, since Virginia was a marchesa by birth and countess by marriage, she could boast of both variants. In the second half of the nineteenth century, *fleurons* were also clover-shaped jewels with a pearl or other precious gem, and it is distinctly possible that this was what Victor Emmanuel gave her.
43. A. Decaux, *La Castiglione*, 70–74.
44. Stanislao Bentivoglio (1821–1889), son of Prospero Bentivoglio and Isabella Poniatowska. A half-brother of Maria Anna Zanobi di Ricci Walewska's, he married Thadée d'Ornano in Paris in 1863.
45. A. Decaux, *La Castiglione*, 77.

## PARIS (1856–1857)

1. "During the Second Empire the situation is very different from the way things had been in the 1830s and 1850s. Industry is expanding. From 1850 to 1870, the French railway network goes from 3,000 to 17,500 km. In the same period, the production of cotton wool increases from 140 to 220 thousand pounds sterling, etc. Savings banks and investment banks are created that encourage the development of businesses." Jean-Jacques Perquel, *L'économie française (1830/1880) vue par Balzac et Zola*, conference for alumni of the École des hautes études commerciales (HEC) in Paris, February 17, 2021.
2. Xavier Mauduit, "La fête imperiale et la comédie du pouvoir. Une histoire politique du Second Empire," in *Spectaculaire Second Empire*, catalog of the exhibition at the Musée d'Orsay, Paris, September 27, 2016–January 15, 2017, edited by Guy Cogeval et al., Milan, Skira, 2016, 46.
3. Ibid., 42.
4. Georges Valance, *Haussmann le grand*, Paris, Flammarion, 2000, 191.
5. Théophile Gautier, "Paris démoli. Mosaïque de ruines, par M. Édouard Fournier," in *Gazette nationale ou le Moniteur universel*, January 21, 1854.
6. Appointed by Napoleon I to develop the etiquette of his new court, the Count of Ségur was inspired by the etiquette of the French monarchy of

the Old Regime. Napoleon III had a grand almoner, a grand palace marshal, a grand chamberlain, a grand squire, a grand hunter, a grand master of ceremonies, a superintendent of the imperial palaces, a superintendent of court entertainment, a director of chapel and chamber music. Less excessive, the empress's household had a first lady-in-waiting, a lady of honor, twelve ladies of the palace, and two readers.

7. Edmond and Jules de Goncourt, *Journal. Mémoires de la vie littéraire*, edited by Robert Ricatte, 3 vols., Paris, Robert Laffont, 1989, vol. 1: 1851–1865, 864.
8. Pierre Milza, *Napoléon III*, Paris, Perrin, 2004, 323.
9. Quoted in Eugenio De Rienzo, *Napoleone III*, Salerno Editrice, Rome 2010, 22–23.
10. Ibid., 22.
11. *Discours, messages et proclamations de S. M. Napoléon III, Empereur des Français. 1849–1860*, Paris, Humbert Mirecourt, 1860, 102.
12. The son of the great Austrian minister, Richard von Metternich was in Paris first as legation secretary (1855–1856), and later as ambassador (1859–1870).
13. *Souvenirs de la princesse Pauline de Metternich (1859–1871)*, preface and notes by Marcel Dunan, Paris, Plon, 1922, 63.
14. Ibid., 65–66.
15. Henri Bouchot, *Les Élégances du Second Empire*, Paris, Librairie illustrée, 1896, x.
16. Rose Fortassier, *Les Écrivains français et la mode. De Balzac à nos jours*, Paris, Presses universitaires de France, 1988, 13.
17. Honoré de Balzac, *Traité de la vie élégante*, Paris, Sillage, 2011, 27.
18. Edmond and Jules de Goncourt, *Journal. Mémoires de la vie littéraire*, vol. 1, 843.
19. Stéphanie Tascher de la Pagerie, *Mon séjour aux Tuileries. Première série, 1852–1858*, Paris, Paul Ollendorff, 1894, 164.
20. Cf. Charles-Éloi Vial, "Une Altesse impériale en République: Mathilde, maîtresse de maison de l'Élysée," in *Un soir chez la Princesse Mathilde. Une Bonaparte et les arts*, catalog of the exhibition at Palazzo Fesch, Ajaccio, June–September 2019, edited by Carole Blumenfeld et al., 2019, 47–49.
21. Adrien Goetz, *Mathilde, une Bonaparte en quête d'auteurs*, in *Un soir chez la Princesse Mathild*e, 229.

22. Émile Ollivier, *L'Empire libéral. Études, récits, souvenirs*, 18 vols. Paris, Garnier Frères, 1895–1918, vol. 5, 432.
23. Ibid., 534.
24. Cf. P. Milza, *Napoléon III*, 342.
25. É. Ollivier, *L'Empire libéral*, vol. 5, 434–35.
26. Built by the architect Alfred-Nicolas Normand between 1856 and 1860, modeled on a Roman house and entirely decorated in Greek Revival style, the residence was designed by Prince Napoleon after the Pompejanum of Ludwig I of Bavaria, built by Friedrich von Gärtner in Aschaffenburg between 1840 and 1848, on the model of the House of the Dioscuri. See Audrey Gay-Mazuel, "Un décor neogrec: la maison pompéienne du Prince Napoléon," in *Spectaculaire Second Empire*, 148.
27. Ibid.
28. For more on the relationship between Virginia and Plon-Plon, see their correspondence at the BNF, "Lettres du Prince Jérôme Napoléon à la comtesse, avec réponses," NAF 25068.
29. Cf. S. Tascher de la Pagerie, *Mon séjour aux Tuileries*, 130.
30. Powdered, in the style of the Old Regime.
31. Quoted in A. Decaux, *La Castiglione*, 82.
32. Ernest Barthez, *La famille impériale à Saint-Cloud et à Biarritz*, Paris, Calmann-Lévy, 1913, 72, quoted in P. Milza, *Napoléon III*, 324.
33. Rodolphe Apponyi, *De la Révolution au coup d'État, 1848–1851*, introduction and notes by Charles Samaran, Geneva, La Palatine, 1948, 114.
34. See *Souvenirs de la princesse Pauline de Metternich*, 85: "His naturalness and bonhomie made him likeable and beloved by everyone. He was the very picture of the gentleman; he had absolutely nothing of the parvenu about him."
35. Letter from Queen Victoria to Augusta of Prussia, April 29, 1855, in *Further Letters of Queen Victoria from the Archives of the House of Brandenburg-Prussia*, translated from the German by Mrs. J. Pudney and Lord Sudley, edited by Hector Bolitho, London, Thornton Butterworth, 1938, 55. Cf. Laure Chabanne and Gilles Grandjean, *L'Impératrice Eugénie*, Collections du château de Compiègne, Paris, Flammarion, 2020, 42.
36. Quoted in A. Decaux, *La Castiglione*, 83. See also Giuseppe Massari, *Diario dalle cento voci, 1858–1860*, preface by Emilia Morelli, Bologna, Cappelli, 59: "November 6, 1858 . . . The viscount recounts a lovely witticism from

No. III regarding the beautiful Countess of Castiglione: "*Elle est très jolie, mais elle n'a pas de charme.* [She is very pretty, but she lacks charm.]"

37. From Virginia's diary, Saturday the 26th [January 1856], AFC.
38. Cf. Madame Carette, *Deuxième série des souvenirs intimes de la Cour des Tuileries*, Paris, Paul Ollendorf, 1890, 237.
39. From Virginia's diary, Saturday the 26th [January 1856], AFC.
40. Arthur-Léon Imbert de Saint-Amand, *La Cour du Second Empire (1856–1868)*, Paris, Dentu, 1898, 171.
41. Quoted in Robert de Montesquiou, *La divine comtesse. Étude d'après Madame de Castiglione,* preface by Gabriele D'Annunzio, Paris, Goupil & Cie, 1913, 205.
42. From Virginia's diary, March 29, AFC.
43. From Virginia's diary, quoted in A. Decaux, *La Castiglione*, 90.
44. A.-L. Imbert de Saint-Amand, *La Cour du Second Empire*, 171–72.
45. This is what, according to Marquise Oldoini, Cavour called Virginia. See her letter to her daughter, December 18, 1855, AST, bundle 1, file 4, letter 34.
46. See the passages from Virginia's diary quoted by A. Decaux, 90–92, and also the diary page of March 5, [1856], in AFC, 7.
47. Quoted in A. Decaux, *La Castiglione*, 90.
48. Letter from Camillo Cavour to Luigi Cibrario, Paris, February 22, 1856, in C. Cavour, *Epistolario*, vol. 13, 105.
49. Letter from Luigi Cibrario to Camillo Cavour, Turin, February 25, 1856, ibid., 122.
50. Letter from Camillo Cavour to Urbano Rattazzi, [Paris, February 22, 1856]: "If I don't succeed it won't be for lack of zeal. I pay visits, dine, go out in society, write notes, intrigue with the Palais Royal, do everything I know how to do, I even tried to rouse the patriotism of the lovely Castiglione, to seduce the emperor," ibid., 107.
51. On February 21—the same day as the concert—Virginia noted in her diary that she had received a visit from Villamarina and Cavour, and it had been decided "to send him to Russia as first secretary"; cited in A. Decaux, *La Castiglione*, 91.
52. "My dear cousin, last night I received a letter for you from a high-ranking person. After pocketing it I went to Lady Holland's where I hoped to see you. But being in one of your moody days you had already gone to bed.

I'll send it to you this morning." Letter from Camillo Cavour to Virginia, [Paris, March 12, 1856], in C. Cavour, *Epistolario*, vol. 13, 215 [French].

53. Letter from Camillo Cavour to Victor Emmanuel II, Paris, March 16, 1859, ibid., 244 [French].

54. "In the meantime, be good to Ninì, don't annoy her and arrange something for her father somehow." Letter from Victor Emmanuel II to Camillo Cavour, March 25, 1856, in *Le lettere di Vittorio Emanuele II*, edited by Francesco Cognasso, 2 vols., Turin, Deputazione Subalpina di Storia Patria, 1966, vol. 1, 453.

55. Letter from Camillo Cavour to Victor Emmanuel II, Paris, March 4, 1856, in C. Cavour, *Epistolario*, vol. 13, 171 [French].

56. P. Milza, *Napoléon III*, 396.

57. A.-L. Imbert de Saint-Amand, *La Cour du Second Empire*, 415.

58. A. Decaux, *La Castiglione*, 86; see also P. Milza, *Napoléon III*, 358. "Probably also said aloud, this exhortation to 'do it' by any means necessary, to which Virginia herself refers several times in her letters, is reported by numerous historians."

59. Cf. A. Decaux, *La Castiglione*, 109.

60. Letter from Costantino Nigra to Virginia, Saturday, no place specified, undated, AST, bundle 3, fascicle 12, letter 4 [French].

61. Letter from Costantino Nigra to Virginia, Paris, Friday, no place specified, undated, *ibid.*, letter 14.

62. General Fleury reports Cavour's remarks to Laffitte concerning his meeting with Rothschild, when he aimed to "*tirer les vers du nez*," in *Souvenirs du Général Cte Fleury*, vol. 2, 412.

63. Adriano Viarengo, *Cavour*, Rome, Salerno Editrice, 2010, 324.

64. Ibid., 327.

65. Letter from Virginia to her father, [Paris], [May 36 1856], ASD, binder 3 [French].

66. Cf. letter from Salvatore Pes di Villamarina to the Count of Cavour, Paris, September 20, 1856, in C. Cavour, *Epistolario*, vol. 13, 742 [French].

67. Nicole G. Albert offers a broad overview of the articles dedicated to the countess by the society pages in her biography *La Castiglione. Vies et métamorphoses*, Paris, Perrin, 2011.

68. Cosmetic made from the mucilage of quince seeds, used to straighten hair.

69. Letter from Prosper Mérimée to Madame de Montijo, Paris, May 28 [1856], in Prosper Mérimée, *Correspondance générale*, edited and annotated by Maurice Parturier, second series, Toulouse, Privat, 1957, vol. 2: 1856–1858, 51.
70. Letter from Prosper Mérimée to Jean-Jacques Ampère, March 8, 1856, *ibid.*, 26.
71. *Souvenirs de la princesse Pauline de Metternich*, 60–61.
72. Letter from Emanuele d'Azeglio to Camillo Cavour, Park Lane, May 31, 1856, in C. Cavour, *Epistolario*, vol. 13, 505 [French].
73. S. Tascher de la Pagerie, *Mon séjour aux Tuileries*, vol. 1, 131.
74. "Wednesday July 23 . . . At the latest gathering at Villeneuve-l'Étang, the Countess of Castiglione disappeared with the Emperor for a long time on a small island in the center of the lake; she emerged, it would appear, a little rumpled, and the empress was unable to hide her displeasure," Horace de Viel-Castel, *Mémoires sur le règne de Napoléon III* (1851–1864), edited by Éric Anceau, Paris, Robert Laffont, 2005, 494.
75. Henry Richard Charles Wellesley, Earl Cowley, *The Paris Embassy during the Second Empire, from the Papers of Earl Cowley*, edited by Col. the Hon. F. A. Wellesley, London, Thornton Butterworth, 1928, 130. See also P. Milza, *Napoléon III*, 360.
76. Quoted in Éric Anceau, *Ils ont fait et défait le Second Empire*, Paris, Tallandier, 2019, 135.
77. Madame Carette, *Deuxième série des souvenirs intimes*, 12–13.
78. Ibid., 138.
79. Letter from Prosper Mérimée to Madame Xifré, May 8, 1855, in P. Mérimée, *Correspondance générale*, vol. 6, 481. The Bal Mabille was a popular open-air dance hall, where the cancan had been introduced some years earlier.
80. See Robert Sencourt, *The Life of the Empress Eugénie, with a Foreword by His Grace the Duke of Berwick and Alba*, New York, Charles Scribner's Sons, 1931, 116.
81. Nancy Mitford, "A Queen of France," in *A Talent to Annoy: Essays, Journalism and Reviews, 1929–1971*, London, Capuchin Classics, 1986, 147–50.
82. Quoted in Raphaël Dargent, *L'Impératrice Eugénie. L'obsession de l'honneur*, Paris, Belin, 2017, 276.

83. See Madame Carette, *Deuxième série des souvenirs intimes*, 155. See also *Journal du docteur Prosper Ménière, publié par son fils le Dr. E. Ménière*, Paris, Plon, 1903, 255–56, where the terrible details of the delivery are reported by Eugénie's doctor.
84. P. Milza, *Napoléon III*, 338.
85. See H. R. C. Wellesley, *The Paris Embassy During the Second Empire*, 96.
86. See *Papiers secrets et correspondance du Second Empire. Documents authentiques annotés. Réimpression complète de l'édition de l'Imprimerie Nationale, annotée et augmentée de nombreuses pièces publiées à l'étranger et recueillies par A. Poulet-Malassis*, 13 volumes compiled in a single volume, Office de Publicité, Brussels, 1870–1871. Castiglione figures on the list of those monitored by the police, since it appears that her letters were intercepted by the Cabinet Noir: "During the Emperor's stay in Plombières and Biarritz, Madame de Castiglione's letters were opened and read by the agents of the ministry of the interior" (vol. 5, chapter 6, "Le Cabinet Noir," 34, and 46–48). See also Howard C. Payne, "Theory and Practice of Political Police during the Second Empire in France," in *The Journal of Modern History*, XXX, 1, March 1958, 14–23.
87. See Nicole G. Albert, *La Castiglione*.
88. Ferdinand Bac, in *Intimités du Second Empire*, 3 vols., Paris, Hachette, 1931, vol. 2: *Les femmes et la comédie d'après des documents contemporains*, the chapter "Souvenirs de Madame de Castiglione," 47. On Ferdinand Bac see, in this volume, note 4 on p. 429.
89. A.-L. Imbert de Saint-Amand, *La Cour du Second Empire*, 173.
90. *Souvenirs du Général Cte Fleury*, vol. 2, 210.
91. Madame Carette, *Deuxième série des souvenirs intimes*, 236.
92. *Souvenirs de la princesse Pauline de Metternich*, 61.
93. Laurent Theis, *François Guizot*, Paris, Fayard, 2008, 143.
94. Madame Carette, *Deuxième série des souvenirs intimes*, 237.
95. Ferdinand Bac, *La Cour des Tuileries sous le Second Empire*, Paris, Hachette, 1930, 112.
96. The photograph was intended for Paul Granier de Cassagnac, who showed it to Loliée after Virginia's death. See Frédéric Loliée, *Les Femmes du Second Empire*, 2 vols., Paris, Tallandier, 1927, vol. 1, 25.
97. Letter from Salvatore Pes di Villamarina to Camillo Cavour, in C. Cavour, *Epistolario*, vol. 13, 778.

98. *Souvenirs du Général Cte Fleury*, vol. 2, 205.
99. *Souvenirs de la princesse Pauline de Metternich*, 78–79.
100. *Souvenirs du Général Cte Fleury*, vol. 2, 204.
101. *Souvenirs de la princesse Pauline de Metternich*, 88–89.
102. See *Souvenirs du Général Cte Fleury*, vol. 2, 213.
103. Madame Jules Baroche [Céleste Baroche Le Tellier], *Second Empire. Notes et souvenirs*, Paris, Les Éditions G. Gres et Cie, 1921, 45.
104. *Souvenirs du Général Cte Fleury*, vol. 2, 212.
105. A letter from Francesco Verasis to his father-in-law states that on Wednesday, in Pierrefonds, after the "lunch among the ruins, the Ladies and the Knights started playing cat and mouse, a game in which you have to run ... apparently Niny tripped over her skirt and fell ... the Emperor's doctor who came to see her diagnosed a serious fracture, all night long Niny made arnica compresses and immersed her arm in ice water," shedding fresh light on the events of that day. Determined not to cut short her stay in Compiègne, Virginia had gritted her teeth and, with her broken arm in a sling, had cheerfully and smilingly taken part in all the social entertainments that followed. "Finally, on Sunday morning, after Mass and breakfast," the Castiglione couple returned to Paris with all the other guests on the famous Espresso train made available to all invitees. (Paris, November 7, 1856, ASD, folder 4 [French]).
106. Letter from her mother to Virginia, [Florence], November 9, 1856, AST, bundle 1, fascicle 4, letter 37.
107. Letter from her mother to Virginia, [Florence], November 22, 1856, ibid., letter 38 [French].
108. Letter from Francesco Verasis to his father-in-law, Paris, November 14, 1856, ASD, binder 4.
109. Letter from Francesco Verasis to his father-in-law, Paris, December 24, 1856, ibid. [French].
110. See A. Decaux, *La Castiglione*, 120.
111. The original of the letter appeared in the Drouot auction, and the catalog (16, 22) contains a long excerpt, but with no indication of the date. Decaux must have seen it before it was sold, given he offers a more complete transcription and also reports the date as Thursday, March 15, without, however, specifying the year. In 1856, March 15 fell on a Saturday, and to have a Thursday that coincides with that date you would have

to wait until 1860; we know, however, that in the spring of 1860, when she briefly returned to Paris after a long absence, Virginia was no longer serving as an intermediary between Turin and Paris, and Costantino Nigra by then was in charge of relations with the emperor. Hence the supposition that the scrupulous Decaux may have transcribed an inaccurate date and the letter instead dates back to the spring of 1857 or 1858. Regardless of the date, the letter remains eloquent proof of Virginia's activity as a secret agent.

112. A.-L. Imbert de Saint-Amand, *La Cour du Second Empire*, 171–73.
113. Madame Jules Baroche, *Notes et souvenirs*, 58.
114. H. de Viel-Castel, *Mémoires sur le règne de Napoléon III*, 538–39.
115. Madame Jules Baroche, *Notes et souvenirs*, 60.
116. Ibid., 59.
117. In *Les Modes parisiennes*, Éliane de Marsy speaks of "a light blue mantle of heavy satin with stripes of ecru silk, dotted with brocaded carnations. The dress was white, also made of satin, and covered by a high flounce of English lace . . . The bodice, embellished with the same lace and beautiful strings of pearls, was decorated on the left side with a bouquet of enormous carnations, just the way the beautiful countess likes them—and a specialty of the Compagnie Floréale. On the right side a riot of gemstones, diamonds, and emeralds sparkled. A light ruche ran over the shoulders. And in her powdered, very voluminous hair were clever combinations of diamond and emerald barrettes, alternating with simple carnations" (quoted in Nicole G. Albert, *La Castiglione*, 80–81).
118. Madame Jules Baroche, *Notes et souvenirs*, 57 and 59.
119. Ibid., 61–62.

## THE ASSASSINATION ATTEMPT (1857–1858)

1. See E. De Rienzo, *Napoleone III*, 210.
2. Avenue Montaigne 24 had been mentioned in a letter from Francesco Verasis to Marquis Oldoini dated November 14, 1856. It was a luxurious, fully furnished *hôtel particulier*, whose astronomical rent was around 48,000 francs a year.
3. See *Papiers secrets et correspondance du Second Empire*, vol. 5, 64: "There can now be no question that during the Second Empire the police had trans-

formed into a veritable hothouse of plots, conceived, organized, or provoked by the prefects Lagrange and Piétri. With the exception of the Orsini and Pianori attacks and the last Villette insurrection, the hand of the imperial police can be seen at work behind all the trials and tribulations that so contributed to the consolidation of the former regime." The attack on avenue Montaigne was evoked imaginatively and in great detail in the *Mémoires de Griscelli, Agent secret de Napoléon III (1850–58), de Cavour (1859–61), d'Antonelli (1861–62), de François II (1862–64), de l'Empereur d'Autriche (1864–67)*, Brussels, 1867, and in the *Mémoires de Monsieur Claude, chef de la police de sureté sous le Second Empire*, 10 vols., Paris, Jules Rouff, 1881–1883. Both works—although probably apocryphal and prone to fictional reimaginings—bear the traces of rumors circulating at the time regarding the activity of different and often rival secret services. According to Griscelli—who boasted of having saved the emperor's life by killing the assassin lurking on the stairs of the house on avenue Montaigne—it was an Italian-instigated attack carried out with the help of Virginia, who was consequently arrested by the police and expelled from the country. Which would not have been pleasing to anyone except Eugénie. The thesis put forward in the *Mémoires of Monsieur Claude* (vol. 1, 319–26) is different: the instigation was still much as it had been described by Griscelli, but here the target of the attack is not the emperor but Virginia. And the mysterious Madame X——, who hatches the intrigue to ingratiate herself with the empress, suggests a cousin of the emperor, Marie-Laetitia Bonaparte Wyse, then Princess Solms, then Madame Rattazzi, then Madame de Rute Giner, an upper-crust international adventuress, a multifaceted dark lady whose metamorphoses were reconstructed by Lucia Lazzerini in *La fée et la diablesse. Histoire d'une hantise poétique et mondaine de "Flamenca" à "Calendau" et "Pinocchio" jusqu'à "La recherche du temps perdu,"* Carrefour Ventadour, Moustier-Ventadour, 2018.

4. The Austrian-born French artist, Ferdinand-Sigismund Bach (1859–1952) was the grandson of an illegitimate son of Jérôme Bonaparte. Settling in Paris a few years after the fall of Napoleon III, under the pseudonym Ferdinand Bac, he collected the reminiscences of Arsène Houssaye, a key witness to the society of the Second Empire, who had, in his turn, collected the confessions of Prosper Mérimée.
5. F. Bac, *La Cour des Tuileries sous le Second Empire*, 105–15.

6. Also see, in this volume, the chapter "Odio et amo."
7. That the Hollands and the Castigliones saw each other frequently is also confirmed by this passage from the Parisian diary of Nassau William Senior, an English economist and friend of Tocqueville: "I dined with Lord Holland, and met . . . the Count and Countess Castiglione. I thought her wonderfully beautiful, more so than when I saw her last year at Holland House. She is a Louis-Quinze beauty: tall, round, well-formed, with large dark eyes, long eyelashes, straight eyebrows, a clear white complexion, and a mouth which, as I saw it, always smiling, was charming. She sat in the evening, filling with her crinoline a whole sofa, to receive and certainly to enjoy the homage of all around her." The beautiful vision is dated "Saturday, April 11, [1857]." *Conversations with M. Thiers, M. Guizot and other Distinguished Persons during the Second Empire by the Late Nassau William Senior,* edited by his daughter M. C. M. Simpson, 2 vols., London, Hurst and Blackett, 1878, vol. 2, 104–105.
8. Letter from Emanuele Taparelli d'Azeglio to Camillo Cavour, July 10, [1857], 25 Park Lane, in C. Cavour, *Epistolario*, vol. 14, 303–304 [French].
9. "Correspondance du prince Joseph Poniatowski et de la princesse de Castiglione," entry 2901, AP/340 (I)/21.
10. Louis Philippe's wife died in exile in England on March 24, 1866. *Correspondances inédites et archives privées de Virginia Vérasis, comtesse de Castiglione*, with a preface by André Maurois, 25 [French].
11. Maria Carolina Augusta of Bourbon died at Twickenham on December 6, 1869.
12. On the subject of the Italian unification, which was putting French politics in a fix, Virginia brazenly changed her position even with regard to her illustrious cousin: "I was a friend of Monsieur de Cavour's, I admired him, I respected him, but now I'm quite cross with him, really quite cross, for all the blunders he committed—in any case, we've already had a fight. He has sent me proposals for reconciliation from every corner of the world, but I don't want to hear it . . . I once loved Italians, now I despise them, I find them absurd, devoid of moral principles, full of stupid ambitions, unbearable; they would like to drag us down with them into an abyss that is baneful to our country." Letter from Virginia to the Duke of Aumale, offered for sale with other handwritten letters; it appears in one of the catalogs of the Librairie Les Neuf Muses, edited by Alain Nicolas [French].

13. The accompanying notes read: "To the Countess Castiglione. / A lovely gift I fain would send to thee, / What I deem loveliest in this mirror see!—Holland." Quoted in "The Romance of a Favourite: Comtesse de Castiglione," *The Lotus Magazine* 4, 2 (November 1912), 59–71.
14. A. Decaux, *La Castiglione*, 132.
15. The portrait of Virginia, based on a photograph of her by Pierre François Eugène Giraud, one of Princess Mathilde's favorite painters.
16. Quoted in *La Divine Comtesse. Photographs of the Countess of Castiglione*, catalogue of the exhibition of the same name at the Metropolitan Museum of Art, New York, September 18–December 31, 2000, edited by Pierre Apraxine and Xavier Demange, with Françoise Heilbrun and Michele Falzone del Barnabò, New Haven-London, Yale University Press, 2000, 166.
17. Bernard Berenson, knowing Montesquiou was on the hunt for any and all documents about the Countess of Castiglione, pointed him toward the Watts portrait in the Holland collection. See R. de Montesquiou, *La divine comtesse*, 51.
18. Ibid., 50–51, and, for Countess Greffulhe, 199.
19. Letter from Virginia to Costantino Nigra, AST, bundle 3, fascicle 12, letter 11.
20. "I, the undersigned, declare that the conduct of the Lord Count toward the dear Lady Countess Nicchia has been *wondrous* for a month for the aforementioned count has shown himself extremely patient, good, gentle, free of rage . . . in short, a veritable angel. In accordance with her request, he has sent her this legal certificate. Paris, July 25, 1858, Francesco Verasis," FP, "Count Verasis" file.
21. *Souvenirs du Général Cte Fleury*, vol. 2, 210.
22. See H. de Viel-Castel, *Mémoires sur le règne de Napoléon III*, 563; see also Madame Jules Baroche, *Notes et souvenirs*, 62.
23. Letter from Francesco Verasis to his father-in-law, Paris, December 24, 1856, ASD, binder 4.
24. Letters from Francesco Verasis to Virginia, Basil, August 17, 1856, 10 p.m., and Genoa, August 21, 1856, Hotel Feder, midnight, AST, bundle 2, fascicle 5, letters 21 and 22.
25. Letter from Francesco Verasis to Virginia, Costigliole, September 5, 1856, ibid., unnumbered letter [French].

26. Letter from Francesco Verasis to Virginia, Nizza, January 26, 1857, ibid., letter 28. Pollenzo was a residence long owned by the House of Savoy.
27. Letter from Francesco Verasis to Giuseppe Poniatowski, March 27, 1857, FP, fascicle "Conte Verasis."
28. Letter from Francesco Verasis to Virginia, AST, fascicle 5, letter 20 [French].
29. Letter from Francesco Verasis to Virginia, Paris, May 26, 1857, ibid., letter 29 [French].
30. Francesco undertook to pay his wife an annual pension and allowed her to see her son whenever she wished, on the condition that she did not live in Turin and that she "behaved honorably, so as not to tarnish the name she bears." Otherwise the count reserved the right to legal action. "Acte de séparation," ibid., letter 30 [French].
31. "(1) Refusal on the part of the countess to fulfill her marital duties under the pretext that she no longer wishes to become pregnant... (2) Absolute lack of obedience toward her husband, whom the countess treats with the utmost harshness, having moreover, even in front of strangers, the air of considering him an imbecile good-for-nothing. (3) Complete absence of religious feeling... (4) Frequently reprehensible conduct, especially in public, with a continuous display, on the part of the countess, of intimate manners with all and sundry, perhaps even in perfect innocence, but after all, in the eyes of the world, this does damage to the husband and therefore is intolerable to him. (5) Unbridled luxury in matters of appearance and in a thousand other things... which exceeds the husband's financial means... (6) Lack of affection for her son whom she treats like a toy, dedicating herself to him exclusively in her rare moments of leisure and constantly leaving him in the hands of strangers. (7) Outbursts of unmotivated anger in which the countess says incredible things, putting her husband's patience to the test. (8) In short, a total disregard for the ways of the world, with the end result that the husband himself appears to be a boor." Ibid., file 7, letter 1 [French].
32. Letter from the Francesco Verasis to Isabella Oldoini, Paris, June 1857, ibid., letter 31 [French].
33. Ibid.

34. Letter from Isabella Oldoini to her husband, June 10, 1857, ASD, binder 3.
35. Karl Philipp Bach's testimony is recorded by his son Ferdinand, in *Intimités du Second Empire*, 52.
36. Comte de Reiset, *Mes souvenirs*, vol. 1, 429.
37. H. de Viel-Castel, *Mémoires sur le règne de Napoléon III*, 624.
38. Ibid., 714.
39. See Romano Paolo Coppini, "Cuori e denari: le amicizie intime dei Rothschild," in *Virginia Oldoini. I giorni e il mito della contessa di Castiglione*, catalog of the exhibition at Museo Lia, La Spezia, 1999, edited by Adriana Beverini and Pia Spagiari, La Spezia, Luna, 1999, 31.
40. Auctioned by Drouot in 1951, seventeen letters from the Count of Nieuwerkerke have recently reappeared on the market.
41. Edmond and Jules de Goncourt, *Journal. Mémoires de la vie littéraire*, vol. 1, 797.
42. H. de Viel-Castel, *Mémoires sur le règne de Napoléon III*, 624.
43. Judging by a letter Virginia wrote to Victor Emmanuel, the Italian and French secret services were perfectly aware of Orsini's intentions and believed they had taken adequate measures: "From Turin today came a warning that F. Orsini had arrived to assassinate the emperor and everyone is on guard here to avert this tragedy... It is terrible that the Italians think of nothing but killing!" (AST, bundle 3, file 14, letter 16). The letter introduces a surprising element that seems to have been previously overlooked by historians of the Risorgimento.
44. A. Viarengo, *Cavour*, 358.
45. Letter from Victor Emmanuel II to Enrico Morozzo Della Rocca, Turin, February 8, 1858, in *Le lettere di Vittorio Emanuele II*, vol. 1, 465–67, quoted in A. Viarengo, *Cavour*, 361.
46. *Lettere di Felice Orsini*, edited by Alberto Maria Ghisalberti, Vittoriano, Rome 1936, 255.
47. As early as 1851, when Walewski was ambassador to London, Massimo d'Azeglio hit the nail on the head, writing to his nephew: "I am also of the opinion that W[alewski] is not one of our friends. In any case he doesn't strike me as all that bright." Letter to Emanuele d'Azeglio, [Turin], October 2, 1851, in M. d'Azeglio, *Epistolario*, vol. 7, 6.

48. Letter from Camillo Cavour to Napoleon III, August 25, 1858, in C. Cavour, *Epistolario*, vol. 15, 598 [French].
49. Letter from Francesco Verasis to Virginia, Paris, July 31, 1858, AST, bundle 2, fascicle 5, letter 36 [French].
50. Letter from Camillo Cavour to Giuseppina Alfieri di Sostegno, [Chambéry], July 13, 1859, in C. Cavour, *Epistolario*, vol. 15, 486.
51. Letter from Francesco Verasis to his father-in-law, Turin, November 14, 1858, ASD, binder 4 [French].
52. Rough draft of the letter sent by Filippo Oldoini to his daughter, La Spezia, November 1, 1857, ASD, binder 3 [French].
53. Letter from Francesco Verasis to his father-in-law, Paris, December 21, 1858, ibid.
54. If, as everything leads us to believe, the Virginia who signs the two letters addressed to Eugenio [di Carignano] and dated "Paris, March 28, 1859" is our countess, then it is clear there are many things we don't know about her. It would seem that Castiglione, whom we believed to be confined to Villa Gloria, returned to the French capital for a few days and was desperately looking for money; that she was in close contact with one of the most authoritative members of the Savoy royal family, who could not have been ignorant of her activities as a secret agent; that she was in turn spied on by those who ordered those activities; and finally, like any professional spy, she had more than one iron in the fire. The letter, entrusted to Cavour—who in the last week of March had gone to Paris to see the emperor and avert the convening of a peace congress—was opened, copied, and perhaps translated by the count's secretary, Isacco Artom, in whose archive it can still be found today. The question remains whether the original was in French and in code, though the text in our possession is in Italian. A prominent political figure, a former general commander and, later, admiral of the Sardinian navy, Eugenio Emanuele di Savoy-Villafranca, Prince of Carignano (1825–1888), prepared himself in case of war—as had previously happened to his cousin Charles Albert—to assume the regency while Victor Emmanuel was on the battlefield. Virginia, as we will see later, had made sure she would be protected, and the two were on such intimate terms that she addressed him using the informal *tu*. Cryptic though they are, the two letters, which perhaps allude to the ongoing negotiations between Cavour and Russia in anticipation of

the war against Austria, show her dealing with her "enemies"—a term that refers both to the French police and to Virginia's creditors.

## VILLA GLORIA (1859)

1. Throughout this chapter, all phrases in quotation marks and without endnote references are taken from "Correspondance du prince Joseph Poniatowski et de la Comtesse de Castiglione," FP, Supplément 3: Famille Poniatowski, Joseph Poniatowski (340AP)-AP/340 (I)/21. An inventory of these letters, kept in a box containing eight envelopes, is not yet available.
2. See the entry on Józef Poniatowski in *Polski Słownik Biorafiiczny, Polska Akademia Nauk*, Wrocław, Instytut Historii, vol. 28, 1983, 437–38.
3. Letter of instructions (January 2, 1849) from the foreign secretary Giuseppe Mortarelli, FP, cited in Ryszard Daniel Golianek, "Politics, Music and Cosmopolitism: The Operatic Output in Joseph Poniatowski (1816–1873) in Its Social and Political Contexts," in *Studia Musicologica*, LII, issue 1/4, December 2011, 160, note 8.
4. Letter from Stanislao Poniatowski to Virginia, no place specified, undated, AST, bundle 4, fascicle 1, file 5, letter 1 [French].
5. In a letter to Alexandre Michaud, the jeweler from whom he'd ordered a ring to give Virginia, d'Azeglio confirmed: "We call Madame de Castiglione *Nicchia*, a typically Florentine diminutive meaning *shell*," in M. d'Azeglio, *Epistolario*, vol. 5, III, 303 [French].
6. Included in the 1951 Drouot auction, the 348 autograph letters from Giuseppe Poniatowski to Virginia (file 71, 52–55) are, as far as we know, not currently available.
7. As early as July 1857 Virginia wrote from London complaining that she had no news from Il Vecio [a Venetian term meaning "the Old Man"], adding: "I'm just waiting for two lines, but a little saltier." "Salt" and "salty" were the terms she often used with him to indicate amorous intimacy.
8. A. Decaux, *La Castiglione*, 176.
9. "My thirst for Nicchia is starting to become so fierce that I fear I am going to go insane," ibid., 175.
10. Letter from Camillo Cavour to Giuseppina Alfieri di Sostegno, December 15, 1858, in C. Cavour, *Epistolario*, vol. 15, 926 [French].

11. See notarized title deed of July 26, 1859, FP, fascicle "Conte Verasis."
12. September 6, 1859; see A. Decaux, *La Castiglione*, 174.

## BABY

1. Letter from Giorgio to his mother, no place specified, undated, AST, bundle 2, fascicle 8, letter 1 [English]. There are about sixty letters sent from Giorgio to Virginia between 1859 and 1866 preserved at the Fondo Castiglione at the State Archives of Turin.
2. Letter from Giorgio to his mother, no place specified, undated, ibid., letter 2 [originally written in English, as are many of Giorgio's letters to "Mina"].
3. Virginia had a mania for nicknames: this one was perhaps suggested to her by Poniatowski, who had been a diplomat in China.
4. Letter from Giorgio Verasis to his mother, no place specified, undated, ibid., letter 3 [English].
5. Letter from Filippo Oldoini to his wife, Paris, November 16, [1854], ASD, binder 4.
6. "At 10 a.m., when the labor pains grew stronger, Dominici had me lie down in the little bed next to mine, where Francesco held my hand and Luisa and Dominici held my legs, for I was in a great deal of pain. At noon I gave birth to a son who was washed and dressed. When everything was over I got up, changed my shirt, and went back to my bed alone, where I sipped broth. I slept until 6, when the priest from the Angeli came in to give holy water to the baby who has been named Giorgio and lay in the pink cradle next to my bed." Quoted in A. Decaux, *La Castiglione*, 48.
7. Letter from Francesco Verasis to his father-in-law, Turin, March 22, 1855, ASD, binder 4 [French].
8. Letter from Francesco Verasis to his father-in-law, Turin, March 9, 1855, ten o'clock in the morning, ibid. [French].
9. Ibid. [French].
10. Letter from Francesco Verasis to his father-in-law, Turin, March 30, 1855: "Niny, who grows bored whenever she's alone, wants me to be her constant companion, but I owe my wife a great deal for having made me the father of such a magnificent child." Ibid., folder 3 [French].

11. See also, in this volume, note 31 on p. 432.
12. H. d'Ideville, *Journal d'un diplomate en Italie*, 94.
13. Ibid., 84.
14. Ibid., 94.
15. P. Apraxine and X. Demange, *La Divine Comtesse. Photographs of the Countess of Castiglione*, 161.
16. Anonymous, *Giorgio Verasis,* 1858, oil on canvas, private collection, La Spezia; see also *Virginia Oldoini. I giorni e il mito della contessa di Castiglione*, file 26, 198.
17. P. Apraxine and X. Demange, *La Divine Comtesse. Photographs of the Countess of Castiglione*, 161.

## THE WAR OF INDEPENDENCE

1. One of the three drafts of Cavour's famous note is preserved in the Fondazione Biblioteca Benedetto Croce, XCIV, C21, and represents—along with another handwritten version preserved in the State Archives of Turin and the text of the speech reported by Giuseppe Massari in *Diario dalle cento voci*, 98—the third slight variant of the famous passage suggested by Napoleon III. The abundance of corrections is proof of how difficult the drafting of this text was. See *Tutti gli scritti di Camillo Cavour*, selected and edited by Carlo Pischedda and Giuseppe Talamo, 4 vols., Turin, Centro Studi Piemontesi, 1976–1978, vol. 4, 2005–2006, note.
2. See Piero Pieri, *Storia militare del Risorgimento*, Turin, Einaudi, 1962, 619.
3. Letter from Virginia to Poniatowski, [Turin, May 1, 1859]: "I saw the count who is leaving with the king today for the front. We embraced. Barba [Uncle Cigala] and all his friends have gone too."
4. In communicating her decision to Poniatowski, Virginia informs him: "The Prince di Carignano writes to tell me that they have decided to *défendre* Turin with the national guard. The army is prepared to be massacred but not to abandon the country. Cavour is right to make the best use of what armed citizens he has."
5. Letter from Cigala to Virginia, Calcinato, [May 22, 1859], AST, bundle 3, fascicle 13, letter 50.
6. Guido Rupigné sees, in Cigala's letters from the front, coded indications about the imminent end of the war. Guido Rupigné, "La storia ci aveva

ingannati sulla contessa Castiglione," in *L'Europeo*, DLXV, August 12, 1956, 47.

7. "I feel I love you too much" (AST, bundle 3, file 13, letter 27); "I love you so much. Write to me it is the only pleasure I have" (ibid., letter 29); "I would like to see you happy because you are good and sometimes delectable" (ibid., letter 34); "I have kissed your dear little face a thousand times" (ibid., letter 36); "I will certainly be thinking of you in the heat of the action" (ibid., letter 40); "don't torment yourself so, dear Nicchia..." (ibid., letter 50).
8. Letter from Cigala to Virginia, [1859]: "Salopa is here with Farfo—may the devil whisk her away. Nobody must know..."; "Salopa is fine and Farfo fucks all day. Well. Viva l'Italia," ibid., letters 34 and 35.
9. In 1856, Cigala asked the king to open an investigation into Rosa Vercellana's behavior. See A. Viarengo, *Vittorio Emanuele II*, 206.
10. Letter from Cigala to Virginia, [1859], AST, bundle 3, fascicle 13, letter 39.
11. On the conditions of the Piedmontese army in 1859, see R. Romeo, *Cavour e il suo tempo* vol. 21, 583–96.
12. Here is the text of the letter: "Torrione, [June 1, 1859]. My dear friend, everyone is well, but the last two days have been hot, we have suffered many wounded, none of whom you know, we have taken more than 800 prisoners, 10 pieces of cannon, many, many enemy deaths. We have suffered heavy losses. We must have more than 1,000 dead and wounded. The Piedmontese army performed honorably. Yesterday we drove back more than 40,000 enemies with the Cialdini division and a Zouaves regiment sent by the emperor of France. Yesterday they distinguished themselves on the battlefield. They took 8 guns and five infantry mortars. Things are going well but there will be a great deal of bloodshed. You cannot imagine how furiously our men charge against the enemies with their bayonets out. The French are shocked to find our soldiers equal to theirs. The count is well but today leaves for Vercelli to rest his foot for two or three days. I am doing very well and see you everywhere I go, dear. Yesterday the emperor asked the king about you, where you were, and the king told me the emperor was practically in *heat*. Whenever he can tell me something about you that might upset me, he does so with such malice, because he thinks I love you. I can take it. I embrace you. Yours always, B. Cigala," FP.
13. Letter from Virginia to Poniatowski, no place specified, undated, ibid.

14. In Virginia's orthography "e" [and] and "è" [is] are interchangeable.
15. Quoted in A. Decaux, *La Castiglione*, 150. Decaux dates the letter May 26, 1859.
16. Ibid. [The word for "stirrup" is *staffa*, which also means "staff" in the organizational sense.—Translator's note.]
17. Protagonist of the eponymous opera by Donizetti.
18. "If they are in Milan, Barba expects a one-day visit and I could conveniently make it with Countess Clemente [Castiglione's sister-in-law]," FP. See also Cigala's letter to Virginia, Milan, in which he informs her that he is looking for an apartment for her, AST, bundle 3, file 13, letter 60.
19. The English minister plenipotentiary to Turin from 1852 to 1863.
20. G. Massari, *Diario dalle cento voci*, 264.
21. The letter Virginia wrote to Poniatowski begins with the following words: "I am sorry not to let you go to sleep hopeful and dream blissful dreams, but *contre le malheur, et pour l'empêcher, il vaut beaucoup mieux être prévenu à temps* [to ward off misfortune, and in order to avoid it, it is much better to be warned in time]."
22. See the letter from Ignace Bauer to Camillo Cavour of April 29, 1851, in C. Cavour, Epistolario, vol. 8, 121.
23. H. de Viel-Castel, *Mémoires sur le règne de Napoléon III*, 863.
24. Letter from Massimo d'Azeglio to Eugène Rendu, July 24, 1859, in M. d'Azeglio, *Epistolari*o, vol. 9, 303–304, letter 47 [French].

## AN UNHAPPY LOVER

1. Letter from La Tour d'Auvergne to Virginia, Berlin, March 5, 1860, AST, bundle 14 C, letter 7.
2. H. d'Ideville, *Journal d'un diplomate en Italie*, 2–3.
3. See A. Decaux, *La Castiglione*, 157–58.
4. *Correspondances inédites et archives privées*, 48–49.
5. Letter from La Tour d'Auvergne to Virginia, Berlin, July 18, 1860, AST, bundle 14 C, letter 54 [French].
6. Letter from La Tour d'Auvergne to Virginia, Genoa, Saturday, [May 14, 1859], ibid., letter 149 [French].
7. Letter from La Tour d'Auvergne to Virginia, no place specified, January 16, [1860], ibid., no number [French].

8. Letter from La Tour d'Auvergne to Virginia, no place specified, undated, ibid., letter 154 [French].
9. Letter from La Tour d'Auvergne to Virginia, no place specified, undated, ibid., letter 61 [French].
10. Letter from La Tour d'Auvergne to Virginia, Friday, no place specified, undated, ibid., unnumbered letter [French].
11. Letter from La Tour d'Auvergne to Virginia, no place specified, undated, ibid., letter 95 [French], ibid.
12. See H. d'Ideville, *Journal d'un diplomate en Italie*, 20–23.
13. Letter from La Tour d'Auvergne to Virginia, [Turin], [January 22, 1860], AST, bundle 14 C, unnumbered letter [French].
14. Letter from La Tour d'Auvergne to Virginia, Berlin, March 18, [1860], Sunday evening, ibid., letter 10 [French].
15. Letter from La Tour d'Auvergne to Virginia, [Berlin], July 25, 1860, ibid., letter 57 [French].
16. Letter from La Tour d'Auvergne to Virginia, [Berlin], February 19, [1860], ibid., letter 2 [French].
17. Letter from La Tour d'Auvergne to Virginia, [Berlin], February 22, 1860, ibid., letter 3 [French].
18. Letter from La Tour d'Auvergne to Virginia, Berlin, March 5, 1860, ibid., letter 7 [French].
19. Letter from La Tour d'Auvergne to Virginia, [Berlin], February 22, [1860], ibid., letter 3 [French].
20. Letter from La Tour d'Auvergne to Virginia, Berlin, February 18 [1860], ibid., letter 1 [French].
21. Letter from La Tour d'Auvergne to Virginia, [Berlin], February 22 [1860], ibid., letter 3 [French].
22. Letter from La Tour d'Auvergne to Virginia, Berlin, March 5, 1860, ibid., letter 7 [French].
23. "These days you're the only one I can turn to expecting to feel anything at all." Letter from La Tour d'Auvergne to Virginia, [Berlin], February 22, 1860, ibid., letter 3 [French].
24. Letter from La Tour d'Auvergne to Virginia, [Berlin], February 29, 1860, ibid., letter 5 [French].
25. Letter from La Tour d'Auvergne to Virginia, [Berlin], March 22, 1860, ibid., letter 11 [French].

26. Letter from La Tour d'Auvergne to Virginia, Berlin, March 3, 1860, ibid., letter 9 [French].
27. Letter from La Tour d'Auvergne to Virginia, Berlin, March 24, 1860, ibid., letter 12 [French].
28. Letter from La Tour d'Auvergne to Virginia, Berlin, June 28, 1860, ibid., letter 43 [French].
29. Letter from La Tour d'Auvergne to Virginia, Berlin, March 18, [1860], ibid., letter 10 [French].
30. Letter from La Tour d'Auvergne to Virginia, Berlin, August 3, 1860, ibid., letter 60 [French].
31. Letter from La Tour d'Auvergne to Virginia, Berlin, July 3, 1860, ibid., letter 46 [French].
32. Letter from La Tour d'Auvergne to Virginia, Berlin, April 3, [1860], ibid., letter 16 [French].
33. Letter from La Tour d'Auvergne to Virginia, Berlin, July 7, 1860, ibid., letter 48 [French].
34. Letter from La Tour d'Auvergne to Virginia, Berlin, June 28, 1860, ibid., letter 43 [French].
35. Letter from La Tour d'Auvergne to Virginia, Berlin, July 29, [1860], ibid., letter 58 [French].
36. Letter from La Tour d'Auvergne to Virginia, Berlin, June 28, 1860, ibid., letter 43 [French].
37. See the letter from La Tour d'Auvergne to Virginia, Berlin, February 3, 1860: "I would really like it if you would always call me Henri and address me as *tu*," ibid., letter 9 [French].
38. Letter from La Tour d'Auvergne to Virginia, Berlin, November 27, 1860, quoted in *Correspondances inédites et archives privées*, 48 [French].
39. Letter from La Tour d'Auvergne to Virginia, Berlin, July 7, [1860], AST, bundle 14 C, letter 48.
40. Letter from La Tour d'Auvergne to Virginia, Berlin, July 29, [1860], ibid., letter 58 [French].

## IN PURSUIT OF THE EMPEROR (1860)

1. A. Decaux, *La Castiglione*, 166.
2. Ibid., 147, note 1.

3. Letter from Virginia to Poniatowski, [Turin, March 20, 1859; date based on the phrase "doman l'altro ho 22 anni"], FP.
4. See A. Decaux, *La Castiglione*, 166.
5. In another letter, Virginia reminded Poniatowski to put "all her letters on pink and blue paper in a little iron chest."
6. *P.* for *puttana* [whore].—Translator's note.
7. A. Decaux, *La Castiglione*, 166. Poniatowski had also asked Princess Mathilde to intercede for Virginia, but received a clear no. See Jérôme Picon, *Mathilde, princesse Bonaparte*, Paris, Flammarion, 2005, 175.
8. See G. Rupigné," La storia ci aveva ingannati sulla contessa Castiglione," 47.
9. Given the reference to the imminent legal separation from her husband (October 16, 1859), the letter can be dated to September 1859.
10. François Ponsard, with *L'Honneur et l'argent* (1853), and Dumas fils, with *La Question d'argent* (1857), wrote about it for the stage; Jules Vallès and Émile Zola made it the central theme of their novels, from 1857 and 1891 respectively, both entitled *L'Argent*.
11. Letter from her mother to Virginia, Genoa, March 10, 1860, AST, bundle 1, fascicle 4, letter 49.
12. A fragment of a letter Virginia wrote to the emperor also seems to confirm this: "In a letter a few days ago, our friend seemed to have reached a point beyond which there will be nothing for him to do but flee in desperation and, before long, he'll have no choice but to seek an uncertain path to salvation in a faraway land. The abyss that has been gaping at his feet for some time is now yawning wider and wider, and the poor fellow has just issued his final cry for help. I was truly distressed for I have a certain fondness for him, but the arrival of your note took my mind off his misfortunes," FP [French].
13. The count's debts added up to 1,568,000 francs, of which 400,000 were owed to Poniatowski. See A. Decaux, *La Castiglione*, 145.
14. Probable allusion to the reunion duet of Elvira and Arturo in Bellini's opera: "From the day I first beheld you / I burned with one solitary ardor, / faithful to you until it beats its last / my heart will burn away to nothing. / I will consecrate my life to you / in joy and in pain, / and dying for love / will feel sacred and sweet . . ."
15. A. Decaux, *La Castiglione*, 173.
16. Diminutive of the name Vincenzo, in this case Vincenzo Carlo Giuseppe,

Ranieri's eldest son. See the letter of February 25, 1863, in which Isabella Oldoini thanks Virginia on behalf of the "entire Lamporecchi household" after she recommended they consult Dr. Blanche regarding the treatment to be given Cencio, who was by then a "raving madman," AST, bundle 1, issue 4, letter 65. See also note 19 on p. 446.

## A LIBERTINE FRIENDSHIP

1. BNF, "Comtesse de Castiglione. Lettres reçues," "Lettres du Général Estancelin," NAF 17774, folio 243.
2. In the early years of the twentieth century, Frédéric Loliée, Estancelin's personal friend and Castiglione's first biographer, was able to consult more than 1,500 of the countess's letters to Estancelin, and published extensive excerpts; see Frédéric Loliée, *Le Roman d'une favorite. La comtesse de Castiglione, 1840–1900, d'après sa correspondance intime inédite et les "Lettres des Princes,"* Paris, Émile Paul, 1912, viii–xi. But whether out of respect for the general's memory or out of prudery, Loliée maintains that the friendship between Estancelin and Castiglione was purely platonic.
3. Presumably in September 1860, when Virginia returned to France after her time in Turin at Villa Gloria.
4. Letter from Estancelin to Virginia, no place specified, undated, BNF, "Lettres du Général Estancelin," folio 99 [French].
5. Letter from Estancelin to Virginia, no place specified, undated, ibid., folio 100 [French].
6. See F. Loliée, *Le Roman d'une favorite*, 219.
7. Letter from Estancelin to Virginia, no place specified, undated, BNF, "Lettres du Général Estancelin," folio 137 [French].
8. Letter from Estancelin to Virginia, no place specified, undated, ibid., folio 110 [French].
9. Letter from Estancelin to Virginia, no place specified, undated, ibid., folio 128 [French].
10. Letter from Estancelin to Virginia, no place specified, undated, ibid., folio 122 [French].
11. Ibid. [French].
12. Letter from Estancelin to Virginia, [late 1872?], ibid., folio 36.

13. Letter from Estancelin to Virginia, [October 1, 1869], ibid., folio 9 [French].
14. Written in 1850, *Lettre à la présidente* was published posthumously in 1890.
15. *Femme piquée par un serpent*, 1847, Musée d'Orsay, Paris.
16. Letter from Estancelin to Virginia, no place specified, undated, BNF, "Lettres du Général Estancelin," folio 173 [French].
17. Letter from Estancelin to Virginia, no place specified, undated, ibid., folio 162 [French]. The same expressions, "fille de marbre" and "fille de feu," were used in reference to prostitutes by Arsène Houssaye in a conversation with Virginia reported by Ferdinand Bac in *Intimités du Second Empire*, 48.
18. Letter from Estancelin to Virginia, no place specified, undated, BNF, "Lettres du Général Estancelin," folios 163–65 [French].
19. Letter from Estancelin to Virginia, no place specified, undated [January 6], ibid., folios 171–72 [French].
20. Letter from Estancelin to Virginia, no place specified, undated, ibid., folios 167–68 [French].
21. Letter from Estancelin to Virginia, no place specified, undated, ibid., folio 169 [French].
22. Letter from Estancelin to Virginia, no place specified, undated, ibid., folio 136 [French].
23. Letter from Estancelin to Robert de Montesquiou, Paris, Saturday, August 9, [1900?], quoted in R. de Montesquiou, *La divine comtesse*, 29.
24. Ibid.

## A STRANGER IN HER OWN LAND (1859–1861)

1. Letter from her father to Virginia, Saint Petersburg, May 10, [1859], AST, bundle 1, fascicle 2, letter 3 [French].
2. Letter from her father to Virginia, Saint Petersburg, December 11, [1859], ibid., letter 25 [French].
3. See the letters of May 10, June 3, July 14, 17, and 22, ibid., letters 3, 4, 5, 7, and 8.
4. Written from Turin and undated, Virginia's letter to Poniatowski is quite difficult to decipher: Cavour tells her about a conversation he had with the emperor ("I was asked") in which he mentions the Count of Casti-

glione's bankruptcy. It can therefore be hypothesized that the conversation took place in March 1859, during Cavour's last visit to Paris, a visit paid expressly to remind the emperor of his commitments. What interest could Victor Emmanuel II and Cavour have had in sending the countess back to France? They must have intended to go on using her as a spy. But how much latitude could Virginia have had, since, as we have seen, the emperor was keeping her at arm's length?

5. Letter from her father to Virginia, Saint Petersburg, June 17, 1859, and response from Virginia, September 29, 1859, ASD, binder 4.
6. Letter from Virginia to her father, [Turin], January 7, [1860], ibid. Emma Vegezzi Ruscalla's family had a villa, La Vigna, on the hillside of San Vito.
7. See the letter from Camillo Cavour to Virginia in which he declares his displeasure "at having so little influence," Leri, [December 4], 1859, in C. Cavour, *Epistolario*, vol. 16, 1277 [French].
8. Letter from Virginia to her father, [Turin], December 4, 1859, ASD, binder 4 [French, Italian].
9. Letter from Virginia to her father, [December 1859], ibid. [French].
10. A. Viarengo, *Cavour*, 407–408.
11. Letter from Virginia to her father, [Turin], January 7, [1860], ASD, binder 4.
12. Marquis Oldoini vainly urged her to abstain from cryptic language, which he found exasperating: "Above all, don't answer me in oracular fashion, as you often do, for we are no longer in the days of Delphi, and put me in a position to understand things clearly." Letter from Marquis Oldoini to Virginia, Saint Petersburg, May 10, [1859], AST, bundle 1, issue 2, letter 3 [French].
13. Letter from Marquise Oldoini to her husband, September 11, [1860], ASD, binder 4.
14. Ibid.
15. Letter from Virginia to her father, no place specified, undated, ibid. [French].
16. Ibid.
17. Castiglione reported this to his father-in-law in a letter dated September 4, 1860, ibid.
18. Letter from her mother to Virginia, Florence, September 21, 1860, AST, bundle 1, fascicle 4, letter 51.

19. See Laure Murat, *La maison du docteur Blanche. Histoire d'un asile et de ses pensionnaires de Nerval à Maupassant*, Paris, Gallimard, 2013. Murat recalls the bonds of friendship that had united Virginia with Dr. Blanche and his family (pp. 209–58).
20. H. de Viel-Castel, *Mémoires sur le règne de Napoléon III*, 925. The notes about Virginia that the Countess of Agoult, on a visit to Italy, received from France are quite different in tone: "Clearly beyond doubt is the triumphal return of the C[astiglione], who, thanks to Fould, is living in a place on the Champs-Élysées. Hence the anger, outbursts, and threats on the side of Livia [Eugénie], who would have liked to return to Spain but was only permitted Scotland." Letter to Félix Henneguy, [Nice], December 26, 1860, in Marie de Flavigny, Countess of Agoult, *Correspondance générale*, edited by Charles F. Dupêchez, 11 vols., Champion, Paris, vol. 11: 1860, 2021, 396.
21. "You are quite right, my dear, to be in mourning; this death is a misfortune for the whole world." Letter from Valentine Delessert to Virginia, Friday 7 [June 1861], AST, bundle 15, "Valentina de Laborde Delessert" file, letter 1 [French].
22. Letter from Valentine Delessert to Virginia, Monday the 18th [?], ibid., letter 2, in which she also thanks Virginia for her gift, a photographic portrait: "Those beautiful eyes that promise to remember me reveal a heart as affectionate as any heart that has ever beat."
23. See the numerous letters from Virginia to Poniatowski on this subject.
24. Letter from her mother to Virginia [circa 1863], AST, bundle 1, fascicle 4, letter 228 [French].
25. See *La comtesse de Castiglione par elle-même*, catalog of the exhibition at the Musée d'Orsay, Paris, October 12, 1999–January 23, 2000, edited by Pierre Apraxine and Xavier Demange, in collaboration with Françoise Heilbrun, Paris, Éditions des musées nationaux, 1999, 171.
26. By the early 1860s, the emperor's health had visibly declined. In 1865, the surgeon Félix Hippolyte Larrey diagnosed "the presence of a stone in the bladder" which caused him terrible suffering. In June 1870, the illustrious clinician Germain Sée confirmed the diagnosis, insisting he needed surgery to extract the stone. The emperor confronted the war against Prussia in a disastrous physical condition, unable even to ride a horse, and would die in England of complications from the surgery.

## THE BURGLARIZED BANKER

1. Letter from Charles Laffitte to Virginia, [October 1865], BNF, "Comtesse de Castiglione. Lettres reçues," "Lettres de Charles Laffitte et minutes de quelques réponses de la comtesse," NAF 17775, folio 112 [French].
2. Letter from Laffitte to Virginia, November 14, 1866, ibid., folio 31 [French]. In total Laffitte's loans to Virginia amounted to 450,000 francs.
3. Letter from Virginia to Poniatowski, [Paris, 1862?], FP.
4. Ibid.
5. After the failure of his first bank, Charles Laffitte, Blount & Co. (1834–1848), Laffitte had founded another in 1851, Charles Laffitte & Co. Limited, "which does not play a leading role in the financial world but nevertheless enjoys a reputation for seriousness." See Georges Gugliotta, *Le général de Galliffet. Un sabreur dans les coulisses du pouvoir, 1830–1909*, Paris, Bernard Giovanangeli, 2014, 65–66.
6. See R. Romeo, *Cavour e il suo tempo*, vol. 21, 362–68.
7. See A. Viarengo, *Cavour*, 93.
8. Letter from Laffitte to Virginia, Paris, December 11, 1863, BNF, "Lettres de Charles Laffitte," folio 1 [English].
9. Letter from Laffitte to Virginia, [1862|], ibid., sheet 66 [English]. The banker's letters are rife with allusions to potential deals, for which Virginia acted as a go-between. "I don't think your friends are interested, and there's nothing worse than trying to draw blood from a stone. But come at a quarter to five (on the dot), and I will put you in touch with my man." He also sends her, through his colleague Louis Le Provost, a few "notes" for Turin (ibid., folio 141) and provides her with confidential information to help her play the stock market, all the while appealing to her discretion: "Mind, dear Nicchia, to the rue Laffitte [the Rothschild house] on my source of information about the Mexican Bond." ibid., sheet 177 [English in the original].
10. In an 1865 letter to Virginia, Laffitte recalled his "three years of devotion" to her. Ibid., sheet 162 [English].
11. Ibid.
12. See Laffitte's note to Virginia: "There is not a cat with me," ibid., folio 131 [English].

13. See the letter from Laffitte to Virginia, midnight, no place specified, undated, ibid., folio 148.
14. Letter from Laffitte to Virginia, Sunday, [March 1865], ibid., folio 110 [French].
15. Letter from Laffitte to Virginia, Thursday, [1865], ibid., folio 162 [English].
16. Letter from Virginia to Laffitte, [1865], ibid., folio 237 [English, French]. "The bad storm," etc. is written in English in the original.
17. Letter from Laffitte to Virginia, Dieppe, Sunday, [1865], ibid., folio 197 [French].
18. See the letter from Louis Le Provost to Virginia, [1865], BNF, "Comtesse de Castiglione. Lettres reçues," "Lettres de Louis Le Provost et minutes de quelques réponses de la comtesse," NAF 17775, folio 263 [French].
19. Letter from Le Provost to Virginia, [December 5, 1867], ibid., folio 270.
20. Letter from Le Provost to Virginia, [1865], ibid., folios 261–62.
21. Letter from Virginia to Laffitte, [August–September 1865], not sent, BNF, "Lettres de Charles Laffitte," folio 218 [English, French].
22. Letter from Virginia to Laffitte, [1865], ibid., folio 220 [French].
23. Letter from Le Provost to Virginia, [1865], BNF, "Lettres de Louis Le Provost," folio 263 [French].
24. Letter from Le Provost to Virginia, [1865], ibid., folio 252 [French].
25. Letter from Le Provost to Virginia, [1865], ibid., folios 311–12 [French].
26. Letter from Virginia to Le Provost, [1865], ibid., folio 427 [French].
27. See letter from Laffitte to Virginia, Salon de Compiègne, 11 o'clock, [1865], BNF, "Lettres de Charles Laffitte," folio 152.
28. Letter from Virginia to Laffitte, no place specified, undated, ibid., folio 240.
29. Letter from Virginia to an unknown correspondent, January 29, 1869, BNF, "Comtesse de Castiglione. Lettres reçues," "Varia," NAF 17775, folio 433 [French].
30. Letter from Laffitte to Virginia, [June 1872], BNF, "Lettres de Charles Laffitte," folio 54 [French].
31. See the two letters from Le Provost to Virginia of January 6 and March 2, [1869], in which he asks her to send a letter of recommendation to

Alphonse de Rothschild, BNF, "Lettres de Louis Le Provost," NAF 17775, sheets 273 and 276.

32. Letter from Le Provost to Virginia, no place specified, undated, ibid., folio 307.

## A SON IN CONTENTION

1. Letter from Cavour to Victor Emmanuel II, Turin, December 3, 1860, in C. Cavour, *Epistolario*, vol. 17, 2834: "The Duchess of Genoa instructed me to ask Your Majesty to allow her to take advantage of the passing of Marchesa di Villahermosa in order to lodge the Countess of Castiglione in a part of the apartment that this event left available. This request seems reasonable to me thus I hope V.M. will deign to look favorably on it." Response from Victor Emmanuel II, Naples, December 9, 1860: "As for my sister-in-law's apartment, go ahead," ibid., 2894.
2. Letter from Francesco Verasis to his father-in-law, Milan, December 19, 1859, ASD, binder 4 [French].
3. Letter from Francesco Verasis to Giuseppe Poniatowski, Turin, November 4, 1858, FP [French].
4. Letter from Isabella Oldoini to her husband, May 15, 1861, ASD, binder 3.
5. Letter from Isabella Oldoini to her husband, no place specified, undated, ibid.
6. Letter from Filippo Oldoini to Giuseppe Poniatowski, La Spezia, 20 [?], FP.
7. Letter from Virginia to her father, [Paris, 1863], ASD, binder 3.
8. Letter from Francesco Verasis to Giuseppe Poniatowski, Turin, May 1, 1861, FP, fascicle "Conte Verasis."
9. Letter from Virginia to Giuseppe Poniatowski, no place specified, undated, FP.
10. Copy of a letter from Giuseppe Poniatowski to Count Cigala, Paris, [May 1861], ibid., fascicle "Conte Verasis."
11. Copy of a letter from Francesco Verasis to Giuseppe Poniatowski, Turin, May 6, 1861, ibid.
12. Poniatowski called Castiglione's proposal "simply ridiculous." Copy of a

letter from Prince Poniatowski to Count Cigala in Turin, Paris, June 10, 1861, ibid. [French].

13. Letter from Giuseppe Poniatowski to Francesco Verasis, Paris, May, ibid. [French].
14. On June 17, *Le Temps* reported the presence of the Countess of Castiglione, Princess Solms, and the Comtesse d'Agoult at the funeral ceremony. See Lucia Lazzerini, *La fée et la diablesse*, 130. See also the letter in which Marquise Oldoini rejoices that her daughter has paid homage to the memory of the count, as she herself had done in Florence, defying the accusations of the "reactionaries." AST, deck 1, file 4, letter 54.
15. Letter from George Sand to Camillo Cavour, Paris, January 4, 1861, AIA, Inventario, 171.

## WAITING FOR THE MATERNAL KISS (1861–1865)

1. In the letter Virginia asks a friend for advice on a possible tutor for Giorgio; letter from Virginia to an unknown correspondent, no place specified, undated, AST, deck 3, file 13.
2. "Only I have the right to let him see relatives or friends, and no one else has the right to prevent it, or allow it, without my consent," from a forty-eight-page letter from Virginia with no indication of the addressee (1869), quoted in *Correspondances inédites et archives privées*, file 15, 22.
3. See the "Confession générale" in which, while still a child, Giorgio confessed lies, money spent on sweets, stamps, perfumes, small debts contracted in college, quoted ibid., file 8, 16–17.
4. Letter from Isabella Oldoini to her husband, [La Spezia, September 11, 1861?], ASD, binder 3.
5. Letter from Isabella Oldoini to Virginia, June 23, 1865, AST, bundle 1, fascicle 4, letter 271.
6. Letter from Virginia to Giuseppe Poniatowski (no place or date), FP.
7. Letter from Giorgio Verasis to his mother, [Dieppe, autumn 1861], AST, bundle 2, fascicle 8, letter 46.
8. "My dearest Mina, I am sorry I was not good when Mina went away because I was sorry and angry to be left in Dieppe." Giorgio to Virginia, undated, AST, bundle 2, fascicle 8, letter 49 [English].
9. Quoted in A. Decaux, *La Castiglione*, 288. See the forty-eight-page letter

from Virginia with no indication of the addressee, quoted in *Correspondances inédites et archives privées*, 22.

10. Letter from Giorgio Verasis to his grandfather, Paris, May 24, 1865, ASD, binder 3.
11. Letter from Lina Rauch to Filippo Oldoini, Paris, June 3, 1865, ibid. [French].
12. Letter from Giorgio Verasis to his mother, Dieppe, AST, bundle 2, fascicle 8, letter 7 [English].
13. Letter from Giorgio Verasis to his mother, Dieppe, ibid., letter 8 [English]. Virginia's birthday was March 22..
14. Excerpt from a letter dating back to 1866, quoted in *Correspondances inédites et archives privées*, file 54, 44.
15. See letter from Isabella Oldoini to Virginia, June 23, 1865, AST, bundle 1, fascicle 4, letter 271.
16. See letter from Giorgio Verasis to his mother, Dieppe, July 19, 1865, ibid., bundle 2, fascicle 8, letter 39.
17. Ibid.
18. See Giorgio Verasis's letter to his mother, Dieppe, July 3, 1865 and Sunday [undated], ibid., letters 31 and 34.
19. See Virginia's letter to an unknown correspondent: "Not long ago, on a walk through a cemetery, Baby picked this beautiful pansy which made me think . . . of you," quoted in *Correspondances inédites et archives privées*, file 32, 30.
20. Letter from Giorgio Verasis to his mother, Dieppe, July 19, [1865], AST, bundle 2, fascicle 8, letter 39 [English].
21. See letter from Giorgio Verasis to his mother, Dieppe, Sunday, ibid., letter 34.
22. See Giorgio Verasis's letters to his mother, Dieppe, July 11 and 19, 1865, ibid., letters 37 and 39.
23. Letter from Giorgio Verasis to his mother, Dieppe, July 7 1865, ibid., letter 33.
24. Letter from Giorgio Verasis to his mother, Dieppe, undated, ibid., letter 8 [English].
25. See letter from Giorgio Verasis to his mother, Dieppe, July 5, 1865, ibid., letter 32 [English].

26. Giorgio Verasis to his mother, Dieppe, July 11, 1865, ibid., letter 37 [English].
27. Letter from Giorgio Verasis to his mother, [Dieppe], July 13, 1865, ibid., letter 35 [English].
28. Letter from Giorgio Verasis to his mother, Dieppe, July 15, 1865, ibid., letter 38 [English].
29. Letter from Giorgio Verasis to his mother, Dieppe, July 19, [1865], ibid., letter 39.
30. Letter from Giorgio Verasis to his mother, Dieppe, July 23, 1865, ibid., letter 17 [English].
31. Letter from Giorgio Verasis to his mother, Dieppe, July 25, 1865, ibid., letter 18 [English].
32. Letter from Isabella Oldoini to her husband, December 12, 1865, ASD, binder 4.
33. Letter from Isabella Oldoini to her husband, May 4, 1866, ASD, binder 3.
34. Ibid.
35. See letter from Giorgio Verasis to his mother, Florence, March 12, 1866, AST, bundle 2, fascicle 8, letter 61.
36. See the letters that Giorgio Verasis wrote from Florence to his mother between March and April 1866, ibid., letters 60–70.
37. Letter from Giorgio Verasis to his mother, [Florence, May–June? 1866], ibid., letter 62. The letter must have reached Giorgio shortly before June 24, when Giorgio informed his grandfather about his mother's health. See Giorgio's letter to the Marquis Oldoini, Turin, June 24, 1866, ASD, folder 3.
38. Letter from Giorgio Verasis to his mother, [Florence, May–June? 1866], AST, bundle 2, fascicle 8, letter 62 [English].
39. The third Italian war of independence (June 20–August 12, 1866).
40. "Today I'm very happy because I heard there will probably be war, and then Papa will have to leave and I hope to come live with Mina, if Mina will allow it." Letter from Giorgio Verasis to his mother, [Florence, May–June? 1866], ibid., letter 9 [English].
41. Marcel Proust, Questionnaire, in *Contre Sainte-Beuve*, Bibliothèque de la Pléiade, Paris, Gallimard, 1971, 335.

## A MAN'S AMBITIONS (1861–1866)

1. Unsent draft of letter from Virginia to her husband, AST, deck 1, new accessions, letter 4 [French, English].
2. Letter from Francesco Verasis to his wife, Milan, June 11, 1861, ibid., bundle 2, fascicle 5, letter 15 [French].
3. From a letter in which Virginia invites Prince Napoleon for breakfast on rue Marivaux, BNF, "Lettres du Prince Jérôme Napoléon à la comtesse, avec réponses," NAF 25068.
4. F. Bac, *Intimités du Second Empire*, vol. 2, 61.
5. F. Bac, *La Cour des Tuileries sous le Second Empire*, 123.
6. See *Correspondances inédites et archives privées*, file 11, 19.
7. H. de Viel-Castel, *Mémoires sur le règne de Napoléon* III, 538–39.
8. See F. Bac, *La Cour des Tuileries sous le Second Empire*, 60.
9. Ibid., 19.
10. Even if the Countess of Castiglione's name never appears either in Zola's letters or in the *notes préparatoires* for *Son Excellence Eugène Rougon* (see the marvelous critical edition by Éléonore Reverzy, Paris, Classiques Garnier, 2019), there are numerous indications that Clorinda Balbi—the main female character in the novel—is a portrait *à clef.* Who else could have inspired the beautiful and mysterious Italian adventuress introduced into Parisian high society—an emissary of Cavour's who exults in extraordinary outfits and jewelry, becomes Napoleon III's lover, and works to organize "a secret meeting between the emperor and a foreign statesman, the draft of a treaty of alliance whose details were still being discussed, and a war for the following spring" (p. 350)? Though he never met Virginia, Zola was able to collect countless bits of gossip—beginning with those bandied about by his friend Edmond de Goncourt—regarding the countess's political intrigues. And the precise way he describes her as she poses for a portrait, half-naked and dressed as Diana the huntress, is astonishing: "With her other hand she leaned on her bow, the calm and powerful expression of the ancient huntress, heedless of her nakedness, disdainful of the love of men, cold, haughty, immortal" (p. 114); as is his perception of her talent as an actress: "She told him she would have loved to be an actress on the stage; she could have depicted anything: anger, tenderness, modesty, terror" (p. 115); his intuitive prediction—given

that the novel was published in 1876—of the decor in the entresol on the Place Vendôme: "One day she had taken the strange whim into her head to have her room hung in black... and to receive her close friends lying in bed and buried under the covers, which were likewise black" (p. 71); and his insistence on the cache of furniture and objects of all kinds, and on the dirt and desuetude that would characterize the apartment on rue Cambon.

11. Clorinda is a female Saracen warrior in Torquato Tasso's *Jerusalem Delivered*.—Translator's note.
12. Letter from Isabella Oldoini to Virginia, no place specified, 8 February 1862, AST, bundle 1, fascicle 4, letter 56 [French].
13. "Deed of settlement between the Count and Countess de Verasis di Castiglione," Turin, February 8, 1862, ibid., bundle 3, file 9, document 8. Virginia had to "pay [the count] an annual sum of 2,500 lire on her dowry assets, payable every six months starting January 1, 1862" as long as he had custody of his son, and continue to pay for Giorgio's insurance, "having the receipts remitted to [the count]." See also the "Progetto di separazione con correzioni a lato di Virginia," ibid.
14. In a letter to her father dated February 17, [1862], Virginia informed him: "Yesterday we signed [the settlement] by telegraph... the deed of settlement, countersigned by the count with witnesses, in which it is written that I will be able to live where I wish, keeping the child with me, and that I will give him to him for one month a year." In this way Virginia regained her "property," above all the much talked-about dowry, and could finally "leave the Castiglione house, which is to say enjoy a position of my own in my own name and truly be at home," ASD, folder 4 [French].
15. Letter from Isabella Oldoini to her husband, no place specified, February 22, 1862, ibid.
16. Letter from Francesco Verasis to his father-in-law, no place specified, March 23, 1862, ibid. [French].
17. Letter from Virginia to her father, [Paris, March 1862], ibid. [French].
18. Letter from Isabella Oldoini to Virginia, no place specified, [March 27, 1862], AST, bundle 1, fascicle 4, letter 59.
19. See, in this volume, note 21 on p. 411.
20. Letter from Isabella Oldoini to Virginia, no place specified, [March 27, 1862], AST, bundle 1, fascicle 4, letter 59.

21. Letter from Francesco Verasis to his wife, [Turin, April 10, 1862], ibid., bundle 14, fascicle B, unnumbered letter [French].
22. "Dear Countess, the king will come between 10 and 11. I promised him that you will receive him with all your good grace. He greatly admired the portrait front and back. Your most devoted," quoted in A. Decaux, *La Castiglione*, 176 [French].
23. See the letter from Francesco Verasis cited above.
24. Letter from Giuseppe Poniatowski to Virginia, July 13, 1862, cited above.
25. Ibid.
26. Letter from Virginia to an unknown correspondent, no place specified, undated, quoted in *Correspondances inédites et archives privées*, 29.
27. See A. Poggiolini, *La contessa Verasis di Castiglione*, 86.
28. A. Decaux, *La Castiglione*, 178.
29. Ibid., 179.
30. The marriage had been celebrated by proxy in Turin on September 27, 1862.
31. See, in this volume, note 54 on p. 434.
32. The address of Poniatowski's Parisian residence.
33. Quoted in A. Decaux, *La Castiglione*, 183–84.
34. P. Apraxine, "The Model and the Photographer," in *La Divine Comtesse: Photographs of the Countess de Castiglione*.

## BACK ON THE SCENE (1863–1866)

1. A. Decaux, *La Castiglione*, 186. The handwritten draft of this note from Virginia to Count Baciocchi has recently resurfaced on the antiquarian market.
2. Virginia had probably had the opportunity to admire the Etruscan and Magna Graecia jewels from the famous Campana collection purchased by Napoleon III in 1861–1862 for the Louvre. The fashion of jewelry in imitation of ancient styles had been launched in Rome by the goldsmith Fortunato Pio Castellani as early as 1814, and in 1860 his son Alessandro had opened a branch of their jewelry shop in Paris. During the Roman republic of 1849, Alessandro and his brother Augustus had joined the unification movement, becoming advocates for a renaissance of Italian goldsmithing through the rediscovery and remaking of ancient models.

Convicted of conspiracy against the papal state, Alessandro was forced to move abroad in 1860, living on the money made by the family business. Considering all this, the "Etruscan" jewels worn by Virginia might be interpreted as a patriotic statement; they also encouraged the "archaeological" jewelry craze in Paris, which, following the example of the Castellanis, began to be produced by well-known Parisian jewelers, such as Mellerio (also of Italian origins) and Fontenay. See Lia Lenti and Maria Cristina Bergesio, *Dizionario del gioiello italiano del XIX e XX secolo*, s.v. "Oldoini Virginia, countess of Castiglione," Turin, Umberto Allemandi, 2005.

3. See Xavier Demange, "Roman-photo d'une vie," in *La comtesse de Castiglione par elle-même*, 61. Written in 1854 for the famous actress Rachel, Ernest Legouvé's three-act tragedy was revived two years later, again in Paris but in an Italian translation, with Adelaide Ristori in the part of Medea.
4. R. de Montesquiou, *La divine comtesse*, 78.
5. From the diary of Virginia, AFC; see also A. Decaux, *La Castiglione*, 186. Virginia, whose first diary ended in 1856, kept a second in February–March 1863.
6. From Virginia's diary, quoted in Elena Henrisch and Costantino Nigro, *Virginia di Castiglione. La contessa della leggenda, attraverso la sua corrispondenza intima, diari e documenti inediti, 1837–1899*, Florence, Marzocco, 1912, 186.
7. Henri de Pène, quoted in A. Decaux, *La Castiglione*, 187.
8. Flaubert's *Salammbô* had appeared the previous year.
9. Letter from Mérimée to Madame de Montijo, Paris, March 7, [1863], in P. Mérimée, *Correspondance générale*, vol. 5, 356–57.
10. Letter from Isabella Oldoini to Virginia, February 20, [1863], AST, bundle 1, fascicle 4, letter 214 [French].
11. *Correspondances inédites et archives privées*, 15.
12. Letter from Francesco Verasis to his wife, June 1, [1863], AST, bundle 2, fascicle 5 [French].
13. Letter from Francesco Verasis to his wife, quoted in A. Decaux, *La Castiglione*, 189.
14. Letter from Virginia to her husband, AST, bundle 3, fascicle 9, letter 9 [French].
15. *Journal de la comtesse de La Pagerie*, quoted in R. de Montesquiou, *La divine comtesse*, 82–83.
16. Ibid., 83–84.

17. BHVP, MS 3036, folios 305–306.
18. See the negative report sent to the countess, dated March 14, 1864, by Frédéric Weill's Laboratoire de chimie et cabinet d'ingénieur, ibid., sheet 307.
19. Letter from Isabella Oldoini to Virginia, [Florence], October 10, 1863, AST, bundle 1, fascicle 4, letter 69.
20. Letter from Isabella Oldoini to her husband, no place specified, December 12, 1863, ASD, binder 4.
21. Letter from Isabella Oldoini to her husband, no place specified, July 3, [1866], ibid., binder 3. "Malevolence" in the sense of others being ill-disposed toward her.
22. Letter from Isabella Oldoini to her husband, no place specified, [August 23, 1866], ibid., binder 4. This date is based on the mention of Garibaldi's victory at Azzo the previous day.
23. See, in this volume, note 16 on p. 442.
24. Letter from Isabella Oldoini to Virginia, no place specified, [1863], AST, bundle 1, fascicle 4, letter 228.
25. See Alain Decaux, *La Castiglione*, 170.
26. See the extracts from the letters exchanged by Virginia and Dr. Arnal between 1864 and 1870, which appear in *Correspondances inédites et archives privées*, file 42, 33–34. Here is one example: "I'm at my wits' end, I can't sleep, I can't eat, for six days I haven't even lifted my head off the pillow... now my eye it is so inflamed that nothing, neither rose water nor eye drops, can stop the tears. The pain from the *hair* in my eye is terrible... I can't stand it anymore... I don't have the strength to lift an arm and dress myself... If you could come..." See also Arnal's letter to Virginia, AST, bundle 12, file 34, letter 13.
27. See A. Decaux, *La Castiglione*, 178.
28. "Gounod will come spend his Saturday evening in Passy tomorrow. I have promised him that he will have the pleasure of seeing you. You will help me keep my promise," Blanche wrote to her on March 24, 1865. *Correspondances inédites et archives privées*, file 47, 37.
29. Letter from Charles-Adolphe Huteau to Filippo Oldoini, Paris, October 3, 1864, ASD, binder 4.
30. Letter from Isabella Oldoini to her husband, no place specified, [summer 1862], ibid.

31. Letter from Virginia to her father, no place specified, undated, ibid. [French].
32. F. Bac, *Intimités du Second Empire*, 58 and 55.
33. Letter from Virginia to her father, no place specified, undated, ASD, binder 4.
34. Letter from Virginia to her father, no place specified, undated, ibid.
35. F. Bac, *Intimités du Second Empire*, 63.
36. Ibid., 55.
37. Letter from Isabella Oldoini to Virginia, [1865], AST, bundle 1, fascicle 4, letter 92.
38. See A. Decaux, *La Castiglione*, 224.
39. Letter from Virginia to her husband, AST, bundle 3, fascicle 10, letter 5 [French].
40. Letter from Isabella Oldoini to her husband, Florence, [July 11, 1866], ASD, binder 4.
41. Costantino Ressmann served as secretary of legation in Paris between 1871 and 1878, and during this period Virginia had an intense four-year affair with him. See Virginia's farewell letter to Ressmann: "Paris made us . . . Sulina unmade us . . . Long live Ressmann!" No place specified, undated, AST, bundle 16, single file, sub-file with annotation: "The last letters of her loves," letter 1.
42. Letter from Virginia to Count Puliga, no place specified, undated [1866|], ibid., bundle 4, file 2, card 3, letter 1.
43. In her letter to the lawyer Cléry quoted by Montesquiou, to which reference is made in note 11 on p. 478, Virginia observes, among other things: "For men, justice is done; for women, injustice." [French].

## FINALLY FREE? (1867–1872)

1. Letter from Costantino Nigra to Virginia, Paris, May 31, 1867, AST, bundle 3, fascicle 12, letter 66.
2. "I myself had come to give you the bitter news and offer you my deepest condolences" stated another note written shortly after the previous one (Costantino Nigra to Virginia, Paris, May 31, 1867, ibid., letter 65).
3. Amedeo d'Aosta, second son of Victor Emmanuel II, had married Princess Maria dal Pozzo della Cisterna.

4. See letter from Cigala to Virginia, Turin, Sunday, [June 1867], ibid., fascicle 13, letter 67.
5. Quoted in A. Decaux, *La Castiglione*, 218.
6. Letter from Virginia to her father, Paris, June 12, 1867, ASD, folder 4 [French]. Since the marquis complained about her indecipherable writing, Virginia, given the solemnity of the occasion, had her friend Puliga serve as her scribe.
7. Letter from Isabella Oldoini to her husband, La Spezia, June 5 [1867], ibid., binder 3.
8. Letter from Isabella Oldoini to Virginia, [Florence, May 1867], AST, bundle 1, fascicle 4, letter 87 [French].
9. Letter from Isabella Oldoini to her husband, [Florence, June 1867], ASD, binder 3.
10. Letter from Virginia to her husband, no place specified, Friday [undated], AST, bundle 3, fascicle 9, letter 2 [French].
11. "I alone know the true wounds of his heart," Isabella Oldoini wrote to her husband upon their son-in-law's death, La Spezia, June 5, [1867], ASD, folder 3.
12. Letter from Francesco Verasis to Giuseppe Poniatowski, Lombardy, Vimercate, June 12, 1859, FP, fascicle "Conte Verasis."
13. Letter from Virginia to her husband, no place specified, Friday [undated], AST, bundle 3, fascicle 9, letter 2 [French].
14. Victor Emmanuel wrote to Prince Napoleon that Verasis's death had filled him with "profound sorrow"; see A. Viarengo, *Vittorio Emanuele II*, 358.
15. C. d'Azeglio, *Lettere al figlio*, vol. 2, 1762, Monday, January 16, 1860 [French].
16. Comte de Reiset, *Mes souvenirs*, vol. 1, 332.
17. Carlo Dossi, *Note azzurre*, edited by Dante Isella, Milan, Adelphi, 2010, 616–17.
18. Letter from Countess Mary Casanova to Filippo Oldoini, ASD, binder 4.
19. The king is probably making reference to a Mass commemorating the death of Charles Albert (28 July 1849), held in La Spezia in 1853.
20. Letter from Virginia to her father, received by him August 4, [1868], ibid. [French].
21. *La comtesse de Castiglione par elle-même*, 179–80.

22. Telegram from Vittorio Emanuele to Virginia, September 15, [1867], AST, bundle 3, fascicle 14, letter 31 [French].
23. Letter from Virginia to Victor Emmanuel II, [1867], ibid., letter 13.
24. See A. Decaux, *La Castiglione*, 226.
25. Letter from Virginia to Victor Emmanuel II, AST, bundle 3, fascicle 14, letter 9 (encrypted).
26. Ibid.
27. See the letters Filippo Antonio Gualterio sent to Virginia, ibid., bundle 4, fascicle 1, file 23, letters 1–24.
28. A. Viarengo, *Vittorio Emanuele II*, 345–46.
29. Ibid.
30. Quoted in A. Decaux, *La Castiglione*, 239.
31. Ibid.
32. Telegram from Victor Emmanuel II to Virginia, no place specified, September 15 [1868?], AST, bundle 3, fascicle 14, letter 32.
33. Letter from Virginia to Victor Emmanuel II (no place or date), ibid., letter 21.
34. Marquis Giacomo Filippo Spinola (1828–1872), who, in 1868, had married Vittoria, the daughter of Victor Emmanuel II and Rosa Vercellana, served directly under his father-in-law.
35. Letter from Virginia to Victor Emmanuel II, no place specified, Sunday evening [undated], ibid., letter 15.
36. Letter from Virginia to Victor Emmanuel II, no place specified, December 31, 1869, ibid., letter 27.
37. Ibid.
38. See A. Viarengo, *Vittorio Emanuele II*, 346, and E. De Rienzo, *Napoleone III*, 461–62.
39. Letter from Virginia to Victor Emmanuel II, no place specified, undated, AST, bundle 3, fascicle 14, letter 33.
40. On the unsatisfactory "diplomatic report," see Virginia's encrypted telegram of protest to Victor Emmanuel II, La Spezia, June 5, 1870, ibid., letter 82.
41. On January 4, 1871, the countess had obtained the concession "of a stretch of sandy land and water in the municipality of Spezia for fifteen years in exchange for payment to the State Treasury of an annual fee of one hun-

dred lire." Her objective was to "transform a part of the vast area of land she owned—including the whole Cappuccini hill, on which the beautiful Villa Oldoini stood, all the way to the walls of the Castello di San Giorgio—into a municipal park that was to bear her name and be open to the public twice a week . . . These projects, aimed at promoting tourism, were thwarted by a series of expropriations in support of the 'war administration,' which began in 1877 and continued until 1886 and beyond, to build the upper and lower parts of the Capuchin Battery," Gabriella Chioma, "La contessa di Castiglione e le 'Joli Golfe': splendore e decadenza. Il mistero dei documenti scomparsi" in *Virginia Oldoini. I giorni e il mito della contessa di Castiglione*, 80–83.

42. See Marzia Ratti, *I documenti relativi alla contessa di Castiglione conservati nelle Civiche Istituzioni Culturali*, ibid., 65.
43. Letter from Auguste-Charles-Joseph de Morny to his father, Charles-Joseph, Count of Flahaut, quoted in Jean-Marie Rouart, *Morny. Un voluptueux au pouvoir*, Paris, Gallimard, 1995, 200.
44. Letter from Virginia to Victor Emmanuel II, [Florence, 1871?], bundle 3, fascicle 14, letter 41.
45. The name of the Countess of Castiglione, however, does not figure in the indices of the archives of the Secretariat of State of the Vatican City, nor in those of the Vatican Apostolic Archives.
46. "Why insist on birth? daughter of the Napoleons of Florence? of the houses of Savoy, Turin, and the Grand Dukes of Tuscany? And why not the Pope? or Antonelli? Occult, unfathomable; indecent to accuse Mother." Facsimile copy of a handwritten letter to General Estancelin (who asked the countess for clarifications about her birth with a view to a possible biography), reproduced in F. Loliée, *Le Roman d'une favorite*, 318.
47. See Federico Engel Janosi, "La questione romana nelle trattative diplomatiche del 1869–1870," in *Nuova Rivista Storica*, XXV, 1941, 28–38; Renato Mori, *Il tramonto del potere temporale, 1866–1870*, Edizioni di Storia e Lettertura, Rome 1967, 521–30; Giacomo Martina, *Pio IX*, 3 vols., Rome, Pontificia Università Gregoriana, 1990, vol. 21: 1867–1878, 234–47.
48. See R. de Montesquiou, *La divine comtesse*, 26–27.
49. The Law of Guarantees was promulgated on July 13, 1871.

## THE SIEGE (1870–1872)

1. The government was presided over by Émile Ollivier, who took office on January 2, 1870.
2. See letter from Virginia to Adolphe Thiers, [January–February 1870], BNF, "Lettres d'Adolphe Thiers et de Mme Thiers à la comtesse de Castiglione," NAF 25068, folios 113–115 [French].
3. Quoted in A. Decaux, *La Castiglione*, 248.
4. The meeting was held on September 19 and 20 in Ferrières, at the Rothschilds' château, which Napoleon III had inaugurated with a gala in 1862, and where Bismarck was quartered.
5. See Charles de Moüy, "La délégation des Affaires étrangères à Tours et à Bordeaux (1870–1871)," in *Souvenirs et causeries d'un diplomate*, Paris, Plon-Nourrit, 1909, second edition, 1–37.
6. Quoted in A. Decaux, *La Castiglione*, 257.
7. Joseph Maria Anton Brassier de Saint-Simon-Vallade (1798–1872), ambassador to the King of Sardinia from 1854–1862, to Florence in 1869, and for the Reich in Rome in 1871.
8. In 1862, Bismarck had briefly been an ambassador in Paris.
9. Letter from Adolphe Thiers to Virginia, December 21, 1872, quoted in R. de Montesquiou, *La divine comtesse*, 150.
10. See the letter from Virginia to Adolphe Thiers, BNF, "Lettres d'Adolphe Thiers," folio 40.
11. See A. Decaux, *La Castiglione*, 251.
12. See BNF, "Lettres d'Adolphe Thiers," "Chiffres Thiers, Bonne Copie," October 12, 1870, folios 40–47 [French].
13. F. Loliée, *Le Roman d'une favorite*, 118.
14. Telegram from Adolphe Thiers to Virginia, BNF, "Lettres d'Adolphe Thiers," folio 87 [French]. With cipher in hand, we can translate "safe and sound" as "provisions found favorable to my meeting with Bismarck and to peace"; "with baggage" as "necessary to confer with Favre in Paris, send me what is needed [a laissez-passer] to cross Paris, enter, and exit"; "without baggage" as "obtained the assignment in Tours with no need to go to Paris. Send me what is needed [a second laissez-passer] to cross the Prussian lines and go to Versailles without passing through Paris."

Probably the two passes (one to enter and exit Paris, and the other to travel from Tours to Versailles) would have been sent to Thiers through Brassier de Saint-Simon.

15. See A. Decaux, *La Castiglione*, 257.
16. See the text of the dispatch, BNF, "Lettres d'Adolphe Thiers," folio 38 [French].
17. Letter from Virginia to Adolphe Thiers, [Florence], undated, ibid., folio 60 [French].
18. Letter from Virginia to Adolphe Thiers, [Florence], undated, ibid., folios 107–108 [French].
19. Extremist republicans who did not want to surrender threatened to set Paris on fire—something the Prussians did not want to see happen.
20. Letter from Virginia to Bismarck, quoted in A. Decaux, *La Castiglione*, 258–59. See also *Correspondances inédites et archives privées*, 26.
21. Letter from Virginia to Costantino Ressmann, AST, bundle 3, fascicle 12, letter 9.
22. He was living at the Pension Comte, at 124 rue Malakoff.
23. Letter from Virginia to Ettore Calderai, [Florence or Venice], Saturday, September 23, 1870, BNF, dossier "Calderai, passateur à Venise. Lettre(s) reçue(s)," sheet 171.
24. See A. Decaux, *La Castiglione*, 263, note 1.
25. See BNF, dossier "Lualdi, Raffaello" and dossier "Cecchi, Giuseppe," folios 162–282.
26. Letter from Virginia to Costantino Nigra, no place specified, August 14, 1870, AST, bundle 3, fascicle 12, letter 68.
27. Letter from Costantino Nigra to Virginia, Paris, August 17, 1870, ibid., letter 69.
28. Letter from Costantino Nigra to Virginia, Paris, August 21, 1870 ibid., letter 70. On October 21, the foreign minister Emilio Visconti Venosta informed the countess that Nigra, before leaving Paris for Tours, had taken steps to secure all her belongings at the legation; ibid., bundle 4, file 1, card 1, letter 4.
29. Letter from Virginia to Adolphe Thiers, Turin, September 8, 1870, BNF, "Lettres d'Adolphe Thiers," folio 94 [French].
30. Ch. de Moüy, *Souvenirs et causeries d'un diplomate*, 11.

31. The recognition of the French republic by the kingdom of Italy was officially announced by Nigra on February 17, 1871.
32. Letter from Virginia to Adolphe Thiers, no place specified, undated, BNF, "Lettres d'Adolphe Thiers," folios 74–75 [French].
33. Letter from Virginia to Adolphe Thiers, Turin, February 20, 1871, ibid., folios 101–102 [French].
34. Quoted in A. Decaux, *La Castiglione*, 76.
35. See the two letters Poniatowski sent to Virginia about Bentivoglio, [September 12 and 24, 1871], BNF, folios 121–123.
36. Letter from Virginia to Adolphe Thiers, Florence, July 29, 1871, ibid., "Lettres d'Adolphe Thiers," folios 159–160 [French].
37. Letter from Virginia to Adolphe Thiers, draft in pencil by Virginia with marking in pen: "Copié par Demoiseau" [Giorgio's nickname], Florence, July 2, 1871," ibid., dossier "Imbert de Saint-Amand, Arthur-Léon dit Baron de, ministre plénipotentiaire," sheet 140 [French].
38. *Correspondances inédites et archives privés*, 45–46.
39. Quoted in A. Decaux, *La Castiglione*, 235.
40. "I love you still, sad, desolate, / No longer singing but speaking softly, / Consecrated queen of pain, / Oh, please, no, don't abandon me! / Come to me, thoughtful and serious soul, / Muse of Melancholy, / I am ready to receive you. / I loved you at dawn, / Already the day is fleeting, I love you still, / Muse, come back, behold, already the sun is setting . . ." quoted in *Correspondances inédites et archives privés*, entry 60, 45–46.
41. Letter from Virginia to Imbert de Saint-Amand, Florence, July 2, 1871, draft in pencil in Virginia's hand with pen marking "Copié par Demoiseau," BNF, dossier "Imbert de Saint-Amand," sheet 142. See also A. Decaux, *La Castiglione*, 270.
42. According to Decaux, the fact that both the letter to Thiers and the accompanying letter to Saint-Amand are present among Castiglione's papers suggests that Saint-Amand returned both letters to sender (ibid.). In fact, Virginia was in the habit of keeping a copy of her letters—both the handwritten ones and those transcribed by her son.
43. Ibid.
44. See A.-L. Imbert de Saint-Amand, *La Cour du Second Empire (1856–1858)*, 171–73.

## MOTHER AND DAUGHTER

1. In a letter dated June 2, 1871, Nigra had let her know the state of "all her things, which is to say: (1) the boxes left at the Legation, (2) the effects from rue de Castiglione [where Virginia rented an apartment], (3) all the things left on rue Nicolo. All of this is in perfect condition, well kept and neat. Nobody has touched it. No damage has occurred . . . and no one will touch it unless you order it. In return, when I see you, you will give me your most beautiful photograph," AST, bundle 3, file 12, letter 79.
2. See A. Decaux, *La Castiglione*, 271.
3. Telegram from Giorgio Verasis to his grandfather, ASD, binder 4.
4. Letter from Isabella Oldoini to her grandson, Florence, 22 [January 1868], AST, bundle 1, fascicle 4/2, letter 167.
5. Letter from Isabella Oldoini to her husband, August 6, 1871, ASD, binder 4.
6. Letter from Marquis Oldoini to Virginia, no place specified, undated, quoted in *Correspondances inédites et archives privées*, file 2, 10–11.
7. Letter from Virginia to Carlo Poniatowski, quoted in A. Decaux, *La Castiglione*, 272.
8. "In order to lay the groundwork for a peaceful old age," Virginia had addressed the problem of dividing the properties in La Spezia already, in a long letter sent to her father in the summer of that year, ASD, folder 4 [French].

## THE THIRD REPUBLIC

1. Benedetto Croce, *Storia d'Italia dal 1871 al 1915*, edited by Giuseppe Galasso, Milan, Adelphi, 1991, 147.
2. Letter from Virginia to her father, [Paris, summer 1872], ASD, binder 4 [French].
3. Telegram from Virginia to her father, Rome, September 29, 1872, ASD, binder 4.
4. See the letters Félix Martelli wrote to the Countess of Castiglione, AST, bundle 15, fascicle "Joseph Poniatowski."
5. Letter from Giuseppe Poniatowski to Virginia, February 1865, ibid., letter 5.

6. Letter from Giuseppe Poniatowski to Virginia, February 1865, ibid., letter 6. As we have already seen, the term "Lisetta" alludes to one of Virginia's private parts.
7. Letter from Virginia to Giuseppe Poniatowski, [Turin, 1858], FP.
8. Letter from Virginia to Giuseppe Poniatowski, [Paris, 1865], AST, bundle 16, single fascicle, sub-fascicle with annotation at the top "3 long letters from Nicchia with reference to the prince," letter 1.
9. Quoted in A. Decaux, *La Castiglione*, 272–73.
10. See the final letter in the chapter "In Pursuit of the Emperor," in which Virginia asks him to account for his boasting about having made love to her.
11. Letter from Princess Poniatowski to Virginia, no place specified, undated, quoted in *Correspondances inédites et archives privées*, entry 71, 54.
12. Four years after Virginia's death, Jacques Bainville noted that the Second Empire had been "a mélange of Offenbach, Mérimée, Mme. de Castiglione, and the Duke of Morny, Biarritz, the boulevard and Compiègne, all of which hovers rather vaguely in the imagination, but sufficiently so to enchant..." Jacques Bainville, *Journal, 1901–1918*, Paris, Plon, 1948, 10.
13. One can hear an echo of the political discussions between the countess and the Duke of Aumale in *Le Roman d'une favorite* by Frédéric Loliée.
14. F. Loliée, *Le Roman d'une favorite*, 127.
15. Ibid., 128.
16. Letter from Henri d'Orléans, Duke of Aumale, to Virginia, Chantilly, September 25, 1872, quoted in *Correspondances inédites et archives privées*, file 43, 34.
17. F. Loliée, *Le Roman d'une favorite*, 128.
18. Ibid., 172, note 1.
19. Five copies of the note are still extant: four written in pencil by Virginia (BNF, "Comtesse de Castiglione. Lettres reçues," "Lettres du Général Estancelin," sheets 252–255) and one, in pen, transcribed by Giorgio (sheet 257) [French].
20. F. Loliée, *Le Roman d'une favorite*, 168, note 1.
21. Ibid., 171, note 1.
22. *Correspondances inédites et archives privées*, file 21, 24.
23. The few excerpts from their letters that appear in the Drouot auction catalog are enough to make one wish to read them someday in full. The

catalog mentions ninety-two handwritten letters, adding up to roughly two hundred pages. Ibid., file 50, 39.

24. A. Decaux, *Amours,* Paris, Hachette, 1958, 73.
25. Quoted in A. Decaux, *La Castiglione,* 278.
26. Quoted ibid., 279.
27. *Correspondances inédites et archives privées,* 39.
28. Letter from Virginia to Estancelin dictated to her son, Giorgio, no place specified, undated, BNF, "Comtesse de Castiglione. Lettres reçues," "Lettres du Général Estancelin," folio 250 [French].
29. Quoted in F. Loliée, *Le Roman d'une favorite,* 217. [The "color of hope" is blue.—Translator's note.]
30. Letter from Virginia to Estancelin, no place specified, undated, BNF, "Comtesse de Castiglione. Lettres reçues," "Lettres du Général Estancelin," folio 259 [French].
31. Quoted in A. Decaux, *La Castiglione,* 283.
32. See Alain Decaux, who had the opportunity, before it was sold at auction, to read the correspondence between Virginia and Cassagnac, consisting of forty-five letters from Cassagnac and three handwritten letters from Castiglione. See also *Correspondances inédites et archives privées,* file 48, 38.
33. Quoted in A. Decaux, *La Castiglione,* 286.
34. Ibid., 286–87.

## THE SLAVE

1. BHVP, MS 3036, letter 246 [French].
2. The only dated letter from L'Esclave, who lived and worked in Paris, is from January 1, 1874 (ibid., letter 283), and around this same time he announces to Virginia the publication of his new newspaper, *Le Nouvelliste.* In the 1870s, various newspapers with this title appeared, especially in the provinces, and in 1874 *Le Nouvelliste de Paris* was published in the capital; its director was Xavier Eyma.
3. Ibid., letter 245 [French].
4. Ibid., letter 246 [French].
5. Ibid., letter 248.
6. Ibid., letter 249 [French].
7. Ibid.

8. Ibid., letter 253 [French].
9. Ibid., letter 255 [French].
10. Ibid., letter 260 [French].
11. Ibid., letter 261 [French].
12. Ibid., letter 266 [French].
13. Ibid.
14. Ibid., letter 278 [French].
15. Ibid., letter 298 [French].

## "LOVE WHICH IS NOTHING AND EVERYTHING AT ONCE"

1. "... with [love], everything is possible, everything is desirable, everything seems beautiful, everything seems good. With [love], everything is done, everything is accepted, everything is given, in time, in action, in speech and writing." Letter from Virginia to Costantino Ressmann, [Paris, 1878?], AST, bundle 16, single fascicle, sub-fascicle with annotation at the top "Letters and notes from Nicchia," letter 12.
2. Of the four hundred letters that Ignace Bauer sent to Virginia between 1862 and 1872 we only have a few passages, thanks to Decaux and Drouot's auction catalog. See A. Decaux, *La Castiglione*, 182–84 and 203–206 and *Correspondances inédites et archives privées*, entry 46, 36–37.
3. Letter from Virginia to an unknown correspondent, no place specified, undated, quoted ibid., file 32, 29.
4. Letter from Virginia to Count Puliga, [1866], AST, bundle 4, fascicle 1, file 43, letter 1.
5. See *Correspondances inédites et archives privées*, files 26–35, 27–31.
6. Letter from Virginia to Ignace Bauer, quoted ibid., file 27, 27.
7. Reported by Loliée, it can only come from the correspondence between Virginia and Estancelin, to which the biographer had access. F. Loliée, *Les femmes du Second Empire*, vol. 1, 48.
8. The Baron de Malaret said that he admired her naked in a "performance as a beautiful statuette... for a few privileged spectators," quoted in F. Loliée, *Le Roman d'une favorite*, 112–13. There was also a rumor of a performance for Laffitte's son-in-law, General de Galliffet, who, when questioned by friends about how he'd felt about the experience, said that

she "smelled of sweat." See A. Decaux, *La Castiglione*, 210–11 and G. Gugliotta, *Le général de Galliffet*, 73–74.

9. *Correspondances inédites et archives privées*, file 27, 27.
10. Ibid., file 33, 30.
11. Ibid., file 29, 28.
12. Letter from Virginia to Giuseppe Poniatowski, no place specified, Wednesday at noon [undated], AST, deck 16, single fascicle, sub-fascicle with annotation at the top. Unnumbered letter.
13. AFC, letter 2.
14. Eleven-page draft of a letter in pencil, no place specified, undated, AST, bundle 16, single fascicle, sub-fascicle with annotation "Letter from a restless soul," letter 1. The identification of the unknown correspondent as Poniatowski is mine.
15. Letter from Virginia to Giuseppe Poniatowski, no place specified, December 1, ibid., sub-fascicle with annotation "letter written 1 December," unnumbered letter.
16. Letter from Virginia to Giuseppe Poniatowski, ibid., unnumbered letter.
17. In fact it is not "to an unknown lover" (as the catalog claims) but to Cassagnac (who figures in it under the nickname *Pays*) whom she addresses the unsigned, undated thirty-eight-page diary, auctioned by Drouot (*Correspondances inédites et archives privées*, card 26, 27) and today preserved in AST, deck 1, file 4, card H, letter 25 [French].

## THE REBELLIOUS CHILD (1866–1879)

1. *Correspondances inédites et archives privées*, 38.
2. Letter from Isabella Oldoini to her husband, Florence, [June 1867], ASD, binder 3.
3. Letter from Isabella Oldoini to her husband, [Florence, summer 1868], ibid., binder 4.
4. See Isabella's letter to her husband, Florence, [July 11, 1866], ibid., in which Virginia is furious with Mademoiselle Rauch and Huteau, her faithful steward, who is guilty of going over to her husband's side and of flirting.
5. Letter from Isabella Oldoini to her husband, [Florence, summer 1868], ibid.

6. Quoted in L. Murat, *La maison du docteur Blanche*, 219.
7. Letter from Isabella Oldoini to her husband, [Florence, summer 1868], ASD, binder 4.
8. Letter from Isabella Oldoini to her husband, [Florence, summer 1868], ibid., binder 3.
9. Letter from Isabella Oldoini to her husband, [La Spezia, summer 1868], ibid., binder 4.
10. See the letters that Giorgio Verasis wrote to his grandfather, Ferrières, December 8 and 15, 1867, ibid.
11. Letter from Betty de Rothschild to Virginia, quoted in *Correspondances inédites et archives privées*, 56.
12. See the statement the widow Bellande gave to the police, ADPP, "Comtesse de Castiglione de Verazi [*sic*] (Virginie)" folder, B a/1002.
13. Pierre-Dominique-Omer Maurette, chaplain of the Refuge de Sainte-Anne, was very fond of Giorgio and took care of him when he was ill or his mother was in Italy. See Giorgio's letter to Filippo Oldoini dated April 15, 1870, in which he implores his grandfather, then serving in Lisbon, to have the abbot awarded the Portuguese decoration of the Order of Christ as a sign of gratitude. ASD, folder 4.
14. For example, the letters from the countess to Thiers (preserved in the Bibliothèque nationale de France) are from Giorgio's hand, as are all the letters relating to the surveillance of the house in Passy and the shipment of baggage during the Franco-Prussian War.
15. Letter from Giorgio Verasis to his mother, no place specified, undated, AST, bundle 2, fascicle 8, letter 56.
16. Letter from Giorgio Verasis to his grandfather, Turin, January 27, 1874, ASD, binder 4.
17. See Giorgio Verasis's letter to his grandfather, Paris, January 29, 1875, ibid., in which he takes stock of the matter.
18. Ibid.
19. Quoted in *Correspondances inédites et archives privées*, 17. See ADPP, dossier "Comtesse de Castiglione de Verazi [*sic*] (Virginie)."
20. A. Decaux, *La Castiglione*, 190.
21. See the dossier sent on May 1, 1875, to the prefect of police by "M. Macé, Commissaire de Police, Préfecture de Police, Délégations judiciaires,"

ADPP. The dossier contains documents relating to Sol, part of the "proceedings initiated against the widow Bellande, accused of blackmail and inciting a minor to vice."

22. See the letters sent by the abbé to the pupil and preceptor in an attempt to reprimand and call them to order, AST, bundle 12, file 34, letters 86–97.
23. See letter from Genulphe Sol to Virginia, December 14, 1873, ADPP, dossier "Comtesse de Castiglione de Verazi [*sic*] (Virginie)."
24. Letter from Virginia to Cléry, quoted in R. de Montesquiou, *La divine comtesse*, 118.
25. Letter from Giorgio Verasis to his grandfather, Genoa, December 21, 1873, ASD, binder 4 [French].
26. Letter from Giorgio Verasis to his grandfather, January 29, 1874, ibid. [French].
27. Copy of the letter, dictated to her amanuensis and sent by Virginia to Genulphe Sol, no place specified, undated, AST, bundle 14, file C, sub-file with annotation "Giorgio Verasis," letter 1.
28. Letter from Virginia to Genulphe Sol, [Paris, late November–early December 1873], ibid., unnumbered letter [French]; see also the pencil copy of another letter to Sol, no place specified, undated, bundle 14, "Famiglia Verasis di Castiglione" file, bundle 4, V475p.
29. Letter from Giorgio Verasis to Genulphe Sol, Genoa, December 9, 1873, ADPP, folio 122 [French].
30. Letter from Giorgio Verasis to Genulphe Sol, no place specified, December 15, 1873, ibid., folio 127 [French].
31. Letter from Giorgio Verasis to Genulphe Sol, December 16, 1873, ibid., folio 131 [French].
32. Letter from Giorgio Verasis to Genulphe Sol, December 20, 1873, ibid., folio 132 [French].
33. Letter from Giorgio Verasis to Genulphe Sol, Genoa, December 25, 1873, Christmas Day, 3 o'clock in the morning, ibid., folio 139 [French].
34. Letter from Giorgio Verasis to his grandfather, no place specified, January 29, 1874, ASD, binder 4 [French].
35. Letter from Giorgio Verasis to his grandfather, Turin, March 20, 1874, ibid. [French].

36. See letter from Lina Rauch to Isabella Oldoini, no place specified, May 23, 1872, ibid., binder 3.
37. Letter from Giorgio Verasis to his grandfather, Turin, June 12, 1875, ibid., binder 4 [French].
38. Letter from Giorgio Verasis to his grandfather, Turin, December 28, 1874, ibid.
39. Letter from Giorgio Verasis to his grandfather, Turin, February 15, 1875, ibid.
40. Letter from Filippo Oldoini to his grandson, rough draft, Lisbon, February 3, 1875, ibid. [French].
41. See the original of this letter, sent to Virginia on March 9, 1875, in which the marquis repeats the idiom "every man for himself," in *Correspondances inédites et archives privées*, entry 2, 11.
42. Letter from Virginia to her father, Paris, March 31, 1875, ASD, binder 4 [French].
43. According to the agreement, Virginia would give her son his portion of his father's inheritance, and Giorgio would agree not to meddle any further in his mother's affairs.
44. See letter from Giorgio Verasis to his grandfather, Turin, March 17, 1875, ibid.
45. Letter from Giorgio Verasis to his grandfather, Turin, February 15, 1875, ibid. [French].
46. Quoted in A. Decaux, *La Castiglione*, 299–300.
47. Letter from Virginia to her father, Paris, May 31, 1875, ASD, binder 3 [French].
48. Draft of a letter from Marquis Oldoini to Virginia, ibid., binder 4 [French].
49. Letter from Filippo Oldoini to Isacco Artom, Lisbon, July 5, 1875, AIA, fascicle 138.
50. Letter from Giorgio Verasis to Virginia, Buenos Aires, October 9, 1875, quoted in *Correspondances inédites et archives privées*, file 8, 16.
51. See the letter from Isabella Oldoini to her husband, ASD, binder 4.
52. It can be deduced from two letters to her friend in La Spezia, Agostino Fossati, that Virginia had gone to Turin to attend the wedding of her son. And this was when she gave him the famous 100,000 francs she had

received as a dowry from her father at the time of her marriage. See Adriana Beverini, "La contessa di Castiglione: momenti di una vita. Gli anni settanta tra Parigi e la Spezia. Lettere inedite," in *Virginia Oldoini. I giorni e il mito della contessa di Castiglione*, 72–75.

53. Quoted in *Correspondances inédites et archives privées*, file 8, 17.

## ODIO ET AMO

1. See H. d'Ideville, *Journal d'un diplomate en Italie*, 240. See also *Souvenirs du Général Cte Fleury*, vol. 2, 214.
2. Letter from Costantino Nigra to Virginia, Turin, March 23, [1856], AST, bundle 3, fascicle 12, letter 2.
3. Federico Chabod, "Costantino Nigra," in *Storia della politica estera italiana dal 1870 al 1896*, Bari, Laterza, 1962, 2nd edition, 673.
4. Adriano Viarengo, "Il '48 in Piemonte e le élites giovanili," in *L'opera politica di Costantino Nigra*, edited by Umberto Levra, Bologna, Il Mulino, 2008, 108. See also Luigi Mascilli Migliorini, "Il racconto della formazione giovanile di Nigra," ibid., 53–61.
5. See Carlo Richelmy, "Il silenzio di Costantino Nigra," in *Il Mondo*, July 16, 1949, 11–12. Giovenale Vegezzi Ruscalla had participated in the uprisings of 1821 and fought, in his writings and in parliament, for the independence of all peoples; his uncle Saverio Vegezzi was an important lawyer and a loyal supporter of Cavour, who had been part of his government as minister of finance and, later, minister of justice.
6. See the portrait of Emma drawn by Flore Richelmy Bonnet, the wife of a cousin of the Vegezzis, in *Second Empire et Unité Italienne*, Rome, A.L.E.C., 1981, 47–140.
7. É. Ollivier, *L'Empire libéral*, vol. 5, 187.
8. Maxime Du Camp, *Souvenirs d'un demi siècle. Au temps de Louis-Philippe et de Napoléon III*, 1830–1870, 2 vols., 24th edition, Paris, Hachette, 1949, vol. 2, 99.
9. Comte de Maugny, *Souvenirs du Second Empire. La fin d'une société*, Paris, Ernest Kolb, 1889, 122–23.
10. Quoted in F. Richelmy Bonnet, *Second Empire et Unité Italienne*, 135.
11. Ibid.

12. Letter from Prosper Mérimée to Filippo Palizzi, Château de Compiègne, November 16, [1861], quoted in *Correspondance générale de Prosper Mérimée*, vol. 4, 397 [French].
13. Ibid., 397–98.
14. Letter from Nigra to Virginia, Turin, March 23, [1856], AST, bundle 3, fascicle 12, letter 2.
15. The photographs all come from the Parisian studio Mayer & Pierson, apart from a few portraits taken by a Piedmontese photographer.
16. See Michele Falzone del Barbarò, "Nota sull'album fotografico," in *L'album della contessa di Castiglione*, Milan, Longanesi, 1980, 105–11.
17. Letter from Nigra to Virginia, Wednesday, no place specified, undated, AST, bundle 3, fascicle 12, letter 41.
18. P. Apraxine, "The Model and the Photographer."
19. Letter from Virginia to Nigra, no place specified, undated, AST, bundle 3, fascicle 12, letter 11 [French].
20. More specifically, she asked which color dress—white or black?—she should wear to a ball being thrown by the Prussian general Baron Wilhelm Leopold Colmar von der Goltz. See *Correspondances inédites et archives privées*, file 18, 23.
21. Letter from Nigra to Virginia, AST, no place specified, undated, bundle 3, fascicle 12, letter 13.
22. Letter from Virginia to Nigra, [Paris], Sunday. May 22. [1864], ibid., letter 53.
23. Letter from Nigra to Virginia, [Paris], Monday, [May 23, 1864|], ibid., letter 5 [French] The date in this case has been calculated based on the days of the week that appear at the head of the various letters.
24. Letter from Virginia to Nigra, no place specified, Monda, [May 1864|], ibid., letter 7.
25. Letter from Nigra to Virginia, no place specified, undated, ibid., letter 51.
26. Letter from Nigra to Virginia, no place specified, undated, ibid., letter 27.
27. Letter from Nigra to Virginia, [Paris], Thursday, ibid., fascicle 4, letter 19.
28. Letter from Nigra to Virginia, no place specified, Wednesday, ibid., fascicle 12, letter 41.
29. Letter from Nigra to Virginia, no place specified, Sunday, ibid., letter 47 [French].
30. Letter from Nigra to Virginia, no place specified, Friday, ibid., letter 40.

31. The existence of these letters is suggested by Flore Richelmy Bonnet, who scrupulously reconstructed Nigra's life up to 1870. See F. Richelmy Bonnet, *Second Empire et Unité Italienne*, 222–23.
32. We can take, as a terminus post quem, a letter in which Nigra tells Virginia that she must "give up Dieppe" and in which reference is also made to Marquis Oldoini's promotion to chargé d'affaires in Saint Petersburg, which happened in August 1862.
33. Letter from Nigra to Virginia [February 1863]: "Don't be in a hurry. My arm is yours. If you wish to come to the Legation I will go with you. If you wait for me on the staircase, I will find you there. But I warn you that, once inside, I will let you go greet her [the empress] alone. I will tell you in person why I will not do the same," AST, deck 3, file 12, letter 15.
34. Nigra writes to Virginia: "I saw the master today. He will go to the Tuileries this evening. I think you would do well to find a woman to accompany you. No matter what, my arm is yours as far as the stairs. Once inside, I leave you to the admiration of others. I'm only going there to make an appearance and then will leave straightaway. I will be at the Legation until half past 9," ibid., letter 12.
35. Letter from Virginia to Nigra, no place specified, undated, ibid., letter 18.
36. Letters from Virginia to Nigra, ibid., letters 20, 51, 55.
37. Ibid., letters 23, 25, 30. In August 1864, Victor Emmanuel's eldest son went to visit Paris and was received at Saint-Cloud. The society columns had reported the presence of the Countess of Castiglione, wearing an "ostentatious" outfit, at the official lunch given by Napoleon III and his wife in honor of the heir to the Italian throne. "It was one of her last appearances at court. She was dressed in a very eye-catching way, with a high pouffed hairstyle . . . Her figure and her face were irresistibly beautiful, her eyes magnificent, her mouth enchanting, her bulging, slightly sloping brow, but the haughtiness that emanated from every inch of her person did not dispose anyone to forgive her that beauty which has been so much discussed," in *Le Gaulois*, August 24, 1890, quoted in Nicole G. Albert, *La Castiglione*, 167.
38. Letter from Nigra to Virginia, Paris, March 23, 186[2]: "Screw up your courage before you read the dispatch enclosed. The news continues to be bad, and the doctors have little hope," AST, deck 3, file 12, letter 70.
39. Letter from Nigra to Virginia, Paris, September 21, 1863, ibid., letter 64.

40. Letter from Nigra to Virginia, no place specified, May 27, 186[?], ibid., letter 26.
41. Letter from Nigra to Virginia, no place specified, Saturday [undated], ibid., letter 36.
42. Letter from Nigra to Virginia, no place specified, March 30, 1865, ibid., letter 66.
43. Letter from Nigra to Virginia, no place specified, Sunday, [April 1865], ibid., letter 67.
44. Letter from Nigra to Virginia, December 19, [1865], ibid., letter 33.
45. Letter from Nigra to Virginia, no place specified, Tuesday [undated], ibid., letter 34.
46. Letter from Nigra to Virginia, no place specified, Saturday [undated], ibid., letter 43.
47. Letter from Nigra to Virginia, no place specified, undated, ibid., letter 44.
48. See Prosper Mérimée's report to Filippo Panizzi, June 25, [1863], evening, Castle of Fontainebleau, in P. Mérimée, *Correspondance générale*, vol. 5, 406–407.
49. "I was baptized by the Adriatic sea / and its wrathful waves. / The fatal queen of the Doges / sent me to you. / The anger, hopes, and tears / Of an unhappy people, / O blond empress, / I shall place before you . . ." in Costantino Nigra, *Poesie originali e tradotte, aggiuntovi un capitolo dei suoi ricordi diplomatici*, edited by Alessandro D'Ancona, Florence, Sansoni, 1914, 29–31.
50. The barcarolle "Sopra una gondola" was later set to music by Antonio Santacroce and published in Milan by Francesco Lucca in 1864.
51. Letter from Eugénie de Montijo to Francesco Arese, Saint-Sauveur, August 26, 1859, in "Napoleone III, Eugénie de Montijo e Francesco Arese in un carteggio inedito," *Nuova Antologia*, Rome 1921, 23.
52. M. Du Camp, *Souvenirs d'un demi-siècle*, vol. 1, 243.
53. Quoted in C. Richelmy, "Il silenzio di Costantino Nigra," 12.
54. Ibid.
55. Letter from Cavour to Nigra, May 9, 1860, cited ibid., 11. Probably lost, the letter does not appear in Cavour's correspondence. It was quoted, according to Richelmy, in an article by Costantino Rinaudo, which appeared in the *Domenica del Corriere* in the 1920s.
56. The September Convention—a treaty signed on September 15, 1864.
57. See M. Du Camp, *Souvenirs d'un demi-siècle*, vol. 1, 242.

58. Letter from Virginia to Nigra, copy of unsigned draft in pencil, Thursday, June 1, AST, bundle 3, fascicle A, letter 53.
59. Letter from Virginia to Nigra, copy of unsigned draft in pencil, no place specified, undated, ibid., fascicle 12, letter 73.
60. See Virginia's lengthy impeachment of Nigra and "his ugly, infamous, dirty habit of never being honest," ibid., item 16, single fascicle, sub-fascicle with pencil annotation "Sunday, Monday snow, snow, snow."
61. Letter from Nigra to Virginia, Paris, September 14, [1863–1864], ibid., bundle 3, fascicle 12, letter 63.
62. Letter from Nigra to Virginia, no place specified, Tuesday, [June 26, 1866], ibid., letter 68.
63. Letter from Nigra to Virginia, Paris, January 1, 1867, ibid., letter 69.
64. Madame Carette, *Deuxième série des souvenirs intimes*, 297–98.
65. Ibid., 284.
66. A. Viarengo, *Vittorio Emanuele II*, 373–74.
67. F. Chabod, "Costantino Nigra," 672–82.
68. Letter from Nigra to Visconti Venosta, June 24, 1871, ibid., 677.
69. Ibid.
70. Letter from Virginia to the Duke of Chartres (which dates to sometime between the end of 1873—when the countess returned to Paris—and May 1876, the end of Nigra's time in France), transcribed by an unknown hand in Genoa on behalf of the Trigones, the Genoese heirs of the countess, before the auction of her archive, AFC, letter 8 [French].
71. The Fondazione Camillo Cavour Santena has a transcription of several pages of Virginia's diary, which must date to sometime after the death of her son (on November 14, 1879).
72. *Glossae Hibernicae veteres Codicis Taurinensis* (1869), which would be followed by *Reliquie celtiche* (1872) and *Fonetica del dialetto di Val Soana* (1874). See the letter from Prosper Mérimée to Antonio Panizzi, Paris, June 9, 1869, in P. Mérimée, *Correspondance générale*, vol. 14, 514.
73. *La chioma di Berenice*, translated and with a commentary by Costantino Nigra, Milan, Hoepli, 1891; *Inni di Callimaco su Diana e sui lavacri di Pallade*, edited, translated, and with a commentary by Costantino Nigra, Turin, Loescher, 1892.
74. Vittorio Santoli, *I canti popolari italiani: ricerche e questioni*, Florence, Sansoni, 1940, new edition, 1968, 90, cited in G. Galasso, "Nigra: una veduta

d'insieme," in *L'opera politica di Costantino Nigra*, 191–92. See Costantino Nigra, *Canti popolari del Piemonte*, edited by Franco Castelli, Emilio Jona, and Alberto Lovatto, Vicenza, Neri Pozza, 2020.

75. Letter from Melchior de Vogüé to Nigra, September 9, 1892, quoted in F. Chabod, *Storia della politica estera italiana*, 617–18.
76. See Delfino Orsi, "Il mistero dei 'Ricordi diplomatici' di Costantino Nigra," in *Nuova Antologia*, LXIII, fascicle 1360, November 16, 1928, 137–54.
77. See *Nuova Antologia*, LVI, March 1895, 5–25.

## THE SUPREME SHAME OF DECLINE

1. Letter from Virginia to Léon Cléry, [Paris, 1874], quoted in R. de Montesquiou, *La divine comtesse*, 118.
2. See AST, bundle 15, fascicle "Ricevuta per l'acquisto del pugnale di Mlle Rachel," April 28, 1858.
3. Ibid., bundle 14, file C, subfile with annotation "Important document dealing with her separation from her husband."
4. Quoted in R. de Montesquiou, *La divine comtesse*, 120.
5. Letter from Virginia to Léon Cléry, [Paris, December 29, 1895], quoted ibid, 142–43.
6. See the letters that Cléry sent to Virginia, AST, bundle 12, fascicle 34, letters 106–107.
7. Léon Cléry, *Notes et souvenirs*, quoted in R. de Montesquiou, *La divine comtesse*, 22–23.
8. This is how Cléry described the countess's letters, ibid., 109.
9. In the interviews he conducted after Castiglione's death, Montesquiou was able to take down Cléry's testimony and view several letters that Virginia had written to the lawyer.
10. Letter from Madame de Sévigné to her daughter, May 18, 1671, in Madame de Sévigné, *Correspondance*, edited by Roger Duchêne, 3 vols., Paris, Gallimard, Bibliothèque de la Pléiade, 1972–1978, vol. 1, 258. The "five-penny" style was that of the epistolographic manuals sold at bookstalls.
11. R. de Montesquiou, *La divine comtesse*, 138.
12. Ibid., 141–42.

13. Ibid., 114.
14. Ibid., 135.
15. Ibid., 139.
16. Ibid., 133.
17. ADPP, Préfecture de Police, Police municipale, Brigade Recherches, Rapport, Paris, February 13, 1881.
18. In the inventory of objects drawn up after her death were "21 marble paperweights taken from the ruins of the Tuileries," R. de Montesquiou, *La divine comtesse*, 167.
19. One Carnival night, on her way back from a ball, Lady Walburga Paget says that she and her companion had seen "a dark figure flitting along under the shadow of the palaces; it stopped for a moment, and then crossed over into the moonlight." The man with her, Lady Paget then goes on to say, begins walking faster: "'I think I know! It must be she,'" he says to me as we approach, and putting a hand on the lady's arm he adds: 'Ninì! Since when are you here?' She turns and reveals in the white light of the moon that face which for ten years had drawn crowds around her in every capital of Europe. She moved her arm as if she wished to keep my companion at a distance, and as her long black cloak fell back I saw beneath it, covering her from throat to waist, the famous necklace of white-and-black pearls which I knew could only belong to the celebrated Countess C——. 'What are you doing here alone at this house and with all those pearls on? What new folly is this?' exclaimed my friend impatiently. But instead of answering, the countess only drew a stiletto from her bosom." Lady Walburga Paget, *Scenes and Memories*, London, Murray, 1913, 278–279.
20. See the letter on Laffitte's death quoted on p. 360.
21. "My troubles are burning up my brains . . . and *you know* that writing is my only consolation," quoted in F. Loliée, *Le Roman d'une favorite*, 282.
22. Letter from Virginia to an unknown correspondent [Costantino Ressmann?], AST, bundle 16, single fascicle, "At dawn (supplement to a night of aquatic dreams)," sub-fascicle with annotation "Letters and notes from Nicchia."
23. Quoted in R. de Montesquiou, *La divine comtesse*, 132.
24. See ADPP, Cabinet de M. Macé, February 9, 1873.
25. See her correspondence with Thiers quoted on pp. 262–273.

26. The first to dedicate a long portrait to her was Henry d'Ideville in his *Journal d'un diplomate en Italie*, 83–94, which appeared in 1872. In sending the book to Virginia, who had expressly requested it, the foreign minister Visconti Venosta wrote to her: "I don't know what sort of smile will play upon your lips when you read the pages about the Countess of Castiglione. I will not tell you my own opinion in writing, I would prefer to say it in person, when I have the pleasure of seeing you," [Rome], June 1, 1872, AST, bundle 4, issue 22, letter 3. Destined to become an obligatory reference for all of Castiglione's biographers, Ideville's portrait is more than flattering—the French diplomat remembers her as mysterious, haughty, and disillusioned from her days at Villa Gloria—especially since, when he had given her the pages in question to read, Virginia had inserted a few lines, which Ideville, with good reason, defines as "curious": "The Eternal Father did not know what was being done the day he brought her into the world; he kneaded and kneaded and when he had finished, he lost his mind looking at his marvelous work, and left it there in a corner, not putting it in place. Meanwhile he was called elsewhere, and when he returned he found it out of place" (p. 90). The series of unfavorable opinions of her began with the Count of Viel-Castel's *Mémoires sur le règne de Napoléon III* (1884), followed by the *Souvenirs intimes de la Cour des Tuileries* (1889) by Madame Carette, Eugénie's first reader. Montesquiou—who examined a copy of the book in which Virginia made marginal corrections to statements concerning her—speaks of the "comically dissonant duet, alternating between careless inaccuracy, rather than deliberate malevolence, and furious recriminations, rising up from the bottom of a well like the voice of Truth transformed into Anger," *La divine comtesse*, 40. *Mon Séjour aux Tuileries (1852–1858)* by Stéphanie Tascher de la Pagerie (1894) and *Souvenirs du Général Cte de Fleury* (1897–1898) were published next. A year before Virginia's death, Imbert de Saint-Amand's *La Cour du Second Empire (1856–1858)* appeared (1898).
27. F. Loliée, *Le Roman d'une favorite*, 241.
28. Ibid., 242.
29. Ibid., 246, note 2.
30. Ibid., note 1.
31. Ibid., 247.
32. Ibid., 231.
33. Quoted in R. de Montesquiou, *La divine comtesse*, 125–26.

34. Ibid., 134.
35. Quoted in A. Decaux, *La Castiglione*, 315.
36. R. de Montesquiou, *La divine comtesse*, 147.
37. Ibid., 135.
38. F. Loliée, *Le Roman d'une favorite*, 255, note 2.
39. Virginia's deep and problematic emotional bond with La Spezia is at the heart of many of the critical contributions in *Virginia Oldoini. I giorni e il mito della contessa di Castiglione*, the catalog of the exhibition that the Ligurian town dedicated to her on the first centenary of her death. Working from documents preserved in the city's public and private collections, Carlo Biossi, Marzia Ratti, Pia Spagiari, Adriana Beverini, Gabriella Chioma, and Graziano Tonelli reconstruct her plans to fight against the transformation of the small town of farmers and fishermen into an important mercantile and military center, her conflicts with the city administration, and the tortuous state of her assets. It is a valuable contribution to our understanding of—as the people of La Spezia called Virginia—Rapallina's love-hate relationship with the *joli golfe*.
40. Marquis Oldoini died in La Spezia on January 14, 1889.
41. The entire legal process has been reconstructed in detail by Alfredo Poggiolini: "The ancestral palace, the villa called Isabella, a relic of the Lamporecchi patrimony, with the adjacent lands and rustic houses, were awarded to a naval commander, the cavalryman Emanuele de Negri, for 167,000 lire," A. Poggiolini, *La contessa Verasis di Castiglione nel romanzo e nella realtà*, 74–75.
42. On January 7, 1893, the Credito Fondiario dell'Opera Pia di S. Paolo of Turin granted her a loan of 80,000 lire, see ibid., 76.
43. See ibid., 76–80.
44. See AFC. These six letters have come down to us thanks to an unknown copyist who was given permission by the countess's heirs to view her papers when they were still in Genoa. The pages that he was able to transcribe include, among other things, multiple letters addressed to a single recipient in May 1894 and various fragments from other letters dating to the same period.
45. We can be sure these letters are from 1894 because Virginia says that Pentecost Sunday fell on May 13, the same day as the death of Valentine Delessert, whose funeral is described in the fifth letter.

46. The devoted friend may well be Agostino Fossati, a gifted landscape painter, who, in addition to being Virginia's steward and loyal advisor, had long been her friend. See "Ferruccio Battolini, Agostino Fossati, consigliere della Contessa, artista da consacrare e Maria Giuliana Zucchini, Agostino Fossati in una lettera della Contessa a Léon Cléry," in *Virginia Oldoini. I giorni e il mito della contessa di Castiglione.*
47. One of the attacks carried out by anarchists in Paris during those years.
48. Letter from Virginia to an unknown correspondent, [May 1894], AFC, letter 1.
49. Letter from Virginia to an unknown correspondent, [May 13, 1894], ibid., letter 2.
50. In penal colonies under the Restoration, those sentenced to fixed terms wore a green cap, while those sentenced to life wore a red cap. The distinction lasted long enough for it to become proverbial. See André Zysberg, "Galere, bagni penali, deportazione in Francia tra settecento e ottocento," in *La scienza e la colpa. Crimini, criminali, criminologi: un volto dell'ottocento*, edited by Umberto Levra, Milan, Electa, 1985, 206.
51. Letter from Virginia to an unknown correspondent, [May 13, 1894], AFC, letter 2.
52. See Édouard Grenier, "L'Elkovan," in *Petits poèmes*, Paris, Charpentier, 1859. Probably inspired by the myth of Ceyx and Alcyone, the poem speaks of the unhappy love between a boatman and an odalisque, the unfortunate Aina, who, on the verge of drowning, entrusts her soul to a halcyon, which then comes to rest on the arm of his beloved. [An "elkovan" is, according to Grenier, "a gull of the Bosporus."—Translator's note.]
53. The "idealistic and compassionate poet" may be Robert de Montesquiou, "Les Vraies immortelles," XXXIV, in *Les Paons*, Paris, Charpentier, 1901.
54. Letter from Virginia to an unknown correspondent, [May 1894], AFC, letter 3.
55. Letter from Virginia to an unknown correspondent, ibid., letter 7.
56. Letter from Virginia to an unknown correspondent, ibid., letter 5.
57. Letter from Virginia to Jacques Blanche, September 15, 1893, Bibliothèque de l'Institut de France, Fonds Blanche, MS 6281, quoted in L. Murat, *La maison du docteur Blanche*, 455–57.
58. Quoted in A. Decaux, *La Castiglione*, 316.
59. P. Apraxine, "The Model and the Photographer."

60. Marcel Escoffier will remember this and have Alida Valli wear a similar burnoose in Visconti's *Senso*.
61. Jacques-Émile Blanche, *Propos de Peintre*, Paris, Émile-Paul Frères, 1921, xxv–xxvi, quoted in L. Murat, *La maison du docteur Blanche*, 457.
62. There are two versions of the portrait. The first, entitled *La Comtesse de Castiglione, souvenir de 1893*, at the Musée Carnavalet, was completed after the publication of the biographies by Loliée and Montesquiou, and is based on the photographic portrait *Rachel*. The painting "has the merit of establishing for the benefit of posterity a certain image of the countess—that of a woman dressed all in black, eccentric and solitary, whose expression contains all the desperation in the world." The second, *Comtesse de Castiglione 1893*, is in a private collection and was painted between 1921 and 1925. On the back is a label: "J. É. Blanche—after the study made in August 1893 in Auteuil in my room when the countess came to see me after my father's death." It is inspired by a photograph of Castiglione in profile, also from the "Sainte Cécile et Rachel" series. See *La Comtesse de Castiglione par elle-même*, entries 91 and 93, 185.
63. Ibid., entry 88, 184.
64. R. de Montesquiou, *La divine comtesse*, 163.
65. See A. Poggiolini, *La contessa Verasis di Castiglione nel romanzo e nella realtà*, 80.
66. P. Apraxine, "The Model and the Photographer." The photograph was taken on August 1, 1894.
67. See, above, the letter from Virginia to Sol, 471, note 28.
68. P. Apraxine, "The Model and the Photographer."
69. "The painted photograph is one of the hallmarks of Mayer & Pierson, which offers its customers a team of retouchers, miniaturists, and painters . . . Furthermore, the procedure allows the countess to intervene directly in the image, with pencil or brush, and gives her complete power over the final form of her portrait," ibid., 42–43.
70. The negatives of the photographs all remained in Pierson's studio.
71. In a letter dated [January 24], 1861, Lord Clarendon thanks "her for the gift of a photograph of herself bearing the single word 'Remember,'" AST, deck 15, file 'Lord Clarendon', letter 1. In 2019 the museum of the Château de Compiègne acquired an album put together in 1866 by Maria Anna Walewska and containing seventeen photographs, which come from the

collection of Robert de Montesquiou. See *+Photographie #2: les acquisitions des collections publiques*, Marseille, Le Bec en l'air, 2021, 234–35.

72. Nicole G. Albert, *La Castiglione*, 167.
73. Ernest Daudet, *Les Coulisses de la Société Parisienne*, Paris, Ollendorff, 1895, 181–85.
74. Letter from Virginia to an unnamed correspondent [Giuseppe Poniatowski], no place specified, undated, AST, bundle 16, single fascicle, sub-fascicle with the annotation "Letter of a restless soul," letter 1. See, in this volume, note 14 on p. 469.
75. Letter from Virginia to an unnamed correspondent [Giuseppe Poniatowski], no place specified, undated, ibid., bundle 16, single fascicle, sub-fascicle with the annotation "This is one of my dreams," letter 12.
76. AFC, fragment.
77. A. Decaux, *La Castiglione*, 320–22.

## POSTMORTEM

1. "Last night I had such a high fever that if I didn't die it's because God doesn't want me: he's afraid I'll set Paradise ablaze," loose sheet, quoted in R. de Montesquiou, *La divine comtesse*, 173.
2. *Virginia Oldoini. I giorni e il mito della contessa di Castiglione*, 204.
3. "Catalog of beautiful jewels: MAGNIFICENT FIVE-ROW PEARL NECKLACE, beautiful pearls on paper, jewels, bracelets, brooches, earrings, rings, diamond and colored gemstone brooches; silver, fans, ornaments, lace, books, souvenirs of the Second Empire; portraits, landscapes, furniture, and objets d'art, will be put up for sale, following the death of the Countess of Castiglione, Hôtel Drouot, room no. 1, on Wednesday the 26th, Thursday the 27th, Friday the 28th and Saturday the 29th of June 1901, at two o'clock." See F. Loliée, *Le Roman d'une favorite*, 263, note 1.
4. F. Bac, *Intimités du Second Empire*, 16–17.
5. R. de Montesquiou, *La divine comtesse*, 10.
6. Montesquiou would acquire this volume in the auction of 1901.
7. The doctor was Arthur Christophe Hugenschmidt, a renowned dentist who looked after Virginia in the last months of her life. Born in Paris on September 22, 1861, he was the third child of a clerk and a wardrobe

mistress of the Tuileries; his older brothers had died in infancy. After the defeat at Sedan, his father continued to serve the exiled sovereign as a butler, while Arthur, who remained in Paris with his mother, studied dentistry under the guidance of Thomas W. Evans, the American dental surgeon who had treated the imperial family, hidden Eugénie in his house on September 4, 1870, and organized her escape to England. The young Arthur had visited Chislehurst more than once when the emperor was still alive, and after her son's death in 1879, Eugénie often invited him to her new residence on Farnborough Hill, welcoming him into her inner circle. Arthur's resemblance to the Prince Imperial was undeniable and substantiated the rumors that he was the natural son of Napoleon III. Arthur himself would always avoid speaking of it, outside of confiding in a colleague that Virginia was his mother. There were (a few) supporters of this hypothesis, which Alain Decaux proceeded to dismantle (*La Castiglione*, 324–26), and for which Sampiero Sanguinetti, who recently resurrected this idea of Virginia's secret maternity in *L'Enfant* (Montacher-Villegardin, Le Charmoiset, 2017), provides no documentary proof. The countess regularly gave her friends, acquaintances, and servants fanciful nicknames, and the fact that she called Arthur "l'Enfant" is not in itself significant; nor is Virginia's friendship with Dr. Evans, on whose behalf she petitioned Nigra, among others, for an Italian title. She was also close with Dr. Arnal, the imperial family's trusted doctor. It is also not at all clear how Virginia could have hidden her pregnancy during a time (1860–1861) when her life was under scrutiny. If in her letters to Poniatowski from Italy she fleetingly mentions a "Baby," it's because she had led the emperor to believe that her gynecological problems were the result of a miscarriage. Furthermore, if she had really given birth to Napoleon's son, her silence would have been worth its weight in gold, and it is hard to imagine why she wouldn't have made him her heir, or at least bequeathed some tangible proof of gratitude for the care he'd given her. Of course, we cannot rule out that the uncovering of new documents might lead us to change our minds.

8. R. de Montesquiou, *La divine comtesse*, 16–17.
9. Philippe Jullian, *Robert de Montesquiou, un prince 1900*, Paris, Librairie académique Perrin, 1965, 63.
10. Dorian Gray in Oscar Wilde's eponymous novel (1890), Count Muzarett

in Jean Lorrain's *Monsieur de Phocas* (1901), and Viscount Jacques de Serpigny in Henri de Régnier's *Le Mariage de Minuit* (1903).

11. "Souverain des choses transitoires": a line that opens "Maëstro," a poem in *Les Chauves-souris*, which Montesquiou recycles in a dedication to Proust written at the bottom of a photograph of himself. See M. Proust, *Contre Sainte-Beuve*, 409.
12. Élisabeth de Clermont-Tonnerre, *Robert de Montesquiou et Marcel Proust*, Paris, Flammarion, 1925, 73.
13. See *Robert de Montesquiou ou l'art de paraître*, catalog of the exhibit at the Musée d'Orsay, Paris, October 12, 1999–January 23, 2000, edited by Philippe Thiébaut and Jean-Michel Nectoux, Paris, Réunion des musées nationaux, 1999.
14. R. de Montesquiou, *La divine comtesse*, 3–4.
15. Preface by G. D'Annunzio, ibid., i–ii.

# Index

BENEDETTA CRAVERI is a professor of French literature at the University Suor Orsola Benincasa, Naples. She is a corresponding member of Accademia dei Lincei and contributes to *The New York Review of Books* and to the cultural pages of the Italian newspaper *La Repubblica*. Her books include *The Age of Conversation* and *The Last Libertines* (both available from New York Review Books). She is married to a French diplomat and was awarded the Prix mondial Cino Del Duca by the Institut de France.

ALEX ANDRIESSE has translated several books from French and Italian, including François-René de Chateaubriand's *Memoirs from Beyond the Grave* and Cristina Campo's *The Unforgivable and Other Writings* (both available as NYRB Classics).